T0205982

# Lecture Notes in Computer Science 14723

Founding Editors

Gerhard Goos
Juris Hartmanis

## Editorial Board Members

The series Lecture Notes in Computer Science (LNCS), including its subseries Lecture Notes in Artificial Intelligence (LNAI) and Lecture Notes in Bioinformatics (LNBI), has established itself as a medium for the publication of new developments in computer science and information technology research, teaching, and education.

LNCS enjoys close cooperation with the computer science R & D community, the series counts many renowned academics among its volume editors and paper authors, and collaborates with prestigious societies. Its mission is to serve this international community by providing an invaluable service, mainly focused on the publication of conference and workshop proceedings and postproceedings. LNCS commenced publication in 1973.

Panayiotis Zaphiris · Andri Ioannou

Editors

# Learning and Collaboration Technologies

11th International Conference, LCT 2024
Held as Part of the 26th HCI International Conference, HCII 2024
Washington, DC, USA, June 29 – July 4, 2024
Proceedings, Part II

Springer

*Editors*
Panayiotis Zaphiris ⓘD
Department of Multimedia and Graphic Arts
Cyprus University of Technology
Limassol, Cyprus

Andri Ioannou ⓘD
Department of Multimedia and Graphic Arts
Cyprus University of Technology
Limassol, Cyprus

Research Center on Interactive Media, Smart
Systems and Emerging Technologies
(CYENS)
Nicosia, Cyprus

ISSN 0302-9743                    ISSN 1611-3349 (electronic)
Lecture Notes in Computer Science
ISBN 978-3-031-61684-6          ISBN 978-3-031-61685-3 (eBook)
https://doi.org/10.1007/978-3-031-61685-3

This Springer imprint is published by the registered company Springer Nature Switzerland AG
The registered company address is: Gewerbestrasse 11, 6330 Cham, Switzerland

If disposing of this product, please recycle the paper.

# Foreword

This year we celebrate 40 years since the establishment of the HCI International (HCII) Conference, which has been a hub for presenting groundbreaking research and novel ideas and collaboration for people from all over the world.

The HCII conference was founded in 1984 by Prof. Gavriel Salvendy (Purdue University, USA, Tsinghua University, P.R. China, and University of Central Florida, USA) and the first event of the series, "1st USA-Japan Conference on Human-Computer Interaction", was held in Honolulu, Hawaii, USA, 18–20 August. Since then, HCI International is held jointly with several Thematic Areas and Affiliated Conferences, with each one under the auspices of a distinguished international Program Board and under one management and one registration. Twenty-six HCI International Conferences have been organized so far (every two years until 2013, and annually thereafter).

Over the years, this conference has served as a platform for scholars, researchers, industry experts and students to exchange ideas, connect, and address challenges in the ever-evolving HCI field. Throughout these 40 years, the conference has evolved itself, adapting to new technologies and emerging trends, while staying committed to its core mission of advancing knowledge and driving change.

As we celebrate this milestone anniversary, we reflect on the contributions of its founding members and appreciate the commitment of its current and past Affiliated Conference Program Board Chairs and members. We are also thankful to all past conference attendees who have shaped this community into what it is today.

The 26th International Conference on Human-Computer Interaction, HCI International 2024 (HCII 2024), was held as a 'hybrid' event at the Washington Hilton Hotel, Washington, DC, USA, during 29 June – 4 July 2024. It incorporated the 21 thematic areas and affiliated conferences listed below.

A total of 5108 individuals from academia, research institutes, industry, and government agencies from 85 countries submitted contributions, and 1271 papers and 309 posters were included in the volumes of the proceedings that were published just before the start of the conference, these are listed below. The contributions thoroughly cover the entire field of human-computer interaction, addressing major advances in knowledge and effective use of computers in a variety of application areas. These papers provide academics, researchers, engineers, scientists, practitioners and students with state-of-the-art information on the most recent advances in HCI.

The HCI International (HCII) conference also offers the option of presenting 'Late Breaking Work', and this applies both for papers and posters, with corresponding volumes of proceedings that will be published after the conference. Full papers will be included in the 'HCII 2024 - Late Breaking Papers' volumes of the proceedings to be published in the Springer LNCS series, while 'Poster Extended Abstracts' will be included as short research papers in the 'HCII 2024 - Late Breaking Posters' volumes to be published in the Springer CCIS series.

I would like to thank the Program Board Chairs and the members of the Program Boards of all thematic areas and affiliated conferences for their contribution towards the high scientific quality and overall success of the HCI International 2024 conference. Their manifold support in terms of paper reviewing (single-blind review process, with a minimum of two reviews per submission), session organization and their willingness to act as goodwill ambassadors for the conference is most highly appreciated.

This conference would not have been possible without the continuous and unwavering support and advice of Gavriel Salvendy, founder, General Chair Emeritus, and Scientific Advisor. For his outstanding efforts, I would like to express my sincere appreciation to Abbas Moallem, Communications Chair and Editor of HCI International News.

July 2024                                                    Constantine Stephanidis

# HCI International 2024 Thematic Areas and Affiliated Conferences

- HCI: Human-Computer Interaction Thematic Area
- HIMI: Human Interface and the Management of Information Thematic Area
- EPCE: 21st International Conference on Engineering Psychology and Cognitive Ergonomics
- AC: 18th International Conference on Augmented Cognition
- UAHCI: 18th International Conference on Universal Access in Human-Computer Interaction
- CCD: 16th International Conference on Cross-Cultural Design
- SCSM: 16th International Conference on Social Computing and Social Media
- VAMR: 16th International Conference on Virtual, Augmented and Mixed Reality
- DHM: 15th International Conference on Digital Human Modeling & Applications in Health, Safety, Ergonomics & Risk Management
- DUXU: 13th International Conference on Design, User Experience and Usability
- C&C: 12th International Conference on Culture and Computing
- DAPI: 12th International Conference on Distributed, Ambient and Pervasive Interactions
- HCIBGO: 11th International Conference on HCI in Business, Government and Organizations
- LCT: 11th International Conference on Learning and Collaboration Technologies
- ITAP: 10th International Conference on Human Aspects of IT for the Aged Population
- AIS: 6th International Conference on Adaptive Instructional Systems
- HCI-CPT: 6th International Conference on HCI for Cybersecurity, Privacy and Trust
- HCI-Games: 6th International Conference on HCI in Games
- MobiTAS: 6th International Conference on HCI in Mobility, Transport and Automotive Systems
- AI-HCI: 5th International Conference on Artificial Intelligence in HCI
- MOBILE: 5th International Conference on Human-Centered Design, Operation and Evaluation of Mobile Communications

# List of Conference Proceedings Volumes Appearing Before the Conference

1. LNCS 14684, Human-Computer Interaction: Part I, edited by Masaaki Kurosu and Ayako Hashizume
2. LNCS 14685, Human-Computer Interaction: Part II, edited by Masaaki Kurosu and Ayako Hashizume
3. LNCS 14686, Human-Computer Interaction: Part III, edited by Masaaki Kurosu and Ayako Hashizume
4. LNCS 14687, Human-Computer Interaction: Part IV, edited by Masaaki Kurosu and Ayako Hashizume
5. LNCS 14688, Human-Computer Interaction: Part V, edited by Masaaki Kurosu and Ayako Hashizume
6. LNCS 14689, Human Interface and the Management of Information: Part I, edited by Hirohiko Mori and Yumi Asahi
7. LNCS 14690, Human Interface and the Management of Information: Part II, edited by Hirohiko Mori and Yumi Asahi
8. LNCS 14691, Human Interface and the Management of Information: Part III, edited by Hirohiko Mori and Yumi Asahi
9. LNAI 14692, Engineering Psychology and Cognitive Ergonomics: Part I, edited by Don Harris and Wen-Chin Li
10. LNAI 14693, Engineering Psychology and Cognitive Ergonomics: Part II, edited by Don Harris and Wen-Chin Li
11. LNAI 14694, Augmented Cognition, Part I, edited by Dylan D. Schmorrow and Cali M. Fidopiastis
12. LNAI 14695, Augmented Cognition, Part II, edited by Dylan D. Schmorrow and Cali M. Fidopiastis
13. LNCS 14696, Universal Access in Human-Computer Interaction: Part I, edited by Margherita Antona and Constantine Stephanidis
14. LNCS 14697, Universal Access in Human-Computer Interaction: Part II, edited by Margherita Antona and Constantine Stephanidis
15. LNCS 14698, Universal Access in Human-Computer Interaction: Part III, edited by Margherita Antona and Constantine Stephanidis
16. LNCS 14699, Cross-Cultural Design: Part I, edited by Pei-Luen Patrick Rau
17. LNCS 14700, Cross-Cultural Design: Part II, edited by Pei-Luen Patrick Rau
18. LNCS 14701, Cross-Cultural Design: Part III, edited by Pei-Luen Patrick Rau
19. LNCS 14702, Cross-Cultural Design: Part IV, edited by Pei-Luen Patrick Rau
20. LNCS 14703, Social Computing and Social Media: Part I, edited by Adela Coman and Simona Vasilache
21. LNCS 14704, Social Computing and Social Media: Part II, edited by Adela Coman and Simona Vasilache
22. LNCS 14705, Social Computing and Social Media: Part III, edited by Adela Coman and Simona Vasilache

**https://2024.hci.international/proceedings**

# Preface

In today's knowledge society, learning and collaboration are two fundamental and strictly interrelated aspects of knowledge acquisition and creation. Learning technology is the broad range of communication, information, and related technologies that can be used to support learning, teaching, and assessment, often in a collaborative way. Collaboration technology, on the other hand, is targeted to support individuals working in teams towards a common goal, which may be an educational one, by providing tools that aid communication and the management of activities as well as the process of problem solving. In this context, interactive technologies not only affect and improve the existing educational system but become a transformative force that can generate radically new ways of knowing, learning, and collaborating.

The 11th International Conference on Learning and Collaboration Technologies (LCT 2024), affiliated with HCI International 2024, addressed the theoretical foundations, design and implementation, and effectiveness and impact issues related to interactive technologies for learning and collaboration, including design methodologies, developments and tools, theoretical models, and learning design or learning experience (LX) design, as well as technology adoption and use in formal, non-formal, and informal educational contexts.

Learning and collaboration technologies are increasingly adopted in K-20 (kindergarten to higher education) classrooms and lifelong learning. Technology can support expansive forms of collaboration; deepened empathy; complex coordination of people, materials, and purposes; and development of skill sets that are increasingly important across workspaces in the 21st century. The general themes of the LCT conference aim to address challenges related to understanding how to design for better learning and collaboration with technology, support learners to develop relevant approaches and skills, and assess or evaluate gains and outcomes. To this end, topics such as extended reality (XR) learning, embodied and immersive learning, mobile learning and ubiquitous technologies, serious games and gamification, learning through design and making, educational robotics, educational chatbots, human-computer interfaces, and computer-supported collaborative learning, among others, are elaborated in the LCT conference proceedings. Learning (experience) design and user experience design remain a challenge in the arena of learning environments and collaboration technology. LCT aims to serve a continuous dialog while synthesizing current knowledge.

Three volumes of the HCII 2024 proceedings are dedicated to this year's edition of the LCT 2024 conference. The first focuses on topics related to Designing Learning and Teaching Experiences, and Investigating Learning Experiences. The second focuses on topics related to Serious Games and Gamification, and Novel Learning Ecosystems, while the third focuses on topics related to VR and AR in Learning and Education, and AI in Learning and Education.

The papers of these volumes were accepted for publication after a minimum of two single-blind reviews from the members of the LCT Program Board or, in some cases, from members of the Program Boards of other affiliated conferences. We would like to thank all of them for their invaluable contribution, support, and efforts.

July 2024                                                          Panayiotis Zaphiris
                                                                        Andri Ioannou

# 11th International Conference on Learning and Collaboration Technologies (LCT 2024)

Program Board Chairs: **Panayiotis Zaphiris**, *Cyprus University of Technology, Cyprus*, and **Andri Ioannou**, *Cyprus University of Technology, Cyprus* and *Research Center on Interactive Media, Smart Systems and Emerging Technologies (CYENS), Cyprus*

- Miguel Angel Conde Gonzalez, *University of Leon, Spain*
- Fisnik Dalipi, *Linnaeus University, Sweden*
- Camille Dickson-Deane, *University of Technology Sydney, Australia*
- David Fonseca, *La Salle, Ramon Llull University, Spain*
- Alicia Garcia-Holgado, *Universidad de Salamanca, Spain*
- Francisco Garcia-Penalvo, *University of Salamanca, Spain*
- Aleksandar Jevremovic, *Singidunum University, Serbia*
- Elis Kakoulli Constantinou, *Cyprus University of Technology, Cyprus*
- Tomaz Klobucar, *Jozef Stefan Institute, Slovenia*
- Birgy Lorenz, *Tallinn University of Technology, Estonia*
- Nicholas H. Müller, *Technical University of Applied Sciences Würzburg-Schweinfurt, Germany*
- Fernando Moreira, *Universidade Portucalense, Portugal*
- Anna Nicolaou, *Cyprus University of Technology, Cyprus*
- Antigoni Parmaxi, *Cyprus University of Technology, Cyprus*
- Dijana Plantak Vukovac, *University of Zagreb, Croatia*
- Maria-Victoria Soule, *Cyprus University of Technology, Cyprus*
- Sonia Sousa, *Tallinn University, Estonia*

The full list with the Program Board Chairs and the members of the Program Boards of all thematic areas and affiliated conferences of HCII 2024 is available online at:

**http://www.hci.international/board-members-2024.php**

# HCI International 2025 Conference

The 27th International Conference on Human-Computer Interaction, HCI International 2025, will be held jointly with the affiliated conferences at the Swedish Exhibition & Congress Centre and Gothia Towers Hotel, Gothenburg, Sweden, June 22–27, 2025. It will cover a broad spectrum of themes related to Human-Computer Interaction, including theoretical issues, methods, tools, processes, and case studies in HCI design, as well as novel interaction techniques, interfaces, and applications. The proceedings will be published by Springer. More information will become available on the conference website: https://2025.hci.international/.

General Chair
Prof. Constantine Stephanidis
University of Crete and ICS-FORTH
Heraklion, Crete, Greece
Email: general_chair@2025.hci.international

**https://2025.hci.international/**

# Contents – Part II

## Novel Learning Ecosystems

# Serious Games and Gamification

# DOMUS: An Educational Multiplayer Game for Touch Tables Using a Tangible User Interface

Gennaro Costagliola⬛, Mattia De Rosa(✉)⬛, Vittorio Fuccella⬛,
Alfonso Piscitelli⬛, and Parinaz Tabari⬛

Department of Informatics, University of Salerno, Via Giovanni Paolo II,
84084 Fisciano, SA, Italy
matderosa@unisa.it

**Abstract.** Educational video games enable participants to actively engage with a specific topic, leading to improved educational processes and learning outcomes. This methodology can also enhance critical thinking while providing an attractive learning environment and discussion platform. This paper introduces DOMUS, an educational video game inspired by ancient Roman history. The game was developed for museums and designed for multi-touch tables. It uses a Tangible User Interface (TUI) that allows users to move physical game pieces, simulating a real board game. Each participant receives a game piece, with which they have to perform tasks and read information about Roman history related to the task they are performing. Subsequently, we conducted a user study involving 12 participants in game sessions. After the game session, each participant completed a learning outcome questionnaire to assess the learning impact of a single session with DOMUS. The study found that participants answered 6.41 out of 9 questions on the learning outcomes questionnaire correctly. The average System Usability Scale score was 87.29.

**Keywords:** Educational Game · Touch Table · Usability · User Study · Human-Computer Interaction · HCI

## 1 Introduction

Active methodologies such as game-based education can cause learning and critical thinking improvements. This learning strategy enhances the educational process and provides an attractive learning environment for players. It also allows discussion among players [20]. Due to these advantages, this technique has gained increased attention from researchers and trainers all over the world [23]. In recent years, the ubiquity of touchscreen devices, such as smartphones, tablets, smartwatches, and interactive kiosks, has made interaction with these tools a common practice, and many studies have investigated ways to improve their HCI [1,9,11,14–18,31,35]. These devices include tables equipped with multi-touch screens. They offer several advantages, such as the ability to be used simultaneously by multiple people, promoting collaboration and interaction among users.

P. Zaphiris and A. Ioannou (Eds.): HCII 2024, LNCS 14723, pp. 3–16, 2024.
https://doi.org/10.1007/978-3-031-61685-3_1

One distinctive feature of these devices is their ability to not only interact through fingers or a stylus but also to allow objects to be placed on their surface due to their horizontal arrangement and generous size. This mode of interaction is a part of Tangible User Interfaces (TUIs) [28] which aim to turn physical information into digital information and vice versa by utilizing the users' natural ability to manipulate objects while interacting with computing devices. Numerous examples of TUIs [19,26,27,31,34] use dedicated hardware or computer vision to recognize the objects with which interaction takes place.

The focus of this paper is to present DOMUS, an educational video game designed for multi-touch tables that exploits a TUI. The game is primarily designed for use in museum settings, in an attempt to provide an experience that combines educational and playful aspects. It was previously observed [31] that, compared to a traditional multi-touch interface, a TUI encourages touching and manipulation, attracting more groups of visitors. An early version of DOMUS was presented in Coppola et al. [12]; the new contribution in this paper consists of an enhanced version of DOMUS and its evaluation through a user study.

The remainder of the article follows this structure: Sect. 2 presents related works. Section 3 describes the DOMUS application, game structure, and information about the implementation, and Sect. 4 presents the user study describing apparatus, participants, and procedure. Section 5 illustrates the results of the user study and discusses them. Finally, Sect. 6 summarizes this study and highlights directions for future research.

## 2   Related Work

In exploring the intersection of technology and culture, Popleteev et al. [36] designed a cultural collaborative game for multi-touch tables. The context was the museums of Luxemburg and Athens and the researchers intended to raise cross-cultural awareness and knowledge of the visitors about those two European cities, incorporating game concepts like jigsaw/mosaic, put-in-order, memory, and treasure hunt. These researchers also examined the impact of video-to-video streaming on user behavior. However, unlike our study, their focus was not on testing usability or evaluating learning outcomes, which are central to our research. In another approach, Antle et al. [4] developed Futura, an interactive game, using a multi-touch table, about land use planning, which teaches the balance between human and environmental needs. The context of the game was design evaluation techniques in land use planning for a population. The objective was to teach users how they can provide a balance between human and environmental needs.

Similarly, educational applications of multi-touch technology have been the focus of several other studies. Heinemann et al. [21] delved into the realm of analyzing eye-tracking in multi-touch educational games within computer science education, aiming to understand participants' behavior through this technology. Complementing this, other studies explored the use of multi-touch tables to enhance collaborative learning and engagement in educational settings. Holz et al. [22] explored serious games in computer science studies. The researchers aimed to improve collaborative learning outcomes using muti-touch tables. The usage modes were classified into "Learning, Playing, Creating" categories. The implementation adhered to tabletop design principles. On the other hand, Ardito et al. [5] focused on interactive learning experiences in school environments, using games based on geography and flags that provided two educational games to students about class lessons via a multi-touch screen. The idea was to install the screen in the school hall and let students interact with it during their breaks. The game had four modalities including playing with capital cities, flags, countries, or mixed. The researchers then evaluated the social and educational aspects of this approach. Yu et al. [39] implemented four prototypes for an educational and competitive game. The context was children's famous cartoons and stories. The device was a large multi-touch display and the players had to play in pairs on the right and left sides of the screen. Langner et al. [29] introduced PhysicsBox, a collection of educational games simulating physics lessons, showcasing a Java library for hardware independence. Their study, however, primarily discussed game design and implementation, without delving deeply into learning outcomes or usability, a gap our study aims to fill.

In the realm of special needs education, Cascales-Martínez et al. [10] presented a cooperative game designed for students with special needs, focusing on money management skills. The researchers assessed learning improvements through pre- and post-tests, to some extent similar to our approach in which we have an initial knowledge self-assessment and a learning outcome questionnaire at the end. Bottino et al. [7] developed a serious game called "SMART VIEW" for mobility support of mentally impaired teenagers using touch screen tables. The participants were specifically trained in spatial orientation. Furthermore, the role of multi-touch technology in planning and rehabilitation was explored in other studies. Lloréns et al. [30] developed a game called "The Awareness Climbing" to enhance self-assessment and role-playing skills in patients post-brain injury, employing the Intrinsic Motivation Inventory (IMI) and the System Usability Scale (SUS) scales; we also used the latter to assess usability.

Lastly, some studies explored the use of cutting-edge technologies to enhance the educational process through interactivity and immersion. Ayed et al. [6] utilized Microsoft Kinect to investigate students' understanding of the periodic table. This approach allowed students to interact with the educational content through body gestures, such as hand, eye, or hip movements, enriching the learning experience with auditory and visual feedback. This method not only made the learning process more engaging but also catered to different learning styles by incorporating kinesthetic and visual elements. Similarly, Martín-SanJosé et al. [32] employed innovative engagement methods in teaching history to children. They used an autostereoscopic system in 3D mode and a frontal projection on a table in 2D mode, which was comparable to a touch table. The use of Microsoft Kinect in both methods further enhanced the interactive experience.

Each of these studies contributes to the growing understanding of how multi-touch technology can be innovatively used in educational, cultural, and rehabilitative contexts, demonstrating the versatility and impact of this technology. Our study builds upon these foundations, focusing particularly on usability testing and evaluating learning outcomes, areas that have been less emphasized in previous research.

**Fig. 1.** DOMUS players.

## 3   DOMUS

DOMUS is a museum-focused interactive game that serves both educational and recreational purposes. The main purpose of DOMUS is to educate users about the atmosphere of a wealthy Roman family's domus (i.e., house). In this game, participants take on different character roles such as the *matron* (wife of the dominus, i.e., householder), the *dominus' trusted slave*, or the *dominus' eldest son*. The game is intended for two or more players to participate simultaneously, such as a family, to promote comparison and knowledge sharing. The game rules are straightforward, similar to those of traditional board games. This allows for a game session to be completed within a reasonable amount of time, considering the museum environment. Each character must perform certain tasks, and the player's goal is to complete their activities before the other participants. During

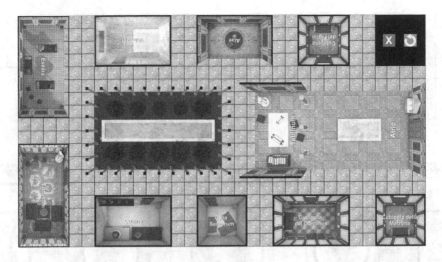

**Fig. 2.** DOMUS game board (tangibles not placed on the table).

the game, multimedia information is provided about the rooms and the tasks, allowing learning about the customs, traditions, and history of ancient Rome. The game is designed in such a way that even after a participant has won by having completed all the assigned tasks, other players can continue playing to gain additional historical knowledge. Compared with the previous version of DOMUS described in [12], the software has been improved by adding new descriptions of ancient Roman history, fixing bugs, and improving the UI.

Hardware-wise, DOMUS has been developed using a touch table manufactured by Ideum [24], with a 43-inch 80-point multi-touch screen and a personal computer running Windows 10. The Tangible Engine 2 SDK [25], which is included with the hardware, allows for the use of tangibles. Tangibles are objects with a nonconductive part and conductive feet that are uniquely recognized when placed on the screen. The game was created with the Unity platform [38] and Cinema 4D [33] was used to model the Domus rooms.

### 3.1 Interface and Interaction

The design of the game board, shown in Fig. 1 and 2, draws inspiration from a Roman domus from the 1st century AD. Specifically, it takes cues from the luxurious villas of Pompeii, such as the renowned "House of the Tragic Poet" and "House of the Faun".

Tangibles are used as game pieces that users can place or move on the screen. On the screen, around the edges of these pieces, contextual menus are displayed to allow users to perform actions by touching them with their fingers. Not only do these menus move along with the tangibles, but they also adjust their orientation based on the rotation of the tangibles. This ensures that users can easily read the menus by rotating them as necessary.

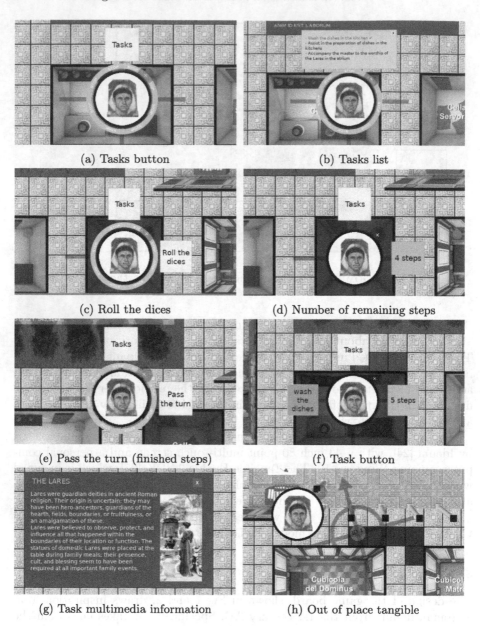

(a) Tasks button

(b) Tasks list

(c) Roll the dices

(d) Number of remaining steps

(e) Pass the turn (finished steps)

(f) Task button

(g) Task multimedia information

(h) Out of place tangible

**Fig. 3.** Domus GUI.

The game begins by prompting users to position their game pieces within the room that corresponds to their character. Once each user has completed this step, a button located in the center of the screen can be clicked to initiate the game. Since the game operates on a turn-based format, the system also determines the order of players and allocates tasks to them at this point. These tasks encompass various activities commonly performed in a domus, such as enjoying a meal in the triclinium or honoring the Lares.

Figure 3 shows the different states of a piece and its contextual menus. Specifically, when the players are waiting for their turn, they can access the "tasks" button, as shown in Fig. 3a. By pressing it, the player can view the list of tasks that need to be completed (and those that have already been completed) within the rooms of the Domus, as shown in Fig. 3b.

When it is the user's turn, they will see the "roll the dice" button in the contextual menu (Fig. 3c). Pressing this button will cause the system to roll two virtual dice. The player can then move their piece on the playing area for some steps on the playing board boxes equal to the rolled number (Fig. 3d). After completing their moves, the player can pass the turn to the next player by clicking the corresponding button (Fig. 3e). If the player reaches a room before using up all the available steps, they can perform a task associated with that room (Fig. 3f). When a task is performed, the system will display multimedia content (such as text, images, and videos) that provides more information about the task in the Roman civilization (Fig. 3g). If the piece is moved or lifted in a way that is not supposed to happen, the system will hide the contextual menu and display a placeholder until the user repositions it (Fig. 3h). Finally, after a player completes all the tasks, the system will display a message to declare their victory and ask if the remaining players wish to continue playing or begin again.

## 4   User Study

To test the usability/effectiveness of Domus, we conducted a user study where participants played a game with Domus in groups of three. After the experiment, participants completed a Learning Outcomes Questionnaire (LOQ) with questions about what is told in Domus about ancient Rome, a SUS questionnaire [8], and a free-form comments questionnaire.

### 4.1   Participants

For the user study, we recruited 12 participants (3 females), divided into four groups. The participants who volunteered for the study were students with ages between 20 and 30 years old (mean 25.17, SD 2.82).

### 4.2   Apparatus

The experiment was conducted entirely in person, under the supervision of a member of the research team. Participants used a 43" Ideum multi-touch table with 80 multi-touch points connected to a personal computer with Windows 10, Intel i7 processor, and 16 GB RAM. The system ran the Domus version described in Sect. 3.

### 4.3   Procedure

At the beginning of each experiment session, we explained the objectives and procedures to the participants and assigned the roles for the game session using a randomizer. Each participant then completed a preliminary questionnaire about their age, gender, experience with multi-touch tables, knowledge of smartphones, and their level of knowledge about Roman history.

After the preliminary questionnaire, we introduced participants to the game session, both presenting the rules of the game and playing a test round. At the end of the introductory phase, each participant took their place around the touch table in their character's initial position, and they started the game session. All participants had to complete the three tasks given to each character, and when a participant completed a task, they had to read a descriptive text regarding the completed task (from a historical point of view) shown in the center of the DOMUS interface. For example, when a participant completed a task about the *Tablinium*, they read a description of what the tablinium was and which activities were performed. The game did not end when one participant won by being the first to complete all assigned tasks; it continued until all participants completed their tasks. The game duration was recorded for each group of participants.

At the end of the game session, participants filled out a multiple-choice questionnaire about ancient Roman history. It consisted of nine questions related to the text read during the game session, each with four possible answers, of which only one was correct. Subsequently, each participant completed the SUS questionnaire, utilizing a five-point Likert scale on alternating positive and negative statements. Finally, we asked participants to give their free-form comments and suggestions.

## 5   Results and Discussion

All participants completed the experiment. For each participant, the experiment lasted about 25 min, including the introductory session. The average time required for the only game session was 8:57 min (S.D. 0:55 min).

### 5.1   Learning Outcomes Questionnaire

After the game session, each participant filled out a questionnaire about the content learned during the game session in order to assess whether this game can improve learning. The LOQ had an average of 6:41 correct answers (S.D. 1:50) out of 9. Table 1 shows the results obtained by each participant. It can be seen that all participants answered more than half of the questions correctly.

### 5.2   SUS Questionnaire

At the end of the game session and after the completion of the Learning Outcome Questionnaire, all involved people compiled a SUS questionnaire to measure participant satisfaction with the DOMUS application. For each filled questionnaire, the SUS score was calculated, which ranged from 0 to 100; the participants collectively achieved an average SUS score of 87.29 (S.D. 8.22), a very good value [37].

**Table 1.** Number of correct answers to learning outcomes questionnaires (*LOQ/9*), and game session duration. The last columns also report responses to the preliminary questionnaire (*SA Rome* stands for the initial self-assessment of knowledge about ancient Rome).

| Participant | Group | LOQ/9 | Game dur. | Gender | Age | SA Rome/5 |
|---|---|---|---|---|---|---|
| 1 | 1 | 5 | 7:31 | M | 22 | 2 |
| 2 | 1 | 9 | 7:31 | M | 21 | 3 |
| 3 | 1 | 5 | 7:31 | F | 20 | 1 |
| 4 | 2 | 6 | 9:40 | M | 27 | 2 |
| 5 | 2 | 6 | 9:40 | F | 27 | 3 |
| 6 | 2 | 9 | 9:40 | M | 27 | 3 |
| 7 | 3 | 8 | 9:42 | F | 24 | 3 |
| 8 | 3 | 7 | 9:42 | M | 27 | 2 |
| 9 | 3 | 5 | 9:42 | M | 29 | 2 |
| 10 | 4 | 6 | 8:56 | M | 27 | 1 |
| 11 | 4 | 5 | 8:56 | M | 26 | 2 |
| 12 | 4 | 6 | 8:56 | M | 25 | 2 |

### 5.3    Free-Form Comments

In free-form comments, participants said they enjoyed their experience with DOMUS, particularly the opportunity to learn about ancient Rome while playing the game, the social aspect of the game, and the fun and curiosity in using a tangible technology. They also suggested some improvements to the game, such as reducing the size of the tangibles (although there are hardware limitations in this regard), and adding additional tasks and some quality-of-life features to further improve and extend the game experience.

### 5.4    Insights and Implications

The initial questionnaire, completed by participants before the game session, revealed that their self-assessment of ancient Roman history averaged 2.17 (SD 0.72) on a scale of 1 to 5. This value indicates a medium to low level of knowledge. At the end of the game session, each participant completed a test on the content suggested in the game: the average number of correct answers was 6.41 (SD 1.50) out of 9 questions; the lowest number of correct answers was five, and two participants answered all questions correctly. These results suggest that DOMUS helps participants to learn content about ancient Roman history.

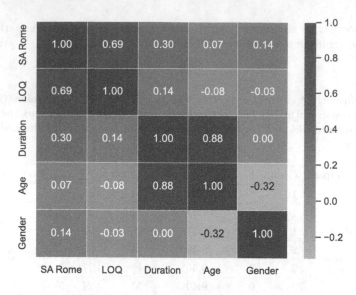

**Fig. 4.** Correlation Matrix computed with Pearson Method.

Figure 4 shows the correlation matrix calculated between *game duration, LOQ correct answers, initial self-assessment of knowledge about ancient Rome, Age, Gender*. From the figure, we can note the following correlations:

- (Age, Game duration) = 0.88
- (SA Rome, LOQ) = 0.69
- (SA Rome, Duration) = 0.30

It can also be seen from the correlation matrix that there is a correlation between the initial self-assessment and the number of correct answers in the learning outcomes questionnaire. This correlation suggests that the game allows participants with little knowledge to acquire the basic knowledge of the proposed content; moreover, people who already know something about the topic of the game were able to improve their knowledge about it through this game. A study in this field observed that a TUI was more effective in facilitating touching and manipulations and also attracted a larger number of visitor groups compared to a traditional multi-touch interface [31].

The correlation between age and duration of the game session seems to indicate that young participants have more confidence in game mode than older ones. Finally, there is also a weak correlation between the duration and the participant's self-assessment of knowledge about ancient Rome. This correlation could indicate that participants who know something about the topic are faster in the game phases (including reading the content) than participants who know little or nothing about the topic of the game.

## 6    Conclusions and Future Work

Educational games, such as Domus, make it possible to support learning activities for different topics. In this study, we analyzed how participants learned new information about ancient Roman history through a Domus game session. The results show that, at the end of the game session, all participants performed well, with an average number of correct answers of 6.41 out of 9, suggesting that the game session helped them learn the proposed content. The results also show some correlations between the initial self-assessment (in knowledge of ancient Roman history) and the number of correct answers to the outcome questionnaire and between the self-assessment and the duration of the game session. These correlations suggest planning further analysis between the user's initial and final knowledge and between both of them and the duration of gaming sessions. We also plan to improve Domus by adding new game scenarios with new objectives (and new characters) and by integrating a text-to-speech service to further the accessibility of the game. Moreover, we will investigate the integration of a Speech Recognition service [2,3,13] to interact with the game (e.g. a virtual assistant) through the voice. Finally, new user studies involving more participants will be performed.

**Acknowledgments.** The authors thank Giuseppe Coppola for his contribution in implementing the first version of Domus. This work was partially supported by grants from the University of Salerno (grant numbers: 300392FRB23COSTA).

**Disclosure of Interests.** The authors have no competing interests to declare that are relevant to the content of this article.

## References

1. Albinsson, P.A., Zhai, S.: High precision touch screen interaction. In: Proceedings of the SIGCHI Conference on Human Factors in Computing Systems, CHI 2003, pp. 105–112. Association for Computing Machinery, New York (2003). https://doi.org/10.1145/642611.642631
2. Allison, F., Carter, M., Gibbs, M.: Word play: a history of voice interaction in digital games. Games Culture **15**(2), 91–113 (2020). https://doi.org/10.1177/1555412017746305
3. Allison, F., Newn, J., Smith, W., Carter, M., Gibbs, M.: Frame analysis of voice interaction gameplay. In: Proceedings of the 2019 CHI Conference on Human Factors in Computing Systems, CHI 2019, pp. 1–14. Association for Computing Machinery, New York (2019). https://doi.org/10.1145/3290605.3300623
4. Antle, A.N., Bevans, A., Tanenbaum, T.J., Seaborn, K., Wang, S.: Futura: design for collaborative learning and game play on a multi-touch digital tabletop. In: Proceedings of the Fifth International Conference on Tangible, Embedded, and Embodied Interaction, pp. 93–100 (2010)
5. Ardito, C., Buono, P., Costabile, M.F., Lanzilotti, R.: Educational games on a large multitouch screen. In: DMS, pp. 242–245. Citeseer (2011)

6. Ayed, I., Jaume-I-Capó, A., Moya-Alcover, B., Perales, F.: Vision based interaction game for revising the periodic table. In: EDULEARN19 Proceedings, pp. 9376–9382. IATED (2019)

7. Bottino, R.M., Canessa, A., Ott, M., Tavella, M.: SMART VIEW: a serious game supporting spatial orientation of subjects with cognitive impairments. In: Stephanidis, C., Antona, M. (eds.) UAHCI 2014. LNCS, vol. 8514, pp. 489–500. Springer, Cham (2014). https://doi.org/10.1007/978-3-319-07440-5_45

8. Brooke, J.: Sus: a "quick and dirty usability" scale. Usability Eval. Ind. **189**(3), 189–194 (1996)

9. Bufano, R., Costagliola, G., De Rosa, M., Fuccella, V.: PolyRec Gesture Design Tool: A tool for fast prototyping of gesture-based mobile applications. Softw. Practice Exp. **52**(2), 594–618 (2022). https://doi.org/10.1002/spe.3024

10. Cascales-Martínez, A., Martínez-Segura, M.J., Pérez-López, D., Contero, M.: Using an augmented reality enhanced tabletop system to promote learning of mathematics: a case study with students with special educational needs. Eurasia J. Math. Sci. Technol. Educ. **13**(2), 355–380 (2016)

11. Cipriano, M., Costagliola, G., De Rosa, M., Fuccella, V., Shevchenko, S.: Recent advancements on smartwatches and smartbands in healthcare. In: Chen, Y.-W., Tanaka, S., Howlett, R.J., Jain, L.C. (eds.) Innovation in Medicine and Healthcare. SIST, vol. 242, pp. 117–127. Springer, Singapore (2021). https://doi.org/10.1007/978-981-16-3013-2_10

12. Coppola, G., Costagliola, G., De Rosa, M., Fuccella, V.: Domus: a multi-user tui game for multi-touch tables. In: Proceedings of the International Conference on Advanced Visual Interfaces. AVI 2020. Association for Computing Machinery, New York (2020).https://doi.org/10.1145/3399715.3399951

13. Corbisiero, E., Costagliola, G., De Rosa, M., Fuccella, V., Piscitelli, A., Tabari, P.: Speech recognition in healthcare: A comparison of different speech recognition input interactions. In: Chen, Y.W., Tanaka, S., Howlett, R.J., Jain, L.C. (eds.) Innovation in Medicine and Healthcare, pp. 142–152. Springer, Singapore (2023)

14. Costagliola, G.; De Rosa, M., D'Arco, R., De Gregorio, S., Fuccella, V., Lupo, D.: C-QWERTY: a text entry method for circular smartwatches. In: The 25th Int. DMS Conference on Visualization and Visual Languages, pp. 51–57 (2019). https://doi.org/10.18293/DMSVIVA2019-014

15. Costagliola, G., De Rosa, M., Fuccella, V.: Gesture-Based Computing, chap. 32, pp. 397–408. John Wiley & Sons, Ltd. (2023). https://doi.org/10.1002/9781119863663.ch32

16. Costagliola, G., De Rosa, M., Fuccella, V., Martin, B.: Bubbleboard: a zoom-based text entry method on smartwatches. In: Kurosu, M. (ed.) Human-Computer Interaction. Technological Innovation, vol. 13303, pp. 14–27. Springer (2022). https://doi.org/10.1007/978-3-031-05409-9_2

17. De Rosa, M., et al.: T18: an ambiguous keyboard layout for smartwatches. In: 2020 IEEE International Conference on Human-Machine Systems (ICHMS) (2020). https://doi.org/10.1109/ICHMS49158.2020.9209483

18. De Rosa, M., Fuccella, V., Costagliola, G., Albanese, M.G., Galasso, F., Galasso, L.: Arrow2edit: a technique for editing text on smartphones. In: Kurosu, M., Hashizume, A. (eds.) HCII 2023. LNCS, vol. 14011, pp. 416–432. Springer (2023). https://doi.org/10.1007/978-3-031-35596-7_27

19. Duranti, D., Spallazzo, D., Petrelli, D.: Smart objects and replicas: a survey of tangible and embodied interactions in museums and cultural heritage sites. J. Comput. Cult. Herit. **17**(1), January 2024.https://doi.org/10.1145/3631132

20. Ghanatpisheh, M.A., Amini, M., Tabari, P., Moosavi, M.: The effect of game-based learning technique on the knowledge of health-volunteers in 2017. J. Adv. Pharmacy Educ. Res. **9**(2), 95–98 (2019)
21. Heinemann, B., Ehlenz, M., Schroeder, P.D.U.: Eye-tracking in educational multi-touch games: design-based (interaction) research and great visions. In: ACM Symposium on Eye Tracking Research and Applications, pp. 1–5 (2020)
22. Holz, J., Bergner, N., Schäfer, A., Schroeder, U.: Serious games on multi touch tables for computer science students. In: CSEDU (2), pp. 519–524 (2012)
23. Hosseini, H., Hartt, M., Mostafapour, M.: Learning is child' play: Game-based learning in computer science education. ACM Trans. Comput. Educ. (TOCE) **19**(3), 1–18 (2019)
24. Ideum: Ideum multitouch tables. https://ideum.com/products
25. Ideum: Tangible engine. https://tangibleengine.com
26. Ishii, H.: The tangible user interface and its evolution. Commun. ACM **51**(6), 32–36 (2008). https://doi.org/10.1145/1349026.1349034
27. Ishii, H., Ratti, C., Piper, B., Wang, Y., Biderman, A., Ben-Joseph, E.: Bringing clay and sand into digital design-continuous tangible user interfaces. BT Technol. J. **22**(4), 287–299 (2004)
28. Ishii, H., Ullmer, B.: Tangible bits: Towards seamless interfaces between people, bits and atoms. In: Proceedings of the ACM SIGCHI Conference on Human Factors in Computing Systems, CHI 1997, pp. 234–241. Association for Computing Machinery, New York (1997). https://doi.org/10.1145/258549.258715
29. Langner, R., Brosz, J., Dachselt, R., Carpendale, S.: Physicsbox: playful educational tabletop games. In: ACM International Conference on Interactive Tabletops and Surfaces, pp. 273–274 (2010)
30. Lloréns, R., Alcañiz, M., Navarro, M.D., Ferri, J., Noé, E.: Self-awareness rehabilitation through a multi-touch virtual game board after acquired brain injury. In: 2013 International Conference on Virtual Rehabilitation (ICVR), pp. 134–138. IEEE (2013)
31. Ma, J., Sindorf, L., Liao, I., Frazier, J.: Using a tangible versus a multi-touch graphical user interface to support data exploration at a museum exhibit. In: Proceedings of the Ninth International Conference on Tangible, Embedded, and Embodied Interaction, TEI 2015, pp. 33–40. Association for Computing Machinery, New York (2015). https://doi.org/10.1145/2677199.2680555
32. Martin-SanJose, J.F., Juan, M.C., Mollá, R., Vivó, R.: Advanced displays and natural user interfaces to support learning. Interact. Learn. Environ. **25**(1), 17–34 (2017)
33. Maxon: Cinema 4D. https://www.maxon.net/en/cinema-4d
34. Nathoo, A., Bekaroo, G., Gangabissoon, T., Santokhee, A.: Using tangible user interfaces for teaching concepts of internet of things. Interactive Technol. Smart Educ. **17**(2), 133–158 (2020). https://doi.org/10.1108/ITSE-09-2019-0061
35. Parhi, P., Karlson, A.K., Bederson, B.B.: Target size study for one-handed thumb use on small touchscreen devices. In: Proceedings of the 8th Conference on Human-Computer Interaction with Mobile Devices and Services, MobileHCI 2006, pp. 203–210. Association for Computing Machinery, New York (2006). https://doi.org/10.1145/1152215.1152260
36. Popleteev, A., McCall, R., Molnar, A., Avanesov, T.: Touch by touch: promoting cultural awareness with multitouch gaming. In: 2013 International Conference on Smart Communications in Network Technologies (SaCoNeT), vol. 4, pp. 1–4. IEEE (2013)

37. Sauro, J.: 5 ways to interpret a sus score. https://measuringu.com/interpret-sus-score/
38. Unity Technologies: Unity real-time development platform. https://unity.com
39. Yu, X., Zhang, M., Ren, J., Zhao, H., Zhu, Z.: Experimental development of competitive digital educational games on multi-touch screen for young children. In: Zhang, X., Zhong, S., Pan, Z., Wong, K., Yun, R. (eds.) Edutainment 2010. LNCS, vol. 6249, pp. 367–375. Springer, Heidelberg (2010). https://doi.org/10.1007/978-3-642-14533-9_38

# The Use of Gamification in Mathematics Education: Enhancing Geometry Comprehension with High School Students

Carlos Alberto Espinosa-Pinos[1]($\boxtimes$) (iD), Alex Mauricio Mazaquiza-Paucar[1] (iD), and Clara Augusta Sánchez Benítez[2] (iD)

[1] Universidad Indoamerica, Bolívar 20-35 and Guayaquil, Ambato 180103, Ecuador
`carlosespinosa@indoamerica.edu.ec`
[2] Universidad Técnica de Ambato, Colombia and Chile Avenue, Ambato 180215, Ecuador
`ca.sanchez@uta.edu.ec`

**Abstract.** The non-existence or non-application of strategies, methodologies, innovative techniques such as gamification, which offers a more attractive and dynamic way of approaching the mathematical topic about the equation of the line, a concept that is often abstract and difficult to understand for many students. The present study aims to analyze the effectiveness of gamification in the pedagogical process between educators and learners in relation to the understanding of the equation of the line in students of the tenth year of higher EGB. This analysis was carried out through a quantitative approach that included the administration of a knowledge test before and after applying gamification to 92 GBS tenth grade students. These students were divided into two groups of 46 students each, one experimental group (EG) worked on gamification activities and the other control group (CG) employed traditional techniques. The purpose of this division was to determine if there were significant differences in performance means between the two groups. The gamified proposal incorporates elements of games, challenges, rewards and competitions, taking into account the learners in a dynamic way, providing them with a sense of purpose and achievement. After the T-Student application, it was concluded that the proposal not only significantly increases the academic performance of the students, but also develops logical thinking and reasoning, and favors autonomous and collaborative work.

**Keywords:** Gamification · Teaching and Learning · Mathematics · Educational Technology

## 1 Introduction

### 1.1 Justificación

The rationale for this research is based on the need to integrate new technologies and innovative strategies in education, particularly in the teaching of mathematics. Traditional methodology has become obsolete, and teachers are looking for new ways to

P. Zaphiris and A. Ioannou (Eds.): HCII 2024, LNCS 14723, pp. 17–30, 2024.
https://doi.org/10.1007/978-3-031-61685-3_2

motivate students and develop their mathematical skills in a meaningful and lasting way. The study of mathematics continues to be of great interest worldwide, and educators are striving to adopt playful and motivating approaches. This project is based on meaningful and constructive learning, using instructional design to develop mathematical skills through a gamified didactic sequence Hoffman [1]. The objective is to enable students to understand and apply the equation of the straight line in different contexts, improving their mathematical skills and preparing them to face current educational challenges, as shown by the PISA results, which highlight the weaknesses in mathematical performance in Latin America. In this context, PISA assessments measure students' ability to apply mathematical concepts in diverse environments and promote mathematical reasoning and problem solving in real situations. Suradika, Dewi, & Nasution [2].

The evolution of educational theories has been a topic of interest in educational research, as it reflects a significant change in the pedagogical approach over time. From behavioral theories to constructivism and social constructivism, a transition from a behavioral approach to an emphasis on the active construction of knowledge by the learner has been observed. This evolution has been analyzed in diverse contexts, which supports the importance of understanding the historical trends in educational theory as mentioned by: García, Pérez, González, & Rodríguez [3]; Gómez-Carrasco, López-Facal, & Castro-Fernández [4]. In addition, the need to integrate educational theory more effectively with pedagogical practice has been highlighted, which poses challenges and opportunities for teacher training and curriculum design, according to Bernaschina [5]. In this sense, the evolution of educational theories has not only influenced the understanding of the teaching-learning process, but has also impacted the way in which the relationship between educational theory and practice is conceived. Hoffman [1].

The central problem addressed in this text is related to the low performance in mathematics, specifically in solving straight-line equations, among students in Latin America, as evidenced in OECD reports. It highlights that traditional education and the lack of technological classroom resources hinder effective mathematics learning. In addition, the lack of teacher training in gamified strategies limits incorporation of innovative teaching methods. It is recognized that gamification, through technological resources and interactive approaches, can be an effective solution to improve students' performance and enthusiasm for mathematics. Despite the challenges, it is noted that some institutions and teachers in Ecuador are exploring gamification as a strategy for learning.

The main purpose of educational theories is to provide a detailed explanation of educational phenomena and, in turn, to offer pedagogical approaches that encourage the active participation of students and the achievement of meaningful learning. These theories seek to understand and predict educational policies and practices, encompassing various branches such as pedagogy, curriculum, learning, and educational policy, according to Lang, Tebben, Luckey, Hurns, Fox, Ford, Ansari, and Pasque [6]. By combining theory with reflective practice, educators can adapt and customize their pedagogical approaches to promote meaningful and enriching learning, taking into account the individual needs of students. El-Attar, El-Ela, and Awad [7]. Ultimately, the main purpose of educational theories is to improve the quality of education by providing students with the necessary tools and skills to meet current challenges, as mentioned by Gates, Teasdale, Shim, and Hubacz [8].

Understanding these theories provides educators with a sound theoretical framework and a basis for designing strategies that contribute to the creation of enriching and stimulating educational environments, as referred to by Zhang and Zhou [9]. By using teaching theories as a guide, educators can inspire and empower students, recognizing the importance of the diversity of pedagogical approaches and the non-exclusion of any theory. Hashmi et al. [10]. It is important to recognize that no theory is exclusive and that, on the contrary, the combination of diverse theories can enrich educational practice, providing educators with the necessary tools to promote meaningful and enriching learning.

The theory of self-regulation has become a topic of interest in educational research, since it has been shown to influence students' intrinsic motivation. According to alenzuela, Codina, Castillo and Pestana [11], self-regulation refers to students' ability to control and direct their own learning, which implies the activation of learning strategies necessary to achieve learning objectives. Intrinsic motivation, associated with autonomy, competence, and socialization, is a key factor influencing students' self-regulation and engagement in educational activities, as recommended by Kingsford-Smith and Zhou [12]. Evans et al. [13] refer to the flow theory, proposed by Csikszentmihalyi, describes a state of absorption in an intrinsically pleasurable activity, leading to joy and success, which is also mentioned by Jimenez Torres [14]. The relationship between engagement and flow suggests that adequate engagement can generate a favorable flow state, which in turn can enhance students' performance and engagement with the subject matter. Rativa [15].

Self-regulation theory, intrinsic motivation and flow are closely related, as they all influence students' active engagement in the learning process, as suggested by Gates et al. [8]. In conclusion, self-regulation theory, intrinsic motivation and flow are key concepts in educational research, as they influence students' engagement and performance. Self-regulation refers to students' ability to control and direct their own learning, while intrinsic motivation is associated with autonomy, competence and socialization. On the other hand, extrinsic motivation is linked to external regulation. Flow theory describes a state of absorption in an intrinsically pleasurable activity, leading to joy and success. The relationship between engagement and flow suggests that adequate engagement can generate a favorable flow state, which in turn can enhance students' performance and engagement with the subject matter.

Gamification has become an increasingly popular learning technique in various fields, such as entrepreneurship, medicine, and education. In education, gamification aims to improve student engagement by incorporating game elements into the design of learning processes, as mentioned by Khasawneh [16]. Gamification is defined as the introduction of game elements and experiences in the design of learning processes, with the purpose not only to improve learning, but also to develop skills and attitudes such as collaboration, self-regulation and creativity according to Barata et al. [17].Gamification has become an innovative strategy to improve intrinsic and extrinsic motivation of students, providing immediate feedback, exploration and learning from mistakes in the view of Alkhawalde & Khasawneh [18].

Intrinsic motivation is associated with autonomy, competence and socialization, while extrinsic motivation is linked to external regulation according to Evans et al. [13]. Gamification is presented as a strategy that encourages the creative process of teachers in the design of learning environments, allowing them to customize activities and content according to the needs of each student, favoring the acquisition of knowledge and improving attention, Barata et al. say [17]. There are different gamification models, but Werbach and Hunter's model is one of the most widely used. This model includes dynamics, mechanics and components, and focuses on creating game experiences that involve students and motivate them to actively participate in the learning process, for Barata et al. [17].

According to Alkhawalde & Khasawneh [18], gamification is presented as a technique that contributes to improve the teaching-learning process, since it allows to generate meaningful learning in students, facilitating the internalization of content and increasing their motivation and participation. In conclusion, gamification is presented as an innovative and effective strategy to improve students' motivation and engagement with educational activities, which in turn can enhance their performance and learning, referred by Rojas et al. [33] (Table 1).

**Table 1.** Summary of Relevant Research on Gamification in Mathematics Education

| References | Scope | Results |
|---|---|---|
| Elmawati et al. [19] | To assess the level of gamification in Italian secondary schools in the field of mathematics | Teachers, albeit unconsciously, apply gamification in their classrooms without having received any training on the subject |
| Čubela et al. [20] | Exploring the integration of problem-based learning, gamification, and data-driven approaches in engineering education | It resulted in student motivation, enrichment of students' STEM prespectives, and development of skills needed for students' future careers |
| Chen et al. [21] | Studies the impact of a gamified approach in a mobile self-regulated learning environment on students' self-regulated learning skills | In conclusion, there was improvement in students' academic performance, improvement in students' performance in defining objectives and reflection; however, the students who used the proposed approach did not achieve a higher monitoring performance than the students who learn without gamification |

*(continued)*

**Table 1.** (*continued*)

| References | Scope | Results |
|---|---|---|
| Chen et al. [22] | Design an online gamified learning game activity that incorporates multi-representational scaffolding and compare the differences in learning achievement and motivation for the gamified activity and general synchronous distance learning | The gamified learning activity was not significantly effective in terms of improving learning. In terms of motivation for learning, a significant increase was found |
| Dehghanzadeh et al. [23] | Understand how gamification has been used to engage students in peer review activities and summarize the empirical evidence of its effectiveness | Although the existing peer review literature reports positive effects of gamification on student engagement, this range remains low. Student reflection on the feedback received has been largely unexplored with respect to gamification |
| Sanmugam et al. [24] | Discuss the role of gamification as an educational technology tool to engage and motivate students | Highlights the importance of educational technology in teaching and learning, and how gamification can be an effective tool to engage and motivate the learner |

# 2   Methodology

## 2.1   Justification

The present research is developed from a quantitative perspective, since the results are measured and subjected to statistical analysis using the IBM SPSS Statistics software tool. Data obtained through a questionnaire with two dimensions are used: knowledge acquisition through gamification by developing activities related to the equation of the straight line together with its applications. The study focuses on particularizing the benefits of gamifying activities in mathematics and recognizing the characteristics of educational treatments within the Educational Unit. Inquiry is used through a questionnaire applied to teachers and students to obtain information about the contribution of gamified activities in the mathematical context of the equation of the straight line. The research is based on statistical testing to test the hypothesis that gamification improves students' academic performance, which involves collecting and analyzing relevant data on students' academic performance. The sample consists of 7 teachers and 92 students through a field exploration in the Educational Unit "Luis Alfredo Martínez" to collect data in real time and directly to its target population of study through surveys applied to managers, teachers and students.

The statistical instrument of satisfaction applied to 92 schoolchildren in the tenth year of higher EGB is based on three areas such as: Gamification, motivation and teamwork, problem development and logical thinking, a technique that measures the impact on students the new and innovative methodology such as motivation.

The following gamification validation questionnaire was applied to the students of the tenth grade of EGB superior of the Educational Unit "Luis Alfredo Martinez" which was approved by two experts of the Education Area, being the following fellow teachers: Mg. Marlene Guaigua, Rector of the Unit; and Msc. Enrique Toapanta Vice Rector. The content of the instrument was validated by the group of experts acting as judges, since they meet the necessary requirements in terms of experience and knowledge. It is possible to verify the importance and the range of approval of the playful procedure on the part of the students, 74.29% indicate that the impact of gamification is very evident not only in the performance but also in the change of attitude with the subject of calculus and particularly with the relevant subject "Equation of the straight line", they consider the resources, the personalization, the challenges and prizes as adequate and motivating.

Motivation and teamwork are essential components in mathematics gamification, especially with straight line equality content. Motivation drives students to actively participate and overcome challenges, while teamwork fosters collaboration, mutual support, and friendly competition. These elements contribute to a more beneficial and effective education skill in the gamification environment, concluding that 80% of the sample considered motivation and teamwork to be highly evident and recommended. Problem solving and the development of reasonable understanding are paramount aspects in the formation and development of calculus processes, including content on straight line equality. These skills allow students to apply concepts, develop critical and analytical thinking, transfer skills, sequence steps, analyze relationships, and justify their reasoning. Their mastery in these aspects contributes to a deeper and more meaningful mathematical learning, enhancing these skills with gamification resulting in 70% considering it very evident to obtain favorable, accurate and correct results by developing logical reasoning, 23.33% considering it quite evident and 0% considering it not evident, see Table 2.

**Table 2.** Participant Satisfaction and Perceived Learning Outcomes

| Dimension | Question | Percentages (levels) |
|---|---|---|
| Gamification | What was your overall level of satisfaction with the incorporation of gamification in the training process? | 90% (very evident) 10% (fairly evident) |
| | To what extent do you think gamification improved your understanding of the theoretical background and skills related to the topic of study? | 70% (very evident) 20% (fairly evident) 10% (evident) |

(*continued*)

**Table 2.** (*continued*)

| Dimension | Question | Percentages (levels) |
|---|---|---|
| | How would you rate the personalization of learning provided through gamification? | 60% (very evident)<br>20% (fairly evident)<br>10% (evident)<br>10% (not very evident) |
| | In general, would you recommend the use of gamification with the Genial.ly platform in training to other students? | 90% (very evident)<br>10% (fairly evident) |
| | Indicate your level of satisfaction with the playful part of the gamification of the equation of the line | 70% (very evident)<br>20% (fairly evident)<br>10% (not very evident) |
| | Mention your level of satisfaction with the resources used in the gamification of the equation of the line | 80% (muy evidente)<br>10% (fairly evident)<br>10% (evidente) |
| Motivation and teawork | State your level of satisfaction with the correctness of the challenges, prizes, medals, benefits, and additional contents of the gamification part of learning the equation of the line | 60% (very evident)<br>20% (fairly evident<br>10% (evidente)<br>10% (not very evident) |
| Solving calculation difficulties and increasing reasonable understanding | Do you consider that gamification promoted your active group participation in the learning process? | 70% (very evident)<br>10% (bastante evidente) |
| | How would you rate the effectiveness of gamification in fostering your engagement and motivation during the learning process? | 10% (evident)<br>10% (not very evident)<br>80% (very evident)<br>20% (fairly evident |
| | To what extent do you think the teamwork contributed to your understanding of the equation of the line? | 90% (very evident)<br>10% (fairly evident) |

(*continued*)

**Table 2.**  (*continued*)

| Dimension | Question | Percentages (levels) |
|---|---|---|
| | How would you rate your level of reasoning and solving skills in calculus difficulties related to the equality of the line after using the learning approach? | 70% (very evident) 20% (fairly evident) 10% (evident) |
| | How would you evaluate the level of development of your logical thinking after using gamification in training on straight line equality? | 70% (very evident) 20% (fairly evident) 10% (not very evident) |
| | In general, would you recommend the application of gamification in obtaining knowledge of straight line equality to solve calculation difficulties and increase reasonable understanding? | 70% (very evident) 30% (fairly evident) |

## 3   Results and Discussion

The links presented below are part of the gamified proposal that I hope you will enjoy and that they will generate the required favorable impact on each of the people who access the gamified presentation: Equation of the straight line: https://acortar.link/gykiNL. Escape to the educational recess: https://acortar.link/sVF6ar. The Deserted Island: https://aco rtar.link/UStwpa. It is recommended to first review the contents and then access the gamification.

Evaluation of the innovative proposal. When evaluating the impact of the gamification of the equation of the line in Genial.ly, the following indicators or criteria specified in the gamification assessment questionnaire for students described below are considered Lozada Ávila & Betancur Gómez [25]. Active participation: Observes the level of effective intervention of learners during the gamified activity. The amount of interactions performed can be measured, such as time spent solving challenges, completing activities or engaging in the game related to the equation of the line.

Knowledge retention: Evaluates the sufficiency of the schoolchildren to remember and apply the contents of the equation of the straight line after gamification. Tests or questionnaires are used to measure their understanding and applicability of the concepts learned during the gamified activity. Motivation and engagement: Observes the range of enthusiasm and engagement of tenth grade students during the gamification. It collects comments, conducts surveys or uses evaluation scales to measure their degree of enthusiasm, interest and commitment during the activity.

Improved academic performance: Analyze whether the gamification of the equation of the line in Genial.ly has had a positive impact on learners' academic productivity.

Compares the grades or results obtained before and after the activity to identify significant improvements as demonstrated in the T-Student test. Collaboration and teamwork: Evaluates the suitability of students to collaborate and perform as a team during gamification. The degree of interaction and cooperation among students is observed, as well as the quality of the solutions or answers they generate together.

Student feedback: Collects feedback from students about the gamification experience in Genially. It uses surveys or interviews to obtain information about their perception of the activity, the aspects they found most useful or fun, and suggestions for improvement. Knowledge transfer: Assesses whether learners have the competence to transfer the cognition acquired during gamification to real situations or problems related to the equation of the line. Practical problems or application situations are provided to verify their ability to apply the concepts learned. It is recalled that these indicators were adapted to the specific needs and objectives of the gamification in Genially on the equation of the straight line. It is also important to mention the data collection to reach a global perception of the impact of the activity through the T-Student test and the gamification assessment questionnaire for students.

According to the quantitative paradigm the post-test was developed with the students of tenth grade of EGB being the probalistic sample of 92 students who, divided in two groups of 46 each one of them, in two weeks receive the application of the gamification with the experimental group (GE) and the execution of techniques, traditional in the control group (GC) to obtain the significant divergence of the means between groups. With the execution of traditionalism in the CONTROL group, the pre-test reflects an average of 8.26 out of 10 points in school productivity of parallels A and B, with the memoristic teaching added with master classes after talks, conversations and monitoring-control of the planning of the teachers of these parallels, an average of 8.42 is obtained, reflecting a significant difference of 0.16, i.e. the improvement in performance is too small or minimal, see Table 3.

Table 3. Student Productivity of the initial pilot (Pre-Test) and the final pilot (Post-Test) of the Control Group

| | Rendimiento grupo de control | Font size and style | | Diferencia significative |
|---|---|---|---|---|
| Estadístico descriptive | Pre-Test | Post-Test | NE | |
| Media | 8.26 | 8.42 | 46 | |
| Diferencia significative | | | | 0.16 |

Before the implementation of gamification in the study group in the tenth parallel C and D, an average of 7.19 is reflected after the two weeks of work with the gamming methodology, the average of 9.59 is obtained, being the significant difference of 2.40 comparing the two groups, it can be clearly observed that gamification in mathematics can encourage the development of skills to solve mathematical difficulties. By presenting challenges, challenges and competencies related to the equations of the line, students have the opportunity to exercise and apply their understanding to find solutions. This promotes critical thinking and logical reasoning. This finding is similar to that found by Lee, Pyon and Woo [26] as well as Rincon-Flores et al. [27], see Table 4.

**Table 4.** Experimental Group Results

| Descriptive statistics | Performance of the expert group (study) | | | Diferencia significative |
|---|---|---|---|---|
| | Pre-Test | Post-Test | NE | |
| Media | 7.19 | 9.59 | 46 | |
| Significant difference | | | | 2.40 |

The statistical comparison with the T - Student test in SPSS determines that there are significant differences in the two groups as with the value of the variable (p > 0.05) in agreement with the quantitative statistics the application of learning through fun and game in the sciences of the theoretical models applied, specifically the topic "The equation of the straight line" notably raised the academic performance of the experimental group, existing minimal or null changes in the learning of the control group, according to Luzuriaga et al. [31]. The significance of the application of gamification in higher GBS levels, especially in tenth grade, is proven because gamification increases the commitment of schoolchildren by turning the acquisition of knowledge into an interactive and fun experiment, using game elements, such as rewards, levels and challenges, students can be motivated to intervene dynamically and to strive to achieve their goals, see Table 5.

To give validity to the T-Student demonstration, the homogeneity test must be similar, apart from being numerical, generating the hypothesis: Ho: Groups with equal variance, H1: Groups with different variances; the Levene test is applied where the p_value is 0.595, therefore there is no statistical evidence to reject Ho, therefore the experimental and control groups are homogeneous, according to Espinosa et al. [32]. To demonstrate the efficiency of the gamification of the equality of the line we have Ho: the averages (means) are equal, H1: The averages (means) are not equal. Since the p_value is less than 0.05 there is no statistical evidence to reject H1, see Table 5.

Regarding the importance and the range of approval of the ludic procedure by the learners, 74.29% consider the resources, personalization, challenges and rewards as adequate and motivating. This coincides with the findings of Lee et al. [26], and Rincón-Flores et al. [27]. This factor should be taken into account in the design of this type of activities. Speaking of Motivation and teamwork are essential components in the gamification of mathematics, especially with the contents of straight line equality, 80% of the participants consider it recommendable, this is similar to what was found by Park et al. [28] and Park et al. [29].

Finally, problem solving and the development of reasonable understanding are essential aspects in the formation and development of calculation processes, 70% considered very evident the obtaining of favorable, precise and correct results by developing logical

**Table 5.** T-test for independent models of the GC and GE FP

| Post-Control | Levene's Test for Equality of Variances | | t-test for equality of means | | | | | 95% for interval confidence interval | |
|---|---|---|---|---|---|---|---|---|---|
| | F | Sig | T | gl | Sig. Bilateral | Diff. of averages | Standard error diff | lower | upper |
| Equal variances are assumed | 18.288 | 0.000 | −5.233 | 90 | 0.000 | −1.163 | 0.222 | −1.605 | −0.722 |
| Equal variances are not assumed | | | −5.233 | 90 | 0.000 | −1.163 | 0.222 | −1.609 | −0.718 |

reasoning, 23.33% considered quite evident and 0% considered not evident. In general, we observe similarities with the research conducted by Subiyantoro [30], as enthusiasm when performing the gamification activities. However, during the sessions some students lost interest in the results of their teams. Therefore, it is worth reflecting on the design of the activities and their dosage.

## 4 Conclusions

The results obtained conclude that the general objective was met, since it is evident that teaching based on gamification with the interactive platform Generally favored both autonomous and collaborative learning, where creativity was developed and above all the motivation of the students of the tenth grade EBG to learn the subject of mathematics in an interactive way.

The objective of this study was to check if the teachers and students fulfilled the same, when applying the surveys, the following results were obtained 74.29% mentioned that if they are attracted to work with gamification especially in the area of mathematics to improve the teaching of the equation of the straight line through the use of different resources, where the benefit of gamification within the learning of students is that they are able to visualize the concept of what is being taught. This will allow teachers to better understand and work with the use of strategies to work in a practical way.

Thanks to the technologies that have been implemented in education have undoubtedly been evolving and creating challenges within educational institutions and especially in teachers, these tools as in generally have proved to be very effective and easy to access and use, since they facilitate the teaching-learning process, as something innovative in the classroom, especially nowadays it is very important to apply this type of platforms since they generate in the student a new way of learning about the equation of the straight line and thus motivate and encourage students to improve their knowledge and academic performance, since mathematics is learned by playing.

As recommendations for future research, it is suggested to prepare teachers about gamification topics related to education, in order to generate and facilitate its use in the development of mathematics classes, where the student will be the only protagonist of his own learning, in the same way the proposed objectives will be fulfilled, encouraging an effective participation of the student.

It is recommended to use gamification very frequently in educational activities, especially in subjects that are complicated for students, especially in the subject of Mathematics, where they are offered very fun tasks, so that teachers can capture the concentration and creativity of the same, so that they can achieve the objectives set through the implementation of educational platforms easily accessible to students.

Encourage teachers to propose the proper use of interactive platforms and they should be kept in constant training, so that when teaching students they can develop in the best way, in this way with the constant use of this tool can respond positively to the educational needs, where the student learns in an interactive and especially innovative way so that students grasp and have fun learning mathematics.

**Disclosure of Interests.**  The authors have no competing interests to declare that are relevant to the content of this article.

# References

1. Hoffmann, M.K.H.: Applying a Flipped Classroom Model for an International School in Taiwan: Overcoming Amotivation and Anxiety in Algebra (Doctoral dissertation, University of Saskatchewan Saskatoon) (2023)
2. Suradika, A., Dewi, H.I., Nasution, M.I.: Experimental of project based learning and problem based learning models in students' critical and creative categories in coloid chemistry subject. J. Pendidik. IPA Indonesia **12**(1) (2023)
3. Toledo Jofré, M., Magendzo Kolstrein, A., Gutiérrez Gianella, V., Iglesias Segura, R.: Enseñanza de'temas controversiales' en la asignatura de historia y ciencias sociales desde la perspectiva de los profesores. Estud. Pedag. (Valdivia) **41**(1), 275–292 (2015)
4. Gómez-Carrasco, C., López-Facal, R., Castro-Fernández, B.: Educación histórica y compe-tencias educativas. Educar em Revista **35**(74), 145–171 (2019). https://doi.org/10.1590/0104-4060.64402. FapUNIFESP (SciELO)
5. Bernaschina, D.: GIF y net. art en las TIC: nueva aplicación educativa para la escuela inclusiva. Rev. Avenir **6**(1), 7–15 (2022)
6. Lang, S.N., et al.: Early childhood teachers' dispositions, knowledge, and skills related to diversity, inclusion, equity, and justice. Early Childhood Res. Quart. **67**, 111–127 (2024)
7. El-Attar, N.E., El-Ela, N.A., Awad, W.A.: Integrated learning approaches based on cloud com-puting for personalizing e-learning environment. Int. J. Web-Based Learn. Teach. Technol. **14**(2), 67–87 (2019). https://doi.org/10.4018/ijwltt.2019040105. IGI Global
8. Gates, E.F., Teasdale, R.M., Shim, C., Hubacz, H.: Whose and what values? Advancing and illustrating explicit specification of evaluative criteria in education. Stud. Educ. Eval. **81**, 101335 (2024). https://doi.org/10.1016/j.stueduc.2024.101335. Elsevier BV
9. Zhang, S., Zhou, A.: The construction and practice of a TPACK development training model for Novice University Teachers. Sustainability **15**(15), 11816 (2023). https://doi.org/10.3390/su151511816. MDPI AG

10. Hashmi, S., et al.: Perspectives on embedding inclusive pedagogy within a BSc psychology curriculum. Cogent Educ. **11**(1) (2024). Informa UK Limited
11. Valenzuela, R., Codina, N., Castillo, I., Pestana, J.V.: Young university students' academic self-regulation profiles and their associated procrastination: autonomous functioning requires self-regulated operations. Front. Psychol. **11** (2020). Frontiers Media SA
12. Evans, P., Vansteenkiste, M., Parker, P., Kingsford-Smith, A., Zhou, S.: Cognitive load theory and its relationships with motivation: a self-determination theory perspective. Educ. Psychol. Rev. **36**(1) (2024). Springer Science and Business Media LLC
13. Michou, A., Altan, S., Mouratidis, A., Reeve, J., Malmberg, L.-E.: Week-to-week interplay between teachers' motivating style and students' engagement. J. Exp. Educ. **91**(1), 166–185 (2021). https://doi.org/10.1080/00220973.2021.1897774. Informa UK Limited
14. Jiménez Torres, M.G.: Experiencias de flow en niños y jóvenes: Influencias en distintos indicadores de rendimiento y bienestar (2016)
15. Rativa, D.S.: Estrategia metodológica orientada desde la Gamificación para la promoción de hábitos saludables, en la comunidad del Barrio Diana Turbay de Bogotá DC (2021)
16. Khasawneh, M.A.S.: Beyond digital platforms: gamified skill development in real-world scenarios and environmental variables. Int. J. Data Netw. Sci. **8**(1), 213–220 (2024). https://doi.org/10.5267/j.ijdns.2023.10.002. Growing Science
17. Barata, G., Gama, S., Jorge, J., Gonçalves, D.: Identifying student types in a gamified learning experience. Gamification 541–558 (2015). https://doi.org/10.4018/978-1-4666-8200-9.ch026. IGI Global
18. Alkhawalde, M.A., Khasawneh, M.A.S.: Designing gamified assistive apps: a novel approach to motivating and supporting students with learning disabilities. Int. J. Data Netw. Sci. **8**(1), 53–60 (2024). Growing Science
19. Elmawati, E., Martadiputra, B.A.P., Samosir, C.M.: Gamification research focus in learning mathematics. In: 2023 the 5th World Symposium on Software Engineering (WSSE) (WSSE 2023). ACM (2023). https://doi.org/10.1145/3631991.3632012
20. Čubela, D., Rossner, A., Neis, P.: Using problem-based learning and gamification as a catalyst for student engagement in data-driven engineering education: a report. Educ. Sci. **13**(12), 1223 (2023). https://doi.org/10.3390/educsci13121223. MDPI AG
21. Chen, Y.-C., Hwang, G.-J., Lai, C.-L.: Motivating students to become self-regulatory learners: a gamified mobile self-regulated learning approach. Educ. Inf. Technol. (2024). https://doi.org/10.1007/s10639-024-12462-z
22. Chen, M.-F., Chen, Y.-C., Zuo, P.-Y., Hou, H.-T.: Design and evaluation of a remote synchronous gamified mathematics teaching activity that integrates multi-representational scaffolding and a mind tool for gamified learning. Educ. Inf. Technol. **28**(10), 13207–13233 (2023). https://doi.org/10.1007/s10639-023-11708-6. Springer Science and Business Media LLC
23. Dehghanzadeh, H., Farrokhnia, M., Dehghanzadeh, H., Taghipour, K., Noroozi, O.: Using gamification to support learning in K-12 education: a systematic literature review. Br. J. Educ. Technol. **55**(1), 34–70 (2024). https://doi.org/10.1111/bjet.13335. Wiley
24. Sanmugam, M., Mohd Zaid, N., Mohamed, H., Abdullah, Z., Aris, B., Md Suhadi, S.: Gamification as an educational technology tool in engaging and motivating students. An analyses review. Adv. Sci. Lett. **21**(10), 3337–3341 (2015)
25. Lozada Ávila, C., Betancur Gómez, S.: La gamificación en la educación superior: una revisión sistemática. Rev. Ingenier. Univers. Medellín **16**(31), 97–124 (2017). https://doi.org/10.22395/rium.v16n31a5. Universidad de Medellin
26. Lee, J.Y., Pyon, C.U., Woo, J.: Digital twin for math education: a study on the utilization of games and gamification for University Mathematics Education. Electronics **12**(15), 3207 (2023). https://doi.org/10.3390/electronics12153207. MDPI AG

27. Rincon-Flores, E.G., Santos-Guevara, B.N., Martinez-Cardiel, L., Rodriguez-Rodriguez, N.K., Quintana-Cruz, H.A., Matsuura-Sonoda, A.: Gamit! icing on the cake for mathematics gamification. Sustainability **15**(3), 2334 (2023). https://doi.org/10.3390/su15032334. MDPI AG

28. Park, S., Kim, S.: The avaritia: entrepreneurship practice to understand the problem of information control through gamification. Sustainability **15**(8), 6738 (2023). https://doi.org/10.3390/su15086738. MDPI AG

29. Park, S., Kim, S.: Learning performance styles in gamified college classes using data clustering. Sustainability **14**(23), 15574 (2022). https://doi.org/10.3390/su142315574. MDPI AG

30. Subiyantoro, S., Degeng, I.N.S., Kuswandi, D., Ulfa, S.: Developing gamified learning management systems to increase student engagement in online learning environments. Int. J. Inf. Educ. Technol. **14**(1), 26–33 (2024). https://doi.org/10.18178/ijiet.2024.14.1.2020. EJournal Publishing

31. Jaramillo, H.A.L., Pinos, C.A.E., Sarango, A.F.H., Román, H.D.O.: Histograma y distribución normal: Shapiro-Wilk y Kolmogorov Smirnov aplicado en SPSS: Histogram and normal distribution: Shapiro-Wilk and Kolmogorov Smirnov applied in SPSS. LATAM Revista Latinoamericana de Ciencias Sociales y Humanidades **4**(4), 596–607 (2023)

32. Espinosa-Pinos, C.A., Villota-Zambrano, J.C., Luzuriaga-Jaramillo, H.A.: Algoritmo para clasificar la resolución de conflictos en aspirantes automotrices. Revista Tecnológica-ESPOL **35**(2), 170–180 (2023)

33. Rojas-López, A., Rincón-Flores, E.G., Mena, J., García-Peñalvo, F.J., Ramírez-Montoya, M.S.: Engagement in the course of programming in higher education through the use of gamification. In: Universal Access in the Information Society, **18**(3), 583–597 (2019). https://doi.org/10.1007/s10209-019-00680-z. Springer Science and Business Media LLC

# A Gamified Learning Experience for Teaching European Values in English Lessons

Lucía García-Holgado(✉) ⓘ, Francisco José García-Peñalvo ⓘ,
and Andrea Vázquez-Ingelmo ⓘ

GRIAL Research Group, Research Institute for Educational Sciences,
Universidad de Salamanca, Salamanca, Spain
{luciagh,fgarcia,andreavazquez}@usal.es
https://ror.org/02f40zc51

**Abstract.** This study presents an eLearning course that synergizes gamification with game-based learning methodologies to enhance the educational experience within the framework of the European Project Gamified Values Education for Fostering Migrant Integration at Schools (GAMIGRATION). This paper explores the innovative application of gamified learning within the context of English language instruction, specifically designed to inculcate European values among students. The primary goal is to foster inclusion and improve the integration of immigrant students in European schools. Each level consists of modules emphasizing values such as cultural diversity, respect, tolerance, and solidarity, leveraging game-based learning resources to enhance interactivity and engagement. This work presents the pedagogical design by implementing the gamified course, illustrating its potential as an effective tool for integrating European values into language learning.

**Keywords:** Gamification · eLearning · European Values · Game-based-learning

## 1 Introduction

In the contemporary landscape, children are inherently immersed in a digital world, with adolescents demonstrating significant interest in video and mobile gaming. Although this tendency could raise concerns, we aim to transform it into a solution that facilitates the integration of immigrant students. Our approach involves leveraging gamified eLearning courses to enable immigrant and local students to deepen their understanding of European Values. We aim to provide educators with tangible teaching materials embedded within authentic contexts, fostering the instruction and reinforcement of shared European Values. This initiative is facilitated through Gamified English Lessons, applying gamification principles that encompass the integration of gameplay elements within non-game applications, particularly in consumer-centric web and mobile interfaces [1]. This strategy incentivizes user adoption of these applications and encourages the desired behaviors associated with them. In essence, gamification, synonymous with engagement, has been substantiated by numerous researchers as a powerful catalyst for enhanced learner engagement, utilizing elements that are fundamental to the gamification process [2, 3].

P. Zaphiris and A. Ioannou (Eds.): HCII 2024, LNCS 14723, pp. 31–44, 2024.
https://doi.org/10.1007/978-3-031-61685-3_3

This study operates within the scope of the European project Gamified Values Education For Fostering Migrant Integration at Schools (GAMIGRATION) [4]. Its primary goal is to introduce an innovative framework for enhancing inclusion within educational settings, particularly in English classes [5]. This is achieved by integrating gamification and game-based-learning methodologies and teaching European values, presenting a novel approach to promoting and enriching the educational environment.

Following this objective, the project is structured around four outcomes developed through the consortium's expertise. To achieve this, a perception study on inclusion in educational institutions has been conducted [6]. Additionally, an eLearning [7] course gamified around European values will be developed alongside creating branching scenarios to enhance students' understanding of cultural diversity. These initiatives aim to strengthen the educational environment, promote respect, and enhance mutual understanding between immigrant and local students.

This paper presents the gamification approach adopted in an eLearning course specifically designed and implemented to emphasize European Values. It highlights incorporating game-based learning resources within the course content as a pivotal aspect of the design and implementation process.

This work is organized into six sections. Section 2 introduces the project, offering an overview of GAMIGRATION. Section 3 details the design of the eLearning course. Section 4 describes the gamification strategy employed in the courses. Section 5 discusses the implementation of the educational plan. Finally, Sect. 6 summarizes the conclusions drawn from this study.

## 2 Project Description

The GAMIGRATION project represents a concerted effort to transform the educational experience for migrant students by integrating European Union citizenship values and eLearning strategies. This initiative seeks to provide new approaches and resources designed to make the transition for these students into new educational environments. Using gamification in English language teaching, the project intends to make the learning process more engaging and less intimidating [8].

The GAMIGRATION project has two key objectives that drive its progress:

- *Facilitating the adaptation process.* The project aims to ease the adaptation process for immigrant pupils, rendering it more enjoyable and stress-free. By introducing gamification techniques in English classes, the project seeks to create a more dynamic and supportive learning environment.
- *Teaching EU citizenship values.* An implicit goal within the English curriculum is to convey core European Union citizenship values, which encompass Respect for Human Dignity, Equality, Human Rights, Inclusion and Tolerance, and Respect for Diversity. Through this approach, the project not only teaches language but also cultivates a sense of shared values among students.

To achieve these overarching goals, GAMIGRATION has set forth four specific objectives:

- *Understanding integration challenges.* Initiating a comprehensive analysis of the factors that impede the integration of students with migrant backgrounds to develop targeted educational strategies.
- *Supporting English educators.* Assisting English teachers in imparting European citizenship values to both immigrant and local learners in a manner that complements the explicit teaching of the English language.
- *Providing practical teaching materials.* Supplying educators with tangible, real-life teaching resources that facilitate the teaching and reinforcement of shared European values.
- *Enhancing mutual understanding.* Enhancing the mutual comprehension among native and immigrant students by sharing knowledge about each other's daily lives, familial backgrounds, cultural customs, and values systems.

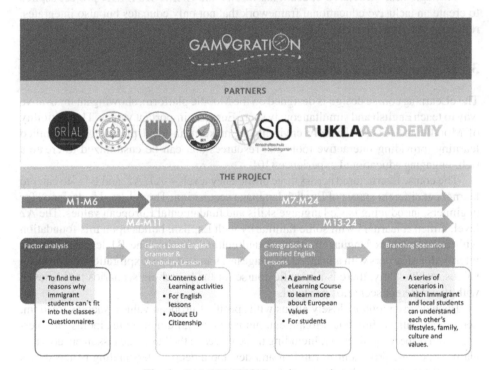

**Fig. 1.** GAMIGRATION results overview.

The GAMIGRATION project, led by the University of Salamanca throughout the GRIAL Research Group [9], unites a consortium of educational institutions, including IES Ruiz de Alda, Bursa İl Millî Eğitim Müdürlüğü, Nesrin Fuat Bursali İlkokulu, UKLA AKADEMI, and Wirtschaftsschule am Oswaldsgarten. This collaborative initiative aims to leverage gamified learning to facilitate the integration of immigrant pupils into European educational systems with the development of four educational outcomes (Fig. 1):

- *Factor analysis.* Using questionnaires, this first outcome aims to recognize the different challenges that can affect the smooth integration of immigrant students into new schools.
- *Game-based English lessons about EU citizenship.* The second output supports English educators in teaching EU citizenship values while focusing on the clear objectives of language learning.
- *E-integration via gamified English lessons.* The third outcome offers a gamified eLearning course for the students to provide educators with effective didactic materials that enrich the learning experience and reinforce common European values.
- *Branching scenarios.* Lastly, the project develops branching scenarios to foster personalized learning situations that enable immigrant and local learners to better understand each other's personal and cultural backgrounds.

Through these structured educational results, the GAMIGRATION project aspires to create an inclusive educational framework that not only educates but also integrates, reflecting the great diversity in Europe.

## 3   Design of the eLearning Course

The eLearning course design is designed on the Moodle platform, showing an innovative way to teach English and simultaneously share Europe's important values. The flexibility of Moodle and its user-friendly environment make it an ideal platform for gamified learning, providing interactive tools and resources that can be customized to create a rich, engaging educational experience [10].

The course is structured across three proficiency levels—A1, A2, and B1—to cater to learners at different stages of English language acquisition. The A1 level is designed for beginners, introducing basic language skills and fundamental European values. The A2 level, aimed at learners with some familiarity with English, builds upon this foundation with more complex language structures and cultural details. The B1 level challenges intermediate learners with advanced language tasks and a deeper exploration of European values. Additionally, there is a specific course for the branching scenarios to this level, with two different scenarios per level.

Each course module closely aligns with specific European values, such as freedom, democracy, citizenship, equal treatment, human dignity, human rights, inclusion, tolerance, and respect for diversity. Including these values in the language lesson ensures that learners become proficient in English and develop a deep understanding of the values essential to European identity.

Within each block of the course, students are provided with a comprehensive suite of activities focusing on key areas of language acquisition: Grammar, Vocabulary, and Skills. These activities are carefully designed to teach the mechanics of the English language and enhance the practical application of these elements in real-world contexts. After completing these activities, students undertake an evaluation specifically tailored to assess their understanding of the content covered in that block. This evaluative step is crucial as it ensures that students have effectively assimilated the knowledge before progressing, reinforces their learning, and provides a clear way for their achievements (See Fig. 2).

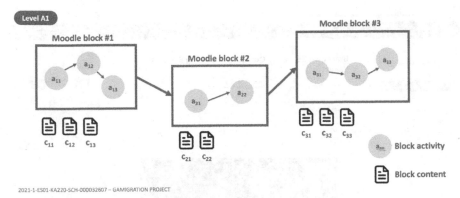

**Fig. 2.** Course design structure

A crucial component of the course design was the English proficiency test, which was employed by our target groups to verify the levels for working in the course. This test is thoughtfully crafted to evaluate the learners' abilities, ensuring that we can provide the level that matches their skills, thus guaranteeing an optimal learning trajectory. Despite the majority being at an A1 level, we decided to create more levels to provide learning tailored to each student's individual proficiency to foster motivation. It is important to match students with the right level so everyone feels comfortable and challenged enough to learn effectively.

Within this framework, game-based learning resources are key elements, enhancing interactivity and immersion. These resources are strategically integrated into different modules, fostering engagement through interactive quests and also one course only for the branching scenarios. Each module corresponds to a particular European value, ensuring comprehensive coverage and practical application across proficiency levels.

One of the core innovations lies in fostering collaborative learning environments, where both immigrant and local students interact within the gamified course. This approach facilitates language acquisition and fosters mutual understanding and respect among learners from varied backgrounds.

This eLearning course is more than just a language program; it is an immersive journey through language and values designed to foster collaboration and unity among learners from diverse backgrounds. Confidence is held in the approach that combines the capabilities of the Moodle platform (Fig. 3) with innovative gamification techniques [11], which is expected to significantly enhance the educational experience and facilitate the integration of immigrant students into the European educational landscape.

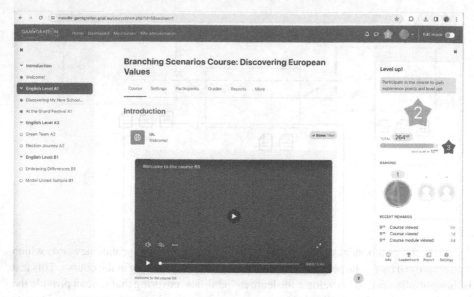

**Fig. 3.** Gamified course in the GAMIGRATION Moodle platform

# 4 Gamification Strategy

## 4.1 Gamification Elements

The design of the GAMIGRATION courses thoughtfully incorporates various gamification techniques to enrich the educational journey of learners. This section delves into the specific gamification elements [12] that are woven into the course structure, each selected to bolster engagement and facilitate a deeper connection with the course material (Fig. 4):

- *Progression badges.* The courses use a badge system [13] to mark progression, which is a common gamification technique to motivate learners and provide them with tangible evidence of their achievements. Each course level, from A1 to B1, and the additional Branching Scenarios (BS) course, is structured to award badges upon completing modules, branching scenarios, and assessments. This visual reward system can help keep students engaged and motivated to progress through the courses.

- *Modular structure with EU value themes.* Each course is divided into modules focused on specific European Union values. This modular structure allows for a focused exploration of each value, making the learning experience manageable and rewarding. By completing a module, students earn a badge, which gamifies the learning process and can foster a sense of accomplishment.

- *Assessments with rewards.* Students are assessed to ensure comprehension and retention after completing certain activities and resources within the modules. Successful completion of assessments is rewarded with badges, reinforcing the knowledge acquired and incentivizing the mastery of the course content [14].

- *Engagement through play.* The B1 level course includes a feature labeled "Play ENGAME" [15, 16] with the integration of a game or interactive activity designed to deepen the learning experience through play. This aligns with game-based learning principles, where the act of playing itself facilitates education.
- *Branching scenarios.* The courses include branching scenarios, which are interactive learning experiences where students make choices that influence the outcome. Completing these scenarios earns students' badges, promoting active learning and decision-making. This approach can deepen the student's engagement with the course content and provide a personalized learning experience. Beyond the main language proficiency courses, there are different scenarios with themes such as "Discovering My New School," "Election Journey," and "Embracing Differences." These likely represent specialized content that caters to various aspects of cultural and social integration, using gamification to make these important topics more engaging.
- *Leaderboards.* The reference to leaderboards [17] in each course is a competitive element where students can compare their progress with peers. This can encourage learners to engage more deeply with the course material to improve their standing on the leaderboard.
- *Levels.* The color-coded levels indicate a progression system within each course. This tiered approach allows learners to move through stages, experiencing a structured learning journey. Completing each level is likely associated with earning a badge, adding to the gamified experience.

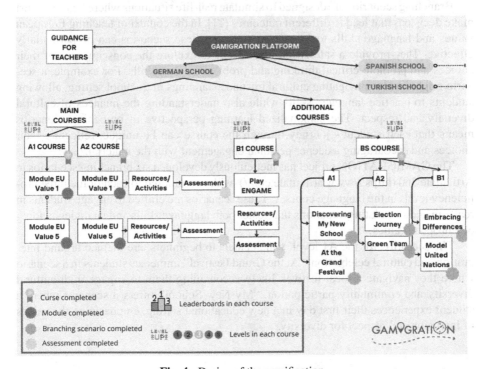

**Fig. 4.** Design of the gamification

- *Avatars.* Avatars are vital in enhancing the learning experience and protecting student identities [18]. Each student can automatically generate a simple image for their profile, thus eliminating the need to upload personal photographs, which could infringe on their privacy. Additionally, the course will provide a selection of optional, predesigned avatars that students can choose from according to their preferences. This approach encourages creativity and individual expression and adheres to strict digital privacy and security policies, ensuring that uploaded images are thoroughly reviewed and verified for appropriateness and safety within the educational environment.

In conclusion, the GAMIGRATION course design utilizes a comprehensive gamification strategy that includes progression badges, modular learning, branching scenarios, interactive assessments, thematic play, and competitive leaderboards. These elements are designed to work in synergy to create an immersive and motivating educational environment that teaches English and European values and promotes inclusion and the integration of immigrant students [19].

### 4.2 Branching Scenarios

One of the strengths of the design is the branching scenarios. Branching scenarios [20] is a powerful gamification element that can transform traditional learning into a dynamic and engaging experience, particularly within the context of the GAMIGRATION project's eLearning courses.

Branching scenarios are designed to simulate real-life situations where learners must make decisions that lead to different outcomes [21]. In the context of teaching European values and language skills to immigrant students, these scenarios can be particularly effective. They provide a safe space for learners to explore the consequences of their choices and promote critical thinking and problem-solving skills. For example, a scenario might involve navigating cultural misunderstandings in a school setting, allowing students to practice language skills while also understanding the nuances of cultural diversity and respect. The personalized learning perspective of branching scenarios means that each student's journey through the course can be unique, reflecting their choices and encouraging a deeper personal engagement with the material.

The GAMIGRATION project has meticulously developed six branching scenarios in Articulate 360 (https://www.articulate.com/), with two tailored to each of the three proficiency levels in the language courses. These scenarios are crafted to engage students in real-life and stimulating situations that foster both language skills and an understanding of European values.

The scenarios for the A1 level, which caters to beginners, are themed around integration and cultural celebration. "At the Grand Festival" immerses students in a scenario where they navigate a local festival, likely encouraging them to engage with cultural diversity and community participation. "My New School" offers a scenario where a student experiences their first day in a new educational setting, emphasizing the values of inclusion and respect for diversity.

The scenarios become more complex at the A2 level, designed for students who are slightly more advanced in their language proficiency. "Green Team" could involve students in environmental initiatives, promoting teamwork and responsibility, while "Election Journey" likely simulates a school election process, teaching democratic values and the importance of active participation.

For the intermediate B1 level students, "Embracing Differences" likely challenges them to engage with scenarios that require understanding and appreciation of diverse perspectives, fostering a deeper sense of tolerance and solidarity. "Model United Nations (MUN)" is a scenario that simulates participation in a Model UN conference (Fig. 5), encouraging students to debate and negotiate on global issues, reflecting the EU values of human dignity and rights.

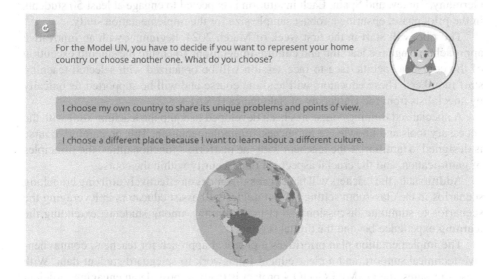

**Fig. 5.** Branching Scenario: Model of United Nations

These branching scenarios are an integral part of the GAMIGRATION project's course design, offering students the opportunity to apply language skills in contextually rich settings that reflect their learning and the societal values they are being encouraged to embrace.

### 4.3 Game-Based Resources

The selection of game-based resources for the GAMIGRATION project's course is strategically aimed at fostering an engaging and motivating learning environment. These resources require active participation, thereby ensuring better retention and practical application of knowledge. The immersive nature of game-based learning allows for contextual and experiential learning, where students can practice European values within realistic scenarios. Immediate feedback within games helps students quickly grasp and correct their understanding while problem-solving aspects encourage critical thinking. Collaboration in the game settings enhances communication and teamwork skills, which are critical for integrating immigrant students. Additionally, the adaptability of game-based resources caters to varied learning styles and proficiency levels, providing a personalized learning journey. Crucially, the safe and low-pressure environment of games permits students to learn from failures, fostering resilience and confidence in their language learning and cultural integration.

## 5 Expected Implementation and Impact

The GAMIGRATION course will be rolled out across three educational institutions in Germany, Turkey, and Spain. Each institution is expected to engage at least 50 students in the pilot phase, ensuring a robust sample size for the implementation study.

The pilot will start in the first week of March 2024, beginning with an innovative approach to language learning and cultural integration. To ensure the smooth execution of the course, a specific face-to-face session will be organized with selected teaching staff members. These educators will lead the course and will be supported technically by specialists from the University of Salamanca (USAL).

A specialized training course has been developed to equip the teaching staff with the necessary tools and knowledge for successful implementation. This preparatory course is designed to familiarize the teachers with the platform's functionalities, the principles of gamification, and the crucial aspects of data security within the course.

Additionally, the teachers will have access to guides on effectively utilizing branching scenarios in the classroom setting. These guides will assist educators in leveraging the scenarios to stimulate discussion and critical thinking among students, extending the learning experience beyond the digital screen.

The implementation plan prioritizes a practical approach for teachers, comprehensive technical support, and a clear ethical framework to safeguard student data. With these measures, the GAMIGRATION project is ready to provide an engaging, efficient educational program that meets the highest standards of educational quality and ethical practice.

The gamified learning experience is expected to strongly impact students, particularly in promoting inclusion and integration. By participating in a curriculum that combines language learning with European values, students will likely improve their language skills and gain a better understanding and respect for diversity and cultural differences. The interactive nature of the course should encourage students from various backgrounds to work together, thereby breaking down barriers and promoting a sense of community. This inclusive environment is designed to help immigrant students feel welcomed and valued, facilitating smoother integration into the school system and society at large.

However, implementing such an innovative educational approach comes with challenges. One potential difficulty is the varying levels of digital literacy among students and educators, which could impact the effectiveness of gamification strategies. To mitigate this, comprehensive training and ongoing technical support will be crucial. Another challenge could be the engagement level across different cultural contexts; what motivates students in one country may not resonate in another. This can be addressed by tailoring gamification elements to be culturally responsive and offering flexibility in the course content.

Additionally, technical issues such as server downtime or software glitches could disrupt the learning process because the course depends directly on technology. Establishing a robust technical support system and having contingency plans in place are essential solutions to this challenge. Lastly, measuring the effectiveness of such a program in real-world settings will require careful consideration and development of appropriate assessment tools that go beyond traditional testing methods to capture how of inclusion and integration progress.

Overall, while there are challenges to anticipate, with careful planning and a focus on adaptability, the GAMIGRATION project stands to make a meaningful impact on the educational and social experience of students, particularly in fostering an inclusive environment that supports integration.

## 6 Discussion and Conclusions

Implementing gamified courses in educational settings has shown considerable potential in actively engaging students. This engagement is not solely attributed to the novelty of gaming elements but also to their ability to contextualize learning in an interactive framework. The gamified courses in the GAMIGRATION project are expected to take advantage of this, creating an informative and engaging learning experience. The courses use gaming elements like scoring points, having competitions, and putting students in different scenarios to keep them interested and motivated. These are key factors in successful language acquisition and value internalization.

Teaching European values through games is a special chance to share these ideas in a way that makes sense to the digitally native student population. The anticipated benefits include a deeper, more intuitive understanding of such values, as the learning process is both experiential and reflective. Values like tolerance, democracy, and human rights are not merely taught as abstract concepts but are experienced through gameplay and decision-making processes within the course.

The course design is grounded in educational theory, emphasizing active learning, student engagement, and the contextual application of knowledge. Its theoretical contributions lie in its practical application of gamification within an educational framework, which is expected to yield insights into effective pedagogical strategies for digital learning environments.

For educators, this approach means a paradigm to change the teaching methodology, embracing more facilitative roles in guiding students through the learning process. Policymakers may consider the implications of such innovative methods on broader educational practices, potentially advocating for more resources to be allocated toward technology-driven learning solutions. Curriculum developers are encouraged to consider integrating gamified elements in curriculum design to cater to diverse learning needs and preferences.

However, this design has limitations. The efficacy of gamification in education is contingent upon the balance between educational content and game elements, which can be challenging to achieve. Additionally, the dependence on technology raises concerns about accessibility and the digital gap. Future research directions include exploring the long-term impact of gamified learning on student outcomes, the scalability of such courses across different educational contexts, and the development of best practices for integrating gamification into the curriculum.

In conclusion, the GAMIGRATION gamified courses represent a step towards an immersive learning experience that teaches English and instills European values in students. While its full impact remains to be seen, the potential benefits and theoretical contributions offer promising directions for the future of educational practices.

**Acknowledgments.** This study has been carried out in the framework of the project, supported by the European Union's Erasmus+ Programme under its Key Action 2: Partnership for Cooperation in School Education. Gamified Values Education for Fostering Migrant Integration at Schools – GAMIGRATION project (Reference number: 2021-1-ES01-KA220-SCH-000032607). The content of the publication is the sole responsibility of the author, and neither the European Commission nor the Spanish Service for the Internationalization of Education (SEPIE) is responsible for any use that may be made of the information contained therein. This research work is done under the University of Salamanca PhD Programme on Education in the Knowledge Society scope (http://knowledgesociety.usal.es) [22].

# References

1. Llorens-Largo, F., Gallego-Durán, F.J., Villagrá-Arnedo, C.J., Compañ-Rosique, P., Satorre-Cuerda, R., Molina-Carmona, R.: Gamification of the learning process: lessons learned. IEEE Revista Iberoamericana de Tecnologias del Aprendizaje **11**, 227–234 (2016). https://doi.org/10.1109/RITA.2016.2619138
2. Roa González, J., Sánchez Sánchez, A., Sánchez Sánchez, N.: Evaluación de la implantación de la Gamificación como metodología activa en la Educación Secundaria española. Rei-DoCrea. Revista de investigación y Docencia Creativa **10**, 1–9 (2021). https://doi.org/10.30827/Digibug.66357
3. Alonso de Castro, M.G., García-Peñalvo, F.J.: Systematic review of Erasmus+ projects labelled as good practice and related to e-learning and ICT: some case studies. Heliyon **9**, e22331 (2023). https://doi.org/10.1016/j.heliyon.2023.e22331
4. García-Holgado, L., et al.: Gamified values education for fostering migrant integration at schools. In: Proceedings of the Tenth International Conference on Technological Ecosystems for Enhancing Multiculturality (TEEM 2022), Salamanca, 19–21 October 2022, pp. 1117–1123. Springer, Singapore (2023). https://doi.org/10.1007/978-981-99-0942-1_118
5. García-Holgado, L., et al.: La gamificación en la enseñanza de inglés como lengua extranjera para el fomento de valores europeos. In: Fernández-Sánchez, A.J. (eds.) Resúmenes de conferencias y comunicaciones. XIII Congreso ACLES Centros de lenguas universitarios e internacionalización: nuevos desafíos. Salamanca, del 29 de junio al 1 de julio de 2023, Salamanca, España (2023)
6. García-Holgado, L.: Estudio sobre la percepción de la inclusión en Instituciones Educativas Europeas. (Master Thesis). Máster Universitario en Estudios de la Ciencia, la Tecnología y la Innovación. Universidad de Salamanca. Salamanca, España (2023)
7. García-Peñalvo, F.J. (ed.): Advances in E-Learning: Experiences and methodologies. Information Science Reference (formerly Idea Group Reference), Hershey (2008)

8. Erling, E., Foltz, A., Siwik, F., Brummer, M.: Teaching English to linguistically diverse students from migration backgrounds: from deficit perspectives to pockets of possibility. Languages **7**, 186 (2022). https://doi.org/10.3390/languages7030186

9. García-Peñalvo, F.J., Rodríguez-Conde, M.J., Therón, R., García-Holgado, A., Martínez-Abad, F., Benito-Santos, A.: Grupo GRIAL. IE Comunicaciones. Revista Iberoamericana de Informática Educativa 33–48 (2019)

10. dos Reis, S.C., Machado Linck, A.J., Flores Figueiredo, M., Lopes Pfeifer, D.: Gamification into the design of the e-3D online course. Front. Educ. **8** (2023). https://doi.org/10.3389/feduc.2023.1152999

11. Cornellà Canals, P., Estebanell Minguell, M.: GaMoodlification: moodle at the service of the gamification of learning. Campus Virtuales **7**, 9–25 (2018)

12. Nah, F.F.-H., Zeng, Q., Rajasekhar Telaprolu, V., Padmanabhuni Ayyappa, A., Eschenbrenner, B.: Gamification of education: a review of literature. In: Nah, F.F.-H. (ed.) HCI in Business (HCIB 2014), pp. 401–409. Springer, Cham (2014). https://doi.org/10.1007/978-3-319-07293-7_39

13. Hamari, J.: Do badges increase user activity? A field experiment on the effects of gamification. Comput. Hum. Behav. **71**, 469–478 (2017). https://doi.org/10.1016/j.chb.2015.03.036

14. Sanneman, L., Shah, J.A.: Validating metrics for reward alignment in human-autonomy teaming. Comput. Hum. Behav. **146**, 107809 (2023). https://doi.org/10.1016/j.chb.2023.107809

15. Afxentiou, A., et al.: A case study on gaming implementation for social inclusion and civic participation. In: Lopata, A., Gudonienė, D., Butkienė, R. (eds.) Information and Software Technologies (ICIST 2022), pp. 305–314. Springer, Cham (2022). https://doi.org/10.1007/978-3-031-16302-9_25

16. Dambrauskas, E., Gudonienė, D., García-Holgado, A., García-Peñalvo, F.J., Kiourti, E., Fruhmann, P., Kyriakidou, M.: Understanding user perspectives on an educational game for civic and social inclusion. In: Lopata, A., Gudonienė, D., Butkienė, R. (eds.) Information and Software Technologies (ICIST 2023), pp. 222–234. Springer, Cham (2024). https://doi.org/10.1007/978-3-031-48981-5_18

17. Daineko, L.V., Goncharova, N.V., Zaitseva, E.V., Larionova, V.A., Dyachkova, I.A.: Gamification in education: a literature review. In: Bylieva, D., Nordmann, A. (eds.) The World of Games: Technologies for Experimenting, Thinking, Learning. XXIII Professional Culture of the Specialist of the Future, vol. 1, pp. 319–343. Springer, Cham (2023). https://doi.org/10.1007/978-3-031-48020-1_25

18. Ratinho, E., Martins, C.: The role of gamified learning strategies in student's motivation in high school and higher education: a systematic review. Heliyon **9** (2023). https://doi.org/10.1016/j.heliyon.2023.e19033

19. Mateus, C., Campis, R., Jabba, D., María Erazo, A., Romero, V.: Gamification as a tool for inclusion. In: Altınay, F., Altınay, Z. (eds.) Intellectual and Learning Disabilities - Inclusiveness and Contemporary Teaching Environments. IntechOpen (2023). https://doi.org/10.5772/intechopen.113229

20. Pujolà, J.T., Argüello, A.: Stories or scenarios: implementing narratives in gamified language teaching. In: Arnedo-Moreno, J., González-González, C.S., Mora, A. (eds.) Proceedings of the 3rd International Symposium on Gamification and Games for Learning (GamiLearn 2019), Barcelona, 22 October 2019. CEUR-WS.org, Aachen (2019)

21. Argueta-Muñoz, F.D., Olvera-Cortés, H.E., Durán-Cárdenas, C., Hernández-Gutiérrez, L., Gutierrez-Barreto, S.E.: Instructional design and its usability for branching model as an educational strategy. Cureus **15** (2023). https://doi.org/10.7759/cureus.39182
22. García-Peñalvo, F.J.: Education in knowledge society: a new PhD programme approach. In: García-Peñalvo, F.J. (ed.) Proceedings of the First International Conference on Technological Ecosystems for Enhancing Multiculturality (TEEM 2013), 14–15 November 2013, Salamanca, pp. 575–577. ACM, New York (2013). https://doi.org/10.1145/2536536.2536624

# Spatial Cognition Through Gestural Interfaces: Embodied Play and Learning with Minecraft

Jannah Issa⬤, Vishesh Kumar(✉)⬤, and Marcelo Worsley⬤

Northwestern University, Evanston, IL 60208, USA
jannahissa2026@u.northwestern.edu,
{vishesh.kumar,marcelo.worsley}@northwestern.edu

**Abstract.** Increasingly accessible gesture-based interfaces offer powerful but underexplored potential for facilitating inclusive and engaging learning experiences. In this work, we explore creating and testing a hand and body pose-based gestural control interface for playing Minecraft. This work aims to be a starting point for making Minecraft (and other video games) based learning and play more inclusive and engaging by moving away from just keyboard-mouse controls. We study the viability and user-friendliness of our initial designs through surveys, interviews, and early co-design sessions, shaping gestures that resonate with diverse youth, enriching the learning and assessment of spatial cognition skills among them.

**Keywords:** Multimodal Interfaces · Gesture Based Control · Spatial Thinking · Game-based Learning

## 1 Introduction

Educational video games spanning homes, schools, and various out-of-school contexts have become indispensable tools for learning [16]. Their applications in diverse fields such as STEM, Social Sciences, and Special Needs education are well-documented [2,8]. Minecraft, in particular, stands out due to its extensive usage across disciplines, as well as its potential for enhancing spatial cognition skills [16].

Video games in general and Minecraft in particular have been recognized for supporting development of a variety of spatial cognition skills [13,15], a fundamental aspect of human intelligence. [4] highlight the potential design space for engaging spatial cognition using embodied interfaces. Gestural interfaces also offer increased access for children with physical disabilities limiting motor control corresponding to keyboard and mouse control, addressing the need for more inclusive game-based learning experiences [3].

There is significant and increasing evidence suggesting that incorporating gesturing into educational practices enhances learning outcomes [9]. In this work

P. Zaphiris and A. Ioannou (Eds.): HCII 2024, LNCS 14723, pp. 45–56, 2024.
https://doi.org/10.1007/978-3-031-61685-3_4

we identify hand and body based gestural moves captured through web cameras to interact with Minecraft play. This innovative approach enables a unique combination of leveraging the greater accessibility of physical actions for young audiences, while also engaging sensory-motor interactions facilitating an embodied engagement with spatial reasoning.

## 2  Methods

In this study, we use observation, survey, and interview data to explore the viability of such a design in terms of ease of learning and use. We highlight the potential for how such a system can provide deeper insights into how different gestures connect to learning and deepening spatial reasoning skills [12]. Qualitative and thematic analysis of survey data from earlier work helped us identify and categorize various gesture types: interactive, involving direct manipulation of the virtual environment, and control, focusing on user input and navigation. These corresponded to vista and environmental forms of embodiment [4]. We chose gestures to control movement (walking & jumping), game view (panning the camera sideways), and in-game actions (breaking/mining) in Minecraft, and created a system that can convert gestures into Minecraft-based actions in real-time - using MediaPipe's hand pose recognition system.

### 2.1  Technical Details

Details of the system include a gestural control interface designed for playing Minecraft, offering an alternative to conventional keyboard and mouse controls. The Python program code integrates OpenCV, MediaPipe, and Minecraft libraries to accomplish this. Hand landmarks are identified and categorized through a K-Nearest Neighbors (KNN) classifier. The MediaPipe library is utilized for hand landmark detection, capturing the landmarks for each hand and translating their physical positions into in-game actions. These landmarks undergo processing to extract features contributing to the classification of various gestures. In real-time, the webcam feed is analyzed to detect hand landmarks using the MediaPipe library. The identified landmarks are then input into the trained KNN classifier for predictions. The predicted actions subsequently trigger corresponding in-game actions, enhancing the Minecraft experience through the use of gestural controls. The system is seamlessly integrated with the Minecraft API, allowing the execution of actions within the game world based on recognized gestures. Various gestures, such as walking, breaking/attacking, placing/using, looking, and jumping in Minecraft, trigger distinct actions. This comprehensive system incorporates player movement, block manipulation, and camera control for a more immersive gameplay experience.

### 2.2  User Study

We build on prior work not elucidated in this paper due to IRB limitations, wherein we surveyed 15 participants spanning 6–17 years of age from a summer camp. We collected initial expectations and preferences concerning gaming gestures through a pre-survey. We then presented a preliminary gesture based minecraft play system, explaining to them the specifics of gesture-action relationships to help provide initial insights on the engagement fostered through this system. Post playtesting, participants engaged in a post-survey where we asked them about their preferences for using gestures versus traditional keyboard/mouse controls, the perceived effectiveness of each gesture in gameplay scenarios, and further ideation on gestures they felt would be relevant.

After improvements, we analyze in this study a second round of testing with youth aged 11–14 years old, randomly selected from a Minecraft club organized in a public middle school in the Midwestern United States. Students in this club play after school hours at their school, in an opt-in program through personal interest in Minecraft. The participants in our study included 4 boys and 1 girl in the context of a common spatial reasoning task recreated in Minecraft [7] – where participants navigate an environment, examine and manipulate complex 3D objects, and are then assessed around their memory of the objects' details and abilities.

## 2.3 Spatial Task

We wanted to evaluate students' spatial cognitive abilities in the spatial challenge and find out how they use gestures to recall information. In order to make this investigation easier, we built a virtual structure in Minecraft that is intended to resemble the commonly used mental rotations test [11]. First, the gestural interface was shown to the students and questions about their preferences in Minecraft were asked. They moved over the standard Minecraft terrain to become accustomed to the virtual world and learn which gestures corresponded to which activities (Fig. 1).

Moving around the virtual world involved spatial awareness, understanding the gestures that triggered actions, and building an understanding of the correspondence between gestures and in-game controls. Following this, students were informed about participating in a memory game, where they would be tested after they finished playing. Placed just outside the meticulously created virtual structure, participants were tasked with identifying items within (a bed, bales of hay, a pumpkin, leaves, and chests), thereby fostering spatial memory. Their challenge was to mentally map the locations of various items strategically placed within the structure. Participants were given explicit instructions to traverse the virtual structure while utilizing the gestural interface to identify and locate objects. This hands-on approach aimed to reinforce the mental representation of spatial information through the physical enactment of movements, providing a comprehensive understanding of the intricate relationship between gestures and spatial memory.

Spatial mapping played a pivotal role in our study, aiming to unravel how students utilized gestures to perceive, comprehend, and mentally represent spatial relationships between objects and environments. Gestural interfaces, identified as crucial tools in this investigation, facilitated kinesthetic learning. This approach

**Fig. 1.** In-Game structure students interacted with, as well as the items to locate

directly linked physical movements to cognitive processes, thereby enriching spatial understanding by incorporating bodily experiences into the learning process [5] (Fig. 2).

After an initial gameplay phase, we transitioned participants to the testing segment. During this phase, we presented them with a visual representation of the structure in its regular orientation, prompting them to recognize its shape. Once the students acknowledged the image as the structure, we asked them a series of questions about item locations within the structure, with notes taken to track the nuances of their gestures. This detailed observation aimed to discern if students naturally incorporated gestures during the recall of spatial information. Adding an additional layer of complexity, an outline of the structure 2 was rotated 90°C either to the right or left. We then queried them again about their ability to recall the locations of items within the altered spatial configuration.

Throughout this process, we underscored the importance of adaptive and flexible interactions with spatial content. Learners demonstrated their ability to dynamically adjust their gestures based on the evolving spatial context, promoting adaptability in spatial thinking. An illustrative example included the use of gestures to rotate through virtual space, demonstrating adaptability to varying spatial scenarios and fostering a flexible spatial mindset.

After the initial series of questions, we further questioned participants about item locations, recall strategies post-rotation, and whether the gestural interface significantly contributed to their memory recall. We asked additional questions to explore general preferences and experiences with the gestural interface, providing a comprehensive understanding of the intricate interplay between spa-

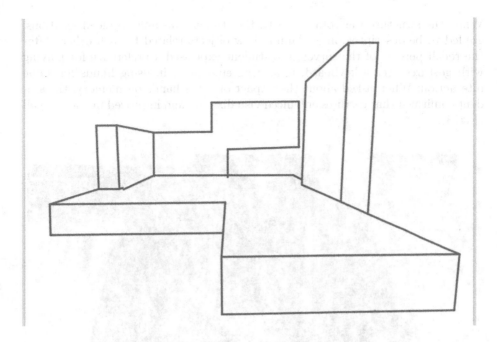

**Fig. 2.** Visual Representation of structure for Recall test

tial cognition, gestures, and memory recall within the virtual environment we meticulously designed.

## 3  Findings

In the post-play survey, we asked participants several questions to provide us with a detailed description of their interaction with the virtual environment. This exploration helped us to better understand how their gestures and descriptive language assisted in their spatial cognition and memory recall abilities within the virtual environment and the spatial task. The detailed exploration of spatial cognition and memory recall abilities within the virtual environment was not limited to individual experiences; rather, it extended across several user studies involving multiple students. As each participant engaged in the post-play survey, we present here a diverse array of strategies employing gestures and descriptive language to navigate and recall elements within the simulated space.

For instance, while prompting a student with questions regarding the location of specific objects, the student used very descriptive direction language, while also turning their body to correspond with the directions they were using to explain the location of the object. The student also utilized other objects as reference points, repeatedly referencing the overall layout of all objects within the structure to further explain instructions for finding each item. Notably, the student used descriptive directional language to articulate depth within the structure, using hands to simulate layers and visually express the spatial relationships.

When the structure was rotated 90°C, the student was able to recall locations, guided to be descriptive in explaining how objects related to each other. After the recall portion of the survey, the student expressed a preference for playing with gestures over a keyboard, indicating enjoyment in using hands for game interaction. When asked about the impact of using hands on memory, the student confirmed that gestures enhanced visualization and improved memory recall (Fig. 3).

**Fig. 3.** Photo of student moving hand down

Similarly, another student was asked to identify the location of the bed without directly pointing at the picture. The student described the bed's location in relation to the length of platforms and shapes on the structure. As the orientation of the structure was changed, the student used hands more while describing the bed's location, noting the shapes and layout of the structure as reference points. Even after the structure was rotated, the student used gestures to provide directions for his description of the bed's new location relative to the new orientation. When asked about how they remembered the bed's location, the student explained breaking down the platform into shapes, faces, and corners, pointing down while describing the bed's position. The student mapped out several pieces of hay and used gestures to convey depth, demonstrating a comprehensive reliance on hand movements for spatial recall (Figs. 4, 5 and 6).

**Fig. 4.** Photos of student moving hand front and back

Other students extensively used hands to outline the overall shape of the structure, employing flat hands to represent faces during recall. After the structure was rotated, the students mimicked the rotation with hands to assist in recall. This particular participant's reliance on gestures suggested a strong connection between hand movements and spatial memory.

## 4  Discussion

The findings from our user studies underscore the impact of integrating gestural interfaces into Minecraft gameplay for enhancing spatial cognition skills among youth. This section summarizes the key findings derived from the user studies, offering a comprehensive exploration of the impact of gestural interactions on spatial description, embodied memory and recall, visualization, orientation, shaping, and depth.

### 1. Spatial Description through Gestures

The adept utilization of body and hand gestures by students showcased a remarkable proficiency in spatial description. For instance, during spatial tasks, students employed sweeping hand motions to vividly illustrate the layers of virtual objects, providing a tangible representation of depth. A notable example emerged where a student effectively used descriptive directional language to explain the precise location of an object, simulating layers and enhancing spatial understanding. Students frequently employed specific hand gestures, such as flattening their hands, to represent faces or surfaces of the virtual structure. This nuanced use of gestures served as a symbolic representation, aiding in the description of the layout and orientation of objects within the Minecraft environment. For instance, students flattened their hands to symbolize the faces of the structure

**Fig. 5.** Student using hands flat to represent faces of structure

**Fig. 6.** Student turning hand faces to represent structures rotation during recall

during recall, providing a visual and kinesthetic reference for the arrangement of virtual elements.

**2. Embodied Memory and Recall** Gestures became a powerful tool in facilitating memory recall, allowing students to embody their mental representations of the virtual environment. Despite the challenges posed by the rotation of the virtual structure, students seamlessly integrated gestures into their recall process. This adaptability underscored the effectiveness of gestural interactions in enhancing spatial memory. For instance, in the observation of one student, the inquiry about the location of an object demonstrated the powerful role of gestures in memory recall. When prompted to remember the position of an object, the student actively turned his body, using physical movement to enhance his mental recall process. The student not only used descriptive directional language like "behind the bed and under the pumpkins" but also employed gestures with his hands to simulate layers, providing a tangible representation of the virtual environment's depth. Additionally, when the structure was rotated, the student's ability to recall locations, guided by descriptive gestures, highlighted the adaptability and effectiveness of gestural interactions in spatial memory. The student's preference for playing the game with gestures further emphasized the positive impact on memory recall, as he confirmed that using his hands helped him visualize the virtual environment more effectively. The gestures served as an aid, enabling the student to anchor their memory in tangible spatial references.

**3. Visualization and Orientation** Beyond spatial description, students used gestures to deconstruct the virtual structure into shapes, corners, and extruding pieces, significantly contributing to memory recall. After the rotation of the virtual structure, students mimicked the rotation with their hands to assist in recall. This gesture served as a simulation technique, allowing students to mentally visualize and recall the reoriented structure. For example, one student illustrated the integration of gestures into the visualization and orientation of the virtual environment. The student, when asked to identify the bed without directly pointing, employed gestures to describe the bed's location in relation to the length of platforms and shapes on the structure. Even after the structure was turned, the student used hand movements to convey directions and elaborate on the bed's new position. The student's breakdown of the platform into shapes and corners, coupled with pointing and mapping with hand movements, demonstrated how gestures contributed significantly to the visualization and orientation of the virtual space. The use of hands to replicate the rotation underscored the interactive and embodied nature of gestural interactions in Minecraft gameplay.

**4. Shaping and Depth** Gestures also assisted in conveying depth, as students employed nuanced hand movements to represent spatial relationships within the virtual environment. In a notable example, a student effectively used gestures to map out the location of objects, providing both visual and kinesthetic cues. The observations of various students provided insights into how gestures played a pivotal role in conveying depth within the virtual environment. One student, in outlining the overall shape of the structure, used hand movements extensively.

Additionally, the use of flat hands to represent the faces of the structure during recall and mimicking the rotation with hands showcased how gestures were employed to provide both visual and kinesthetic cues. The detailed gestures, such as waving hands to map out hay or signaling depth by moving hands forward and back, highlighted the dynamic and multi-dimensional aspects of gestural interactions in shaping spatial understanding. In several instances, students utilized flat hands to symbolize faces or surfaces of the virtual structure during recall. This mapping technique was observed as a means to break down the complex structure into simpler components, aiding in memory recall. Our documented students used flat hands to represent the orientation of platforms, shapes, and objects within the virtual space. This dynamic gesture provided a tangible and interactive way to convey spatial relationships.

The observations of students in Minecraft gameplay, particularly the use of gestures in spatial tasks, corroborate Atit et al.'s findings [1] where students utilized body and hand gestures to articulate spatial information, highlighting the intrinsic connection between gestures and spatial cognition. We built on their work to ask students to describe the layout and depth of a virtual environment, and students effectively used a variety of gestures in doing the same. The use of sweeping hand motions to illustrate layers of virtual objects in Minecraft parallels the students in the research study who used gestures to convey the intricate layers of rock. This shared emphasis on gestures as a means of providing a tangible representation of depth suggests a consistent pattern in the use of gestural interactions for spatial understanding. We also notice a similarity in the gestures used for directions, including pointing upwards for elevation and circular motions for object orientation. Both studies converge on the notion that gestures serve as a dynamic and expressive tool for spatial description and understanding.

We also notice students use gestures while engaged in verbal memory recall and spatial understanding, which also influences their communication within the virtual environment of Minecraft. This connection between gestures and talk mirrors the work by Morsell & Krauss [5] which explicate how gestures, especially in the role of engaging spatial memory, influence speech production.

## 5   Conclusion

Early findings highlight a mix of affordances and limitations. While movement and navigation tasks are sometimes more laborious using hand poses, corroborating ongoing findings around interaction fatigue [10], players report easier viewfinder and object manipulation using gestures. Some participants perceived movement tasks as more laborious when using hand poses. There were instances where the program was not adapted well to the hands of children, and the use of extra fingers posed challenges. These limitations underscore the need for ongoing refinement and adaptation to ensure optimal usability and inclusivity. We find a noticeable increase in usage of embodied gestures in follow-up spatial cognition tasks by players who utilized the gestural interfaces more during gameplay. Youth provided a variety of complex gestures and interactions that connect complex concepts which are often laborious tasks in gameplay to easy to demonstrate gestures, including symbols for loops, multi-step constructions, and multi-axis viewfinder which we are currently working on creating.

By incorporating gesture principles into instructional design, educators can craft more engaging and effective learning environments for students, particularly in spatial thinking and STEM fields, where success is closely linked to spatial abilities. The increased usage of embodied gestures observed in participants who extensively used gestural interfaces during gameplay suggests that integrating such interfaces in educational tasks can enhance spatial cognition. Moreover, when applied to teamwork tasks, gestural interfaces not only bolster spatial understanding but also foster social interaction, collaboration, and innovative learning approaches with richer social manners. The hands-on and interactive nature of gestural interfaces can potentially make learning more enjoyable, leading to heightened participation and sustained interest. Additionally, the gestural interface system serves as a novel tool for educators to assess students' spatial reasoning skills, offering insights into their problem-solving approaches.

By integrating gestural interfaces and spatial tasks, educators are equipped with a potent arsenal that not only nurtures spatial cognition but also fosters social interaction, collaboration, and new ways of learning not only with their whole bodies but also in richer social manners [14]. By considering inclusive and embodied ways of enriching spatial cognition, this research charts a course toward a more equitable, inclusive, and empowering educational landscape.

# References

1. Atit, K., Gagnier, K., Shipley, T.: Student gestures aid penetrative thinking. J. Geosci. Educ. **63**, 66–72 (2015). https://doi.org/10.5408/14-008.1
2. Cai, Y., Goei, S.L., Trooster, W. (eds.): Simulation and Serious Games for Education. GMSE, Springer, Singapore (2017). https://doi.org/10.1007/978-981-10-0861-0
3. Cezarotto, M. A., Chamberlin, B.: Towards accessibility in educational games: a framework for the design team. In: InfoDesign-Revista Brasileira de Design da Informação, vol. 18(2) (2021)
4. Clifton, P.G., et al.: Design of embodied interfaces for engaging spatial cognition. Cogn. Res.: Principles Implications **1**(1), 1–15 (2016). https://doi.org/10.1186/s41235-016-0032-5
5. Morsella, E., Krauss, R.M.: The role of gestures in spatial working memory and speech. Am. J. Psychol. **117**(3), 411–424 (2004). https://doi.org/10.2307/4149008
6. Freina, L., Ott, M.: A literature review on immersive virtual reality in education: state of the art and perspectives. In: The International Scientific Conference Elearning and Software for Education, vol. 1, no. 133, pp. 1000–1007 (2015)
7. Guay, R.B., McDaniel, E.D.: The Purdue spatial visualization tests: a brief history. Educ. Psychol. Measur. **37**(2), 391–397 (1977)
8. Kangas, M.: Creative and playful learning: learning through game co-creation and games in a playful learning environment. Thinking Skills Creative **5**(1), 1–15 (2010)
9. Koumoutsakis, T., et al.: Gesture in Instruction: evidence from live & video lessons (2016)
10. Ma, F., Song, F., Liu, Y., Niu, J.: Quantitative analysis on the interaction fatigue of natural gestures. IEEE Access **8**, 190797–190811 (2020)

11. Shepard, R.N., Metzler, J.: Mental rotation of three-dimensional objects. Science **171**(3972), 701–703 (1971)
12. Skulmowski, A., Rey, G.D.: Embodied learning: introducing a taxonomy based on bodily engagement and task integration. Cogn. Res. **3**, 6 (2018). https://doi.org/10.1186/s41235-018-0092-9
13. Subrahmanyam, K., Greenfield, P.M.: Effect of video game practice on spatial skills in girls and boys. J. Appl. Dev. Psychol. **15**(1), 13–32 (1994)
14. Wang, L.H., Chen, B., Hwang, G.J., Guan, J.Q., Wang, Y.Q.: Effects of digital game-based STEM education on students' learning achievement: a meta-analysis. Int. J. STEM Educ. **9**(1), 1–13 (2022)
15. Worsley, M., Bar-El, D.: Spatial reasoning in minecraft: an exploratory study of in-game spatial practices. In: Computer Supported Collaborative Learning, 2 (2020)
16. Zhonggen, Y.: A meta-analysis of use of serious games in education over a decade. Int. J. Comput. Games Technol. (2019)

# How Hexad Player Types Affect Student Behaviour in Three Versions of a Peer-Quizzing Game

Nafisul Kiron [ID] and Julita Vassileva[✉] [ID]

Computer Science Department, University of Saskatchewan, 176 Thorvaldson Bldg, 110 Science Pl., Saskatoon, SK S7N5C9, Canada
`ni.kiron@usask.ca, jiv@cs.usask.ca`

**Abstract.** In recent years, game-based learning has gained significant attention as an engaging and effective approach to promoting knowledge acquisition and retention. Among various game mechanics, peer quizzing fosters active participation, social interaction, and friendly competition among learners. However, understanding individual preferences and behaviours within this class of educational games setting remains unexplored. Our study investigates how student player types influence their behaviour preferences in three versions of a peer-quizzing game, which differ in the type of support provided to the students. We recruited 136 students from a first-year programming language course. We divided the participants into three groups: two with different supports and one group without support. In the pre-study survey, we collected demographic information about the participants and their Hexad player type. The students played the peer-quizzing game during the academic term, challenging each other to answer questions related to the material taught in the course. We present the findings from the game activity data collected from the students' gameplay through the lens of their Hexad player types. Our findings show that different supports influence different player types differently.

**Keywords:** Game-based learning · Hexad · Peer-quizzing

## 1 Introduction

Game-based learning is an innovative approach to educational technologies that harness the motivational power of games to enhance the learning experience [2]. By integrating educational content into interactive games, students are immersed in a playful learning environment. Game-based learning promotes active participation, problem-solving, critical thinking, collaboration, and decision-making skills. It allows learners to explore complex concepts in a safe and enjoyable environment, making the learning process more engaging and effective. Through meaningful challenges, feedback, and rewards, game-based learning encourages students to stay motivated, persist through difficulties, and achieve a deeper understanding of the learning materials.

Research on video games and game-based learning has explored various aspects of games and players to identify the driving factors of motivation and engagement. Identifying different player preferences for gaming experiences and their frequent behaviours, research in game psychology has developed several taxonomies of player types. Identifying different player types based on preferences and behaviors, enables game designers to create an optimal user experience [3]. Player types help in understanding how different individuals engage with games and what motivates them. For example, the Bartle taxonomy of player types classifies players into Achievers, Explorers, Socializers, and Killers based on their preferred in-game behaviors, such as seeking rewards, interacting with the game world, socializing, or competing with other players [4, 5]. Understanding these player types can help game developers tailor game design to meet the specific needs and preferences of different player groups, ultimately enhancing the gaming experience for a diverse range of users [5, 6]. A recent player typology, Hexad [1] proposed a classification of gamer types based on their motivations for playing; it will be presented with more details in the next section.

Game-based peer-quizzing combines the benefits of games and peer-quizzing for an interactive learning experience [7]. Peer-quizzing as a game-based learning approach offers several benefits to learners. First, it promotes active engagement and participation by involving students in the learning process as both host and participant. Students must deeply understand the content and think critically to create meaningful questions for their peers. Peer quizzing encourages competition and collaboration, as students can discuss improved questions and answers after solving quizzes. It also improves communication skills by encouraging concept explanations and discussions among students. Students become more responsible when they take ownership of their learning and create good questions. Lastly, peer quizzing can boost motivation and self-efficacy as students receive immediate feedback and recognition from their peers or the game, encouraging them to further improve their understanding of the subject matter and helping them prepare for exams.

Analyzing the relation between player behaviours and their Hexad player types in the context of a game-based peer-quizzing game, educators can gain insights into students' motivations and preferences, such as competition, collaboration, exploration, and achievement. This information can be leveraged to tailor the game-based peer-quizzing experience to suit the diverse needs of learners. This paper presents a study that explores if the preferred activities in peer-quizzing gameplay of students are influenced by the supports provided and how they are related to their Hexad player types.

## 2  Background and Related Work

For game-based learning, it is crucial to grasp player types to adapt learning game design to accommodate the different preferences, motivations and typical behaviors of learners. By identifying and accommodating different player types, educational game designers can create an optimal user experience that promotes engagement and effective learning [8]. In this section, we provide a brief overview of the main existing player typologies and existing work on adapting educational games to the player types of learners.

### 2.1  Player Typologies

Bartle's player type model, widely utilized for categorizing player types, is considered one of the oldest models in this field, along with its extensions [9, 10]. These types were established by considering the individual desires and motivations of players in Multi-User Dungeons (MUDs) environments. Bartle's model emerged from the examination of MUDs and established four player types: Achiever, Explorer, Socializer, and Killer.

A more recent player typology called BrainHex was developed by Nacke et al. [11]. By thoroughly reviewing existing literature, this research has identified seven player archetypes that consider neurobiological factors and examine the patterns and emotions evoked by games. The BrainHex model has six distinct archetypes: Seeker, Survivor, Daredevil, Mastermind, Conqueror, Socializer, and Achiever.

Ferro et al. proposed a classification of players consisting of five categories: Dominant, Objectivist, Humanist, Inquisitive, and Creative [12]. This classification was derived by combining the personality traits, player types, and game elements and mechanics. The intention of this model is to assist in the design process of gamified projects, with the ultimate goal of creating a more captivating and motivating experience for users.

Researchers have studied factors that affect how people perceive motivation. Jia et al. studied how personality traits impact gamification customization [13]. The study showed that players' personalities influence how they perceive gamification elements, suggesting that customizing gamified systems to match users' personalities could be beneficial. Orji et al. conducted a study where they investigated the correlation between persuasive strategies and personality traits [14]. Their study further supported the notion that personality traits can impact the perception of persuasive strategies employed in gamification.

The Hexad model of player types was proposed by Marczewski in 2015 [1]. It classifies players into six distinct types: Achiever, Socializer, Disruptor, Player, Philanthropist, and Free Spirit. Achievers find motivation in challenges and rewards, while Socializers thrive on social and collaborative gameplay. Disruptors appreciate open-ended environments that they can shape, and Players thrive in competitive scenarios. Philanthropists feel motivated by helping others, and Free Spirits enjoy designing and creating. Educators and game designers can benefit from understanding the Hexad player types in game-based learning. Tailoring educational games to different player types can create more engaging learning experiences. The Hexad player-type inventory categorizes individuals based on their motivations and preferences when playing games [1].

## 2.2 Using Player Typologies to Tailor Educational Games

Identifying player types can contribute to the design and implementation of educational games. It allows for tailoring game-based learning experiences to the preferences and motivations of different player types, thereby enhancing engagement and learning outcomes. A study conducted by Gholizadeh et al. presents a model of player-game interaction in the mobile game-based learning setting regarding behavioral propensity [15]. The model comprises five different features inherited from the player typology literature, including precision, perfection, punctuality, presence, and pace. According to the authors, gaining insight into these player types can help to improve game design [15].

Another study conducted by Van Galeen et al. on 102 participants identified five distinct patterns in game preferences: the social achiever, the explorer, the socializer, the competitor, and the troll [8]. The study concluded that identifying player types can help future researchers and educators select effective game-based learning game elements purposefully and in a student-centered way [8].

In the context of educational gamification, a study conducted by Abdollahzade & Jafari investigated the relationship between player types based on the Hexad model and the dimensions of the Felder-Silverman Learning Style Model (FSLSM) [16]. The research aimed to determine how player types correlate with learning styles to guide the design of gamified learning environments. By analyzing data from university students (n = 121), the study found significant relationships between certain player types and learning styles, which could inform the design of gamification elements to improve educational outcomes.

## 3   Methodology

The present study contributes to the growing body of research on game-based learning and player types by providing educators and educational game designers with valuable insights into the varied preferences and strengths of players within a peer-quizzing environment. Understanding these differences may help game designers and educators to tailor game mechanics, feedback systems, and learning materials to better accommodate individual needs and maximize engagement. For example, instructors might consider offering customized question templates or prompts that cater to the unique interests and strengths of each player type.

### 3.1   Research Tool: A Peer-Quizzing Educational Game

We designed a peer-quizzing game where the students quiz each other on course topics categorized by their course syllabus [17]. The game had 3 versions: one with instructional tips for questions and answers construction, one with a database of previous players' questions and answers, and a basic version where students create questions and answers independently. The students receive points for asking quiz-style questions and for answering the questions of their peers. In the game, players can do several activities. They can create new quiz questions, where we expect them to exhibit a strong preference for analytical thinking, problem-solving, and creativity, which aligns with their role in designing quiz questions that challenge and engage their peers. Furthermore, they can answer the quiz questions of their peers, displaying inclination towards curiosity, intelligence, and risk-taking. These attributes enable them to quickly recognize patterns and connections between seemingly unrelated pieces of information, allowing them to excel in solving quiz questions. Finally, they can view solved questions, learning from the experience of others by observing the results of their gameplay. We used the three variants of the game in our study. We collected gameplay data to see if the design of the game impacts the predominant types of activities of the players, and if there is any relationship between the player type and preferred activities in each game design.

### 3.2 Study Design

We carried out the study in a first-year Introduction to Programming class at the University of Saskatchewan. The study began in September 2023 and ended in mid-December 2023. Participation in the game was voluntary, and as a reward for participating, the students received a grade weighted 5% marks of their final grade for the course. For students who did not wish to participate 5% weight was added to their final exam. For one academic term, the students played the game alongside studying their course material and doing coursework. At the beginning of the study, after providing informed consent for participation, the students had to complete a pre-study survey which collected demographic data. We also obtained data on the participants' player types using the Hexad validated survey to further investigate player types [1]. Throughout the academic term, we collected game activity data from the peer-quizzing game. Towards the end of the term, the participants completed a post-study survey collecting information about their gameplay experiences. Our study was approved by our university's research ethics board (Beh ID: 101).

The participants were assigned randomly to three groups: Groups 1 and 2 played a version of the game with additional support, and Group 3 played the game without any support. The students in Group 1 received weekly messages when they logged into the game containing instructions and tips for creating better questions. Group 2 did not receive messages but had access to an existing question bank to study from before they posted their questions. Group 3 played the game without any external support and on their own.

## 4 Results

We originally started our study with 143 students in the three groups. However, 7 students opted out of the study, so we had to remove them from their groups. After removing them there were 136 participants.

### 4.1 Comparison Between Activities in the Three Groups

Table 1 shows the summary of the collective gameplay metrics of the students (n = 136) in the peer-quizzing game. The table shows the number of activities in the game: creating, answering, browsing, and attempting to answer quiz questions. The students collectively created 825 quiz questions along with their correct answers. It must be noted, that the three groups shared the same pool of questions to which they could contribute, attempt to answer questions, or browse the answered questions. Of the total number of questions contributed, 770 (93.3%) were correctly answered by other students after 2,104 attempts, which included multiple tries at the same question. While most questions were attempted and answered, there was a small portion that was either too difficult or deemed to be too hard or incomprehensible. Browsing through questions was a particularly popular activity, with 3,642 instances recorded, suggesting that students were actively exploring the available questions, possibly assessing which ones to attempt, or searching for questions that helped them understand the material better. The high level of activity indicates that the game was a dynamic and engaging learning environment where students tested their knowledge and actively engaged in a learning process by creating questions and exploring content made by their peers.

**Table 1.** Summary of participants and data.

|                            | Total |
|----------------------------|-------|
| Participants               | 136   |
| Questions created          | 825   |
| Questions answered         | 770   |
| Views (browsed questions)  | 3642  |
| Questions attempted        | 2104  |

Table 2 shows the size of the three groups and their activities in the game. The unevenness in the size of the groups was due to the few students opting out of the study.

**Table 2.** Breakdown of activities by the three groups.

| Type               | Group 1     | Group 2     | Group 3     |
|--------------------|-------------|-------------|-------------|
| Towers created     | 229 (28%)   | **380 (46%)** | 216 (26%)   |
| Questions answered | 189 (25%)   | 257 (33%)   | **324 (42%)** |
| Questions browsed  | 1004 (28%)  | 1344 (37%)  | 1294 (36%)  |
| Questions attempted| 505 (24%)   | 799 (38%)   | 800 (38%)   |
| **Participants**   | 45 (33%)    | 47 (35%)    | 44 (32%)    |

Group 1, with 45 participants which received instruction and tips on how to create good questions, created 229 questions (27.8% of the total number of questions contributed by the three groups), made 505 attempts, answered 189, and browsed through the solved questions, viewing them 1,004 times. As can be seen in Table 2, the percentages of total number of each activity for each group, Group 1 answered fewer questions than the other groups, made significantly fewer attempts to solve questions and engaged less in browsing than the other two groups, especially the control group 3 that had no supports.

Group 2, with 47 participants, had access to a database of questions for the current topic that they could directly submit as their own, or modify and submit them. Unsurprisingly, this group was the most active in creating questions, totalling 380. The students in this group made 799 attempts, answered 257 questions, and browsed the solved questions with a total of 1,344 views. This group was most engaged in the game, with the highest number of questions created and attempted. Its activity level in questions answered and browsed was the second highest, but very close to that of the control group 3.

Group 3, with 44 participants, which did not have any support, created 216 questions, made 800 attempts, answered the highest number of questions of the three groups - 324, and viewed 1,294 solved questions. Even though they created fewer questions than the other groups, Group 3 was the most successful in answering questions and made nearly the same number of attempts as Group 2. In comparison, Group 2 appears to be the most active in terms of creating and attempting questions, possibly showing a higher level of engagement and enthusiasm. Group 3, while not as active in question creation, was more successful in answering questions, suggesting a strong focus on problem-solving. Group 1, while not leading in any category, maintained a balanced approach to the game, participating evenly across all activities. This data highlights the different strategies and strengths of each group in the peer-quizzing game, reflecting the various ways the students exposed to the different supports or no support at all engaged in the game.

### 4.2 Hexad Player Types in the Three Groups

We observe that in all groups the predominant player type is 'Achiever'. Group 1 (n = 45) had the highest number of 'Free spirits' (13) and 'Achievers' (14), and a moderate number of 'Philanthropists' (9) and 'Socializers' (3). The absence of 'Disruptors' in all three groups suggests that the participants in the study preferred a structured gameplay and adherence to the game mechanics Group 2, with 47 participants, has more 'Achievers' (22), which has the highest count among all groups, followed by a moderate number of 'Free spirits' (9) and 'Philanthropists' (6). Group 3, consisting of 44 participants, has a more balanced distribution with 'Achievers' (16) and 'Socializers' (7).

### 4.3 Hexad Player Types and Engagement in Game Activities

We explored the differences in game activities between the participants in the three groups based on their Hexad player types to see if we could find any interesting patterns that may suggest that specific game conditions are more engaging for students with specific personalities.

We can hypothesize that because 'Achievers' are driven by mastery and accomplishment they will demonstrate it in the three game designs by maximizing the numbers of questions they created and answered. 'Players' are motivated by rewards and extrinsic benefits (the 5% participation marks). We expected that we would also try to maximize the measurable items (number of questions created and answered) in all three groups.

We expected that the 'Philanthropists' would take the opportunity to create many questions for their classmates to practice in all three conditions. 'Socializers' are driven by social interactions and community; we expected that they would prefer to attempt to answer questions and browse the solved questions. The game created conditions for social interaction in all three groups, so we didn't expect a significant difference in the top activities of socializers across the three groups. 'Free spirits' are motivated by autonomy and possibilities for self-expression and creativity, so we expected that they would prefer the condition in Group 3 where there were no instructions or ready questions to use. Notably, none of the groups contained 'Disruptors', who are players that enjoy challenging norms and influencing the game environment, showing that the participants preferred a more structured play within the rules of the game.

Table 3 shows the breakdown of Groups 1, 2, and 3's gameplay activities, categorized by the students' Hexad player types and the number of students of each player type in each group. For convenience, we present the average number of activities per person from each player type and each group in Table 4. This helps to see that some player types excel in specific activities and game conditions.

**Table 3.** Game play performance of the three groups by player type.

| Group 1 | | | | |
|---|---|---|---|---|
| Type (count) | Created | Answered | Browsed | Attempted |
| Philanthropist (n = 9) | 47 | 45 | 107 | 75 |
| Socializer (n = 3) | 9 | 1 | 18 | **7** |
| Free spirit (n = 13) | 49 | **84** | **397** | **231** |
| Achiever (n = 14) | 59 | 48 | 361 | 137 |
| Player (n = 6) | **65** | 11 | 121 | 55 |
| Group 2 | | | | |
| Type | Created | Answered | Browsed | Attempted |
| Philanthropist (n = 6) | 49 | 14 | 135 | 69 |
| Socializer (n = 4) | 15 | 36 | 180 | 113 |
| Free spirit (n = 9) | 101 | 50 | 344 | 189 |
| Achiever (n = 22) | **208** | **120** | **525** | **344** |
| Player (n = 6) | 7 | 37 | 160 | 84 |
| Group 3 | | | | |
| Type | Created | Answered | Browsed | Attempted |
| Philanthropist (n = 6) | 24 | 52 | 154 | 121 |
| Socializer (n = 7) | 9 | 8 | 87 | 34 |
| Free spirit (n = 7) | 19 | 19 | 112 | 63 |
| Achiever (n = 16) | 160 | 239 | 895 | 548 |
| Player (n = 8) | 4 | 6 | 46 | 34 |

In Group 1, 'Free spirits' were the most active across three of the four activities, leading over other player types in number of attempts (mean 17.77 per person), answered questions (mean 6.46 per person) and browsing the answered questions (mean 30.53 per person). In this group 'Players' were leading in creating questions (mean 10.83 per person). 'Free spirits' are motivated by autonomy and possibilities for self-expression and creativity. The conditions in which they played the peer-quizzing game in Group 1 instructional messages with advice on how to create good questions, but without providing them with ready questions, supported their need for challenge and gave them a chance to develop mastery through creating their own questions. It is worth mentioning that although the numbers of achievers and free spirits were about the same in Group 1, achievers still tended to create more questions.

**Table 4.** Game play performance of the three groups by player type.

| Mean Number of Questions Created per person of each type in the three groups | | | |
|---|---|---|---|
| Type | Group 1 | Group 2 | Group 3 |
| Philanthropist | 5.22 | 8.16 | 4 |
| Socializer | 3 | 3.75 | 1.29 |
| Free spirit | 3.77 | **11.22** | **2.72** |
| Achiever | 4.21 | 9.45 | 10 |
| Player | **10.83** | 1.16 | 0.5 |

| Mean Number of Questions Answered per person of each type in the three groups | | | |
|---|---|---|---|
| Type | Group 1 | Group 2 | Group 3 |
| Philanthropist | 5 | 2.33 | 8.67 |
| Socializer | 0.33 | **9** | 1.14 |
| Free spirit | **6.46** | 5.55 | 2.71 |
| Achiever | 3.42 | 5.45 | **14.93** |
| Player | 1.83 | 6.16 | 0.75 |

| Mean Number of Questions Attempted per person of each type in the three groups | | | |
|---|---|---|---|
| Type | Group 1 | Group 2 | Group 3 |
| Philanthropist | 8.33 | 11.5 | 20.17 |
| Socializer | 2.33 | **28.25** | 4.86 |
| Free spirit | **17.77** | 21 | 9 |
| Achiever | 9.79 | 15.64 | **34.25** |
| Player | 9.17 | 14 | 4.25 |

| Mean Number of Browsing (Question Visits) per person of each type in the three groups | | | |
|---|---|---|---|
| Type | Group 1 | Group 2 | Group 3 |
| Philanthropist | 11.89 | 22.5 | 25.67 |

(*continued*)

**Table 4.** (*continued*)

Mean Number of Browsing (Question Visits) per person of each type in the three groups

| Type | Group 1 | Group 2 | Group 3 |
|------|---------|---------|---------|
| Socializer | 6 | **45** | 12.43 |
| Free spirit | **30.54** | **38.22** | 16 |
| Achiever | 25.79 | 23.86 | **55.94** |
| Player | 20.17 | 26.67 | 5.75 |

In Group 2, as shown in Table 4, 'Socializers' dominate in the mean number of questions answered (mean 9 per person), browsed (mean 45 per person) and attempted (mean 28.25 per person). The highest number of questions was created Free Spirits (mean 11.22), followed by Achievers (mean 9.45). Free Spirits also browsed questions a lot (mean 38.22) and attempted to solve questions (mean 21 per person), but less than socializers. The availability of a database with ready question examples motivated the 'Achievers' to strive to submit a high number of questions as their achievement, while the 'Free spirits' were able to modify existing questions or submit new questions of their own.

In Group 3, the Achievers were the most active, leading in all activities. This may suggest that the goal-oriented 'Achievers' are the driving force in this group. 'Philanthropists', who are motivated by purpose and contributing to a greater cause, also show a high level of engagement, particularly in answering and browsing questions.

## 5 Discussion

The initial summary of participants and data revealed a high level of interaction with the game, including question creation, answering, browsing, and attempting, indicating an overall positive engagement with the game. A breakdown of the performance of each group showed that the students in Group 2, which supported the players with a pool of ready questions, were the most active in creating and attempting questions. This result can be easily explained because it was easier to create questions using the ready pool of questions, either directly or with minor changes. This involved less cognitive efforts to think of new questions. The higher number of new questions in this group provided a base for students to make more attempts to solve them, and more questions they could browse compared to the other groups. The students of player-type Socializers were most active in Answering, Attempting and Browsing, and Free Spirit students were most active in creating questions. Still, they were also highly active in attempting to answer and in browsing questions. It is interesting that Socializers were active only in Group 2 and not in the other two groups. Yet they did not make use of the database of questions, as their average number of created questions was the second lowest. It is hard to explain why socializers were so active in Group 2. Possibly, the higher number of questions created conditions for more attempts, answers and browsing, which are more social activities in comparison with question creation.

Free spirits were also active in Group 1, where they excelled in the number of questions answered, attempted, and browsed. Yet in Group 1 the highest number of questions were created by Players. It is possible that the instruction provided about how to construct good questions in this system focused the attention of Players on this activity as the most important, most visible, and consequently most rewarded one. The instruction that students were exposed to in Group 1 focused their attention on the quality of questions and possibly discouraged them from asking not-well-thought-through questions, resulting in fewer questions. The focus of the instruction messages in Group 1 on how to ask good questions can also explain the lower number of attempted and answered questions; consequently, there were fewer solved questions to review. In contrast, it is possible that Free Spirit students were not influenced much by the focus on quality, and participated actively in attempting, answering questions, and browsing the solved questions.

Group 3, which had no added support, excelled in answering questions, browsed a lot of the solved questions, and created a comparable number of questions as Group 1. Achievers were top performers in all activities by a wide margin, which was expected, as they are driven by mastery.

## 6 Conclusion

We conducted an exploratory study to observe the influence of student player types on behavior preferences within a game-based peer quiz tool. We recruited a significant number of students as participants. We divided them into three nearly equally sized groups, exposing them to three versions of the same peer-quizzing game: two versions providing quiz question creation support and one without support. We observe the differences in the preferred activities of learners with different Hexad player types across the three groups. Observing the activities across the three groups of students provides insights into how different motivations influence engagement in educational games with added instruction, with added examples, or without any support. Understanding the player profiles' impact on their engagement can aid in designing more effective educational tools that support various learner needs. The observations from this study underline the importance of considering player types in game design. Future studies can build upon these results by investigating the dynamic interactions between player types, exploring additional game mechanics, and examining the long-term impact of game-based peer quizzing on learning.

**Acknowledgement.** We are grateful to Jeff Long, who, as the coordinator and instructor of the class, provided us with the opportunity to do the study. We would also like to acknowledge Fatima Saberi for providing feedback on a previous draft of the paper.

## References

1. Marczewski, A.: Even Ninja Monkeys Like to Play: Gamification, Game Thinking and Motivational Design, 1st edn. CreateSpace Independent Publishing Platform (2015)

2. Kapp, K.M.: The Gamification of Learning and Instruction: Game-Based Methods and Strategies for Training and Education. Wiley (2012). https://dl.acm.org/citation.cfm?id=2378737. Accessed 02 Feb 2019
3. Brandl, L.C., Schrader, A.: Clustering on player types of students in health science - trial and data analyses. Stud. Health Technol. Inform. **307**, 89–95 (2023). https://doi.org/10.3233/SHT I230698
4. Zuchowska, L., Kutt, K., Nalepa, G.J.: Bartle Taxonomy-based Game for Affective and Personality Computing Research. MRC@IJCAI (2021)
5. Thawonmas, R., Iizuka, K.: Visualization of online-game players based on their action behaviors. Int. J. Comput. Games Technol. **2008**, 1–9 (2008). https://doi.org/10.1155/2008/906931
6. Chapman, J.R., Kohler, T.B., Gedeborg, S.: So, why do students perform better in gamified courses? Understanding motivational styles in educational gamification. J. Educ. Comput. Res. **61**(5), 927–950 (2023). https://doi.org/10.1177/07356331221127635
7. Sung, H.-Y., Hwang, G.-J.: A collaborative game-based learning approach to improving students' learning performance in science courses. Comput. Educ. **63**, 43–51 (2013)
8. Van Gaalen, A.E.J., Schonrock-Adema, J., Renken, R.J., Jaarsma, A.D.C., Georgiadis, J.R.: Identifying player types to tailor game-based learning design to learners: cross-sectional survey using Q methodology. JMIR Serious Games **10**(2), e30464 (2022). https://doi.org/10.2196/30464. https://games.jmir.org/2022/2/e30464
9. Bartle, R.: Hearts, clubs, diamonds, spades: players who suit MUDs. J. MUD Res. **1**(1), 19 (1996)
10. Bartle, R.: Virtual worlds: why people play. In: Massively Multiplayer Game Development, vol. 2, no. 1, pp. 3–18 (2005)
11. Nacke, L.E., Bateman, C., Mandryk, R.L.: BrainHex: Preliminary Results from a Neurobiological Gamer Typology Survey. LNCS, vol. 6972, pp. 288–293 (2011). https://doi.org/10.1007/978-3-642-24500-8_31/COVER
12. Ferro, L.S., Walz, S.P., Greuter, S.: Towards personalised, gamified systems: an investigation into game design, personality and player typologies. In: Proceedings of the 9th Australasian Conference on Interactive Entertainment: Matters of Life and Death, pp. 1–6 (2013)
13. Jia, Y., Xu, B., Karanam, Y., Voida, S.: Personality, targeted gamification: a survey study on personality traits and motivational affordances. In: Proceedings of the Conference on Human Factors in Computing Systems, pp. 2001–2013 (2016). https://doi.org/10.1145/2858036.2858515
14. Orji, R., Nacke, L.E., Di Marco, C.: Towards personality-driven persuasive health games and gamified systems. In: Proceedings of the Conference on Human Factors in Computing Systems, vol. 2017, pp. 1015–1027 (2017). https://doi.org/10.1145/3025453.3025577
15. Gholizadeh, M., Taghiyareh, F., Alvandkoohi, S.: Toward a propensity-oriented player typology in educational mobile games. Int. J. Games Based Learn. **8**(2), 55–67 (2018). https://doi.org/10.4018/IJGBL.2018040105
16. Abdollahzade, Z., Jafari, S.: Investigating the relationship between player types and learning styles in gamification design. Iranian J. Manag. Stud. (2018). https://doi.org/10.22059/IJMS.2018.256394.673107
17. Kiron, N., Adaji, I., Long, J., Vassileva, J.: Tower of questions: a peer-quizzing game to engage students in question and answer posing. In: European Conference on Games Based Learning, pp. 395-XVIII (2019)

# Exploring the Impact of Purposeful Board Games in Higher Education

Naemi Luckner, Michael Pollak[✉], and Peter Purgathofer

Human Computer Interaction Group, TU Wien (Vienna University of Technology),
Argentinierstr. 8/193-5, Vienna, Austria
{naemi,poll,purg}@igw.tuwien.ac.at

**Abstract.** Especially for large classes where personal contact and individual feedback becomes increasingly challenging, educators are continuously developing strategies to get students to engage with the course contents in a meaningful way. Gameful approaches have shown promise to be used as learning tools for students to reflect on a variety of topics. The course *Ways of Thinking in Informatics* is mandatory and offered to first year students of Computing at TU Wien. As part of their coursework in the winter semester of 2023, each student played a minimum of two games designed for and related to the topics of *Ways of Thinking in Informatics*. Some of these games were created in previous semesters especially for the purpose of teaching the content of said lecture, while others were selected from existing, commercial games offering relevant content to reflect on. After playing the games, participating students rated and reviewed whether these games were a promising form of practice-based and in-depth engagement with a specific "way of thinking" and thus in how far this game-based learning and teaching approach for higher education was a successful strategy in introducing the lecture's topics. Initial investigation shows that participants rated the knowledge transfer particularly high in comparison to other activities, as the game-based approach forced interaction and peer-level reflection. Learners who were confronted with a game-based approach challenged each others prejudices and reflected on their understanding. Along with the initial results of the data analysis drawn from one semester of this particular game-based learning and teaching approach, this paper will also present a case study of organising in-person gaming events at scale, which can be utilised as a guideline for other university settings as it shows how to introduce games as addition to regular coursework.

**Keywords:** Gameful Design · Gameful Learning · Gamification · Serious Games · Game-Based Learning · Higher Education · Ways of Thinking

## 1 Introduction

Personal contact and individual feedback becomes increasingly challenging as funding rates decline, teaching staff is reduced and student numbers rise. Especially for mandatory, bachelor-grade classes with huge numbers of participating

© The Author(s), under exclusive license to Springer Nature Switzerland AG 2024
P. Zaphiris and A. Ioannou (Eds.): HCII 2024, LNCS 14723, pp. 69–81, 2024.
https://doi.org/10.1007/978-3-031-61685-3_6

students, motivated educators are continuously intent on developing and deploying new teaching strategies. The goal is to get the students to engage with the course materials on a deeper level that is on the one hand appealing to learners and on the other hand - at least for now - not easily circumvented by the widespread usage of generative AI. Gameful approaches have shown promise to be used as learning tools for students to reflect on various topics [2, 8, 11], however, finding fitting games that deal with exactly the problems discussed in specific lectures is difficult [4, 10]. Facing this challenge and knowing the widespread problem space also from other university contexts, an innovative approach has been chosen. Since there were only a few applicable games available at the time, a collaboration between learners and educators started out to develop new practice based and engaging games.

In the summer semester of 2023, Purgathofer and Luckner offered the course *Gameful Design*, in which 32 students enlisted in Bachelor and Masters programs of Media and Human-Centred Computing created board games specifically aimed at the topics of the interactive lecture called *Ways of Thinking in Informatics* [5]. The course is mandatory and offered primarily to first year bachelor-grade computer science students of the curriculum "BSc. Informatics" at TU Wien. The work developed during the *Gameful Design* course resulted in seven game prototypes created by groups of students over three design iterations. The course focused first on gameplay and game mechanics; then on learning goals and learning transfer. It also included the creation of a framework to be used for deeper reflection regarding the specific "way of thinking". Finally it focused on testing and balancing the games. The detailed course concept along with in-depth descriptions of these prototypes will be published at a later date. Five of these game-based learning prototypes were selected and, along with a number of additional games designed in other contexts but for the same purpose, refined and professionally produced to be played by nearly 700 students as part of the "Games and Labs" exercise of *Ways of Thinking in Informatics* in the winter semester 2023. Additionally, some already existing digital games and board games were selected to widen the students' choices.

Next to a selection of preexisting digital games that could be played alone or in groups, students had the possibility to either borrow from a number of board games to be played at home or participate in large in-person game events where individual students and teams could sign up for a spot to play all of the offered board games in a hosted environment. Each of the participating students played a minimum of two games within a two hour session. The publication at hand will focus on the reception and insights of these participants, who, as part of their coursework, reported on their experience with the exercise, the games, the game event, their learnings and takeaways. This paper will present lessons learned from the initial investigation of this collected pool of data as well as the authors observations.

## 2    State of the Art

The benefit and intrinsic value of gaming has been widely researched in the past. The topic spans a variety of professions, from psychology to education and sociology. The positive impact of playful learning in young minds has lead to increasing interest within different age brackets. One of the first scholars extending the scope of gamification to youth and learning was Piaget [12]. His ideas and the psychological groundwork was utilised by numerous scholars and translated in K-12 and higher education setting [2,8,11,14,16]. As teaching styles progressed into modern forms, new technologies and artefacts were introduced. A lot of the groundwork to gamification and game based learning (GBL) was developed by Resnick et al. [13]. As stated by Subhash and Cudney: "In the field of [higher education], gamified and game-based learning and teaching systems have shown their effectiveness in the promotion of student engagement, motivation, and performance" [15]. Interestingly, despite the large number of publications on the topic of game based learning, a stable definition for a "game" is hard to find. For this work Juul's definition [7] has been the main guide, with the finding that every game needs these six distinct features to be viable: (1) games are rule-based, (2) have variable, quantifiable outcome, (3) offer value assigned to possible outcomes, (4) players invests effort to influence the outcome, (5) they are emotionally attached to outcome, (6) and the consequences are negotiable (see Juul 2003 [7]).

As research progresses and enables new insights, Maratou et al. [9] concluded that the "advantages of analogue [game-based learning] benefit both educators and students. [...] analogue GBL promotes a variety of soft skills that otherwise are hard to induce using traditional methods of teaching. These skills could include collaboration and communication, creativity, problem-solving, and decision-making" [9].

## 3    Research Setting

This case study was conducted at TU Wien, in Vienna - Austria. The university has 26.110 students, 6.000 in the informatics faculty. Each year around 700 of them (including around 120 female and diverse) go through the mandatory course *Ways of Thinking in Informatics* (course number 187.B12[1]). This course has a learners workload of 5.5 ECTS which amounts to 140 working hours for the students. During the "Games and Labs" exercise participating students needed to select one of these eight discussed "Ways of Thinking" as their main focus: Scientific Thinking, Computational Thinking, Design Thinking, Responsible Thinking, Critical Thinking, Criminal Thinking, Policy Thinking, Creative Thinking. Every student had to play two games related to this specific "Way of Thinking" during a play session of at least two hours. Students could either lend games to be played at home or join public in-person game events, which were held in the main building of the university.

---

[1] https://tiss.tuwien.ac.at/course/courseDetails.xhtml?courseNr=187B12

A diverse pool of data concerning the students' experiences was collected based on their perception, and perceived content retention. Students filled out one survey in the beginning of the exercise, collecting basic data. For each game they played, they filled out one survey regarding their perception of games impact and their experience with it. This quantitative research design was based on bloom's taxonomy [3]. Additionally, each student wrote a long form report about playing games and what they learned from them; was asked to formulate two questions other players could asked themselves after playing the game to boost learning transfer and reflection; give explicit feedback about the merit and pitfalls of this type of exercise; and finally write a reflection about their personal takeaways.

Since providing this data was part of their grade, students had to hand in their answers paired with their student identifications. The exercises were graded by someone else as to not make them identifiable by the authors of this paper and were then downloaded without identifiers for the purpose of evaluation. Thus, all data was evaluated anonymously, without students needing to fear repercussions or a negative impact on their grade due to "bad feedback". Due to the short time-frame between data collected throughout the semester and the publication of this paper, we only present results of the initial investigation. The data was collected in German, direct quotes where translated for this publication.

## 4    Evaluation and Lessons Learned

In this section the authors give insights into findings from the data analysis along with lessons learned, operational adaptations that were implemented throughout the semester, as well as (so-far untested) strategies formulated to improve setup, reception and students' experiences in upcoming semesters. The section is structured to first discuss the game selection itself, then focuses on the students' experiences with the exercise and their coursework, and finally outlining the organisational framework underlying the exercise.

### 4.1    Purposeful Board- and Card Games

Many of the board games utilised in this study were created by teams of students in a prior lecture, *Gameful Design*. This will be the topic of a forthcoming publication, but for future reference, the mode that we created groups of Bachelor and Master students who worked together on game prototypes was intensely fruitful. The Bachelor students were still closer to the content of the lecture and could better emphasise with the needs and wants of first semester students. The Master students, however, had a more detailed overall knowledge and feeling in how far the content of *Ways of Thinking in Informatics* supported, impacted and colluded with other courses in their studies, and thus, which aspects they found to be valuable to be put into the games.

However, it is important to select a variety of game format and styles, as some students still struggled with the selection of games available. With a large number of learners it is important to allow for a variety of play styles, interests and account for preexisting knowledge. According to the survey, 6.1% of students play board games "very often" and around 50% "often and sometimes". As a result, a lot of students liked the simple rule set of memory while others felt it was too boring for this purpose. Some found the level of dealing with the lecture topics that the games afforded to be sufficient or surpassing their expectations: "I appreciated the selection of interesting games and the fact that I could choose the games myself" or "I could see that the games were created with passion and highly appreciated this exercise, as it brought variety in the often monotonous study routine". Others found the games' level and challenge superficial: "The games should not be this superficial when it comes to the topic.", "I found the games were drab and would have needed more freedom for the players", "I would have wished for a wider selection of board games about my way of thinking" or "The game was easy, I would have wished for it to be more challenging". To mitigate these shortcomings, students suggested additional exercise modes where they could propose other existing games to add to the pool or create their own games instead of playing pre-selected games.

During the semester it also became apparent, that some game manuals and rule sets lacked detail, were confusing or too long: "The basic idea of the game was good, but reading the manual kept interrupting the flow.", "Some of the terms in the manual were too specific and not explained well" or "The rules were too complex to understand the game within one hour". Additionally especially but not exclusively in regard to the self-designed games, the authors redesigned some rules on the fly, seeing options to improve the rule-set to better support the anticipated impact. Thus, one unexpected downside of analogue games was the necessity to develop, regularly update, print, fold and distribute the games' manuals. For future iteration, digital manuals are developed and included in the games in the form of QR codes, as the need to update the game manuals further over time seems inevitable.

## 4.2 Surveys and Reports

The initial investigation shows that participants appreciated the game-based format as a change: "The format was very entertaining and pleasant, I was able to pick up a lot because of the gameful approach". Students rated the knowledge transfer particularly positive as the game-based approach enabled interaction and peer-level reflection: "I appreciated spending time with new people and learning something new at the same time." and "I experienced the format as very neat and found it great, that I was able to work on my understanding of the subject matter and meet new people at the same time. We had a lot of fun, despite the fact that I didn't know anyone beforehand. I have no complaints". A majority of students (74%) recommended to utilise the approach in other higher education settings and courses as well: "At the game event the atmosphere was very enjoyable and positive and the games are a great opportunity to elaborate on the lectures content. First, I was sceptical if such a balance could be maintained, but all games were well structured and offered a good mix of fun and learning.

*I would wish for more courses to apply this [game-based learning] concept at such a high level."* and *"I find this format very useful, as there are good reasons to use games and entertaining content for learning. In my opinion, not using this format would be a step backwards (well aware that it is not the norm [in other courses and learning environments])".* Experiencing the course topics in this palpable fashion also led to so-called "light bulb moments" or insights, in which students grasped aspects of the course content that they had not realised before: "I made connections [to ways of thinking] during playing, but in reading more about my 'way of thinking' afterwards, I then actually experienced aha-moments", "I had no notion about policy thinking before, but during the game it suddenly made click" or "In my opinion I learned a lot [in this exercise] and some things only sink in, if you find the mistake yourself along with having to find a solution for it".

The collected data overall shows a positive impact of this practical approach of engaging with different "ways of thinking" and allows for playful engagement from unexpected perspectives. Learners that were confronted with a game-based approach challenged each others prejudices and reflected on their own under-standing of their distinct "ways of thinking": *"The question I asked myself [during playing] was how to objectively rate other peoples' opinions as 'good' or 'bad', if every person and every society [...] has a different concept of 'good' or 'bad'".*

Especially the analogue, game-based approach was immensely helpful to fos-ter engagement and discussions among students. It allowed for diverse groups to form and engage in (mostly) positive exchange - be it in cooperative or com-petitive game settings. Of the 197 students who reported on having met new colleagues, 191 indicated positive interactions and only 6 had negative experi-ences. This can also be seen in the recorded reactions, with one particularly striking set of answers to the event's survey: While overall 84% of students agreed that game-based learning is useful in higher education. Diving deeper in these results it seems that the minority groups of female and diverse students especially gained from the benefits of this game-based approach. Within this subgroup around 94% of learners agree with its usefulness, see Fig. 2 in compar-ison to Fig. 1. This effect has been shown in other studies as well and implies a strong correlation between the alternative teaching methodologies and agendas towards more inclusivity in higher education, especially in computer science and engineering curricula [1].

### 4.3   Game Distribution and Game Event Organisation

Organising a system in which up to 700 students get access to a selection of relevant board and digital games over the course of one semester is not a trivial matter. While access to digital games was mostly problematic due to licensing issues for paid games, but otherwise organisationally irrelevant, this section will concentrate on the board game distribution, outlining two tracks of access to board games along with lessons learned and options for improvements.

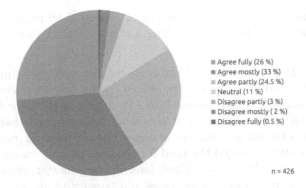

**Fig. 1.** Students perspective on the viability of game-based learning in higher education (n = 426).

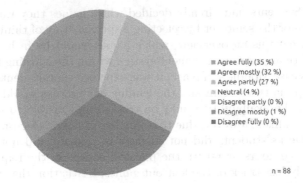

**Fig. 2.** Female and diverse perspective on the viability of game-based learning in higher education (n = 88).

The lecture team offered two tracks: students could either lend out physical board games or they could join one of four live gaming events. Data collected from 495 students showed that 258 students participated in one or more in-person gaming events, while 240 lent out board games or played digital games. Due to the limited number of copies the physical games that were lent out to students had to be returned within three to seven days.

In-person gaming events were designed to allow for random interactions between first year students and were distributed throughout the semester. This section discusses some relevant aspects, which influence the setup of an operational system to offer games that need to be played by 600+ students. This evaluation will report on the practical insights and issues with running these two tracks and thus include some specific advice for other institutions.

### Track One: Game Pickup

One way to access the board games was to use the "game pickup" track. Students could come by the institute, lend out games and return them within an arranged amount of time. The three main factors, relevant for making this system work, were the time investment for the lecture team generated by regular office hours, the game's availability, as well as tracking and retrieving the lent out games.

**Office Hours.** In the beginning of the semester, two two-hour time slots twice a week (Mondays and Thursdays) were offered by the authors during which students could pickup and return games. In the beginning of the semester, students had to return the games within 3–4 days since it was feared that availability would suffer with the limited number of copies of each physical game. However, the team highly overestimated the need for students to lend games, resulting in more effort than actually needed. Thus, later in the semester, office hours were reduced to once a week and in a few cases additional time slots were offered by request, if a students could not come by during the specified office hours.

**Availability.** Students had already decided which games they wanted to play at the beginning of the semester by selecting a specific "way of thinking" for this exercise, which gave us an overview, which games would be in higher demand than others. With an asset management system within the learning management system - in this case Moodle - in place, it was expected that students would individually sign up via the system and the lending out process would be managed digitally. Thus, the availability would be tracked and visible to students and the lecture team alike. However, due to a number of human factors this system became unusable as students did not manage to sign up, did not show up at the specified office hours or return the physical copies on the requested dates. Lecturers quickly lost track of the lent out games, a situation that needed to be mitigated immediately.

**Tracking and Retrieving.** Ultimately the team switched to an analogue "library system" to track incoming and outgoing games. For each game, students had to sign up with name, students ID, and telephone number, so that there was a chance to reach them in case they did not return a game. As luck would have it, one of the students who lent out two games, actually unregistered from their studies in the same week without returning the games first. Only the additional data from the sign up process, i.e. the telephone number, helped in retrieving said games. Later in the semester the pickup date as well as the planned return date were added to the library cards, to make students with their signature more accountable and make it easier for the team to track when to expect the games back and when to start asking for returns if they were late.

If game pickup is offered by an institution, as in this case, the overhead should be taken into account and minimised as far as possible for the students as well as the involved lecture team. Technological solutions of course are a viable option to handle this but need to be enforced and operated, a challenge that should not be underestimated during the planning phase.

**Track Two: Live Gaming Events**
The second option to access the board games was to join in-person gaming events. We offered four of these equally distributed throughout the semester,

using a number of seminar rooms which were located in close proximity to each other for students to play games in.

**Registration.** Students needed to register in the lecture's learning management system if they planned on joining a live gaming event, since the rooms only offered a limited amount of space and we only had a limited amount of copies available for each game (5–9 copies per game). Each of the gaming events was originally planned for 6 h with a room capacity of 80 students per hour. While we had a high amount of registrations for the first two live gaming events, 80% and 53% of the available slots were booked respectively, the six hours for the last two events were hardly needed. Thus, they were shortened to four and two hour long event slots, which were still only filled to 35% and 21% of the room capacity.

The authors have found two main issues with the registration process, both of which could have been fixed easily, if anticipated earlier. Sadly, the registration tool in Moodle did not provide an exportable and usable table for the registration that could have been used on-site during sign up, which made the administration harder than necessary. Additionally, in the registration there was no option to select which "way of thinking" the students intended to play. On the one hand, this made it hard to support the group building process or to keep an overview of which and how many games were needed. On the other hand, some students struggled, because they could not remember which "way of thinking" they had planned to play, thus complicating group building and game distribution even further.

**Event Setting.** The game events took place in four adjacent seminar rooms with movable furniture, which was important to create islands for students to sit around, to play and to create a more gameful atmosphere. One room was utilised as *headquarters* and show room, where games were laid out, participating students could sign in and the individual groups were organised. On average, about four people of the lecture team were present during each game event, so students were able to ask questions about the games, the rules, exercise modes, lecture content and everything in between. Thus, the in-person events additionally provided a low level means of interpersonal interaction between students and the lecture team. Some playing tables were also located directly in the *headquarter* room.

Throughout the event, students were organised in groups and there was a lot of coming and going as new rooms needed to be occupied or tables became available after groups had left the event. As students flocked in the rooms, the events changed their appearance a lot. Full desks and obviously entertained students led to a chain reaction in creating a playful mood and enjoyable experience. While the authors anticipated that their presence in the room would not impact the students' gaming experience, observation showed that the atmosphere tended to be better and lighter in the other rooms in comparison to the *headquarters*. For example, the authors observed more chatting and laughing occurring in other rooms, whereas the main room tended to be quieter and more reserved.

This effect should be taken into account during the preparation stages. Events should be planned concise and short to fill up the available space. Full tables and rooms should be the goal of planning and some waiting-time for students is not detrimental, as eager learners engaged in discussions - especially when already placed in groups - while waiting for a spot to open up. To allow for the necessary space as well as the desired mood to be created, the authors suggest a physical separation between the organisational part of the event - handing out of the games, accounting for participation and answering questions - and the gameful interactions between the students. However, the rooms need to be in close proximity to lessen the organisational overhead.

**Group Organisation.** One of the major issues in organising these in-person gaming events was to create groups of students who planned to play games about the same "way of thinking". Some students were well organised and had already put together groups to play with in advance. However, the majority of students were not yet well connected with their peers and came alone or in groups of two or three. This is partly due to that fact that *Ways of Thinking in Informatics* takes place in the very first semester of their bachelor studies, so many students are completely new to university and have not yet had the opportunity to get to know their colleagues.

Thus, some awkward interactions with students who showed up alone occurred. The main issue occurred when only a few students arrived at the same time and did not have matching "ways of thinking". Often they could not be placed in existing groups and had to wait for other students with suitable "ways of thinking" to arrive. For some, the issue was resolved rather quickly while others had to wait around for 20 min and more and then had to be placed in groups that were already playing and half way through a game. Some groups ended up being composed of students interested in different "ways of thinking", thus negatively impacting their potential takeaways: *"My view on my way of thinking was not greatly impacted, due to the fact that I was in a mixed group and we did not play a game designed for my particular way of thinking"*.

While this issue was not fully resolved, a set of ideas was formulated to be tested in the upcoming semesters: students have to register not only for a time slot but also for a "way of thinking" to provide for a better overview in advance and on-site; the gaming events can be organised by one or two specific "ways of thinking" - this approach creates a more homogeneous pool of participants who can better play with each other; students could be tasked with organising themselves and sign up in groups from the start, however, that just moves the awkward group building process to a different - possibly online - location and might not be easier for the individual students; learners could also be tasked to create teams on-site, before they come to the *headquarters* to sign up, again handing the responsibility for the group building activity to the students; some of the games can be adapted to be played from different points of view, thus making it easier to be played by groups of students who are working on different "ways of thinking".

## 4.4  Preparation and Reflection

In *Ways of Thinking in Informatics* a variety of exercise types are offered throughout the semester. Each student can choose which of these exercises they will complete for the eight distinct "ways of thinking", which are presented and discussed in the lecture. While learners can pick and choose, which exercise they will do for which way of thinking, most of these exercises can only be done after the specific chapter has been discussed in the lecture, creating a tight timetable over the course of the semester.

Playing and analysing the games is one of the only exercise types that can be completed at any time throughout the semester, the thought process being, that some exercises needed to have less restrictions to be able to better fit in, whenever students have spare time. While many students thus moved the exercise to the beginning of the semester, where they had more time - an effect easily noticed in the registration and event capacity - they reported on issues analysing the games in regards to some of the "ways of thinking", e.g. needing to analyse a game from the point of view of "policy thinking" without having a clear understanding what "policy thinking" entails.

This issue is adjacent to issues around the game distribution and event organisation. On the one hand, educators could create more restrictions around the exercise type itself - when and how the game analysis can be done. On the other hand, students do appreciate the option to choose their own deadlines and pace of working and appreciate the freedom that comes along with it. Thus, teaching teams might need to point to more opportunities of independent study - giving a content overview for each chapter with pointers to what might be relevant for deeper reflective activities; providing more guided questions for reflection for each game and the accompanying "way of thinking"; and pointing towards specific resources that need to be read before playing the games.

## 5  Conclusion and Future Research

The authors are inclined to recommend this student-centred and game-based approach to other courses in higher education. At the university level, the utilisation of current, modern and innovative approaches is key to approach the diverse and heterogeneous set of students, higher education strives to teach and introduce to the scientific field and method. We found that, similar to existing studies, "over a quarter of the students are conscious that [game-based learning] sessions allowed them to learn while having fun [...] they do not understand playing as an unproductive or childish activity" [6].

A more diverse selection of exercises can, and in our case did, lead to an improvement in female students engagement; led to a great number of social interaction; and a deeper, more palpable insight in the courses content. Different "ways of thinking" could be practised, explored and discussed with the use of purposeful board games. The setting of in-person, analogue and multiplayer games gave space and time to an incredible amount of personal growth, as can be seen in the students feedback and impressions in the rooms.

This initial case study was a valuable experience that, while highlighting some issues and pitfalls in the selection of games, organisation and setup, also showed the promises of this type of coursework. Students became enthralled in the lecture topics and at the same time the easygoing in-person game events created the means of forming inter-personal, collegial connections and building communities of practice that, if fostered, could support students throughout their studies in higher education.

# References

1. Amer, A., Sidhu, G., Alvarez, M.I.R., Ramos, J.A.L., Srinivasan, S.: Equity, diversity, and inclusion strategies in engineering and computer science. Educ. Sci. **14**(1), 110 (2024). https://doi.org/10.3390/educsci14010110, https://www.mdpi.com/2227-7102/14/1/110
2. Berenice Alfaro-Ponce, A.P., Sanabria-Z, J.: Components of computational thinking in citizen science games and its contribution to reasoning for complexity through digital game-based learning: a framework proposal. Cogent Educ. **10**(1), 2191751 (2023). https://doi.org/10.1080/2331186X.2023.2191751
3. Bloom, B.S., et al.: Reflections on the development and use of the taxonomy. Yearbook: Nat. Soc. Study Educ. **92**(2), 1–8 (1994)
4. Boragine, L.H.: Roll the dice: using game-based learning to teach sustainability in higher education. In: Leal Filho, W., Lange Salvia, A., Pallant, E., Choate, B., Pearce, K. (eds.) Educating the Sustainability Leaders of the Future. World Sustainability Series, pp. 59–73. Springer, Cham (2023). https://doi.org/10.1007/978-3-031-22856-8_4
5. Frauenberger, C., Purgathofer, P.: Ways of thinking in informatics. Commun. ACM **62**(7), 58-64 (2019). https://doi.org/10.1145/3329674
6. Gonzalo-Iglesia, J.L., Lozano-Monterrubio, N., Prades-Tena, J.: Noneducational board games in university education. Perceptions of students experiencing game-based learning methodologies. Revista Lusófona de Educação **41**, 45–62 (2018). https://doi.org/10.24140/issn.1645-7250.rle41.03
7. Juul, J.: The game, the player, the world: looking for a heart of gameness. In: Level Up: Digital Games Research Conference Proceedings, January 2003
8. Kuo, H.C., Weng, T.L., Chang, C.C., Chang, C.Y.: Designing our own board games in the playful space: improving high school student's citizenship competencies and creativity through game-based learning. Sustainability **15**(4), 2968 (2023). https://doi.org/10.3390/su15042968, https://www.mdpi.com/2071-1050/15/4/2968
9. Maratou, V., et al.: Game-based learning in higher education using analogue games. Int. J. Film Media Arts, 68–83 (2023). https://doi.org/10.24140/ijfma.v8.n1.04
10. Mercer, T., Kythreotis, A., Robinson, Z., Stolte, T., George, S., Haywood, S.: The use of educational game design and play in higher education to influence sustainable behaviour. Int. J. Sustain. High. Educ. **18**, 359–384 (2017). https://doi.org/10.1108/IJSHE-03-2015-0064

11. Olayvar, S.: Integration of game-based learning approach as an innovative teaching tool in improving students' academic performance in English. Int. J. Instr. **16**, 677–690 (2023). https://doi.org/10.29333/iji.2023.16336a
12. Piaget, J.: Play, dreams, and imitation in childhood. New York: W. W. Norton & Company, Inc. Psychol. Schools **3**(2), 189–189 (1966). https://doi.org/10.1002/1520-6807(196604)3:2⟨189::AID-PITS2310030222⟩3.0.CO;2-Z
13. Resnick, M.: Lifelong Kindergarten: Cultivating Creativity through Projects, Passion, Peers, and Play. The MIT Press, Cambridge (2017). https://doi.org/10.7551/mitpress/11017.001.0001
14. Smith, E., Golding, L.: Use of board games in higher education literature review. MSOR Connections **16**, 24 (2018). https://doi.org/10.21100/msor.v16i2.624
15. Subhash, S., Cudney, E.: Gamified learning in higher education: a systematic review of the literature. Comput. Hum. Behav. **87**, 192–206 (2018). https://doi.org/10.1016/j.chb.2018.05.028
16. Taspinar, B., Schmidt, W., Schuhbauer, H.: Gamification in education: a board game approach to knowledge acquisition. Procedia Comput. Sci. **99**, 101–116 (2016). https://doi.org/10.1016/j.procs.2016.09.104, https://www.sciencedirect.com/science/article/pii/S1877050916322499, International Conference on Knowledge Management, ICKM 2016, 10–11 October 2016, Vienna, Austria

# Implementation and Usability Evaluation of an Online Videogame for Learning Musical Harmony

Carlos Patricio Meneses Rodríguez[✉] and Jaime Sánchez

Universidad de Chile, Santiago, Chile
cpmeneses94@gmail.com, jsanchezi@uchile.cl

**Abstract.** In the field of music education, harmony represents an important learning challenge, especially for unmotivated students. This obstacle suggests the need for facilitating digital tools. Educational videogames are presented as effective strategies for teaching complex content. This lack of resources is accentuated in university education. In 2020, a multiplayer board game named "Tone Cluster" was developed as a tool for learning musical harmony, with graphic interfaces designed for a future mobile version. This research proposes a digital redesign of the game and interfaces, followed by its implementation and the evaluation of its usability on mobile devices. The application allows for asynchronous games that are accessible anywhere, taking advantage of the versatility of mobile devices. Evaluations with experts and users highlighted the quality and effectiveness of the game in terms of usability, with mostly positive results supporting its potential as a music teaching tool.

**Keywords:** Musical education · educational videogames · harmony learning · usability evaluation

## 1 Introduction

Musical harmony, focused on the study of chords and their interrelationships, constitutes the heart of musical language [1]. However, its understanding presents significant challenges, particularly for students with limited motivation [2]. The pursuit of the state of Flow, where learning is optimal by addressing stimulating challenges aligned with skills [3], is hindered when the formal study of harmony becomes tedious and disconnected from current technologies [4], resulting in frustration.

In the current context of rapid technological advances, the incorporation of educational videogames has flourished in various areas, except in the teaching of musical harmony. In this context, arises the initiative of Medel [2] by proposing an online video game prototype to teach musical harmony.

This study focuses on redesigning, implementing and evaluating the "Tone Cluster" game as an educational tool for musical harmony. The game, conceived as a mobile application, allows users to create accounts, form groups and participate in games of a

P. Zaphiris and A. Ioannou (Eds.): HCII 2024, LNCS 14723, pp. 82–93, 2024.
https://doi.org/10.1007/978-3-031-61685-3_7

musical board game. On each turn, players place tokens representing notes with the goal of forming chords and accumulating points. To facilitate organization, a server platform was developed that allows asynchronous games.

The general objective of this work is to develop and evaluate the usability of the video game "Tone Cluster", seeking more effective and attractive learning compared to traditional methods. Specific objectives encompass the redesign of the game, its implementation on mobile devices with online multiplayer capabilities, and the evaluation of its usability by students and experts in music education.

This innovative approach is oriented towards enriching the teaching of musical harmony, integrating technology and collaborative learning, with the aim of overcoming the traditional barriers of motivation and difficulty in the study of this fundamental musical aspect.

## 2  Related Work

The game developed is educational, mobile and features asynchronous multiplayer mode. In addition, its theme was musical harmony, and its usability was measured. Pedagogies, games and applications related to each of these categories are considered below.

### 2.1  Distance Learning

The pedagogy of distance education can be separated into three generations: Cognitive-Behavioral, Social-Constructivist and Connectivist pedagogy. In Cognitive-Behavioral pedagogy, the student is a passive recipient of the knowledge that is given to him or her.

In Social-Constructivist pedagogy, on the other hand, the student is an active agent of his or her own learning [5]. Finally, in connectivist pedagogy, learning is understood as the process of building networks of information, contacts and resources that are applied to real problems, focusing on the ability to obtain and apply knowledge over memorization.

The game proposed in this study is in the category of Social-Constructivist learning, where learning is applied, in this case, in a game space. This space is shared with other people. With this, it is expected that the user's social activity combined with the use of the application will facilitate significant learning.

### 2.2  Educational Videogames

The videogame that was developed in this report is an educational game made for use by students using mobile devices. Examples of educational games for mobile devices include the games Evolution, Buin Zoo, and Museo. These serious games were developed to be used in the specific context of curricular activities in classes of elementary schools. [6].

These games were used with groups of eighth grade students in learning activities during which they went to Buin Zoo and the National Museum of Natural History. During these activities, students were divided into groups of four and asked to solve the questions posed in the games. Some questions are answered individually and others in groups.

After these activities, the students had to answer a survey and perception scales of problem-solving skills and collaboration skills. The data obtained after this research indicates that the experimental group achieved a greater perception of their collaboration skills.

## 2.3 Educational Music Games

An example of a game aimed at teaching musical harmony is In Harmony [7]. Which is an educational program aimed at primary school children that incorporates two music education software programs: Teach, Learn, Evaluate! (TLE) [8], and Impromptu [9] TLE consists of a series of four musical activity exercises. Impromptu is an application in which the user can organize fragments of known melodies represented in blocks to reconstruct them or to create new melodies.

## 2.4 Musical Harmony Educational Tools

Tools made with the goal of teaching aspects of musical harmony include Harmony Space [10], Harmonic Walk [11], and the MusEdLab [12] Math, Science & Music [13] and Music Lab [14] playgrounds.

Harmony Space is an interface designed to facilitate rapid learning, especially by beginners, of the theory and practical use of tonal harmony. In this tool you can build chords on a "board" of notes arranged at specific intervals. It has at least six general uses: Musical instrument, tool for teaching basic harmonization, learning tool for exploring tonal music theory, discovery learning tool for composing and modifying chord sequences, and notation for non-tonal chord sequences that are not obvious in conventional notations.

Harmonic Walk is an interactive environment where the user's position in a rectangular space generates different chords, where the user's challenge is to generate a harmonious progression by walking the right path. A disadvantage of these two softwares is that for the student to use them, the constant guidance of an educator is necessary.

The playgrounds are similar to each other. Each one with small digital activities aimed at musical education. However, its musical theoretical content is very basic. No games were found for teaching musical harmony at the university level.

## 2.5 Usability on Mobile Devices

The ISO defines usability as "The extent to which a product can be used by specific users to achieve specific objectives with effectiveness, efficiency and satisfaction in a specific context of use" (ISO 9241-11). An important part of making sure users have a positive experience with the game is making sure the interface makes it easy to use the app [15].

The preferred method for measuring usability in games is evaluation through heuristics. [16] Users are asked questions associated with desirable features in the application that serve to measure the experience they have with the application. The answers to these questions are according to your opinion.

There is disagreement as to whether the playability of a game should be considered a criterion of usability. [16] EFlowGame is a heuristic usability questionnaire that considers the enjoyability of the game [17].

Because usability depends on the domain being worked on, there are many possible heuristics to measure the usability of an application. In mobile application contexts, for example, it may be necessary to evaluate the impact that user movement has on the use of the application. [15] There are reviews on the different evaluation models [15] and meta-heuristics to be able to choose which heuristic questions to ask to evaluate games according to the ideas that can be used to describe the game [16].

### 2.6 Asynchronous Games

Multiplayer games can be divided into synchronous and asynchronous. Synchronous games are those where all players are performing actions in the game at the same time, while asynchronous games are those where players play in sequence rather than simultaneously [18].

The game that was developed belongs to the category of asynchronous games. So, it is worth reviewing other asynchronous games and how they use it.

There are games for mobile devices that take advantage of asynchronicity in their experiences. Words with Friends is a Scrabble-based game for mobile devices in which players can take turns without the other players having the game activated. This allows players to play multiple games, in which only one move needs to be made every couple of days. The game's use of asynchronicity is like Words with Friends.

In turn, Pokémon Go allows players to compete for control of gyms, which are points of interest for players. For this, a player can perform a gym capture and then another player can try to defeat a computer-controlled version of the first player to take control of the captured gym from him. This multiplayer is done without both players playing at the same time.

## 3 Game Design

In the initial design phase of the educational video game "Tone Cluster", created by Daniela Medel Sierralta for her master's thesis, rules and interface designs were established. The game, similar to Scrabble but with tiles representing musical notes to form chords, aims to facilitate the teaching of musical harmony to university students and music professionals. The game board is a 15 × 15 grid where players, in turns, place tiles to form chords, starting from the center and connecting to previous chords (Figs. 1, 2, 3, and 4).

The game allows up to 4 players and offers 13 difficulty levels that vary the notes available to build chords. The mobile application has a series of interfaces that include a home with access to multiple functions (such as interactive piano, circle of fifths, and configuration options), user profile, help, settings, a section for friends and modes to choose players and define game options.

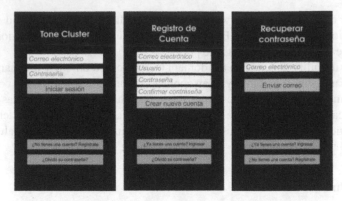

**Fig. 1.** Login, Registration and Password Recovery Screens.

**Fig. 2.** Main Menu, Friends List and Create New Game Screens.

**Fig. 3.** Help, Rules and Technical Support Screens.

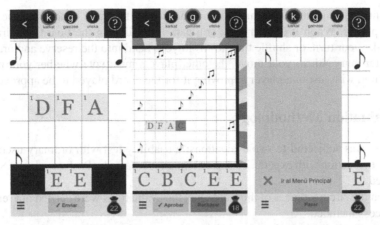

**Fig. 4.** Game screens: During the player's turn, voting on another player's move, displaying the menu.

During the development process, areas were identified to improve and modify the original design, such as the incorporation of buttons separated by phase, an option to zoom in and out of the screen with touch movements, and the creation of a system for entering and registering user accounts, which allowed for more efficient management of user information.

The application was developed following the Rapid Prototyping methodology, [19] which involves the iterative creation of prototypes for constant review and improvement.

The process covers three phases:

Prototyping, where the solution is visually outlined.

Review, presenting the prototype to evaluative users to validate if it meets their expectations.

Refine, adjusting the prototype according to the feedback received.

For this project, the evaluators were the guiding teacher and Daniela Medel, designer of Tone Cluster. This methodology was chosen for its flexibility, the constant feedback it provides, and the close relationship established between the developer and the testers.

## 4 Solution Design

The mobile application, accessible from anywhere, focuses on a client-server architecture. While the client, developed in Unity, operates on the user's mobile device, updating the interface and processing the game logic, the server in PlayFab is responsible for managing the data and maintaining the database. This design makes it easier for users not to interact directly, but rather all game information is centralized and saved on the server. You can see the game in action in the following video: youtu.be/F9gBBoVilZ0.

## 5 Game Controls

Each player must register their own user account within the applications to which their information is associated. Within the main menu of the application the user can enter games already started, accept invitations or create new games. To create a match, the player must add other users to their friends list and then invite them to their match.

Within the game the user can zoom in and out of the game board with the chords already played. When it is your turn, you can place tiles on the board, confirm your move, take your turn, or shuffle the tiles from your hand into the reserve and draw new tiles. After you confirm your move, the other players must vote whether your move is valid or not, with just one player approving it for the chord played to be approved.

## 6  Evaluation Methodology

The game was subjected to two evaluations: a usability test with ordinary users and a heuristic evaluation with experts. Two questionnaires created by Professor Jaime Sánchez were used.

Given the circumstances of the pandemic, the evaluations were carried out remotely. The process included:

Instrument Selection: Use of questionnaires recognized in literature.

Selection of Evaluating Users: Including experts in music and digital applications in said field.

Sending Instruments and Access to the Game: Through links for download and evaluation.

Reception and Analysis: The responses were analyzed to determine the acceptance of the video game by users.

There was a setback with a bug in the interface, but after its correction, the evaluation was carried out successfully, considering factors such as navigability, design, interaction, and usability, among others.

## 7  Evaluation Sample

The evaluation involved two types of users: experts and end users. The expert users were three university music professors with knowledge of digital applications in the musical field, selected by Professor Jaime Sánchez. The usability test with common users was carried out with 10 users, of which there were 3 amateurs, 5 music students and 2 professionals, who were chosen by the game designer and the guiding teacher.

## 8  Instruments

The instruments used to evaluate the usability of the game are described below.

Video Game Usability Questionnaire: This questionnaire, based on Nielsen, aims to evaluate the usability of the game with end users. It consists of questions that address aspects such as navigation, interaction, design and game functionalities. [20].

Heuristic Evaluation: The questionnaire used focused on heuristic evaluation, aimed at expert users. This tool was created to evaluate the usability of videogames based on interface design heuristics, mainly inspired by the studies of Nielsen and Schneiderman. It is made up of questions that cover 13 factors and one additional category, addressing topics from the visibility of the state of the videogame to interactivity [21].

These questionnaires were administered after the players interacted with the game to collect their impressions and feedback.

# 9  Results

Two usability evaluations were carried out: One with common users and one with expert evaluators in heuristics. The results of these are described below.

**Usability Questionnaire Results**

The questionnaire was applied to 10 users, who were 3 amateurs, 5 music students and 2 professionals. The results are described in Figs. 5 and 6.

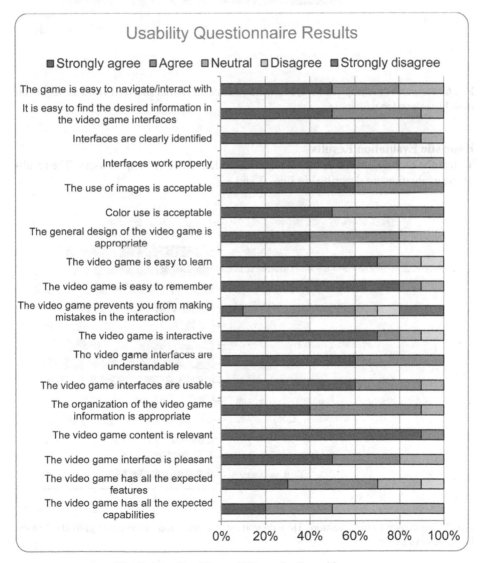

**Fig. 5.** Results of the usability evaluation with users.

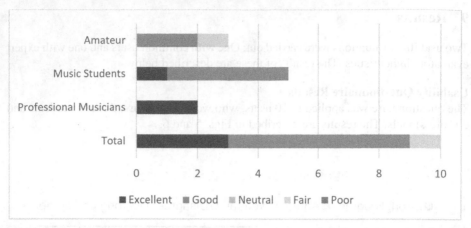

**Fig. 6.** Responses to the question "How would you rate the overall analyzed video game?" in the usability evaluation with users.

## Heuristic Evaluation Results

To test the usability of the application, it was tested with three expert users. The results of the evaluation are described in Figs. 7 and 8.

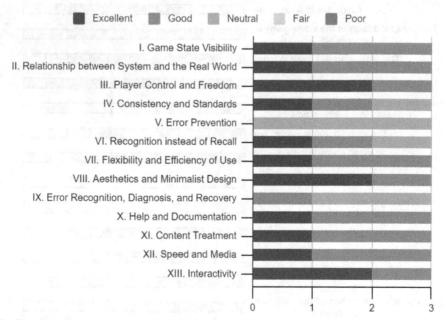

**Fig. 7.** Responses to the question "How do you rate the analyzed video game globally?" in the heuristics evaluation.

**Fig. 8.** Results of the heuristics evaluation.

# 10   Conclusions of the Evaluation

In a usability evaluation with end users, of 14 questions, 11 obtained at least 75% approval, qualifying the evaluation as positive. However, three questions did not meet this threshold. Two were related to the expectation of more in-game functionality. The third, about whether the game avoided errors in interaction, probably had problems due to a bug that arose due to technical differences in capacity between the cell phone used for debugging during development and the users' devices during evaluation. This bug affected the ability to interact with the interface, requiring a reevaluation once fixed, which could have influenced the results. Additionally, the game relies heavily on the internet, which could cause errors. Recommendations included improving feedback, visual appearance and adding a tutorial. Desirable elements, such as a chat, were in the original design but were omitted due to lack of time.

## 11    Discussion

During the project, the video game "Tone Cluster" for cell phones was redesigned and evaluated, which allows online games.

The redesign was simple, focused on the objectives of the game, although a broader future redesign is contemplated. The development presented challenges due to the complexity of the online functionalities, which led to simplification of the application. Unity made things like the user interface and connecting to the server easier, although their impact on device resources had to be considered. PlayFab, used for the server, helped simplify tasks such as account creation, but lacked clear documentation, requiring experimentation. The game was well received by users, but the need for testing on various devices and adding functionalities to improve the experience was identified. In the future, we are looking to strengthen the application, add omitted tools and improve the interface. A more extensive usability evaluation is essential.

**Acknowledgments.** This work was funded by Chilean National Agency for Research and Development (ANID), Basal Funding for Scientific and Technology Centers of Excellence, project FB0003.

## References

1. Nettles, B.: Harmony 1. Berklee College of Music, New York (1987)
2. Medel Sierralta, D.: Proposal for an Online Video Game Prototype for Learning Musical Harmony. Master's Thesis, University of Chile Faculty of Social Sciences Graduate School, Santiago, Chile (2021)
3. Denis, G., Jouvelot, P.: Motivation-Driven Educational Game Design: Applying Best Practices to Music Education, pp. 462–465 (2005). https://doi.org/10.1145/1178477.1178581
4. Savage, J.: Reconstructing music education through ICT. Res. Educ. **78**, 65–77 (2007)
5. Anderson, T., Dron, J.: Three generations of distance education pedagogy. Int. Rev. Res. Open Dist. Learn. **12**(3), 80 (2011). https://doi.org/10.19173/irrodl.v12i3.890
6. Sánchez, J., Mendoza, C., Salinas, A.: Mobile serious games for collaborative problem solving. Stud. Health Technol. Inf. **144**, 193–197 (2009). https://doi.org/10.3233/978-1-60750-017-9-193
7. Portowitz, A., Peppler, K.A., Downton, M.: In harmony: a technology-based music education model to enhance musical understanding and general learning skills. Int. J. Music. Educ. **32**(2), 242–260 (2014). https://doi.org/10.1177/0255761413517056
8. Portowitz, A., Lichtenstein, O., Egorov, L.: Teach, Learn, Evaluate (TLE): A Computer-based Music learning Tool Designed to Foster Musical Understanding, General Learning Skills, and Cross cultural Understanding (Poster) (2015)
9. Bamberger, J.S., Hernandez, A.: Tuneblocks (2002). https://tuneblocks.com/

10. Holland, S.: Learning about harmony with harmony space: an overview. Tech. Rep. STAN-M-88, Stanford University Department of Music (1994)
11. Mandanici, M., Roda, A.: The "Harmonic Walk": an Interactive Educational Environment to Discover Musical Chords (2014)
12. Ruthmann, S.A.: Musedlab (2013). https://musedlab.org/. Accessed 6 Oct 2022
13. NYU Music Experience Design Lab (MusEDLab). (sf). MathScienceMusic. https://mathsc_iencemusic.org/. Accessed 6 Oct 2022
14. Google. Chrome Music Lab. (2018). https://musiclab.chromeexperiments.com/. Accessed 6 Oct 2022
15. Al Fatta, H., Maksom, Z., Zakaria, M.H.: Systematic literature review on usability evaluation model of educational games: playability, pedagogy, and mobility aspects 1. J. Theor. Appl. Technol. Inf. **31**(14) (2018)
16. Yanez-Gomez, R., Font, J.L., Cascado-Caballero, D., Sevillano, J.-L.: Heuristic usability evaluation on games: a modular approach. Multim. Tools Appl. **78**(4), 4937–4964 (2018). https://doi.org/10.1007/s11042-018-6593-1
17. Fu, F.-L., Su, R.-C., Yu, S.-C.: EGameFlow: a scale to measure learners' enjoyment of e-learning games. Comput. Educ. **52**, 101–112 (2009). https://doi.org/10.1016/j.compedu.2008.07.004
18. Bogost, I.: 1 Asynchronous Multiplay Futures for Casual Multiplayer Experience (2004)
19. Jain, A.: A Beginner's Guide to Rapid Prototyping (2018). https://www.freecodecamp.org/news/a-beginners-guideto-rapid-prototyping-71e8722c17df/. Accessed 6 Oct 2022
20. Sánchez, J.: Video Game Usability Evaluation, End User Questionnaire. Department of Computer Science. University of Chile (2016)
21. Sánchez, J.: Video Game Usability Evaluation, Heuristic Evaluation Questionnaire. Department of Computer Science. University of Chile (2020)

# Analysis of Gamification Elements in E-Learning

Boris A. Reif[✉][iD], Karin Schluifer, Cindy Mayas[iD], and Matthias Hirth[iD]

Technische Universität Ilmenau, Fakultät für Elektrotechnik und Informationstechnik, Institut für Medientechnik, Postfach 10 05 65, 98684 Ilmenau, Germany
{boris.reif,karin.schluifer,cindy.mayas,matthias.hirth}@tu-ilmenau.de

**Abstract.** The e-learning market is growing and with it the importance of motivating elements such as gamification. This paper examines the use of gamification elements on e-learning platforms and how they contribute to a positive User Experience for learners. The paper also examines the effects of gamification elements on the motivation of learners. An online survey was conducted among 204 participants. The survey includes the standardised User Experience Questionnaire to assess the User Experience and the ARCS Model to rate motivation based on the two categories relevance and satisfaction. The results show that a controlled embedding of gamification elements reduces the rate of attrition and has positive effects on the user experience for learners. A second study evaluates the effects of selected gaminfication elements in Moodle and Duolingo. This study shows that gamification elements need to be applied in a controlled manner, have clear targets, and be easily understandable to contribute positively towards the motivation and user experience of the learners.

**Keywords:** Gamification · Gamified Learning · E-Learning · User Experience · Motivation

## 1 Introduction

The e-learning market has been consistently growing for several years [23]. Ever more people are advancing their education via online platforms and more and more companies are offering further education and personal development to their staff through *Learning Management Systems*. According to STATISTA, the market for digital education is projected to reach nearly 400 billion U.S. dollars by 2026. In comparison, in 2021 the market size was estimated at only around 200 billion U.S. dollars [68]. Reports by market research companies are equally optimistic [33,57] about the future prospects of e-learning. Further, the COVID-19 pandemic has greatly contributed to this rise in the use of e-learning [27]. Many e-learning products have taken the step to *gamify* their product or service [58] to maintain learners' attention and engagement [2,39] and solve challenges that are faced in e-learning [71] such as high dropout rates [24,39]. Today, *gamification* is seen as growing in importance in education [9,71]. There

P. Zaphiris and A. Ioannou (Eds.): HCII 2024, LNCS 14723, pp. 94–112, 2024.
https://doi.org/10.1007/978-3-031-61685-3_8

is a growing body of research suggesting that well-implemented gamified learning environments can stimulate cognitive and emotional benefits, such as increased problem-solving abilities and resilience [12,13,62,66]. It has turned gamification and *game based learning* into a large business [64]. Several reports by commercial market research companies suggest further growth of the gamification market [15,48]. This is trend is affirmed by academic publications [52,64]. The gamification of e-learning, in particular for higher education, is well established as the literature review by Khaldi, Bouzidi, and Nader [39] demonstrates.

Gamification can improve the *User Experience* (UX) of a product [31,53]. Handayani et al. [30] point out the importance of satisfying UX on e-learning platforms and propose UX criteria for designing gamified e-learning. However, a poor UX of gamification elements or misuse of gamification elements on the e-learning platform can negatively impact the learning experience [26,50]. Due to poor implementation, 80% of gamification applications miss their goals [71].

This paper investigates gamification elements in e-learning regarding their perceived UX and their impact on learners' motivation. We examine the gamification elements of selected e-learning platforms available in Germany in an online survey to answer the following two research questions:

- **RQ1**: Are gamification elements on e-learning platforms experienced as motivating?
- **RQ2**: Which user experience of gamification elements in e-learning is perceived?

The question regarding the UX is answered using the *User Experience Questionnaire* (UEQ) [60]. For measuring the perception of motivation of gamification elements we use selected scales of the ARCS model [37], and further present a comparison between MOODLE and DUOLINGO as a case study using the same method.

## 2   Background and Related Work

### 2.1   On E-Learning

The origins of *e-learning* reach back to *computer-based trainings* and *web-based trainings* [45]. However, it is regularly subject to rapid change of technical and didactic conditions driven by continuous innovation and growing needs [7]. Thus, definitions often need to be revised and adapted [7]. To gain an understanding of the term, Kerres [38] developed a comprehensive definition in which e-learning is described *"as an umbrella term for all variants of using digital media for teaching and learning purposes (including digital storage media and the Internet) to convey knowledge"*. Brehmer and Becker [7] also discuss various types of devices in their definition of e-learning, such as PCs, laptops, tablets, smartphones, projectors, interactive whiteboards, and technology for recording and playing back media. According to Algahtani et al. [3], there are different ways to classify e-learning: either by the *extent of engagement* or by the *timing of interaction*.

This paper concentrates on online e-learning platforms, such as MOODLE, UDEMY, and DUOLINGO. E-learning or more generally using digital media in learning has great potential but is not necessarily fundamentally better than other forms of teaching and learning [21,67,70]. Despite all its commercial success and popularity amongst users, digital learning still requires improvement [14,51]. In particular, keeping people motivated to conclude online e-learning courses successfully is a challenge. Further, it is important to ensure the quality and effectiveness of online courses, especially in combination with traditional methods [5,69]. Proper design helps learners engage with learning [18].

## 2.2   On Gamification

*Gamification* or *gameful design* is often defined as the use of game elements, gamemechanics, and game principles in a non-game context [17]. Today, gamification is described as a *persuasive technology* aimed at influencing user behaviour by activating certain motivational triggers through game design elements [54].

Czikszentmihalyi [16] discovered that in learning environments created by games, people obtain pleasure, engagement, higher levels of inspiration, and creativity. It is mainly in this sense that Kapp [35] created the definition of gamification that we are using in this paper: *"Gamification is using game-based mechanics, aesthetics, and game-thinking to engage people, motivate action, promote learning and solve problems"*. In e-learning, the trend toward a *gamified learning experience* is intended to improve the UX for learners and increase the engagement rate [8,39]. *Engagement* is here to be loosely understood as by Zichermann and Cunningham [74], who define engagement as *"... a series of potentially interrelated metrics that combine to form a whole. These metrics are: recency, frequency, duration, virality, ratings."*.

It goes without saying that gamification does not overcome all challenges that arise in and from e-learning [25,34,40,47,55,63]. More importantly, gamification itself has its shortcomings and when implemented poorly can be ineffective at best Dah et al. [17]. Humans like to play games and like to play [11,28]. Maybe that is why we naturally assume that games can have a motivating effect on us when it comes to learning. However, as Bouchrika et al. [6] point out there is a growing volume of literature calling for a more rigorous examination of the supposedly positive impact of gamification on learning and demanding more evidence on its increase in motivation, e.g. [4,19,41].

Regardless, the significance of UX in commercial areas is increasing, leading to a greater reliance on gamification [31]. Research by Fitz-Walter et al. [22] found that gamification does not negatively affect UX but rather enhances it, making activities more fun and motivating. The challenge lies in considering the context and role of users to fully leverage the effectiveness of gamification. The design process should be user-centred and iterative [22].

# 3   Methodology

## 3.1   Convenience Sampling Through an Online Survey

We examined the perceived motivational character and quality of gamification elements through a quantitative survey. The survey was conducted online in the form of an opportunity sample, also referred to as convenience sampling. Potential participants were passively recruited by making them aware of the survey through an announcement using the active-students email distribution list of the Technical University Ilmenau, Germany. The link to the survey was also shared on social networks. In addition, individuals from personal contacts were recruited by approaching them directly. The online questionnaire reached a total of 240 people during its collection period from 14th February 2022 to 14th March 2022. However, for the analysis, only the participants who fully completed the survey were considered. Participants who answered the survey incompletely were sorted out to achieve a balanced evaluation. This reduced the number to 204 test persons. Of these participants, 52.45% are women and 45.10% are men. The average age is 25 years (SD = 2.66). Most of the participants are students (77.94%). The remaining number of people are employees (16.18%), pupils (3.92%) and others (1.96%). The number of our samples varies during the test. Not all participants were allowed to answer all the questions. Participants who replied that they had never used an e-learning service or product were not allowed to answer the questions about gamification elements in such a  service or product.

For our online-based study, we used the survey software UNIPARK. An online survey brings with it an increased level of anonymity compared to a face-to-face survey. This anonymity has the added benefit of answers being generally less biased due to the reduced pressure created by social desirability [59]. Before the actual data collection, though, the questionnaire was piloted in a pretest with a similar, but smaller, survey group [42]. Subsequently, the arrangement and sequence of explanatory texts were changed. Further, some of the terminologies used in the survey were renamed, for example, from *gamification elements* to *game mechanics*, to increase the comprehensibility of our questionnaire. The questionnaire consists of a combination of two standardized questionnaires: the ARCS model (partial version) and the UEQ.

The questionnaire was supplemented with general questions on the usage behavior of e-learning offers, a sociodemographic query, and open-ended questions to capture further ideas and impressions of the respondents. For the questionnaire, a range of options was provided, from which known e-learning offers could be selected. This list was created during the conception of the questionnaire and included criteria regarding download numbers, special features, and ratings on online portals. Participants were also given the option to name an e-learning platform in an additional field labeled *other*. This option was added as no reliable figures could be found on the usage of e-learning platforms in Germany.

## 3.2    ARCS Model

American educational psychologist John M. Keller developed an instructional model called ARCS [36,37]. The model focuses on motivation, especially in learning environments [36]. In our study, we use it in the context of e-learning platforms. ARCS is an acronym and stands for *Attention, Relevance, Confidence* and *Satisfaction*.

In this context, *attention* refers to the knowledge taught by teachers. It should attract the attention and interest of learners, and make students have *cognitive curiosity* [20,73]. *Relevance* means the presented content should be understandable and should be related to the learners' experiences and knowledge [1,73]. *Confidence* means that learners can increase their self-confidence. Learning should be linked to the learners' personal effort and ability. This is closely related to the idea of self-efficacy which is the belief to have the ability to achieve certain goals [73]. *Satisfaction* refers to the positive emotional experience by learners in learning activities. The learners' expectations are met and a sense of accomplishment is being produced [72,73]. Satisfaction can be acquired from internal reinforcement and external rewards, such as positive feedback [10,73].

These four categories need to be stimulated and maintained to keep the learner's motivation high and the lack of any one of them will lead to a learner's reduced motivation and decrease the overall teaching effect [36,37,73]. They also have several subcategories and provide specific recommendations on how to positively influence the motivation of learners [36,56]. For our study, the ARCS model was abbreviated to the categories of *Relevance* and *Satisfaction* for reasons of efficacy and adapted in wording. This is to ensure that our test persons conclude the test and do not abort the test because they feel it takes too much time to answer. The ARCS categories can be used and evaluated independently of each other [36,46]. However, the content of the items was not changed, as it is based on specific attributes of motivation [36].

The ARCS model offers two measurements, which were developed based on the theories of Keller [37]. The first one is the *Course Interest Survey* (CIS), which evaluates students' reactions to teacher-led instruction and is used in face-to-face teaching or sometimes in synchronous and asynchronous online courses [36,46,49]. The other is the *Instructional Materials Motivation Survey* (IMMS), which examines reactions to self-directed instructional materials. In our study, we use the IMMS because it is designed for self-directed learning, computer-based learning and online courses that are mainly self-directed.

Both measurements, the CIS and the IMMS, are situational measurement tools that measure the level of motivation of learners regarding a specific learning course or material. They do not capture the general level of motivation a learner might have, as these are not trait-related measurements [36]. The IMMS consists of 36 items (abbreviated to 15 items for reasons of efficacy, as mentioned before), which can each be assigned to a scale. A five-point Likert scale (1 = Strongly disagree; 5 = Strongly agree) was used. Among the items, one is reverse coded [36]. Although both measurements have already been used in numerous research works, there are no uniform standards for the values of the scales [46]. To put these in relation, comparative or replication studies must be consulted [36]. For example, the study by [29] determines the motivation-enhancing properties of game mechanics on learning platforms. This study shows significant differences from the control group for the satisfaction scale. However, no comparative values for the relevance scale are presented. Small and Gluck [65] confirmed the reliability as satisfactory, a rating initially given by Keller [37] based on Cronbach's alpha. Recent studies also confirm, alongside the results of Keller [36], the internal consistency and empirical validity of the IMMS [32].

### 3.3 User Experience Questionnaire

The perceived quality of gamification elements in e-learning was determined by the UEQ (Version 8) [60]. The UEQ allows for the quick and direct measurement of UX and has been designed, among other things, for use in online question-naires. To keep the dropout rate as low as possible and to enable quick, intuitive answering, a semantic differential is used as the item format. All 26 items consist of pairs of opposite adjectives that represent a specific aspect of the UX (a total of six scales) and were rated on a seven-point Likert scale (-3 = full agreement with the negative term; +3 = full agreement with the positive term). Half of the items represent positive terms, and the other half negative terms - each in a random order. No inter-dependency is assumed, but rather a general impression of the user is considered. This impression is formed by the attractiveness scale, which in turn should be influenced by the value of the remaining scales [61]. The reliability and validity of the UEQ scales have been examined in several usabil-ity tests and online surveys, resulting in sufficient reliability of the scales [61]. Additional studies have also shown good validity of the scales [43,44].

## 4 Results

### 4.1 Descriptive Statistics

As part of the survey people were asked how frequently they used e-learning platforms. From 204 people questioned 69 (33.82%) replied they had never made use of e-learning. These individuals were not further considered and were filtered out. More than a quarter (25.98%) of the respondents used e-learning platforms several times a week and 31 (15.20%) several times a month. About 30 people (14.71%) reported using e-learning offerings daily and 21 people (10.29%) rarely used e-learning platforms.

The 135 people who stated they are making use of e-learning platforms were asked which platforms they use. Multiple answers were allowed. The results are depicted in Fig. 1. The most used e-learning platform is MOODLE, with more than 100 mentions (74.81%). Fifteen people stated they use DUOLINGO (11.11%), and another 16 reported using UDEMY (11.85%). The least used learning offerings are ONCAMPUS (2.22%), SAP LITMOS (2.22%), and KHAN ACADEMY (1.48%).

The participants in our survey were then asked which gamification elements they are familiar with. The response to this question is visualised in Fig. 2. The

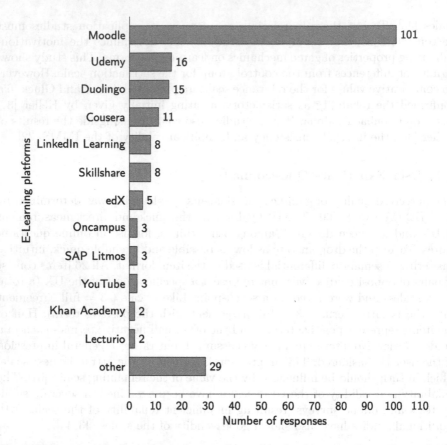

**Fig. 1.** E-learning platforms most frequently used amongst respondents. In total 135 people were considered. The numbers stated here are again absolute numbers. That is, from the 135 people taken into account, 101 used Moodle.

most known gamification element is the progress bar with 50 responses. This was followed by the status bar (39 repsondents) and points based gamification elemnts (34 responses). Achievements based gamification elemnts and challenges received 30 and 28 responses respectively. Goal oriented gamification elements received 26 responses, navigation elements 19, virtual goods 17 and creativity based gamification elements received 13 responses. Combination (Combo-Points) and avatar based gamification elements received 8 responses each. Only two people were familiar with other gamification elements.

### 4.2   Results on RQ 1

The first research question focuses on how gamification elements are perceived as having a positive influence on motivation. As already stated, only the categories *relevance* and *satisfaction* from the standardised questionnaire (ARCS model)

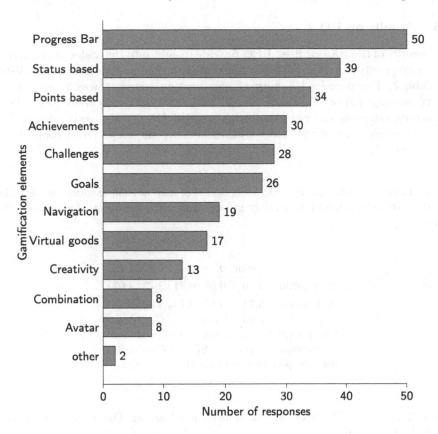

**Fig. 2.** Gamification elements participants were most familiar with. The numbers displayed here are absolute numbers. In total, 58 participants out of the 135 people who used e-learning were familiar with gamification elements. From these 50 participants (18%) named the *progress bar* as an element they are familiar with.

were examined. The results are summarised in Table 1. The mean value for satisfaction is 3.90 and for relevance, it is 3.75. That is, for both scales the perceived motivation-enhancing effect was rated slightly above average (3.0). Therefore, it can be concluded that the use of gamification elements in e-learning offerings is experienced by the respondents as motivation-increasing. The internal consistency of the scales is also computed and displayed as Cronbach's alpha value with $\alpha \geq 0.9$ referred to as excellent, $0.9 > \alpha \geq 0.8$ as good, $0.8 > \alpha \geq 0.7$ as acceptable, $0.7 > \alpha \geq 0.6$ as questionable, $0.6 > \alpha \geq 0.5$ referred to as poor and $0.5 > \alpha$ labeled as unacceptable. Table 1 displays a Cronbach's $\alpha$ of 0.81 (good) for satisfaction, and 0.74 for relevance (acceptable), confirming the internal consistency.

## 4.3   Results on RQ 2

The results of the standardized UEQ provide insight into the scales of attractiveness, perspicuity, efficiency, dependability, stimulation, and novelty and are listed in Table 2. The perceived quality of gamification elements was rated slightly above average (0)for all scales, except for novelty. Gamification elements in e-learning offerings are perceived with a good UX by the respondents. The internal consistency of the scales as indicated by the respective Cronbach's $\alpha$ is unacceptable.

**Table 1.** Perceived motivation enhancing design of gamification elements in e-learning based on the ARCS model. Our study presented here focuses on satisfaction and relevance.

|  | Mean | $\sigma$ | $\alpha$ | 95% CI | |
|---|---|---|---|---|---|
|  |  |  |  | LB | UP |
| Satisfaction | 3.90 | 0.65 | 0.81 | 3.73 | 4.07 |
| Relevance | 3.75 | 0.57 | 0.74 | 3.60 | 3.91 |

Mean: Arithmetic Mean CI: Confidence Interval LB & UB: Lower & Upper Bound $\sigma$: Standard Deviation (SD) $\alpha$: Cronbach's $\alpha$ (tau-equivalent reliability)

**Table 2.** Perceived UX of gamification elements in e-learning. The tests were conducted using the UEQ model.

|  | Mean | $\sigma$ | $\alpha$ | 95% CI | |
|---|---|---|---|---|---|
|  |  |  |  | LB | UP |
| Attractiveness | 1.463 | 0.989 | 0.255 | 1.208 | 1.717 |
| Perspicuity | 1.353 | 0.931 | 0.240 | 1.114 | 1.593 |
| Efficiency | 0.996 | 0.741 | 0.191 | 0.805 | 1.186 |
| Dependability | 1.091 | 0.775 | 0.199 | 0.891 | 1.290 |
| Stimulation | 1.384 | 0.876 | 0.226 | 1.158 | 1.609 |
| Novelty | 0.872 | 0.956 | 0.246 | 0.626 | 1.118 |

Mean: arithmetic mean CI: Confidence Interval LB & UB: Lower & Upper Bound $\sigma$: Standard Deviation (SD) $\alpha$: Cronbach's $\alpha$ (tau-equivalent reliability)

## 4.4   Case Study: MOODLE vs. DUOLINGO

In **RQ1** we ask if gamification elements on e-learning platforms are experienced as motivating in a general sense. **RQ2** asks, also in a general sense, which UX of gamification elements in e-learning is perceived. Here, we delve deeper into these two questions by comparing two specific platforms in regards to these two questions. MOODLE and DUOLINGO were chosen since they were among the most frequently used e-learning platforms among our respondents. Two groups are compared: 29 people for MOODLE and 13 people for DUOLINGO. We first present the result of our comparison between these two platforms and their gamification elements regarding the perceived effect on motivation and then on the perceived UX.

**Motivation.** The result for the test on how much the gamification elements contribute to a motivating learning experience according to the ARCS model can be seen in Table 3. For the scale of satisfaction MOODLE shows a mean of 3.75 whereas DUOLINGO displays a mean of 4.44. For relevance, the mean is 3.59 for MOODLE and 4.02 for DUOLINGO. Cronbach's $\alpha$ value for the scale of satisfaction is questionable (0.60) and acceptable (0.75) respectively for MOODLE and DUOLINGO. For the scale of relevance Cronbach's $\alpha$ is acceptable (0.72) and unacceptable (0.29) respectively.

**Table 3.** ARCS: MOODLE vs. DUOLINGO. Differences in the perception of motivation-enhancing gamification elements in MOODLE and DUOLINGO. Only relevance and satisfaction were tested from the ARCS model.

| | Mean | | $\sigma$ | | $\alpha$ | | 95% CI | | | |
| | | | | | | | LB | | UP | |
| | Mo | Du | Mo | Du | Mo | Du | Mo | Du | Mo | Du |
|---|---|---|---|---|---|---|---|---|---|---|
| Satisfaction | 3.75 | 4.44 | 0.61 | 0.43 | 0.60 | 0.75 | 3.52 | 4.17 | 3.98 | 4.70 |
| Relevance | 3.59 | 4.02 | 0.58 | 0.36 | 0.72 | 0.29 | 3.37 | 3.80 | 3.81 | 4.23 |

Mean: arithmetic meanCI: Confidence Interval $\sigma$: Standard Deviation (SD)
LB & UB: Lower & Upper Bound $\alpha$: Cronbach's $\alpha$ (tau-equivalent reliability)
n for MOODLE = 29 and n for DUOLINGO = 13

To determine whether there is a significant difference in the perceived motivation-enhancing design of gamification elements on these platforms, a *Mann-Whitney U test*, also referred to as *Wilcoxon-Mann-Whitney-Test*, was conducted. This test was chosen due to the two groups not underlying a normal distribution and their variance being in-homogeneous. The result of this test can be seen in Table 4. For the scale of satisfaction the p-value is 0.02, and for the scale of relevance the p-value is 0.0006946. This means, a statistically significant difference in the scales of relevance and satisfaction between these two e-learning platforms was observed ($p < 0.05$). This result also suggests that the game mechanics used in DUOLINGO are seen to contribute more to a motivating learning environment than those in MOODLE.

**User Experience.** In addition to comparing the gamification elements in MOODLE and DUOLINGO regarding their perceived effect on motivation, we also compared them regarding their UX. The result of the investigation of the two platforms gives us insights into the perceived quality of gamification elements for attractiveness, perspicuity, efficiency, dependability, stimulation, and novelty. The results are summarised in Table 5. It shows the mean values for the six categories of the UEQ for MOODLE and DUOLINGO. In all categories DUOLINGO has a higher mean, except for novelty, where it is 0.91 for MOODLE and 0.87 DUOLINGO. For attractiveness the mean is 1.38 (MOODLE) versus 1.87 (DUOLINGO), for perspicuity it is 1.22 versus 1.87, for efficiency it is 0.90 versus 1.06, for dependability it is 1.01 versus 1.23 and for stimulation it is 1.31 versus 1.67. Cronbach's $\alpha$ values for these categories for MOODLE are all between 0.24 and 0.34, i.e. *unacceptable* with regards to internal consistency. The same is true for DULINGO. Here, Cronbach's $\alpha$ value lies between 0.27 and 0.51. The 0.51 are for novelty which is *poor*.

**Table 4.** ARCS: *Mann-Whitney U test*. Results for the *Mann-Whitney U test* that was conducted in our comparison of MOODLE and DUOLINGO with regards to the motivational effect of gamification elements.

|  | W | p | Diff. in location |
|---|---|---|---|
| Satisfaction | 64.50 | 0.02* | −0.33 |
| Relevance | 101.50 | 0.0006976* | −0.67 |

Difference in location = Median of the difference
p denotes the p-value and W denotes the W-Value
n for MOODLE = 29 and n for DUOLINGO = 13  *$p <$ 0.05

**Table 5.** UX: MOODLE vs DUOLINGO. Differences in the UX of motivation-enhancing gamification elements between MOODLE and DUOLINGO according to the UEQ.

|  | Mean | | $\sigma$ | | $\alpha$ | | 95% CI | | | |
|---|---|---|---|---|---|---|---|---|---|---|
|  |  |  |  |  |  |  | LB | | UP | |
|  | Mo | Du | Mo | Du | Mo | Du | Mo | Du | Mo | Du |
| Attractiveness | 1.38 | 1.87 | 0.94 | 0.57 | 0.34 | 0.31 | 1.04 | 1.56 | 1.72 | 2.38 |
| Perspicuity | 1.22 | 1.87 | 0.90 | 0.57 | 0.33 | 0.31 | 0.89 | 1.55 | 1.54 | 2.18 |
| Efficiency | 0.90 | 1.06 | 0.65 | 0.60 | 0.24 | 0.32 | 0.66 | 0.73 | 1.13 | 1.38 |
| Dependability | 1.01 | 1.23 | 0.76 | 0.64 | 0.28 | 0.35 | 0.73 | 0.88 | 1.29 | 1.58 |
| Stimulation | 1.31 | 1.67 | 0.83 | 0.50 | 0.30 | 0.27 | 1.01 | 1.40 | 1.61 | 1.95 |
| Novelty | 0.91 | 0.87 | 0.92 | 0.93 | 0.33 | 0.51 | 0.58 | 0.37 | 1.25 | 1.38 |

Mean: arithmetic mean CI: Confidence Interval $\sigma$: Standard Deviation (SD)
LB & UB: Lower & Upper Bound $\alpha$: Cronbach's $\alpha$ (tau-equivalent reliability)
n for MOODLE = 29 and n for DUOLINGO = 13

To investigate if any of these differences in the perception of the UX of the gamification elements between these two platforms is statistically significant, again a *Mann-Whitney-U-Test* was conducted. The result of this test is summarized in Table 6. The p-values for the six categories of the UEQ are 0.10 (attractiveness), 0.02 (perspicuity), 0.41 (efficiency), 0.44 (dependability), 0.13 (stimulation) and 0.69 (novelty). Thus, a statistically significant difference in the perspicuity scale ($p < 0.05$) was observed. For the remaining values, no significant difference ($p \geq 0.05$) was identified. The perceived quality of gamification elements was rated slightly above average for both platforms.

We added in our survey a final question which asked our test persons to state whether they noticed any effect from the gamification elements. Around fifty (81.03%) of the respondents stated they could notice an effect. Only ten (18.97%) people replied that they could not detect any effect at all. The people who stated that they could notice an effect described it in positive terms. One test person liked the league system: *"Especially a league system has so far motivated me greatly to use the offering regularly"*. Another stated, referring to gamification: *"I find it helpful, it makes learning fun"*. In general, it can be said that people identified mainly the positive effects of gamification elements in e-learning.

**Table 6.** UEQ: *Mann-Whitney U-test.* Results of the *Mann-Whitney U test* of the comparison between MOODLE and DUOLINGO with regards to the user experience of gamification elements.

|  | W | p | Diff. in location |
|---|---|---|---|
| Attractiveness | 129.00 | 0.10 | −0.33 |
| Perspicuity | 101.00 | 0.02* | −0.50 |
| Efficiency | 158.50 | 0.41 | −0.25 |
| Dependability | 160.00 | 0.44 | −0.25 |
| Stimulation | 133.00 | 0.13 | −0.25 |
| Novelty | 203.00 | 0.69 | $-3.155462e^{-0.5}$ |

Difference in location = Median of the difference
p denotes the p-value and W denotes the W-Value
n for MOODLE = 29 and n for DUOLINGO IS 13
*$p < 0.05$

## 5   Discussion

The survey results show that the implementation of game mechanics in e-learning is rated with a good user experience by our participants and seen as motivation-enhancing. A majority of the respondents reported observing positive effects regarding learning duration, learning success, and the regularity of learning, partly due to a pleasant design or increased competitive behaviour through the deployed game mechanics. DUOLINGO was rated higher on average in terms of motivation enhancement and UX than MOODLE. The internal consistency of our survey is very low due to our small sample size. Our survey is therefore not representative. Nonetheless, it appears to confirm findings by others [58] of the positive effects that gamification elements on e-learning platforms have on the UX and motivation of learners. It can be concluded that the use of gamification elements can be a useful method to positively influence the motivation or UX of learning materials. Some opinions by test person differed though. The motivation enhancement was also seen as a negative pressure and stress factor depending on the gamification element. Regarding user experience, it was found that this is perceived differently across age groups and thus varies. Moreover, not only the choice but also the number of used elements is a factor that can influence the UX.

To interpret the results of the ARCS model, it must first be noted that the values of the scales are not related, as there are no norms for the ARCS model yet. In our work, only two of the four scales were used for capturing the motivation-enhancing design of gamification elements. This slightly limits the interpretation of the ARCS model results. Nonetheless, we can state that the perceived motivation-enhancing design of the gamification elements was rated as relevant and satisfactory. The study mentioned by Hamzah et al. [29] confirms this statement. The ratings suggest that game mechanics can partly positively influence the degree of motivation enhancement. The UEQ Handbook provides a benchmark dataset that facilitates the interpretation of the results and relates them to other different products, such as corporate software, websites, webshops, and social networks. This dataset consists of data from around 21000 people from nearly 470 studies. This allows for conclusions on the relative quality of the gamification elements in e-learning offerings compared to other products; see Table 7. Compared to other products, the stimulation scale of gamification in e-learning offers is rated as good, thus forming an important basis for efficient learning. Attractiveness, perspicuity, and novelty achieve a better value than the average of the benchmark dataset. Only efficiency and dependability are rated just a little below average compared to other products. A hint as to why the rating of the scales might be worse is provided by the answers to the open questions. An excess of deployed game mechanics has a disturbing effect on the UX. This suggests that the perceived flexibility of the offerings decreases, thus leading to a more negative rating of the efficiency and dependability scales. Users find the game elements appealing, understandable, and creative. The use is rated as particularly fun and more motivating, although aspects like speed and handling can limit the UX.

The comparison of the two most used e-learning offerings in our survey, identified significant differences regarding all aspects of the perceived motivation-enhancing design. For the perceived quality, such significant differences were only found for the perspicuity scale. To understand how these deviations can be explained, the backgrounds of the learning platforms should be understood. DUOLINGO is a gamified, user-centred educational offering. Its content is

**Table 7.** UEQ value comparison to benchmark. This shows the UX comparison with a benchmark dataset from the UEQ Handbook.

| Scale | Comparison to benchmark | Interpretation |
|---|---|---|
| Attractiveness | above average | 25% of results better, 50% of results worse |
| Perspicuity | above average | 25% of results better, 50% of results worse |
| Efficiency | below average | 50% of results better, 25% of results worse |
| Dependability | below average | 50% of results better, 25% of results worse |
| Stimulation | good | 10% of results better, 75% of results worse |
| Novelty | above average | 25% of results better, 50% of results worse |

n = 58

regularly maintained and evaluated. Whereas, MOODLE depends heavily on the users. They determine how the platform's possibilities are utilised and implemented. Thus, a difference regarding motivational enhancement and UX is understandable and reasonable.

There are some limitations in our study. Our sample is of limited size and representativeness. The test on motivation is not standardised. The response to the survey relates to past experiences and memories of the respondents, which in turn may have been influenced or falsified. The results of our study therefore do not have universal validity and should be seen with caution. Nonetheless, they indicate that gamification elements should be applied in a controlled manner to contribute positively towards the motivation and UX for learners.

## 6    Conclusion

This paper examined the perceived motivational character and quality of gamification elements on e-learning platforms available in Germany. The underlying data for the analysis was collected via an online survey, which consisted of two questionnaires: selected scales from ARCS-Model and the standardised UEQ. In total, 240 people participated in the survey. In response to **RQ1** we conclude that gamification elements on e-learning platforms are indeed perceived by learners as having a positive impact on motivation. Regarding **RQ2** our results suggest that a controlled use of such elements does enhance the UX positively. However, gamification elements should not be seen as a panacea for the challenges that learners face in e-learning. Instead, gamification should be used in a targeted and controlled manner. They should be easy to understand. These elements should enhance the learning experience by adding them within reason on a platform and implementing them in a user centred manner. Only then do they contribute to a positive UX.

**Acknowledgements.** Part of this work was funded by the German Federal Ministry of Education and Research (BMBF) grant number 21INVI2302 within the project NetÖV.

**Disclosure of Interests.** The authors have no competing interests to declare that are relevant to the content of this article.

# References

1. Afjar, A., Syukri, M., et al.: Attention, relevance, confidence, satisfaction (ARCS) model on students' motivation and learning outcomes in learning physics. J. Phys.: Conf. Ser. 012119 (2020). IOP Publishing
2. AL-Smadi, M.: Gameducation: using gamification techniques to engage learners in online learning. In: Immersive Education: 4th European Summit, EiED 2014, Vienna, 24–26 November 2014, Revised Selected Papers 4, pp. 85–97 (2015)
3. Algahtani, A., et al.: Evaluating the effectiveness of the e-learning experience in some universities in Saudi Arabia from male students' perceptions. Ph.D. thesis, Durham University (2011)
4. Attali, Y., Arieli-Attali, M.: Gamification in assessment: do points affect test performance? Comput. Educ. **83**, 57–63 (2015)
5. Ausburn, L.J.: Course design elements most valued by adult learners in blended online education environments: an American perspective. Educ. Media Int. **41**(4), 327–337 (2004)
6. Bouchrika, I., Harrati, N., Wanick, V., Wills, G.: Exploring the impact of gamification on student engagement and involvement with e-learning systems. Interact. Learn. Environ. **29**(8), 1244–1257 (2021)
7. Brehmer, J., Becker, S.: e-learning ... ein neues qualitätsmerkmal der lehre. Georg-August-Universität Göttingen (2017)
8. Burlacu, M., Coman, C., Bularca, M.C.: Blogged into the system: a systematic review of the gamification in e-learning before and during the covid-19 pandemic. Sustainability **15**(8), 6476 (2023)
9. Caponetto, I., Earp, J., Ott, M.: Gamification and education: a literature review. In: European Conference on Games Based Learning, vol. 1, p. 50. Academic Conferences International Limited (2014)
10. Chang, Y.H., Song, A.C., Fang, R.J.: Integrating arcs model of motivation and PBL in flipped classroom: a case study on a programming language. Eurasia J. Math. Sci. Technol. Educ. **14**(12), em1631 (2018)
11. Cheah, I., Shimul, A.S., Phau, I.: Motivations of playing digital games: a review and research agenda. Psychol. Market. **39**(5), 937–950 (2022)
12. Christopoulos, A., Conrad, M., Shukla, M.: Increasing student engagement through virtual interactions: how? Virtual Reality **22**, 353–369 (2018)
13. Christopoulos, A., Mystakidis, S.: Gamification in education. Encyclopedia **3**(4), 1223–1243 (2023)
14. Cojocariu, V.M., Lazar, I., Lazar, G.: The ambivalence of strengths and weaknesses of e-learning educational services. BRAIN. Broad Res. Artif. Intell. Neurosci. **7**(3), 55–74 (2016)
15. Company, T.B.R.: Gamification global market report 2024 (2023). https://www.researchandmarkets.com/report/gamification
16. Czikszentmihalyi, M.: Flow: The Psychology of Optimal Experience. Harper & Row, New York (1990)
17. Dah, J., Hussin, N., Zaini, M.K., Isaac Helda, L., Senanu Ametefe, D., Adozuka Aliu, A.: Gamification is not working: Why? Games Culture (2024)

18. Dahalan, N., Hasan, H., Hassan, F., Zakaria, Z., Noor, W.: Engaging students online: does gender matter in adoption of learning material design. World J. Educ. Technol. **5**(3), 413–419 (2013)
19. Deterding, S., Sicart, M., Nacke, L., O'Hara, K., Dixon, D.: Gamification: using game-design elements in non-gaming contexts. In: CHI 2011 extended abstracts on human factors in computing systems, pp. 2425–2428. Association for Computing Machiner (2011)
20. Durrani, U.K., Kamal, M.M.: Application of arcs model for a blended teaching methodologies: a study of students' motivation amid the covid-19. EAI Endorsed Trans. e-Learn. **7**(21), e2–e2 (2021)
21. Elfaki, N.K., Abdulraheem, I., Abdulrahim, R., et al.: Impact of e-learning vs traditional learning on student's performance and attitude. Int. Med. J. **24**(03), 225–33 (2019)
22. Fitz-Walter, Z., Johnson, D., Wyeth, P., Tjondronegoro, D., Scott-Parker, B.: Driven to drive? investigating the effect of gamification on learner driver behavior, perceived motivation and user experience. Comput. Hum. Behav. **71**, 586–595 (2017)
23. Frank Siepmann, M.F.: Teilstudie elearning-anbieter: Dach vs. international. In: eLearning BENCHMARKING Studie Gesamtstudie: eLearning & Weiterbildung, pp. 66–77 (2018)
24. Jarnac de Freitas, M., Mira da Silva, M.: Systematic literature review about gamification in moocs. Open Learn. J. Open Dist. e-Learn. **38**(1), 73–95 (2023)
25. Fülöp, M.T., Breaz, T.O., Topor, I.D., Ionescu, C.A., Dragolea, L.L.: Challenges and perceptions of e-learning for educational sustainability in the "new normality era." Front. Psychol. **14**, 1104633 (2023)
26. Hadi Mogavi, R., Guo, B., Zhang, Y., Haq, E.U., Hui, P., Ma, X.: When gamification spoils your learning: a qualitative case study of gamification misuse in a language-learning app. In: Proceedings of the Ninth ACM Conference on Learning@ Scale, pp. 175–188 (2022)
27. Haffar, M., et al.: Organizational culture and affective commitment to e-learning' changes during covid-19 pandemic: the underlying effects of readiness for change. J. Bus. Res. **155**, 113396 (2023)
28. Hamayon, R.: Why We Play: An Anthropological Study. Hau Books (2016)
29. Hamzah, W.M.A.F.W., Ali, N.H., Saman, M.Y.M., Yusoff, M.H., Yacob, A.: Influence of gamification on students' motivation in using e-learning applications based on the motivational design model. Int. J. Emerg. Technol. Learn. **10**(2), 30–34 (2015)
30. Handayani, V., Budiono, F.L., Rosyada, D., Amriza, R.N.S., Masruroh, S.U., et al.: Gamified learning platform analysis for designing a gamification-based UI/UX of e-learning applications: a systematic literature review. In: 2020 8th International Conference on Cyber and IT Service Management (CITSM), pp. 1–5. IEEE (2020)
31. Hsu, C.L., Chen, M.C.: How does gamification improve user experience? an empirical investigation on the antecedences and consequences of user experience and its mediating role. Technol. Forecast. Soc. Chang. **132**, 118–129 (2018)
32. Hu, Y.: Motivation, usability and their interrelationships in a self-paced online learning environment. Ph.D. thesis, Virginia Tech (2008)
33. Insights, G.M.: E-learning market size - by technology (online e-learning, LMS, mobile e-learning, rapid e-learning, virtual classroom, others), provider (service, content), application (corporate, academic, government) & forecast, 2023–2032 (2023). https://www.gminsights.com/industry-analysis/elearning-market-size

34. Islam, N., Beer, M., Slack, F.: E-learning challenges faced by academics in higher education. J. Educ. Train. Stud. **3**(5), 102–112 (2015)
35. Kapp, K.M.: The Gamification of Learning and Instruction: Game-Based Methods and Strategies for Training and Education. Wiley (2012)
36. Keller, J.M.: Motivational Design for Learning and Performance: The ARCS Model Approach. Springer, Boston (2010). https://doi.org/10.1007/978-1-4419-1250-3
37. Keller, J.M.: Development and use of the arcs model of instructional design. J. Instr. Dev. **10**(3), 2–10 (1987)
38. Kerres, M.: Mediendidaktik: Konzeption und Entwicklung mediengestützter Lernangebote. Oldenbourg Wissenschaftsverlag (2012)
39. Khaldi, A., Bouzidi, R., Nader, F.: Gamification of e-learning in higher education: a systematic literature review. Smart Learn. Environ. **10**(1), 10 (2023)
40. Kibuku, R.N., Ochieng, D.O., Wausi, A.N.: e-Learning challenges faced by universities in kenya: a literature review. Electron. J. e-Learn. **18**(2), 150–161 (2020)
41. Koppitsch, S.E., Meyer, J.: Do points matter? the effects of gamification activities with and without points on student learning and engagement. Mark. Educ. Rev. **32**(1), 45–53 (2022)
42. Krüger, D., Parchmann, I., Schecker, H.: Methoden in der naturwissenschaftsdidaktischen Forschung. Springer (2014)
43. Laugwitz, B., Schrepp, M., Held, T.: Konstruktion eines fragebogens zur messung der user experience von softwareprodukten. In: Heinecke, A.M., Paul, H. (eds.) Mensch & Computer 2006-mensch und computer im strukturwandel. Oldenbourg Verlag, vol. 125, p. 134 (2006)
44. Laugwitz, B., Held, T., Schrepp, M.: Construction and evaluation of a user experience questionnaire. In: Proceedings of the HCI and Usability for Education and Work: 4th Symposium of the Workgroup Human-Computer Interaction and Usability Engineering of the Austrian Computer Society (USAB 2008), Graz, 20–21 November 2008, vol. 4, pp. 63–76. Springer (2008)
45. Le, S., Weber, P.: Game-based learning-spielend lernen? Lehrbuch für Lernen und Lehren mit Technologien (2011)
46. Loorbach, N., Peters, O., Karreman, J., Steehouder, M.: Validation of the instructional materials motivation survey (IMMS) in a self-directed instructional setting aimed at working with technology. Br. J. Edu. Technol. **46**(1), 204–218 (2015)
47. Maatuk, A.M., Elberkawi, E.K., Aljawarneh, S., Rashaideh, H., Alharbi, H.: The covid-19 pandemic and e-learning: challenges and opportunities from the perspective of students and instructors. J. Comput. High. Educ. **34**(1), 21–38 (2022)
48. Markets, M.: Gamification Market by Component (Solution and Services), Deployment (Cloud and On-premises), Organization Size (SMES and Large Enterprises), Application, End-User (Enterprise Driven and Consumer Driven), Vertical, and Region-Global Forecast to 2025 (2020). https://www.marketsandmarkets.com/Market-Reports/gamification-market-991.html
49. Molaee, Z., Dortaj, F.: Improving l2 learning: an arcs instructional-motivational approach. Procedia Soc. Behav. Sci. **171**, 1214–1222 (2015)
50. Mustafa, A.S., Karimi, K.: Enhancing gamified online learning user experience (UX): a systematic literature review of recent trends. In: Human-Computer Interaction and Beyond-Part I, pp. 74–99 (2021)
51. Nedeljković, I., Rejman Petrović, D.: Student satisfaction and intention to use e-learning during the covid-19 pandemic. Int. J. Inf. Learn. Technol. **40**(3), 225–241 (2023)
52. Nilubol, K., Sitthitikul, P.: Gamification: trends and opportunities in language teaching and learning practices. PASAA J. (2023)

53. Ning, B.: A UX-driven design method for building gamification system. In: Proceedings of the Design, User Experience, and Usability: Theory and Practice: 7th International Conference (DUXU 2018), Held as Part of HCI International 2018, Las Vegas, 15–20 July 2018, Part I 7, pp. 112–124. Springer (2018)
54. Petkov, P., Medland, R., Köbler, F., Krcmar, H., Foth, M.: Engaging energy saving through motivation-specific social comparison. In: Proceedings of the Conference on Human Factors in Computing Systems, pp. 1945–1950 (2011). https://doi.org/10.1145/1979742.1979855, cited by 41
55. Rana, H., Lal, M.: E-learning: issues and challenges. Int. J. Comput. Appl. **97**(5) (2014)
56. Reigeluth, C.M.: Instructional Design Theories and Models: An Overview of their Current Status. Routledge (1983)
57. Research, P.M.: E-learning market share, size, trends, industry analysis report, by provider (content provider, service provider), by deployment model (on-premise, cloud), by course, by end-user (academic, corporate, government); by region; segment forecast, 2022–2030 (2022). https://www.polarismarketresearch.com/industry-analysis/e-learning-market
58. Saleem, A.N., Noori, N.M., Ozdamli, F.: Gamification applications in e-learning: a literature review. Technol. Knowl. Learn. **27**(1), 139–159 (2022)
59. Scholl, A.: Die befragung, vol. 2413. Utb (2014)
60. Schrepp, M.: User Experience Questionnaire Handbook (version 8.0) (2015). https://www.ueq-online.org/
61. Schrepp, M., Thomaschewski, J., Hinderks, A.: Construction of a benchmark for the user experience questionnaire (UEQ). Int. J. Interact. Multim. Artif. Intell. (2017)
62. Serice, L.: Prisms of neuroscience: frameworks for thinking about educational gamification. AI Comput. Sci. Robot. Technol. (2023)
63. Shafiei Sarvestani, M., Mohammadi, M., Afshin, J., Raeisy, L.: Students' experiences of e-learning challenges; a phenomenological study. Interdiscip. J. Virt. Learn. Med. Sci. **10**(3), 1–10 (2019)
64. Sharma, W., Lim, W.M., Kumar, S., Verma, A., Kumra, R.: Game on! a state-of-the-art overview of doing business with gamification. Technol. Forecast. Soc. Chang. **198**, 122988 (2024)
65. Small, R.V., Gluck, M.: The relationship of motivational conditions to effective instructional attributes: a magnitude scaling approach. Educ. Technol. 33–40 (1994)
66. Smiderle, R., Rigo, S.J., Marques, L.B., Peçanha de Miranda Coelho, J.A., Jaques, P.A.: The impact of gamification on students' learning, engagement and behavior based on their personality traits. Smart Learn. Environ. **7**(1), 1–11 (2020)
67. Sofi-Karim, M., Bali, A.O., Rached, K.: Online education via media platforms and applications as an innovative teaching method. Educ. Inf. Technol. **28**(1), 507–523 (2023)
68. Statista. Size of the Global e-Learning Market in 2019 and 2026, by Segment (2022). https://www.statista.com/statistics/1130331/e-learning-market-size-segment-worldwide/#statisticContainer
69. Swan, K., Day, S.L., Bogle, L.R., Matthews, D.B.: A collaborative, design-based approach to improving an online program. Internet High. Educ. **21**, 74–81 (2014)
70. Titthasiri, W.: A comparison of e-learning and traditional learning: experimental approach. In: International Conference on Mobile Learning, E-Society and E-Learning Technology (ICMLEET)–Singapore on November, pp. 6–7 (2013)

71. Wahyuningsih, T., Sediyono, E., Hartomo, K.D., Sembiring, I.: The role of gamification implementation in improving quality and intention in software engineering learning. J. Educ. Learn. (EduLearn) **18**(1), 173–184 (2024)
72. Xia, Y.: Research on human resource development and training design based on arcs model. J. Phys.: Conf. Ser. 022061 (2020). IOP Publishing
73. Yang, Y., Ouyang, T., Zhang, L., Wang, J.: Study on blended teaching mode and its application based on the arcs motivational model: taking bioinformatics course as an example. Medicine **101**(40) (2022)
74. Zichermann, G., Cunningham, C.: Gamification by design: implementing game mechanics in web and mobile apps. O'Reilly Media, Inc. (2011)

# Contextualizing Plans: Aligning Students Goals and Plans During Game-Based Inquiry Science Learning

Megan Wiedbusch[1]($\boxtimes$) , Daryn Dever[1] , Alex Goslen[2] , Dan Carpenter[2] , Cameron Marano[1] , Kevin Smith[1] , and Roger Azevedo[2]

[1] University of Central Florida, Orlando, FL 32832, USA
megan.wiedbusch@ucf.edu
[2] North Carolina State University, Raleigh, NC 27606, USA

**Abstract.** A key aim for science education is the improvement of scientific reasoning through inquiry-based learning which asks students to "think and act like scientists". This requires the regulation of specific skills and abilities such as identifying problems, generating hypotheses and evidence, and drawing conclusions. Goal setting and planning can help learners regulate their learning as they engage with scientific inquiry, especially within investigative exploration. Contemporary work on scaffolds for science inquiry-learning requires we (1) understand how students set goals and plans, (2) measure the quality of goals and plans, and (3) develop adaptive intelligent goal and planning scaffolds. This paper presents the development of a new planning scaffold used by 101 middle school students during interactions with CRYSTAL ISLAND, a game-based learning environment designed to teach students about microbiology and through scientific inquiry. We map student goals and plans from the scaffold to a series of epistemic scientific reasoning activities to use in conjunction with online trace data of student behaviors to analyze student goal setting and planning constructed throughout the game. This study describes the development of an analytical mapping approach between (sub)goals and (sub)activities to measure student plan quality build using a planning scaffold. We report on the use of the scaffold as well as implications for future development of an adaptive and intelligent version of the tool. This work highlights that online-trace data should be contextualized to (sub)goals, and the design of intelligent and adaptive goal and planning tools should be dynamic to account for open-ended exploration that differs across learners.

**Keywords:** Game-based learning · Goal Setting · Planning

## 1 Introduction

STEM education has placed a strong emphasis on the practical use of STEM behaviors, attitudes, and standards in addition to declarative and conceptual knowledge [1]. This can take on the form of developing and fostering scientific reasoning skills (e.g., evaluating evidence, generating hypothesis, etc.) during self-regulated learning within real

P. Zaphiris and A. Ioannou (Eds.): HCII 2024, LNCS 14723, pp. 113–128, 2024.
https://doi.org/10.1007/978-3-031-61685-3_9

and simulated environments (e.g., game-based learning enviornments [GBLEs]). These environments help move the context of science learning from lecture-based abstractions to active learning pedagogies in which learners are active participants rather than passive consumers of knowledge (e.g., inquiry-based learning [2–4]). However, these approaches are not always successful as learners may struggle to self-regulate their learning during scientific reasoning resulting in suboptimal performance [5]. Numerous scaffolding tools have been embedded within these learning environments to further support learners' SRL processes to varying degrees of success [6]. Most of these scaffolds have focused on supporting learners' strategy use learning, neglecting the role of goal setting and planning [6]. As such, we have examined the deployment of a new planning and scaffolding tool to better inform the learning environments' recording and measurement of learner plan quality.

## 2   Scientific Reasoning During Self-regulated Learning

The application, practice, and development of scientific inquiry skills (e.g., identifying the problem, collecting evidence, generating hypotheses, making inferences, drawing conclusions) are fundamental to learning the nature of science and science content by allowing students to "think and act like scientists" [7–9]. This requires students use self-regulated learning (SRL), to engage in the formulation of (sub)goals, develop plans to meet those (sub)goals, and monitor and adapt their (meta)cognition based on their progress towards achieving (sub)goals [10, 11]. However, many students lack the necessary SRL skills to do so effectively [12, 13]. Contemporary work in SRL requires we: (1) understand how students set goals and plans, (2) measure the quality of goals and plans, (3) utilize trace data to capture the dynamics of plan enactment via SRL behaviors, and (4) develop adaptive intelligent goal and planning scaffolds. These requirements are non-trivial as SRL is a temporally dynamic, contextual, and conditional process [14].

### 2.1   Scientific Reasoning

Scientific reasoning and the skills commonly associated with it (e.g., making hypotheses, drawing conclusions) are often conceptualized within cycles of scientific inquiry. That is, the cycle one might go through to problem solve or develop new conceptual knowledge based on empirical testing. There have been several frameworks that model scientific reasoning and inquiry including Scientific Discovery as Dual Space (SDSS; [15]), OPIRR (Orientation, Preparation, Implementation, Reporting, and Reflection) model [16], and Fisher et al.'s [17] epistemic activities of scientific reasoning. These conceptualizations' descriptions refer to skill sets, linked domain-specific and domain-general knowledge, and a cycle of stages that one goes through to generate and modify their knowledge production during complex learning [16]. Considering the complexity of many of these scientific reasoning tasks and activities, research has repeatedly shown that students struggle with efficiently and accurately engaging in scientific reasoning [18, 19]. As such, this study aims to assess a scaffolding tool that assists learners in setting goals and plans for enacting scientific reasoning tasks and activities.

For our study, we focus primarily on Fisher's framework of scientific reasoning activities [17] but draw inspiration from the other models as well (such as the cyclic nature of the OPIRR [16] model or the non-linearity of the SDSS [15] model). According to this framework, there are 8 epistemic activities that one might engage in during scientific reasoning. These are defined below in Table 1.

**Table 1.** Fisher et al.'s Epistemic Activities for Scientific Reasoning [17]

| Epistemic Activity | Definition |
|---|---|
| Problem Identification | A problem representation is constructed by the learner based on a study of a scenario in which a perceived discrepancy or weakness exists with respect to the explanation that is currently provided for a given problem |
| Questioning | Based on the problem representation developed during problem identification, the learner identifies question(s) that may be refined later |
| Hypothesis Generation | The learner derives possible answers to the questions from models, available theoretical frameworks, or empirical evidence they are aware of. If prior knowledge is not enough to allow for prediction, the question may be refined in questioning or there may be an exploratory approach of evidence generation |
| Construction & Redesign of Artefacts | The learner constructs and artefact (e.g., a prototype or axiomatic system) typically based on current theoretical models to be tested in an authentic environment |
| Evidence Generation | The learner collects evidence in various approaches including (1) conducting hypothetico-deductive experimental studies; (2) Induction using observations; (3) General Observations; (4) Deductive Reasoning; (5) Compiling fields of research. What counts as evidence differs among domains |
| Evidence Evaluation | The learner assesses the degree to which evidence that has been generated supports a hypothesis/claim/theory |
| Drawing Conclusions | The learner uses different pieces of evaluated evidence to either support or disprove a hypothesis. This can differ among domain and may refer to the compiling of multiple pieces of evidence for integration |
| Communicating & Scrutinizing | The learner interacts with others to share their findings and converse about the practice, methodology, results, conclusion, and implications |

## 2.2 Self-regulated Learning

For successful scientific reasoning to occur, students need to be effective self-regulators in which students can monitor their progress towards learning outcomes and change how they enact scientific reasoning processes to successfully achieve those outcomes [8, 20, 21]. Self-regulated learning (SRL) involves learners monitoring and changing their cognitive, affective, metacognitive, motivational, and social processes throughout learning [10]. However, scientific reasoning is a notoriously difficult process for students to engage in as they are required to continuously engage in information gathering, hypothesis generation, hypothesis testing, and hypothesis adaptation while increasing their scientific knowledge and modifying mental models of complex scientific topics (e.g., microbiology; [15, 18, 19]). Students' ability to engage in successful scientific reasoning is further hindered by students' inability to self-regulate either due to their inability to efficiently and effectively deploy SRL processes (e.g., planning, goal-setting) in addition to their lack of knowledge about SRL processes and strategies [5, 8, 22, 23]. Because of the compounding difficulties in engaging in both effective SRL and scientific reasoning processes, it is essential that students are externally supported by tools or scaffolds within the learning environment in which learning is taking place.

## 2.3 Goals and Plans

Models of SRL highlight the role of goal setting and planning, often occurring before any learning or interaction with instructional materials with the learning environment [11, 24, 25]. Goals and subgoals provide the context by which we can evaluate one's learning against [11]. Setting goals requires learners to consider what they are being asked to do or learn, and may provide an indirect assessment of task understanding [26]. Plans are the actions by which a learner anticipates they need to take in order to accomplish their set goals [11].

**Capturing Goal Setting and Planning.** Goals and plans can be identified either directly (e.g., self-reported from the learner either in a tool or through discourse) or indirectly (e.g., interpreted from behaviors while learning). For example, Goslen and colleagues [27] used logfiles from learners playing a game to identify plans that were compared against their self-reported plans as validation of the plan recognition models. Their work indicated that plans could be automatically detected from interactions with the system that were aligned with the self-reported plans. However, work on goal setting and planning within the context of self-regulation and scientific reasoning has largely neglected to identify the quality of those set plans and goals.

**Measuring Goal Setting and Planning Quality.** McCardle and colleagues [26] identified that effective goals for regulation should have specific time, content, actions, and standards. They highlight that the more specific each of these features are within a goal, the more effective it is in guiding a learner's self-regulation. This concept has not, however, been expanded to the plans that a learner might make to accomplish those goals or been connected to a specific context such as scientific reasoning.

For our study, we have adopted a multidimensional operationalization of plan quality that we will be able to quantify using our analytical mapping technique in with in future research. In this conceptualization we consider a "good" plan to be one that if enacted will result in completed (sub)goals set by either the planner or an imposed external standard. In this way, we must consider both the (sub)goals and the (sub)actions in conjunction with one another when evaluating a plan. We further contextualized plan quality across three dimensions. These dimensions are:

1. *Temporal Coherence* – The degree to which the temporal order of a plan follows the guidance of scientific reasoning epistemic activities (e.g., [15–17]).
2. *Action-Goal Cohesion* – The degree to which action and goals may refer to a scientific reasoning epistemic activity [17].
3. *Plan Complexity* – The degree of intricacy of one's plans categorized by the number of (sub)actions and (sub)goals as well as the degree of nestedness.

*Temporal Coherence.* We have defined the plan quality dimension of Temporal Coherence as the degree to which the temporal order of a plan follows the guidance of scientific reasoning epistemic activities [15–17]. More specifically, temporal coherence argues that a "good" plan is one that follows general temporal guidance of existing theoretical models of scientific reasoning and scientific inquiry skills. For example, in the OPIRR model [16], there is a clear cyclic nature of the steps one moves through from orientation to reflection. A plan, therefore, using this framework as grounding would argue that a poor plan is one that has a learner moving from non-sequential steps while a good plan is one in which they follow goal-action pairings that move around the iterative OPIRR cycle. For example, a learner who would plan to first set up a research design (preparation) and then orient themselves to the topic of interest (orientation) is a worse plan than a learner who first plans to understand the current state of the field of their chosen topic before preparing for a research design. However, this highlights the limitations of this particular model of scientific reasoning. Specifically, it assumes that a learner may not backstep within their scientific reasoning process until they have completed their cycle instead of regulating their strategies and learning throughout. As such, while this model is valuable and highlights the cyclic nature of scientific reasoning, it may not be the strongest model when quantifying the quality of plans as it is the ideal cycle of scientific reasoning.

In our study, we have chosen to ground our work in a less temporally defined framework of scientific reasoning by amending Fisher and colleagues' [17] framework of scientific reasoning epistemic activities. We propose a state model (see Fig. 1) of these activities with transitions informed by the definitions from the original framework and the cyclic temporal relationships identified in other scientific reasoning models (i.e., SDSS [15] and OPIRR [16]). This model shows only one iteration of one scientific reasoning task. We can imagine that science is often iterative and builds upon itself, after communicating and scrutinizing one task, this may then inform the problem identification of another task, creating a cyclic loop of the state model similar to the OPIRR [16] model. This has been omitted given the context of more constrained problem spaces typical in GBLEs for primary and secondary science education. In future research, we will use this state model to quantify the temporal coherence of learners' plans.

*Action-Goal Cohesion.* We have defined the plan quality dimension of Action-Goal Cohesion as the degree to which action and goals may refer to a scientific reasoning

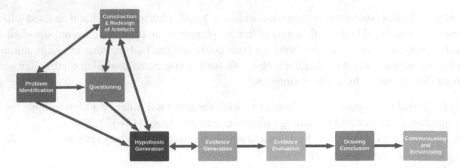

**Fig. 1.** State model of Fischer et al. (2014)'s epistemic activities used in scientific reasoning and argumentation.

epistemic activity. In other words, this refers to how well the (sub)action a learner choses is associated or will help accomplish the paired (sub)goal. For example, if a learner's goal is to determine the correct diagnosis for a patient's health problem in a case-based simulation, a "good" plan would include actions related to evidence evaluation such as determining the relevancy of patient history and lab tests to the reported health issue. A "poor" plan would be one in which a learner pairs unrelated communicating finding actions to this goal. While communicating the correct diagnosis and recommended treatment plan is important in medical interactions, this action would be better paired with the (sub)goal of treating the patient or improving patient outcomes, not on finding the diagnosis.

Within our study's context, our analytical mapping technique identifies the cohesion of all (sub)action-(sub)goal pairings allocated to a learner within the learning environment and planning tool. We review this implementation more closely below (see Sect. 3.1 and Sect. 5.3).

*Plan Complexity.* We have defined the plan quality dimension of Plan Complexity as the degree of intricacy of one's plans categorized by the number of (sub)actions and (sub)goals as well as the degree of nestedness. We highlight that there is no universal standard size of a plan, but rather this is both domain and task specific that must be determined prior to plan evaluation. This may be done with a subject matter expert providing their own plan to the given task to be the "gold standard" by which learners' plans are compared against. Alternatively, this may also be done by defining an acceptable range given the ultimate learning goal for the planner. For example, the minimum of a plan could be one (sub)action-(sub) goal pair for each of the components of one's chosen scientific reasoning framework (e.g., 8 for epistemic activities [17] or 5 for the OPIRR framework [16]). The upper limit could then be defined using the expert model approach, thereby creating a spectrum of plan complexity quality.

In addition, an individual's level of prior knowledge or expertise could be used to determine how nested (e.g., number of subgoals within a goal) the plan should be in which it would be expected the more of an expert a learner is, the less explicitly detailed plan is needed as the learner chunks together steps as expertise research has shown is common [28]. This dimension may also, however, be constrained by environmental factors that may limit the intricacy of the structure of a reported plan, as is the case in our study.

*Additional Dimension of Plan Quality.* We have identified and defined three dimensions of plan quality above based on various models and framework of scientific reasoning. We acknowledge that there are likely additional dimensions that one may wish to consider when evaluating learner plans such as the level of adaptability or flexibility of a plan. These additional dimensions serve as an area for future research and exploration.

## 3 CRYSTAL ISLAND

CRYSTAL ISLAND is a narrative game-based learning environment focused on teaching introductory microbiology and scientific reasoning skills [5]. In this first-person game, players are immersed in a virtual island undergoing an outbreak of a mysterious infection and tasked with discovering (1) what the infection is, (2) what food item caused the infection to spread, and (3) the correct treatment plan. Players are equipped with a virtual notebook tool that allows them to fill in information found throughout the island and hypothesize what infections may be causing certain symptoms. Information about various infectious diseases and their symptoms can be gathered by exploring the island from the first-person point of view and reading posters and books, talking to non-playable characters (NPCs) (e.g., infected patients and other researchers), and testing food items spread throughout various locations on the island.

In addition to the notebook tool, this version of CRYSTAL ISLAND is equipped with a planning support tool that the players can utilize to establish a plan of how they would like to approach the game (see Sect. 3.1). Once the player determines they have all the information they need, they can submit their final diagnosis. If their diagnosis is incorrect, they are prompted to try again and find a new solution, and the game is complete when they submit a correct diagnosis. All in-game activity data was collected through the use of log files, including edits to the planning support tools and diagnosis notebook, time spent on each high level-goal and low-level action, and mouse clicks (e.g., clicking on a book or poster, scanning a food item, and final submission of the diagnosis).

### 3.1 Planning Tool in CRYSTAL ISLAND

Throughout this version of CRYSTAL ISLAND, players have access to a planning support tool (see Fig. 2) that they can utilize to establish their goals and plans to accomplish those goals in their gameplay approach. The planning support tool is on the player's tablet that they carry with them in their backpack that they can reference and edit voluntarily throughout the entire game. Players are prompted to provide at least one plan after the tutorial and encouraged to update their plan at key moments based on time (i.e., every 30 min) and major plot point events (e.g., after talking with a patient about their symptoms).

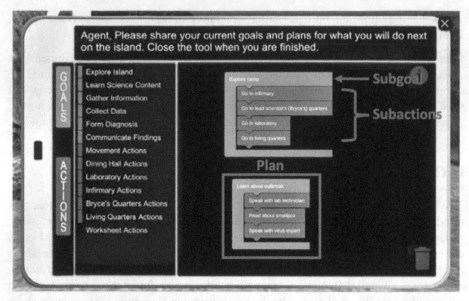

**Fig. 2.** Planning Tool Interface. Goal and Action drop down menus (left) open up to sub-goal and sub-action blocks that players drag and drop to the planning area (right side). Sub-actions (blue blocks) snap into sub-goals (green blocks) to create a plan. Students can have any size plan and as many plans as they like. Plans and blocks can be deleted using the trashcan in the bottom right. When a user opens closes the planning tool after creating a plan, their plan is saved for future reference or editing. (Colour figure online)

The planning tool has a block-based visual interface inspired by visual programming in which players drag and drop sub-goals and sub-actions (retrieved from the left hand side of drop-down goals and action categories) into a planning space (right hand side of the tablet). A "plan" using this tool must consist of a high-level subgoal (green open brackets) with at least 1 sub-action (blue blocks). These sub-actions automatically snap into their assigned sub-goals by the players in whatever order they choose. Players may also utilize the trashcan to remove plans at any point. The size of the plans is unrestricted, and all usage of the tool is logged by the system for post-hoc analysis.

The (sub)actions provided correspond to actions that a player can make in the game (e.g., using the scanner to test a food object for a specific pathogen) while the (sub)goals provided correspond to general scientific reasoning and inquiry skills (e.g., communicating findings to Kim the island's nurse).

## 4  Current Study

Assessing plan quality is a non-trivial task for researchers and educational technology designers. Not only must we develop scaffolding tools grounded in theoretical frameworks, but these tools should then be able to in (near)real-time detect plan quality and make suggestions about how learners should either adapt and modify those plans based on new information or enact their plans most efficiently to accomplish their set goals.

Our work has begun to address this challenge by designing an embedded scaffolding tool into a scientific reasoning GBLE that will ask learners to make their plans explicit so that they can be captured and evaluated. Additionally, above we have conceptualized a multidimensional operational definition of what plan quality is, identifying three features that make up a "good plan". In this study, we than examine a new analytical mapping approach to begin the work of quantifying those dimensions contextualized specifically within CRYSTAL ISLAND. Below, we provide the preliminary results of participants using the new scaffolding tool and discuss the future directions and implications for using our mapping technique moving forward.

## 5   Method

### 5.1  Participants

101 U.S. middle school students (60% female, average age = 13.2 years) played CRYS-TAL ISLAND over a two-day period during remote asynchronous science class (average gameplay time: 94.71 min). Timestamped logfiles capturing participant's interactions with the environment were analyzed for this study. IRB approval was received prior to recruitment and data collection.

### 5.2  Experimental Procedures

Participants, upon providing informed assent (in addition to informed parental/legal guardian consent), were instructed to complete a series of demographic questionnaires (i.e., reporting age, race, experience with playing video games) before completing a 17-item pretest about microbiology. Following this test, all participants were asked to play CRYSTAL ISLAND over a two-day period during their remote asynchronous science class. Upon completing the game, participants were then asked to complete another 17-item posttest about microbiology.

### 5.3  Analytical Mapping Approach

To analyze how students set plans consisting of (sub)actions and (sub)goals using the CRYSTAL ISLAND planning scaffold, we devised an analytical mapping technique that in future research will be used to quantify plan quality across our defined plan quality dimensions (See Sect. 2.3). This mapping technique categories a Goal-Subgoal (rows) and Action-Subaction (Columns) pairing as one of the 8 scientific reasoning epistemic activities (cell color) defined by Fisher and colleagues (2014) of various cohesion levels (cell opacity; see Fig. 3).

That is, striped cells are sub-actions that could be considered partially cohesive with a subgoal but are not necessarily required to be explicitly named while solid colored cells are cells actions that are fully cohesive with its paired goal. For example, if my goal is to "fill in the final diagnosis" on the diagnosis worksheet to share with Kim, the island's nurse, the action "test food and drink patients have consumed" may be one of the actions I must take to make that final diagnosis but is more cohesive with the goal of

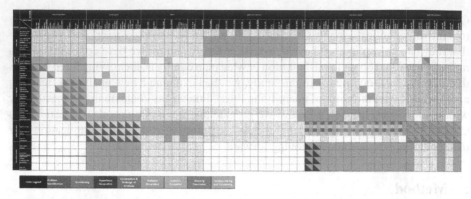

**Fig. 3.** Analytical Mapping Matrix of (Sub)Actions (columns) and (Sub)Goals (rows).

"identify transmission source". That is, while testing the food and drink may lead me to my diagnosis, it also requires I then go through evidence evaluation activities (i.e., determining if that evidence is relevant to the final diagnosis) first. However, it is not entirely unrelated as more expert learners may choose to chunk together evidence collection and evaluation activities into a single explicitly shared plan. As such, in our matrix (see Fig. 4) the cell at the intersection of the sub-action "fill in final diagnosis" and "test food and drink patients have consumed" is striped (partially cohesive). Alternatively, the cell at the intersection of the sub-action "fill in final diagnosis" and "identify transmission source" has a solid fill as it is considered fully cohesive "drawing conclusion" epistemic activity.

| GOAL | | ACTION | evaluate hypothesis | | | | | | | e> | |
|---|---|---|---|---|---|---|---|---|---|---|---|
| | SUB-ACTION | | fill in final diagnosis | fill in prediction about anthrax | fill in prediction about influenza | fill in prediction about salmonellosis | fill in symptoms | fill in test results | fill in tested object | examine poster about botulism | examine poster about ebola |
| collect data | test food drink patients have consumed | | | | | | | | | | |
| | test objects that often spread disease | | | | | | | | | | |
| | test objects patients have touched | | | | | | | | | | |
| | test objects that look dirty | | | | | | | | | | |
| | report evidence- | | | | | | | | | | |

**Fig. 4.** Close up sub-section of the mapping matrix for examples of Goal-Subgoals (rows) and Action-Subactions (Columns) to identify scientific reasoning epistemic activity (cell color) and plan relevancy (cell opacity).

# 6 Preliminary Results

Across the 101 participants, each participant submitted at least 1 plan (required after the tutorial). For the sake of brevity, we have only examined the first plan from participants. Future research will examine changes to the first plan.

Within this first plan, all participants had at least 1 subgoal-sub-action. Total plans ranged from 1–5 subgoals ($M = 1.28, SD = 0.69$). Table 2 reports the average number of sub-actions based on the number of subgoals as the relative plan sizes for the participant's first plan. For example, 14 participants had 2 subgoals in their plan, with an average of 1.89 sub-actions with their second goal and an average of 2.5 sub-actions with their first goal.

**Table 2.** Frequency of First Plan Sizes

| Subgoal | Participant Frequency | Average (SD) frequency of paired sub-actions |
|---|---|---|
| 1 | 82 | 2.50 (1.49) |
| 2 | 14 | 1.89 (0.94) |
| 3 | 2 | 1.2 (0.45) |
| 4 | 2 | 1 |
| 5 | 1 | 1 |

We then examined the most common pairings of subgoals and sub-actions (see Table 3). Within the first plan, there were 298 subgoal-sub-action pairings, with 12 unique sub-goals (out of the possible 21 options).

**Table 3.** Frequency of First Plan subgoals-sub-action Pairings

| subgoal | Frequency | Most Frequently Paired Sub-Action | Frequency |
|---|---|---|---|
| Explore Camp | 140 | Go to Infirmary | 34 |
| Learn about Outbreak | 47 | Speak with Camp Nurse (Kim) | 15 |
| Explore Rest of Island | 33 | Go to Infirmary | 6 |
| Test Objects Patients have Touched | 21 | Use Scanner to Test Object | 3 |
| Learn About Disease | 20 | Go to Infirmary | 4 |

*(continued)*

**Table 3.** (*continued*)

| subgoal | Frequency | Most Frequently Paired Sub-Action | Frequency |
|---|---|---|---|
| Test Food and Drink Patients have Consumed | 14 | Use Scanner to Test Object | 3 |
| Find Sick Individuals | 11 | – | – |
| Test Objects that Often Spread Disease | 4 | – | – |
| Learn how Disease Spreads | 3 | – | – |
| Report Evidence-Based Diagnosis | 2 | – | – |
| Evaluate Influenza Hypothesis | 2 | – | – |
| Test Objects that Look Dirty | 1 | – | – |

Note: Most Frequently sub-action cells that are blank had all unique pairings that are not reported in this table

## 7 Discussion

In this work we report on the use of a new embedded scaffolding planning tool for scientific reasoning in a GBLE that will ask learners to make their plans explicit so that they can be captured and evaluated. Additionally, we conceptualized a multidimensional operational definition of what plan quality is, identifying three features that make up a "good plan". In this preliminary study, we examined a new analytical mapping approach to begin the work of quantifying those dimensions contextualized specifically within CRYSTAL ISLAND.

While we do not report on the plan quality within this study, we are able to draw some preliminary conclusions about this approach and the types of plans our new scaffolding tool generates for learners. These conclusions are essential for future analysis of this tool when quantifying plan quality and in the design of future planning scaffolding tools.

First, our technique highlights that categorizing (sub)actions must be done in context of their (sub)goals. For example, we can see by Table 3, the sub-action "Go to Infirmary" is paired with three different subgoals ("Explore Camp", "Explore Rest of Island", and "Learn about Disease"). While the first two of these pairings, according to our mapping approach, are categorized as the scientific reasoning epistemic activity of "Problem Identification", when paired with the subgoal "Learn about Disease" the action is then categorized as "Evidence Generation". This highlights that when evaluating the quality of a plan or re-inputting this information into the system's underlying architecture for scaffold deployment, it is therefore important to consider what goal the action is in relation to.

Second, our technique highlights that our current scaffolding tool does not encourage learners to develop highly complex or large plans (see Table 2). Most learners have identified 1–2 subgoals they would like to accomplish with only roughly 2 sub-actions associated with each of those subgoals. We believe this behavior could be attributed to two possible explanations. First, the user-interface design of the scaffold itself encourages smaller plans due to the limited planning space relative to the size of the blocks. That is, participants make assumptions about how detailed their plans should be given the space allotment of the tool. Second, the number of options for the participants are provided in the tool immediately following the tutorial may be overwhelming and learners do not have enough prior knowledge about the domain (microbiology) or general knowledge about scientific reasoning to develop more mature plans. There was no instruction provided to learners with the addition of the tool that explained why planning was important, what constitutes a good plan, or how to address solving the mystery. As such, many participants could just not have enough effective self-regulatory skills at their disposal to make the best use of the current scaffolding tool.

Overall, our preliminary findings in conjunction with our expanded framework of scientific reasoning and multidimensional definition of plan quality provide the groundwork for future analysis to develop tools and methods for the automatic quantification of plan quality. We discuss how we plan to address these future directions and the implications it has for the design of future planning tools below.

## 7.1 Limitations

As this is just the preliminary approach to defining and measuring planning quality, we are unable to make any conclusions about the efficacy of the scaffolding tool and its impact on learning outcomes. Additionally, within our definition of plan quality, we have only identified three possible dimensions of quality. Additional dimensions would help provide even more information about the types of plans learners make while self-regulating during scientific reasoning tasks. Finally, we have largely ignored the dynamics of planning. To be a good self-regulator, one must be able to adapt and update their goals and plans. However, within our current approach, we have created an ad-hoc categorization of goal-action plans that do not take into consideration the context by which they are made. For example, the first plan is made immediately after the tutorial, before the learner knows what the island's resources or informational sources are. As they learn what tools they have at their disposal (e.g., the food scanner, patient accounts, etc.) their plans might have changed before they knew this contextual information. Future iterations of this mapping approach should account for the conditional knowledge of learners in addition to prior domain knowledge and knowledge about scientific reasoning to further quantify plan quality.

## 7.2 Future Directions

We have two major avenues for future work that this current study will support. The first is in the continued post-hoc analysis of plan quality based on our conceptualization of plan quality. This requires us to quantify each dimension within the context of CRYSTAL ISLAND and the planning tool reported here. This future analysis will compare learning outcomes across various plan qualities to understand how each dimension of plan quality we have identified might influence one's learning. In addition, we will explore what the plan quality of various subject matter experts may include to understand how different types of expertise (e.g., scientific reasoning, microbiology education, vs. self-regulation) would influence the type of plan one develops, and which should then ultimately act as the "gold standard".

The second major avenue of work this research will support is in the future design of new planning scaffolds for various environments. Our work has been heavily contextualized to a GBLE where inquiry learning and SRL are vital to success and learning outcomes. We anticipate, as such, this planning tool would not be appropriate for other types of learning environments (e.g., a non-simulation based intelligent tutoring system). Additional work is also needed in order to improve upon our current planning tool to encourage plans that support scientific reasoning and SRL processes. We anticipate these changes to range from simple user-interface changes to larger more sophisticated changes that provide individualized and adaptive feedback on plan quality and plan enactment. For example, we can image a planning tool in the future that "checks off" completed actions as the user interacts with the game, prompts the user to reflect on their current plan progress, and accounts for conditional information in a dynamic manner for a more accurate measure of plan quality.

## 8    Conclusion

Our work has begun to explore how a planning tool with an open-ended scientific reasoning GBLE can facilitate students' SRL processes. We will continue to develop a robust and validated measure of goal-setting and plan quality to inform the underlying architecture of CRYSTAL ISLAND to deploy individualized just-in-time feedback and adaptations to the scaffolding tool based on what the learner has accomplished and what they have planned to do. This approach and planning tool may also be applied to other science inquiry-based learning environments with recontextualization to the environments available actions and intended goals. Such work would allow for cross-comparison to understand how different environments foster scientific reasoning epistemic activities. This work and future work contribute significantly to understanding how middle school students engaging in inquiry-based learning can set effective goals and the quality of their plan formations.

**Acknowledgments.** This research was supported by funding from the National Science Foundation under grant DUE-1761178. Any opinions, findings, and conclusions expressed in this material are those of the authors and do not necessarily reflect the views of the NSF. Additionally, the authors would like to thank the members of the UCF SMART Lab and NCSU's Intellimedia Group for their support in this research.

**Disclosure of Interests.** The authors have no competing interests to declare that are relevant to the content of this article.

## References

1. Andrews, T.C., Speer, N.M., Shultz, G.V.: Building bridges: a review and synthesis of research on teaching knowledge for undergraduate instruction in science, engineering, and mathematics. Int. J. STEM Educ. **9**(1), 1–21 (2022)

2. Freeman, S., et al.: Active learning increases student performance in science, engineering, and mathematics. Proc. Natl. Acad. Sci. **111**(23), 8410–8415 (2014)
3. Lombardi, D., Shipley, T.F.: Astronomy team, biology team, chemistry team, engineering team, geography team, geoscience team, physics team: the curious construct of active learning. Psychol. Sci. Publ. Interest **22**(1), 8–43 (2021)
4. Theobald, E.J., et al.: Active learning narrows achievement gaps for underrepresented students in undergraduate science, technology, engineering, and math. Proc. Natl. Acad. Sci. **117**(12), 6476–6483 (2022)
5. Dever, D.A., Amon, M.J., Vrzakova, H., Wiedbusch, M.D., Cloude, E.B., Azevedo, R.: Capturing sequences of learners' self-regulatory interactions with instructional material during game-based learning using auto-recurrence quantification analysis. Front. Psychol. **13** (2022)
6. Azevedo, R., Wiedbusch, M.: Theories of metacognition and pedagogy applied in AIED systems. In: Handbook of Artificial Intelligence in Education, pp. 45–67. Edward Elgar Publishing, United Kingdom (2023)
7. OECD.: Trends Shaping Education 2022. OECD Publishing, Paris (2022)
8. Omarchevska, Y., Lachner, A., Richter, J., Scheiter, K.: It takes two to tango: how scientific reasoning and self-regulation processes impact argumentation quality. J. Learn. Sci. **31**(2), 237–277 (2022)
9. Wallace, C.S., Coffey, D.J.: Investigating elementary preservice teachers' designs for integrated science/literacy instruction highlighting similar cognitive processes. J. Sci. Teacher Educ. **30**(5), 507–527 (2019)
10. Winne, P., Azevedo, R.: Metacognition and self-regulated learning. In: Sawyer, K. (ed.) The Cambridge Handbook of the Learning Sciences, 3rd edn, pp. 93–113. Cambridge University Press (2022)
11. Winne, P.H.: Cognition and metacognition within self-regulated learning. In: Schunk, D.H., Greene, J.A. (Eds.) Educational Psychology Handbook Series. Handbook of Self-regulation of Learning and Performance, pp. 36–48. Routledge/Taylor & Francis Group (2018)
12. Azevedo, R., Mudrick, N., Taub, M., Wortha, F.: Coupling between metacognition and emotions during STEM learning with advanced learning technologies: a critical analysis, implications for future research, and design of learning systems. Teach. Coll. Rec. **119**(13), 114–120 (2017)
13. Lester, J.C., Ha, E.Y., Lee, S.Y., Mott, B.W., Rowe, J.P., Sabourin, J.L.: Serious games get smart: intelligent game-based learning environments. AI Mag. **34**(4), 31–45 (2013)
14. Ben-Eliyahu, A., Bernacki, M.L.: Addressing complexities in self-regulated learning: a focus on contextual factors, contingencies, and dynamic relations. Metacogn. Learn. **10**, 1–13 (2015)
15. Klahr, D., Dunbar, K.: Dual space search during scientific reasoning. Cogn. Sci. **12**, 1–48 (1988)
16. Janssen, E., Depaepe, F., Claes, E., Elen, J.: Fostering students' scientific reasoning skills in secondary education: an intervention study. Int. J. Sci. Math. Technol. Learn. **26**(1), 1–19 (2019)
17. Fisher, F., et al.: Scientific reasoning and argumentation: advancing an interdisciplinary research agenda in education. Frontline Learn. Res. **2**(3), 28–45 (2014)
18. Van Mil, M.H.W., Postma, P.A., Boerwinkel, D.J., Klaassen, K., Waarlo, A.J.: Molecular mechanistic reasoning: toward bridging the gap between the molecular and cellular levels in life science education. Sci. Educ. **100**(3), 517–585 (2016)
19. Woolley, J.S., et al.: Undergraduate students demonstrate common false scientific reasoning strategies. Think. Skills Creativ. **27**, 101–113 (2018)
20. Greene, J.A., Anderson, J.L., O'Malley, C.E., Lobczowksi, N.G.: Fostering self-regulated science inquiry in physical sciences. In: Di Benedetto, M.K. (ed.), Connecting Self-Regulated Learning and Performance with Instruction Across High School Content Areas, pp. 163–183. Springer (2018)

21. Sinatra, G.M., Taasoobshirazi, G.: The self-regulation of learning and conceptual change in science: research, theory, and educational applications. In: Schunk, D., Greene J. (eds.) Handbook of Self-Regulation of Learning and Performance, 2nd edn, pp. 153–165. Routledge (2018)

22. Dever, D.A., Sonnenfeld, N.A., Wiedbusch, M.D., Schmorrow, G., Amon, M.J., Azevedo, R.: A complex systems approach to analyzing pedagogical agents' scaffolding of self-regulated learning within an intelligent tutoring system. Metacogn. Learn. **18**, 659–691 (2023)

23. Greene, J.A., Bernacki, M.L., Hadwin, A.F.: Self-regulation. In: Handbook of Educational Psychology, pp. 314–334. Routledge, New York (2024)

24. Panadero, E.: A review of self-regulated learning: six models and four directions for research. Front. Psychol. **8**, 422 (2017)

25. Zimmerman, B.J., Moylan, A.R.: Self-regulation: where metacognition and motivation intersect. In: Hacker, D.J., Dunlosky, J., Graesser, A.C. (eds.) Handbook of Metacognition in Education, pp. 299–315. Routledge (2009)

26. McCardle, L., Webster, E., Haffey, A., Hadwin, A.: Examining students' self-set goals for self-regulated learning: goal properties and patterns. Stud. High. Educ. **42**(11), 2153–2169 (2017)

27. Goslen, A., Carpenter, D., Rowe, J.P., Henderson, N., Azevedo, R., Lester, J.: Leveraging student goal setting for real-time plan recognition in game-based learning. In: Rodrigo, M., Matsuda, N., Cristea, A., Dimitrova, V. (eds.) International Conference on Artificial Intelligence in Education, LNCS, vol. 13355, pp. 78–89. Springer, Cham (2022)

28. Wirth, J., Stebner, F., Trypke, M., Schuster, C., Leutner, D.: An interactive layers model of self-regulated learning and cognitive load. Educ. Psychol. Rev. **32**(4), 1127–1149 (2020)

# Novel Learning Ecosystems

# Mobile Sensor Interfaces for Learning Science

Jhon Alé[✉] and Jaime Sánchez

University of Chile, Santiago, Chile
jhon.ale@ug.uchile.cl

**Abstract.** In the context of science education, studies frequently highlight experimental practices employing diverse mobile device sensor interfaces for data collection and analysis. Despite the benefits, there is unclearness on sensor integration within science teaching. This study aims to propose a comprehensive model for understanding the interaction between students and mobile device sensors in science education. The model introduces a nested curricular integration approach, focusing on developing scientific skills through stages like observation, research planning, data processing, evidence analysis, and results communication. It also aligns these processes with three levels of technology presence: readiness, use, and integration. The evaluation revealed substantial positive changes in students' expectations of enhanced science learning support, their attitudes toward classroom integration, and intentions to utilize the educational resources. Significant improvements were observed in Expectation of Performance, Attitude, and Intention to use. No significant changes were found in Anxiety-related aspects.

**Keywords:** Mobile Learning · School Education · Science Learning · ICT Integration into Curriculum · Physics Sciences

## 1 Introduction

When mobile technologies are integrated into curriculum responsibly and with proper preparation [1–3] they make it possible for learning not to be confined to textbooks, classrooms, or schools. Rather, it may happen at any time and place, breaking the boundaries of the classroom [4]. Students can interact and engage with different environments, leading to improved teaching and learning experiences [5]. Mobile technology not only provides solutions to longstanding educational issues but also fosters innovation in teaching through more meaningful educational experiences [6].

Particularly in the realm of science education, it is common to come across studies reporting experimental practices using various types of mobile device sensor interfaces to collect and analyze empirical data, including accelerometers [7–9], magnetometers [10, 11], cameras [12], sound sensors [13, 14], and even light sensors [15]. This quality transforms mobile devices into powerful, accessible, and cost-effective tools for conducting rigorous and high-quality scientific experiments. Despite their benefits, the literature is not entirely clear on how sensors can interact with students and be integrated into curriculum within the science teaching context. The literature related to the "use" of mobile sensors presents excellent opportunities for diversifying experimental practices. However, the idea of integration into curriculum entails a more complex process. It aims to assess the didactic possibilities of technologies in relation to educational objectives and needs, taking into consideration diversity, the human context, and nature [2].

The aim of this study is to establish a more complex model that helps understand the interaction between school students and mobile device sensors within the context of science education. Based on a literature review and curriculum integration models [2, 16], we designed of a nested curricular integration model is proposed to incorporate the use of mobile sensors, focusing on the development of scientific skills. This nested model sequentially groups the scientific research and inquiry skills involved in experimental verification. Scientific skills are revealed through five types of learning consistent with the stages of the scientific method: observation and posing questions, planning, and conducting research, data processing, evidence analysis, results communication, and evaluation. This model highlights the research processes that can be enhanced using mobile sensors [16] and links them to three levels of technology presence: readiness, use, and integration [2, 17].

## 2  Related Work

### 2.1  Factors Influencing the Curricular Integration of Technologies

Globalization and the rapid changes of the digital era have driven the integration of technologies in the educational field, with explicit calls from international organizations to incorporate them into curricula, thus promoting equity and accessibility in quality education [18–23]. Adopting technologies under constructivist approaches [1–3] stimulates personalized, timely, and effective learning, improving teaching, student motivation, and closing educational gaps. It can enhance certain learning modalities in specific contexts and contribute to addressing long-standing learning issues [24–26].

Despite reported benefits, there is currently a lack of unbiased evidence regarding the impact of educational technology [24, 27]. The mere incorporation of technology without appropriate educational design can result in distractions for students, emphasizing the importance of adequate training for its use.

This situation is sustained, in part, due to the lack of new educational approaches in educational technology research [28], the absence of new theories, models, and methods for its effective integration into pedagogical practice [29], and the lack of context-specific evidence for regions [24].

Various research works address determining conditions for the effective curricular integration of technologies, highlighting elements such as technological access, technical support, teacher planning, time management, and the positive attitude of the educational community towards technologies [30–33]. Additional moderating factors influencing the educational process with technologies have also been discussed, such as teacher training in technology, the influence of technology use according to curricular plans and programs, and work experiences associated with technology use [34–36].

## 2.2  Mobile Devices and Sensors in Science Education

The incorporation of mobile devices in science education has shown significant improvements in performance, learning efficiency, and feedback processes [37–39]. Particularly, practices involving various mobile technologies based on a socio-constructivist approach have highlighted improvements in learning efficiency, modeling of abstract scientific concepts, and the promotion of student collaboration and creativity [40–42]. Other evidence also demonstrates improvements in student learning efficiency and the modeling of scientific phenomena to enhance the understanding of abstract concepts [41, 43]. There is also evidence linking mobile learning strategies in science with collaborative work, student innovation and creativity, improvements in teacher efficiency, the creation of safe learning spaces for communities, and enhancements in student attention and motivation [44–46].

In the specific context of physics education, there is a wide variety of evidence and educational proposals involving mobile technologies. Some of these propose improvements in the understanding of more abstract physical scientific ideas, such as electric and magnetic field lines [47, 48]. Other mobile resources are designed to simulate objects and phenomena of nature in detail, such as the position of objects in the celestial sphere [49], the characteristics and structure of the Moon, phenomena associated with lunar phases [50], and phenomena related to volcanoes, earthquakes, and plate tectonics [51]. Some software for mobile devices allows virtual journeys to hard-to-reach places, such as the laboratory of the European Organization for Nuclear Research or the European Laboratory for Particle Physics (CERN), as well as visits to observatories or trips to other planets like Mars [52, 53]. Other proposals for scientific education software seek to support experimentation work, for example, by presenting real-time data from sensors in electrical circuits [54], showing the types of connections in electrical circuits [55], or simulating balls that can be thrown as projectiles [56].

Particularly, due to their easy accessibility, mobile sensors are often used as laboratory instruments to assist in data collection or perform data analysis through video analysis. The use of integrated sensors is especially common for learning classical mechanics, with various proposals that utilize the accelerometer [7, 9, 57], magnetometer [10], or other sensors such as the camera [12], sound meter [13, 14], or light meter [58], thus contributing to studies of statics, kinematics, and dynamics.

The qualities described above make mobile devices accessible and cost-effective tools, instruments, and resources with which it is possible to collect and analyze data with high precision and low uncertainty.

## 2.3  Construction of Scientific Models Using Sensor Technology

The reviewed literature guides how technology and mobile sensors can be integrated for the construction of scientific models [59, 60]. School scientific models and modeling processes are crucial aspects of research in science education, and their definitions are not always clear. According to [61], a school scientific model can be understood as school-appropriate versions of scientific models that are theoretical and, at the same time, conceptual in nature, with the ability to describe, explain, predict, and intervene in the world [62]. Scientific models are theoretical and conceptual entities, ideas that emerge to articulate the construction of current scientific knowledge and are fundamental ideas in the sciences, aiming to improve the understanding of phenomena in the world [63].

Constructing scientific models through scientific inquiry is what defines the essence of modeling—a socio-constructive process that involves the use and appropriation of previous scientific models, their evaluation, and transformation. In a representative sense, a scientific model may include physical or abstract objects that are generally smaller than the reference object [64–67].

The construction and validation of scientific models, based on [59, 60] are presented as the axis of scientific activity through a continuous and iterative process of theorization and experimental verification (see Fig. 1).

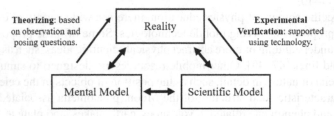

**Fig. 1.** Construction and verification of scientific models with the support of technology, based on [59, 60].

During theorization, ideas, knowledge, and creativity are mobilized through mental and logical models, while during verification, a contrast and fitting are achieved through systematic, coherent, and replicable procedures. During experimental verification, the representativeness of data and evidence is significantly relevant; their scientific validity, reliability, objectivity, replicability in treatment, and analysis. This last factor can be widely supported by technologies and mobile sensors, considering the diversity of measurement instruments they offer.

## 3 Method

### 3.1 Research Strategies

Given that this study focuses on evaluating specific variables related to the use of mobile device sensors for science learning in 15 to 16-year-old students, it is framed within a predominantly applied approach [68]. Based on the reviewed literature, a nested model of ICT curriculum integration was designed for the development of scientific skills and mediated with the use mobile device sensors [16]. The validation of this model included the creation and implementation of "Experimental Activities" and "Guidelines" to mediate its use in the classroom.

The "Experimental Activities" were implemented with a group of 20 students from a school in Chile, using mobile sensors. Simultaneously, each student responded to a survey designed to characterize their intention to use mobile sensors during scientific experimentation (see Annex 1). This survey was adapted from the Technology Acceptance Model (TAM) and the Unified Theory of Acceptance and Use of Technology (UTAUT) [69–72]. The instrument adaptations were made to adjust the language to the age of the participants and consider the context of the science class.

To analyze survey data, Pearson's chi-square tests were conducted to compare expected values with those obtained regarding: Perceived ease of use, perceived usefulness, Attitude toward technology use, facilitating conditions, Self-efficacy, Anxiety, and Intention to use. This procedure allowed for observing significant changes in students' perceptions and attitudes toward the use of mobile sensors in science learning.

The results were cross-referenced to improve the didactic model and experimental activities. Additionally, the application of chi-square tests provided a robust assessment of key instrumental variables, identifying areas of strength and potential intervention points to optimize the acceptance of sensors during science class implementation.

### 3.2  Examples of Experimental Activities with Mobile Sensors

The following three examples are presented as a representative sample of a larger set of experimental activities with mobile sensors. The purpose of these experimental activities is to characterize the period of simple pendulum motion, a phenomenon historically explored by the scientist Galileo Galilei. In these activities, the use of three mobile device sensors is suggested: the light sensor, proximity sensor, and magnetometer. The details of their applications are outlined in Fig. 2.

1. Light sensor: On the device's touchscreen, the location of the light sensor is identified and placed under the shadow of a stationary pendulum mass. The mass is elongated between 5° and 30° without losing tension, generating oscillatory motion. This effect causes the light sensor to be momentarily shaded during the oscillation. Throughout the swing, the light sensor will record variations in light intensity associated with the pendulum's oscillatory motion. Depending on the software, these data can be analyzed using tables or graphs.
2. Proximity sensor: On the device's touchscreen, the location of the proximity sensor is identified and then placed under the stationary pendulum mass, within 5 cm. Again, the mass is elongated between 5° and 30° without losing tension, and it is released to generate oscillatory motion. Each time the mass oscillates within 5 cm of the sensor, variations in sound interference will be recorded. During the oscillation, the proximity sensor will record the reflection of the emitted sound wave due to interference with the mass. Depending on the software, data can be analyzed using tables or graphs.
3. Magnetic field sensor: On the device's touchscreen, the location of the magnetometer is identified, which is placed under the stationary pendulum mass. A small magnet is incorporated into the mass, so each time the mass oscillates and approaches the sensor, it can detect variations in the magnetic field. During the oscillation, the magnetometer will record variations in the intensity of the magnetic field associated with the oscillatory motion of the magnet acting as the pendulum mass. Depending on the software, these data can be analyzed using tables or graphs.

In each of the proposed activities, the aim is to promote the development of essential skills related to observation, question formulation, as well as the design, planning, and

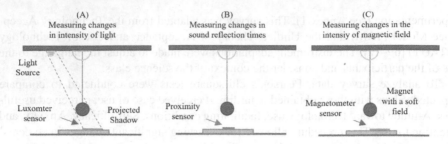

**Fig. 2.** Example of interactions with mobile sensors: Analysis of simple pendulum motion.

execution of scientific investigations. Participants face the task of formulating hypotheses, manipulating variables, and analyzing empirical evidence with the ultimate goal of reaching well-founded conclusions about the oscillation period in the context of pendulum motion.

The activities not only stimulate the practical application of scientific skills but also support the process of experimental verification. By using the instrumental sensitivity provided by mobile sensors, participants can organize, process, and represent data effectively, whether through tables or graphs. This approach not only enriches the practical experience of students but also provides them with a deeper understanding of the physical concepts involved in pendulum motion. The ability to integrate data from mobile sensors into experimental analysis not only entails a practical dimension but also emphasizes the importance of technology in current scientific research.

The three activities with mobile sensors offer flexibility for adaptation by manipulating various control variables, such as elongation (or angle of inclination), the amount of mass, the length of the string, the shape and density of the sphere, the thickness of the string, among others. Figure 3 illustrates three cases that exemplify the possibility of controlling different variables within the research.

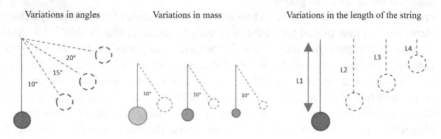

**Fig. 3.** Extension of activities with mobile sensors.

By allowing the variation of these conditions, students can formulate various hypotheses exploring relationships between variables involved in the experiment. This extension of activities not only promotes experimentation and exploration of multiple scenarios but also stimulates students' ability to formulate and test their own theories based on conditions.

# 4   Results

## 4.1   Model for Integrating Mobile Sensors in Science Classes

The proposed nested scientific model in this study is organized sequentially based on the skills and processes of scientific research in the scientific method. These skills encompass observation and question formulation, planning and execution of research, data processing, analysis of evidence, communication of results, and their evaluation.

Figure 4 illustrates the model detailing the research processes that can be enriched by the incorporation of mobile sensors. It also links these processes with three levels of technological presence: readiness, use, and integration.

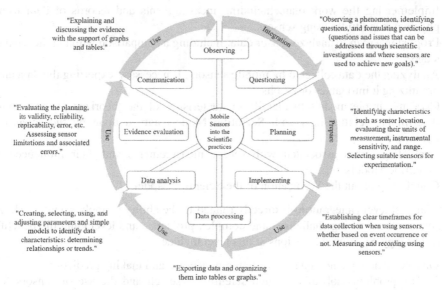

**Fig. 4.**  Nested Model for Integrating Sensors in Science Education.

This nested model, represented in Fig. 1, is based on proposals from [73, 74], adapted to education by [2, 3]. Its aim is to facilitate the progressive development of readiness, use, and integration stages in each phase of school scientific research. The integration of mobile technologies is presented as a key element to enhance these skills, offering students a more complete educational experience aligned with contemporary advances in science education.

In the first level (readiness), an introduction to the use of mobile technologies is proposed without a specific application for learning or scientific activity. Students explore and propose initial steps to understand the functioning of mobile sensors, identifying their characteristics and locations, evaluating the units of measure used, and engaging in activities to understand their operation. Specific suggestions at this level include:

- Identifying the characteristics of the sensor to be used, such as its location on the mobile device.

- Understanding the basic operation of the sensor through explanations and simple experiences.
- Measuring and recording data of physical magnitudes using different sensors.
- Evaluating units of measure, instrumental sensitivity, and range.
- Evaluating the reliability, replicability, and errors associated with sensors.

In the second level (use), skills aimed at collecting, evidencing, and collaborating are cultivated, allowing students to perform specific tasks to support or improve basic research stages. Specific suggestions at this level include:

- Proposing a teaching situation for theorizing about a phenomenon.
- Proposing a work plan, including the times and the way they will collect data from mobile sensors.
- Implementing the work plan, including measurements and records of data from physical magnitudes using sensors.
- Proposing a plan to analyze sensor data, including a comparison with the theorizing stage.
- Analyzing the data collected by mobile sensors. If necessary, exporting the data and organizing it into tables or graphs.
- Creating simple models to identify characteristics of the theorized phenomenon, determining relationships with Scientific Models agreed upon by the scientific community.
- Evaluating errors associated with sensor measurements and their influence on Scientific Models.
- Concluding about the Verification of the Scientific Model.

The last level (integration) is directly related to the ability to apply scientific skills to new contexts, facing challenges and complex problems, and leveraging the benefits of technology. Specific suggestions at this level include:

- Observing new phenomena, formulating questions, and making predictions.
- Posing problems solvable through scientific research and the use of sensors for innovative purposes.

This gradual approach allows teachers and students to progress from basic familiarization to advanced integration of mobile sensors in scientific research, providing a pedagogical structure that aligns with the cognitive processes and progressive skills of students in their scientific learning.

## 4.2 Suggestions for Mediating the Use of Sensors Before Classes

In line with the proposed nested model, pedagogical suggestions based on the analyzed studies are presented. These suggestions provide guidance to facilitate the use of mobile sensors in the educational context. The presented guidelines are implemented before science classes with mobile sensors:

- Relevance Assessment: Before incorporating sensors, it is recommended to assess whether they represent an educational alternative that truly enhances learning achievements compared to other more economical or less complex didactic innovations for implementation. This aspect can be especially crucial in schools or educational centers lacking sufficient access to laboratory resources to conduct experiments. It is preferable to choose the use of sensors with specific and planned activities, aligning them with specific learning objectives and focusing on improving the fulfillment of goals outlined in the curriculum.

- Management with the Educational Community: The importance of informing the educational institution and stakeholders about the pedagogical use of mobile technology is emphasized. Transparency about intended uses and requesting support from the community of educators, teachers, and parents is considered essential for the successful integration of sensors into the educational environment.
- Mutual Agreement with Students and Families: Before implementation, it is proposed to establish a mutual agreement with students and families to ensure proper use of mobile technology. Creating a commitment letter, signed by students and guardians, outlining clear rules about the correct use of mobile technology during classes is suggested.
- Technical Evaluation of Sensors: Before implementation, it is advisable to conduct a technical evaluation to identify the key characteristics of sensors in mobile devices. This includes exploring the types of sensors available in different ranges of devices, identifying the spatial location of sensors, characterizing their instrumental sensitivity and associated errors, and understanding data representation in tables and graphs using different software and hardware available in virtual stores.

The pre-implementation suggestions offer a structured practical foundation to address essential aspects and achieve the integration of mobile sensors in the educational environment, ensuring effective implementation.

### 4.3 Survey Results

Regarding the expected versus observed trends for each construct, Table 1 provides a summary of the Pearson chi-square coefficient value evaluations. Through these tests, associations were identified in three of the constructs: expectation of functionality, attitude, and intention to use, suggesting that they could be influenced by the implementations of the designed didactic activities and their mediation.

**Table 1.** Pearson Chi-square Results for the Intention to Use Mobile Sensors.

| Variable | Bilateral Asymptotic Significance | Interpretation |
|---|---|---|
| Expectation of functionality | .006 | An association is accepted |
| Attitude toward the use of technology | .033 | An association is accepted |
| Anxiety | .077 | No association is accepted |
| Intention to use | .025 | An association is accepted |

According to the survey results, students express their desire to use mobile technology to learn science and indicate their interest in doing so in the coming months, experiencing positive feelings about it. However, the study could not conclusively establish an association with anxiety, making it difficult to determine if students feel nervous or intimidated when using mobile sensors during classes.

## 5 Discussion and Conclusions

The present proposal has successfully achieved its goal of developing a nested model that contributes to understanding the interaction between students and mobile device sensors in the field of scientific education. The design of the nested model, conceived through meticulous literature review, is oriented toward curricular integration through the use of mobile sensors, with a specific focus on fostering scientific skills. This model follows a logical and progressive sequence, organizing essential research and scientific inquiry skills for theorization and experimental verification. Additionally, it highlights the research processes that can be enhanced with the use of mobile sensors, establishing a connection with three levels of technological presence: readiness, use, and integration. Finally, the model incorporates an initial phase of mediation through 'Guidelines,' designed to facilitate the responsible use of mobile device sensors before conducting science classes.

The theoretical foundation of the nested approach aligns with research conducted by [1–3, 16, 17, 30–32, 73, 74]. Special attention has been paid to moderating variables influencing curricular integration processes, as described by [34–36]. Additionally, evidence supporting the hypothesis regarding experimental work with mobile devices has been considered, as presented in the works of [37–44].

The nested model, along with the guidelines and didactic proposals, underwent evaluation through implementation in classrooms with Chilean students aged 15 to 16. The implementations of the proposed activity models, based on the models, had an applied nature, seeking an approach that allowed characterizing students' attitudinal impressions regarding the intention to use mobile devices to learn science.

In the attitudinal self-perception assessments, students expressed that:

- Mobile technology will help them improve their performance in experimental science work.
- Experimental work in science is easier to perform with mobile devices.
- Experimental work in science becomes more interesting or fun with mobile devices.
- Using mobile devices to learn science is in line with the opinions of important people for them and the school community.
- They possess the necessary skills to use mobile devices to learn science.
- They have a clear intention to consciously formulate plans to use mobile devices in science learning over the next 3 months.

Similarly, according to chi-square evaluations, the study could not establish a clear association with anxiety, concerning whether students feel nervous or intimidated when giving pedagogical uses to mobile technology during science classes.

In summary, the experiences associated with the design and evaluation processes allowed intertwining and elaborating on a refined proposal of the proposed model.

These experiences also made it possible to improve guidelines and proposals for didactic activities. All of the above contributes to fulfilling the overall objective set for this work.

## 5.1  Limitations of the Study

Despite the advancements achieved in this study, certain limitations must be acknowledged that could influence the generalization of results and the interpretation of conclusions.

This study focused on a specific group of students aged 15 to 16 in a school in Chile. The homogeneity of the sample and the school context could limit the extrapolation of results to other student populations with different demographic or educational characteristics.

The duration of the implementation of experimental activities and data collection took place over a one-month period. This restriction could influence the depth of observations and capturing possible long-term changes in students' attitudes and expectations towards the use of mobile sensors.

In addition, despite efforts to recognize moderating factors in the implementation, there are other external factors not considered in this study, such as changes in classroom dynamics, unexpected events, or external conditions that could have influenced student responses and the effectiveness of mobile sensor integration.

Moreover, although measures were included to assess students' anxiety when using mobile sensors, the complexity and subjectivity of this construct may limit the accuracy of evaluations. Anxiety could be influenced by individual factors not fully captured in this study, considering other conceptual and operational definitions.

It's also important to note that, while the focus on integrating mobile sensors was on Natural Sciences, specifically physics, the applicability and generalization of the proposed model to other disciplines may require adaptations and additional considerations not fully addressed in this study.

Lastly, it should be considered that, although the implementation of new technologies may generate initial enthusiasm in students due to novelty, this does not imply that it should be sustained over time, and its long-term impact may require more extended monitoring. This is something to be considered for any type of innovative technology, not just for the use of mobile sensors.

Despite these limitations, this study provides a valuable foundation for future research, expanding the understanding of mobile sensor integration in science education and opening the door to new areas of exploration and pedagogical development.

## 5.2  Future Work

With the contribution of this study, the aim was to deepen, from both a theoretical and practical perspective, the relationship between scientific educational practices incorporating mobile sensors. This work lays the groundwork for the design of future field studies or empirical research that demonstrate the impact of learning sequences that integrate sensors in different areas of Natural Sciences disciplines, such as Physics, Chemistry, and Biology; without excluding their incorporation into other disciplines that use the scientific method.

Likewise, the research opens the door to new lines of study focused on the influence of moderating, socio-emotional, and contextual variables that play a crucial role in the process of introducing mobile technologies into the classroom.

Future research could also relate to the study of other types of innovative technologies for the school classroom, different from the use of mobile sensors. For example, emerging technologies such as artificial intelligence, virtual reality, augmented reality, or mixed realities have been little explored in educational environments and offer promising opportunities to support education.

In this sense, the approach proposed in the model of this study aims at a deeper understanding of the complexities involved in the interaction between humans and machines, providing insights into how various social and technological variables interact.

In line with the statements of international organizations, the proposed future research directions not only have the potential to enrich our knowledge in this field but can also significantly contribute to reducing gaps in quality educational practices that use available resources. This is particularly relevant to consider in schools facing limitations in resources for scientific experimentation. Therefore, the research seeks to contribute to the future with new investigations aimed at equal opportunities in access to education, regardless of economic or technological disparities, thereby encouraging more equitable and just teaching for all.

**Acknowledgments.** This work was funded by Chilean National Agency for Research and Development (ANID), Basal Funding for Scientific and Technology Centers of Excellence, project FB0003.

**Disclosure of Interests.** The authors have no competing interests to declare that are relevant to the content of this article.

# References

1. Sánchez, J.: Aprendizaje Visible, Tecnología Invisible. Dolmen Ediciones (2001)
2. Sánchez, J.: Integración curricular de TICS conceptos y modelos. Revista Enfoques Educacionales **5**(1), 51–65 (2017)
3. Sánchez, J.: Bases constructivistas para la integración de TICs. Revista Enfoques Educacionales **6**(1), 75–89 (2018)
4. Cope, B., Kalantzis, M.: Multiliteracies: new literacies, learning, pedagogies. Int. J. **4**(3), 164–195 (2009)
5. Gros, B., Kinshuk, Maina, M.: The future of ubiquitous learning: learning designs for emerging pedagogies. In: Gros, B., Kinshuk, Maina, M. (eds.). LNET, vol. 1, pp. 3–271. Springer, Heidelberg (2016)
6. McQuiggans, S., McQuiggans, J., Sabourin, J., Kosturko, L.: Mobile Learning: A Handbook for Developers, Educators, and Learners. Wiley and SAS Business Series (2015)
7. Kuhn, J., Vogt, P.: Analyzing spring pendulum phenomena with a smart-phone acceleration sensor. Phys. Teacher **50**(8), 504–505 (2012)
8. Monteiro, M., Cabeza, C., Martí, A.: Acceleration measurements using smartphone sensors: dealing with the equivalence principle. Revista Brasileira de Ensino de Física, **37**(1), 1303 (2015)

9. Monteiro, M., Cabeza, C., Martí, A.: The atwood machine revisited using smartphones. Phys. Teacher **53**(6), 373–374 (2015)
10. Pili, U., Violanda, R., Ceniza, C.: Measurement of g using a magnetic pendulum and a smartphone magnetometer. Phys. Teacher **56**(4), 258–325 (2018)
11. Pili, U., Violanda, R., Ceniza, C.: Measuring a spring constant with a smartphone magnetic field sensor. Phys. Teacher **57**(3), 198–199 (2019)
12. Becker, S., Klein, P., Kuhn, J.: Video analysis on tablet computers to investigate effects of air resistance. Phys. Teacher **54**(7), 440–441 (2016)
13. Kuhn, J., Vogt, P., Hirth, M.: Analyzing the acoustic beat with mobile devices. Phys. Teacher **52**(4), 248–249 (2014)
14. Schwarz, O., Vogt, P., Kuhn, J.: Acoustic measurements of bouncing balls and the determination of gravitational acceleration. Phys. Teacher **51**(5), 312 (2013)
15. Silva-Alé, J.: Determination of gravity acceleration with smartphone ambient light sensor. Phys. Teacher **59**(3), 2018 (2021)
16. Wang, T.H., Lim, K.Y.T., Lavonen, J., Clark-Wilson, A.: Maker-centred science and mathematics education: lenses, scales and contexts. Int. J. Sci. Math. Educ. **17**, 1–11 (2019)
17. Sánchez, J.: Successful IT Curriculum Integration: Concepts and Cases. In: Proceedings of ECIS IT Conference, pp. 7–9 (2003)
18. UNESCO. Guidelines for ICT in Education Policies and Masterplans. UNESCO (2022)
19. UNESCO. The International Science and Evidence based Education (ISEE) Assessment: 2.6 Education Technology. UNESCO (2023)
20. The Organization for Economic Co-operation and Development: OECD Future of Education and Skills 2030 OECD Learning Compass 2030 a Series Of Concept Notes. OECD (2020)
21. UNESCO: UNESCO ICT Competency Framework for Teachers. UNESCO (2018)
22. World Economic Forum. Schools of the Future: Defining New Models of Education for the Fourth Industrial Revolution. World Economic Forum (2020)
23. Livingstone, K.: The Place of Information and Communication Technologies in Curriculum Design and Development. Int. J. Educ. Developm. Inf. Commun. Technol. **15**(4) (2019)
24. UNESCO. Global Education Monitoring Report, 2023: Technology in Education: A Tool on Whose Terms? UNESCO (2023)
25. Bogiannidis, N., Southcott, J., Gindidis, M.: An exploration of the possible educational opportunities and the challenges at the intersection of the physical and digital worlds occupied by 10–14-year-old students. Smart Learn. Environ. **10**(26) (2023)
26. Jagust, T., Boticki, I., So, H.-J.: A review of research on bridging the gap between formal and informal learning with technology in primary school contexts. J. Comput. Assist. Learn. **34**(4), 417–428 (2018)
27. Rasheed, R., Kamsin, A., Abdullah, N.: Challenges in the online component of blended learning: a systematic review. Comput. Educ. **144**, 103701 (2020)
28. Chen, X., Xie, H., Zou, D., Hwang, G.J.: Application and theory gaps during the rise of artificial intelligence in education. Comput. Educ. **1**, 100002 (2020)
29. Tang, K.Y., Chang, C.Y., Hwang, G.J.: Trends in artificial intelligence-supported e-learning: a systematic review and co-citation network analysis (1998–2019). Interact. Learn. Environ. 1–19 (2021)
30. Aslan, A., Zhu, C.: Investigating variables predicting Turkish pre-service teachers' integration of ICT into teaching practices. Br. J. Edu. Technol. **48**(2), 552–270 (2016)
31. Aslan, A., Zhu, C.: Influencing factors and integration of ICT into teaching practices of pre-service and starting teachers. Int. J. Res. Educ. Sci. **2**(2), 359–370 (2016)
32. Suleimen, N.: Appraising the attitude towards information communication technology integration and usage in Kazakhstani higher education curriculum. J. Inf. Technol. Educ. Res. **18**(1), 355–378 (2019)

33. Li, S., Yamaguchi, S., Takada, J.: Understanding factors affecting primary school teachers' use of ICT for student-centered education in Mongolia **14**(1), 103–117 (2018)
34. Hammou, Y., Elfatihi, M.: Moroccan teachers' level of ICT integration in secondary EFL classrooms. Int. J. Lang. Literary Stud. **1**(3) (2019)
35. Aksal, F., Gazi, Z.: Examination on ICT integration into special education schools for developing countries. TOJET: The Turkish Onl. J. Educ. Technol. **14**(3), 124–130 (2015)
36. Dong, C., Newman, L.: Ready, steady … pause: integrating ICT into Shanghai preschools. Int. J. Early Years Educ. **24**(2), 224–237 (2016)
37. Xiao, J., Cao, M., Li, X., Hansen, P.: Assessing the effectiveness of the augmented reality courseware for starry sky exploration. Int. J. Distance Educ. Technol. **18**(1), 19–35 (2020)
38. Chun, K.: Pedagogical Innovation Through Mobile Learning Implementation: An Exploratory Study on Teachers' Extended and Emergent Use of Mobile Learning Systems. ProQuest Dissertations Publishing (2019)
39. Lai, C.: Trends of mobile learning: a review of the top 100 highly cited papers. Br. J. Educ. Technol. 1–22 (2019)
40. Laine, T.: Mobile educational augmented reality games: a systematic literature review and two case studies. Computers **7**(1), 19 (2018)
41. Baran, B., Yecan, E., Kaptan, B., Pasayigit, O.: Using augmented reality to teach fifth grade students about electrical circuits. Educ. Inf. Technol. **25**, 1371–1385 (2020)
42. Ozdemir, M., Sahin, C., Arcagok, S., Demir, M.K.: The effect of augmented reality applications in the learning process: a meta-analysis study. Eurasian J. Educ. Res. **18**(74) (2018)
43. Bos, A., et al.: Educational technology and its contributions in students' focus and attention regarding augmented reality environments and the use of sensors. J. Educ. Comput. Res. **57**, 1832–1848 (2019)
44. Coimbra, M., Cardoso, T., Mateus, A.: Augmented reality: an enhancer for higher education students in math's learning? Procedia Comput. Sci. **67** (2015)
45. Guncaga, J., Janiga, R.: Virtual labs and educational software as a tool for more effective teaching STEM subjects. In: The Third International Conference on Computer Science, Computer Engineering, and Education Technologies (2016)
46. Ewais, A., Troyer, O.: A usability and acceptance evaluation of the use of augmented reality for learning atoms and molecules reaction by primary school female students in Palestine. J. Educ. Comput. Res. **57**(7), 1643–1670 (2019)
47. Donhauser, A., et al.: Making the invisible visible: visualization of the connection between magnetic field, electric current, and Lorentz force with the help of augmented reality. Phys. Teacher **58**(6), 438–439 (2020)
48. Bodensiek, O., Sonntag, D., Wendorff, N., Albuquerque, G., Magnor, M.: Augmenting the fine beam tube: from hybrid measurements to magnetic field visualization. Phys. Teacher **57**(4), 262–263 (2019)
49. Heafner, J.: Astronomical apps for teaching astronomy. Phys. Teacher **57**(7), 504–505 (2019)
50. Lincoln, J.: Augmented reality Moon for astronomy lessons. Phys. Teacher **56**(7), 492–493 (2018)
51. Silva-Alé, J.: Learning volcanism through school projects: a pedagogical design using technology in pandemic context. Revista Saberes Educativos **7**, 111–130 (2021)
52. MacIsaac, D.: NYT virtual tour of CERN's Large Hadron Collider. Phys. Teacher **57**(2), 126 (2019)
53. MacIsaac, D.: Perseverance: the new Rover on Mars. Phys. Teacher **59**(4), 303 (2021)
54. Lauer, L., et al.: Real-time visualization of electrical circuit schematics: an augmented reality experiment setup to foster representational knowledge in introductory physics education. Phys. Teacher **58**(7), 518–519 (2020)

55. Kapp, S., et al.: Augmenting Kirchhoff's laws: using augmented reality and smart glasses to enhance conceptual electrical experiments for high school students. Phys. Teacher **57**(1), 52–53 (2019)
56. Chandrakar, M., Bhagat, K., Kumar: Development of an augmented reality-based game for projectile motion. Phys. Teacher **58**(9), 668–669 (2020)
57. Monteiro, M., Cabeza, C., Martí, A.: Acceleration measurements using smartphone sensors: dealing with the equivalence principle. Phys. Teacher **37**(1), 1303 (2015)
58. Silva-Alé, J.: Determination of gravity acceleration with smartphone ambient light sensor. Phys. Teacher **59**(3), 218–219 (2021)
59. Chamizo, J.: Una tipología de los modelos para la enseñanza de las ciencias. Revista Eureka Enseñanza y Divulgación de las Ciencias **7**(1), 26–41 (2010)
60. Chamizo, J.: A new definition of models and modeling in chemistry's teaching. Sci. Educ. **22**(7), 1613–1632 (2011)
61. Soto, M., Couso, D., López, V., Hernández, M.: Promoviendo la apropiación del modelo de energía en estudiantes de 4° de ESO a través del diseño didáctico. Revista de Educación Científica **1**(1) (2017)
62. Hernández, M., Couso, D., Pintó, R.: Analyzing students' learning progressions throughout a teaching sequence on acoustic properties of materials with a model-based inquiry approach. J. Sci. Educ. Technol. **24**(2–3), 356–377 (2015)
63. Greca, M., Moreira, M.: Modelos mentales y aprendizaje de física en electricidad y magnetismo. Enseñanza de las ciencias: revista de investigación y experiencias didácticas **16**(2) (1998)
64. Justi, R.: La enseñanza de la ciencia basada en la elaboración de modelos. Enseñanza de las ciencias **24**(2), 173–184 (2006)
65. Schwarz, C., Gwekwerere, Y.: Using a guided inquiry and modeling instructional framework (EIMA) to support preservice K-8 science teaching. Sci. Educ. **91**(1), 158–186 (2007)
66. Couso, D., Garrido, A.: Models and modelling in elementary school pre-service teacher education: why we need both. In: Cognitive and Affective Aspects in Science Education Research. Springer International Publishing **1**(3), 245–261 (2017)
67. Tünnermann, C.: Modelos Educativos y Académicos. Brevarios Universitarios (2008)
68. Sierra, R.: Técnicas de Investigación Social: Teoría y Ejercicios (2001)
69. Davis, F.: Perceived usefulness, perceived ease of use and user acceptance of information technology. MIS Q. **13**(3), 319–340 (1989)
70. Venkatesh, V., Davis, F.: A theoretical extension of the technology acceptance model: four longitudinal field studies. Manag. Sci. **46**(2), 186–204 (2000)
71. Venkatesh, V., Morris, M., Davis, G., Davis, F.: User acceptance of information technology: toward a unified view. MIS Q. **27**(3), 425–478 (2003)
72. Venkatesh, V., Bala, H.: Technology acceptance model 3 and a research agenda on interventions. Decis. Sci. **39**, 273–315 (2008)
73. Fogarty, R.: Ten ways to integrate the curriculum. Educ. Leadersh. **49**(2), 61–65 (1991)
74. Fogarty, R.: The Mindful School: How to Integrate the Curricula: Training Manual. IRI/Skylight Publishing (1993)

# Optimizing Training Paths Using Bellman Equations to Improve E-Learning with Q-Learning

Karim Elia Fraoua[1,2]([envelope]) and Amos David[2,3]

[1] Université Gustave Eiffel, Equipe Dispositifs d'Information et de Communication à l'Ere Numérique (DICEN IDF), Conservatoire, Champs-sur-Marne, France
`karim.fraoua@univ-eiffel.fr`
[2] National des Arts et Métiers, Université Paris-Nanterre, EA 7339, Nanterre, France
`amos.David@univ-lorraine.fr`
[3] Université de Lorraine, Equipe Dispositifs d'Information et de Communication à l'Ere Numérique (DICEN IDF), Conservatoire, Metz, France

**Abstract.** In this work, we try to explore new perspectives in order to better structure an online and distance training offer. This approach is done on the basis of a training offer based on the design of an adapted offer, named adaptive learning design. Our choice is to introduce more artificial intelligence which can support this project even if it is necessary to remain on fundamental educational elements such as constructivism. This approach allows us to better understand the issue of algorithmic mediation to facilitate online and distance learning.

**Keywords:** E-Learning · Adaptive Learning · Bellman Equation Q-Learning

## 1 Introduction

Since its appearance, e-learning has continued to evolve to meet increasing demand [1, 2]. Several reasons contribute to this. We cite the most recent ones: a problem of acquiring skills throughout life in order to respond to the evolution of professions [3], the question linked to climate change through rethought mobility [4], societal issues in the broad sense [5, 6], etc. Furthermore, we are also seeing an emerging demand from the public for adapted online or distance learning [7], due to digital fatigue [8], the question of boredom in front of the screen [9] and for this, several proposals are made in order to make learning more dynamic and more interactive [10]. Since then, measures have been designed to focus on a more multifaceted communication and informational reading [11].

An approach has been theorized on the name of Adaptive learning design which is a pedagogical approach that aims to personalize the learning experience according to each learner's needs and preferences [7]. Instead of adopting a one approach for all learners, adaptive learning design adapts to the individual characteristics of each learner to deliver an optimal learning path, which is the series of specific activities and content offered to the

P. Zaphiris and A. Ioannou (Eds.): HCII 2024, LNCS 14723, pp. 146–154, 2024.
https://doi.org/10.1007/978-3-031-61685-3_11

learner throughout the learning process [12]. This path is created by considering information about the learner, such as prior knowledge, skills, motivations, and learning preferences. In our case, considering these aspects, we will try to put a track where the learners can decide himself under the supervision of the teachers through quizzes, tests, ...

E-learning is used in many different contexts, including education, professional training, personal development and continuing education. It is also used in more informal contexts, such as massive open online learning (MOOC), which offers, among other things, the flexibility for learners to access online courses and resources at their own pace and according to their own schedule [13]. This can be particularly beneficial for employees, or people who have other commitments.

We have chosen to base our approach on personalizing this learning and meeting the individual needs of learners in a new way. This can be done by providing learning paths tailored to the needs and objectives of each learner, based on the use of the Bellman equation and Q-Learning which is a reinforcement learning technique used to solve optimal learning problems in sequential environments [14]. Bellman equations play an important role in Q-learning. Bellman's equations express a recursive relationship between the state-action Q value of a state s and an action a, and are used to update Q values over time.

## 2   E-Learning

E-learning, or online learning, is a form of learning that uses information and communication technologies (ICT) to provide distance learning resources and activities. It allows learners to access courses, and educational resources online, anytime, anywhere. In this sense, e-learning offers a certain number of advantages compared to traditional learning methods, through flexibility, accessibility, personalization regarding what we have mentioned previously and in a certain sense efficiency [15]. To go back in detail on these aspects, we can summarize it this way:

- Flexibility: Learners can access online courses and resources at their own pace and based on their schedule and availability.
- Accessibility: E-learning is accessible to people regardless of their location when accessing the online or distance course and new devices help to facilitate this access, such as access via mobile phones or better-designed platforms.
- Personalization: E-learning can be personalized to meet the individual needs of learners, and this is the subject of significant research to meet this challenge
- Effectiveness: E-learning can be effective for acquiring new knowledge and skills if it provides a pleasant and simple learning path that meets the needs of each learner.

It is then obvious to think that e-learning is a form of learning that uses information and communication technologies (ICT) to provide resources and distance learning activities [16]. In order to respond to the challenges that have been mentioned. This allows learners to access courses and educational resources online, anytime, and anywhere.

It is useful to remember that e-learning can take many different forms, including:

- **Online Courses:** Online courses are comprehensive courses that can be taken entirely online. They can be offered by universities, colleges, professional training organizations or companies. We find these devices in particular MOOCs and which will generate the complexity of the creation of adapted courses and in which we will be particularly interested.

- **Online Modules:** Online modules are capsules or a shorter learning unit that can be completed independently. They can be used to complete training or to learn new skills. These are often sufficiently short and therefore only chosen by the learner if they need it and can in certain cases be capsules which then form part of a training course.
- **Online educational resources:** Online educational resources include e-books, articles, videos, quizzes, and simulations. They can be used to support online learning or for independent learning.

## 3   Adaptive Learning Design

Adaptive learning design is an educational approach that uses data-driven instruction to personalize and adapt learning experiences to meet the individual needs of each learner [17]. This involves continuously monitoring student progress, engagement and performance and using this information to adjust teaching materials, activities, and assessments to optimize the student's learning journey. This is based on five key principles for adaptive learning design [18]:

1. Personalization: Tailor learning experiences to each student's strengths, weaknesses, learning styles and preferences.
2. Feedback: Provide targeted and timely feedback to help students identify and resolve their errors and misunderstandings.
3. Differentiated instruction: Providing multiple pathways to learning materials to accommodate different learning styles and needs.
4. An adapted pace: Adjust the pace of teaching so that it corresponds to the learning speed and understanding of each student.
5. Flexible Pathway: Give students the opportunity to navigate the learning materials and activities at their own pace and in a way that suits their learning preferences.

This form of learning has several advantages to help design adaptive learning paths:

1. Adaptive learning provides personalized feedback and challenging tasks that engage students and keep them motivated.
2. Improved learning outcomes: Adaptive learning helps students learn more effectively by meeting their individual needs.
3. Adaptive learning can help students master concepts faster by providing targeted instruction and support while reducing boredom and digital fatigue.
4. Adaptive learning can help ensure that all students have access to high-quality education, regardless of their learning difficulties.

The challenges of designing adaptive learning on which we rely to implement our model are based on the collection and analysis of data which will provide information relating to students, at their level but also in their way of doing things learning and also to enable the development of effective adaptive algorithms through the design of algorithms capable of accurately assessing student needs and providing personalized teaching.

Despite the challenges, adaptive learning design has the potential to evolve education by providing personalized and effective learning experiences for all students. It is for this reason that we must understand that AI and machine learning tools are developing every day and today we see to what extent large model languages such as ChatGPT are integrating the space of users, particularly among students, and this is why we continue to participate in this new way of thinking about more innovative adaptive learning solutions [19].

## 4  Le Q-Learning

Q-Learning is a reinforcement learning algorithm that allows an agent to learn the best action to take in a given state. It is based on the Q function, which represents the expected value of an action in a given state. The agent learns the Q function by experiencing and receiving rewards for its actions [14] (Fig. 1).

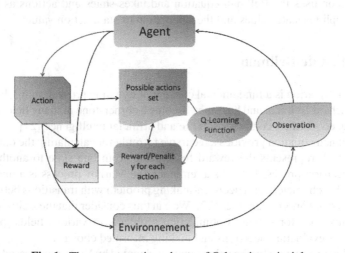

**Fig. 1.** The representative scheme of Q-learning principles

Indeed, to fully understand the principle of how the Q-Learning algorithm works, we must analyze the operating diagram which is as follows:

1. The agent starts with a random Q function.
2. The agent takes an action in its current state.
3. The agent receives a reward for his action.
4. The agent updates the Q function to reflect the reward received.
5. The agent repeats its action until it reaches a terminal state.

We must clarify that this type of algorithm is called off-policy. In fact, this type of method aims to evaluate the policy which has been chosen and to improve it and which is different from that taken to make decisions during learning unlike the on-policy, since in this case the policy that is evaluated and improved is the same one used to make decisions during learning. Off-policy algorithms are therefore algorithms that use a policy different from that of the agent, which makes it possible to make better decisions and collect behavioral data from the agent in order to update its knowledge of the environment [20]. This means that the agent follows a different policy than the one it uses to explore the environment. This explains that the agent will update its action in order to optimize its reward. By thus offering several possibilities to act through different choices and by indicating their degree of difficulty according to the data collected on the agent's behavior. This algorithm makes it possible to solve problems where the agent must learn to make decisions in a complex and uncertain environment, which may be the case when choosing courses to follow online and in which there are several possible choices and that the levels are different or in the courses in which it is necessary to choose learning capsules and choose a learning order.

### 4.1 Q-Function

The Q function uses the Bellman equation and takes states and actions as input. The equation simplifies state values and the calculation of state-action values.

## 5 Equation de Bellman

The Bellman equation is a fundamental concept of dynamic programming. It was introduced by Richard Bellman and has since become a cornerstone in many fields, including engineering, economics, computer science and artificial intelligence [21].

The Bellman equation provides a recursive formula for calculating the optimal value function, which represents the reward for moving from one state to another state in a Markov decision process [21]. As a reminder, the Markov process is a mathematical framework that characterizes a decision-making problem with transitions between states and associated rewards or penalties [22]. We can thus consider that the Bellman equation is an effective tool for solving optimization problems in various fields, providing a framework for evaluating decisions and making informed choices.

The Bellman equation for the value function, denoted by V(s), is expressed as follows:

$$V(s) = R(s) + \gamma \, \Sigma \big[ p(s'|s, \, a) V(s') \big]$$

where:

- V(s): The value function at state s, representing the expected cumulative reward or cost of reaching that state.
- R(s): The immediate reward or penalty received in state s, or the immediate reward or penalty obtained upon reaching the current state
- $\gamma$: The discount factor, which indicates the relative importance of immediate rewards compared to future rewards ($\gamma < 1$ for discounted rewards, $\gamma = 1$ for non-discounted rewards).
- p(s'|s, a): The probability of moving from state s' to state s after performing action a.

## 5.1   4-Bellman's Equations for Q-Learning

In the case of Q-Learning Bellman's equation for the state-action value function (Q-value) is:

$$Q(s, a) = (1 - \alpha) \cdot Q(s, a) + \alpha \cdot \left(r + \gamma \cdot \max_a Q(s', a)\right)$$

where:

- $Q(s, a)$: the state-action value for state s and action a.
- $\alpha$: the learning rate, which controls the updating of Q.
- r: the reward observed after taking action a in state s.
- $\gamma$: the discount factor, which gives priority to short-term rewards versus long-term rewards.
- s: the following state after taking action a.

As we see that Q-learning uses a dynamic approach to estimate the best action. Thus, we can gradually adjust the Q values using the observed rewards to update the estimates. This process of updating Q values based on Bellman's equations makes it possible to converge towards optimal Q values, which represent the best action strategy in each state to maximize the long-term cumulative reward.

This allows the agent to efficiently learn to make the best decisions, leveraging knowledge acquired over time. So, if the agent has not taken the correct capsule, this will allow him to review his choice and thus make the best choice subsequently. It is this dynamic of action that we try to implement in order to achieve optimal learning.

Let's suppose that the agent is currently in a position in the course module matrix and chooses to move to the right. The agent then reaches a new position in the matrix. In fact, the matrix represents the set of choices available once the first module has been acquired, and he receives a reward r accordingly. This situation arises in the case where the learner finishes a training module and chooses a new module, then he can say that he has acquired certification for this module, which will be his reward.

Q-learning repeats this process, adjusting Q-values according to accumulated experience, until the values converge towards optimal values, enabling the agent to make optimal decisions in its environment to maximize cumulative reward. When reinforcement learning problems are formulated as Markov decision processes, Bellman's equations allow us to decompose the value of a state in terms of immediate rewards and expected future rewards. Ultimately, this enables us to build an optimal learning path, thus helping learners to achieve success.

Effectively, the learner is exploring an environment in a matrix of course modules. The matrix has several states represented by cells, and the learner seeks to go from a starting point, which will be his initial state where he has no knowledge, to an end point, which would be the final state where he has acquired sufficient knowledge to pass his exam as illustrated here. The learner can move in four directions: up, down, left and right. The aim is to find the optimum path between the start and finish states, while minimizing the number of steps taken, so as not to make the learning journey boring and tiring. It is for this reason that Q-Learning can be used to solve this type of problem, which can arise for a learner who has several modules in front of him or her, in order to reach the end of the course and avoid failures while enabling an efficient and enjoyable learning path, which we see a lot of in the case of MOOCs or online courses, or in our own online courses. The learner seeks to estimate the value function, which represents the cumulative reward expected when starting from a particular state and implementing specific actions, but in this process, he is sometimes alone to choose, and may start a course only to fail in the middle and give up (Fig. 2).

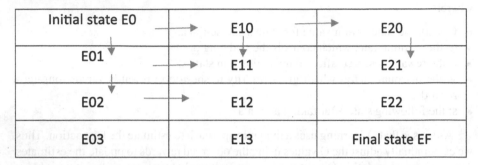

**Fig. 2.** Matrix of action of the learner during learning process

During the learning process, the exploration strategy plays a crucial role in the search for the optimal policy. Initially, the learner must have sufficient information to explore the various state-action pairs to gather information about the environment, before gradually moving on to exploiting the Q-values learned to select actions. This balance between exploration and exploitation is essential for optimum performance. It's at this level that we need to set up support systems to enable assessment devices to be used right from the start of the chosen module, to indicate to the learner whether he or she can access the reward r corresponding to the new target state. We can also set up intermediary devices to enable the learner to take another path if we feel he or she is at risk of failing to reach this new state. Bellman's equations allow us to calculate the value of each state as a function of the immediate reward and the value of successive states. For example, if we're in a state where we have a high probability of winning, the value of that state will be high. On the other hand, if we're in a state where we have little chance of winning, the value of that state will be low.

## 6   Conclusion

In this work we try to show that the use of AI will make it possible in the future to better support learners in their learning in order to be more successful and avoid the problems of boredom and dropping out during online courses. Which for many and although they are interesting and useful are thought of in a linear way, and even if they can be followed by a majority of learners, they constitute a difficulty for many as well. We think that adapted courses need to be put in place and what we are currently trying to put in place by using different platforms, either local by putting courses with different possible choices at each stage or by using platforms open free to university institutions and which make it possible to build learning paths or separate modules which can in themselves constitute learning paths and we thank Datacamp in particular for giving us this opportunity and thus offering our students this possibility of improving their skills.

# References

1. Zhang, D., Nunamaker, J.F.: Powering e-learning in the new millennium: an overview of e-learning and enabling technology. Inf. Syst. Front. **5**, 207–218 (2003)
2. Corbeil, J.R., Corbeil, M.E.: E-learning: past, present, and future. In: International Handbook of E-Learning, vol. 1, pp. 51–64. Routledge (2015)
3. National Research Council. Education for Life and Work: Developing Transferable Knowledge and Skills in the 21st Century. National Academies Press (2012)
4. Henriksen, C.B., Monty, A., Porter, J.R.: E-learning, climate change and carbon footprints. In: IOP Conference Series. Earth and Environmental Science, vol. 6, no. 39. IOP Publishing (2009)
5. Aboagye, E., Yawson, J.A., Appiah, K.N.: COVID-19 and E-learning: the challenges of students in tertiary institutions. Soc. Educ. Res. 1–8 (2021)
6. Olasina, G.: Human and social factors affecting the decision of students to accept e-learning. Interact. Learn. Environ. **27**(3), 363–376 (2019)
7. Gros, B., García-Peñalvo, F.J.: Future trends in the design strategies and technological affordances of e-learning. In: Spector, M., Lockee, B., Childress, M. (eds.) Learning, Design, and Technology, pp. 1–23. Springer, Cham (2016). https://doi.org/10.1007/978-3-319-17727-4_67-1
8. Amponsah, S., van Wyk, M.M., Kolugu, M.K.: Academic experiences of "zoom-fatigue" as a virtual streaming phenomenon during the COVID-19 pandemic. Int. J. Web-Based Learn. Teach. Technol. (IJWLTT) **17**(6), 1–16 (2022)
9. Horton, W., Horton, K.: Bring top classroom features online–no more boredom. e-Learn. Developers' J.–Des. Strategies (2002)
10. Fraoua, S.C., Zara, G., David, A.: Learning by serious game: case study. In: ICERI2020 Proceedings, pp. 5643–5650. IATED (2020)
11. Fraoua, K.E., Leblanc, J.-M., Charraire, S., Champalle, O.: Information and communication science challenges for modeling multifaceted online courses. In: Zaphiris, P., Ioannou, A. (eds.) HCII 2019, Part I. LNCS, vol. 11590, pp. 142–154. Springer, Cham (2019). https://doi.org/10.1007/978-3-030-21814-0_12
12. Ennouamani, S., Mahani, Z.: An overview of adaptive e-learning systems. In: 2017 Eighth International Conference on Intelligent Computing and Information Systems (ICICIS), pp. 342–347. IEEE (2017)
13. (MOOC), which offers, among other things, the flexibility for learners to access online courses
14. Jang, B., Kim, M., Harerimana, G., Kim, J.W.: Q-learning algorithms: a comprehensive classification and applications. IEEE Access **7**, 133653–133667 (2019)
15. Bezovski, Z., Poorani, S.: The evolution of e-learning and new trends. In: Information and Knowledge Management, vol. 6, no. 3, pp. 50–57. IISTE (2016)
16. Yusuf, N., Al-Banawi, N.: The impact of changing technology: the case of e-learning. Contemp.Issues Educ. Res. (CIER) **6**(2), 173–218 (2013)
17. Peng, H., Ma, S., Spector, J.M.: Personalized adaptive learning: an emerging pedagogical approach enabled by a smart learning environment. Smart Learn. Environ. **6**(1), 1–14 (2019)
18. Vesin, B., Mangaroska, K., Giannakos, M.: Learning in smart environments: user-centered design and analytics of an adaptive learning system. Smart Learn. Environ. **5**, 1–21 (2018)
19. Alshahrani, A.: The impact of ChatGPT on blended learning: current trends and future research directions. Int. J. Data Netw. Sci. **7**(4), 2029–2040 (2023)

20. Levine, S., Kumar, A., Tucker, G., Fu, J.: Offline reinforcement learning: tutorial, review, and perspectives on open problems. arXiv preprint arXiv:2005.01643 (2020)
21. Bellman, R.: A Markovian decision process. J. Math. Mech. 679–684 (1957)
22. Dynkin, E.B.: Theory of Markov Processes. Courier Corporation (2012)

# A Real-Time Learning Progress Indicator Updater for Non-reactive Instances in Learning Management System Courses - A User Requirement Based on Evaluation

Tina John[✉]

Technische Hochschule Lübeck, Mönkhofer Weg 239, 23562 Lübeck, Germany
tina.john@th-luebeck.de

**Abstract.** The Onlinecampus Pflege project is developing a learning platform for the acquisition of digital competences for professional nurses. A specific course design for the Moodle instance meets the target group's need for less navigation effort. All activities are needless embedded in the course without links. In this framework, learning progress indicators are not updated as expected, because in the traditional Moodle course design the page and the progress indicators are reloaded frequently whenever a user accesses an activity link. With the special course design, page reloads are not necessary and therefore the indicators are not updated. Evaluations of the platform show that the usability of the platform is high. However, the user misses the real-time updates of the provided progress indicators. The literature supports the positive impact of learning progress indicators. In order to provide the best user experience, the Moodle plugin Live Course Progress UI Updates has been developed that updates learning progress indicators in real-time. The solution preserves the highly rated course design and satisfies the user's desire. The plugin is extensible to any other user interface that needs to respond to activity completion events. This makes it ideal for existing user interfaces. New front-end developments could still try to use Moodle's reactive library. At the very least, frontends should be implemented with unique identifiers and easy-to-call isolated routines for potentially mutating values.

**Keywords:** progress indicator · professional health care · moodle plugin

## 1 Introduction

In the digital age, learning management systems (LMS) like the widely adopted Moodle [1] play a crucial role in delivering online education. The project Onlinecampus Pflege [2, 3] develops an online training that supports the acquisition of digital skills specifically for the success of good care. Nursing is a diverse profession, and so are the digital skills of professional nurses. The learning environment of the target group is characterised by a generally small space for training periods. For the online training a Moodle instance was developed that keeps the navigation effort low and offers quick access to very short learning units to meet the requirements of the target group.

© The Author(s), under exclusive license to Springer Nature Switzerland AG 2024
P. Zaphiris and A. Ioannou (Eds.): HCII 2024, LNCS 14723, pp. 155–169, 2024.
https://doi.org/10.1007/978-3-031-61685-3_12

Development took place iteratively, with the platform being evaluated for each stage of development. Starting with the evaluation of the minimally viable product, through a pre-test for the first test-phase to a third-test phase, which is currently still pending.

A minimum viable product of the platform was created. It contained the platform, one course but no gamification elements. The first MVP was evaluated informally by colleagues. Special attention was paid to the technical functionality of the platform and the self-learning controls, as well as to the media-didactic implementation and the comprehensibility of the content. The main results of the MVP-test confirmed the technical functionality of the platform and the self-learning controls. The media didactic implementation and the comprehensibility of the content were also rated as successful. However, the lack of gamification elements was noted negatively and a specific request was made to add these. As several studies have shown, in most cases a progress indicator motivates the user to complete or continue the task [4–6].

Moodle provides many such indicators. However, the Moodle instance design with low navigation effort does not work well with Moodle's progress indicators. To provide the best possible user experience, the aim of this article is to find the cause of the problem and to present a solution in the form of a Moodle plugin.

## 1.1 Some Features of Moodle LMS

Moodle's flexibility allows for course personalization and customization, accommodating different learning preferences and needs. Instructors can leverage customizable features, such as customizable course formats, themes, and user profiles, to create a visually appealing and personalized learning environment. Customization options empower instructors to adapt course materials to cater to diverse learner requirements, increasing learner motivation and satisfaction.

**Courses and Media-Didactic Preparation of the Learning Material.** One key aspect that contributes to successful online learning experiences is the careful design of courses within Moodle. A well-designed Moodle course starts with clearly defined learning outcomes that align with the educational objectives. By establishing measurable goals, instructors can structure the course content, activities, and assessments in a coherent manner. Breaking down the course into logical sections, topics, or modules enhances navigability and ensures a smooth learning journey for students.

Moodle supports the integration of various multimedia elements, such as videos, audio clips, images, quizzes, and interactive simulations. In addition to the native activities, Moodle offers the embedding of interactive content of the HTML5 package (H5P [7]). Utilizing these tools can stimulate learners' engagement and facilitate diverse learning styles. Instructors can incorporate multimedia content strategically to present information, explain complex concepts or provide real-world examples, fostering active learning experiences.

In practice, a course is a set of multimedia content, activities and assessments arranged in different sections. The most common way to deliver learning material is to provide a link that, when clicked, displays the content in a new page.

**Progress Indicators.** Moodle offers a range of features and tools to track users' learning progress. Moodle allows learners to track their progress in a course or module. With activity information and a table of contents of all tasks (completed and remaining), users are kept informed of their progress within a course. With a gradebook learners have access to their own grades and can monitor their performance throughout the course and get an overview of their personal development.

The course designer can enable different ways of triggering progress. One way is to allow users to manually mark the content they are working on as completed, and another is to set rules such as the activity must be viewed by users, a grade must be received, and a grade must be passed. The latter is often used for activities and assessments.

Although Moodle provides a number of features and tools for tracking users' learning progress, the default theme and course format do not include a progress bar.

## 1.2 Learning Platform for the Acquisition of Digital Competences for Professional Nurses

In order to meet the needs of the target group, with varying levels of digital literacy and generally limited time for training, the platform is designed to break learning down into very short periods of time, keeping navigation effort to a minimum and providing quick access to the very short learning units. The learning offer is divided into modules, module areas and these in turn into very small learning units of 5–20 min workload. In each of these learning units, knowledge, skills and/or attitudes are trained. At the end of each learning unit there is a learning assessment. For the selection of learning units the ISy Metaselect Moodle Plugin [8] is used, which offers filters for modules, module areas and scheduled workload via corresponding metadata using the ISy Meta Moodle Plugin [9]. Alternatively, the system offers predefined learning paths visualized via the learning progress indicator Learning Plans Progress X Version [10] (a further development of the Learning Plans Progress [11]). Each learning path suggests a didactically meaningful order of the learning units based on the competences and the competency framework linked to courses. Learning paths can also be compiled individually by the user according to his or her interests.

**Courses and Media-Didactic Preparation of the Learning Material.** The Moodle instance is customized with the Buttonsx [12] course format. Buttonsx is a version of the Buttons course format [13] specially developed for the Moodle instance. It supports the division of the learning content into even smaller learning bites. "At any time, only one section is visible and the user can change the current section by clicking on the corresponding button" [12]. The content of the learning units is prepared using the variety of multimedia elements Moodle offers. Texts, images, videos with transcripts, podcasts with transcripts and interactive elements from the more than 50 different H5P content types are strung together in different ways, taking into account didactic considerations. H5P provide automatic correction, which is essential for the design as a self-learning tool, and are reusable with less effort - an advantage used for other features of the platform not discussed here.

**Progress Indicators.** Both of Moodle's strategies for marking progress are used. Users must manually mark knowledge acquisition content as completed, while learning assessments are automatically completed when defined criteria are met. The Moodle theme

LearnR [14] provides a progress bar for all course formats. This theme is used to improve the user experience in relation to progress indicators. In addition to the within course progress bar provided by the theme and the basic tools of Moodle for tracking learning progress, Game [15] is used as gamification tool, where user can track their own learning progress and compare it with other users.

**Measures to Keep the Navigation Effort to a Minimum.** The navigation outside and inside a course is designed to keep the effort minimal. Therefore, all activities are embedded in the course with direct access. There are no links provided that opens the activity in a new page. In addition to the advantage, that no extra effort is necessary to access the activity the major advantage is the omitted navigation that is necessary to get back from the activities page to the course content. In addition, all icons and links for H5P contents are hidden through the specially developed option in the Buttonsx course format (see above). That way the elements are needless integrated in the course page thus improving the user experience.

The table of contents is disabled because, on the one hand, it offers links that open activities in new windows, and on the other hand, this link is technically not compatible with the embedding of the activities.

## 2 Evaluation Method Used in the Iterative Development Process

The evaluation was based on questionnaires already tested in other projects, adapted to the current platform in terms of the format of the learning materials and the target group. The evaluation was divided into four categories. To assess the subjective usability of the learning platform, the 10-item SUS (System Usability Scale) was integrated into the evaluation as a standardised instrument [16]. In addition, the evaluation questionnaire included a short scale to assess technical readiness [17]. The participants' readiness to use the technology is assessed as a potential factor influencing response behavior. The platform was evaluated using a psychometric scale (Likert-type).

SociSurvey [18] were used for the General Data Protection Regulation (GDPR)-compliant implementation and data collection. The evaluation was embedded as activity within a course of the Moodle instance. After data collection, data were analysed using the R programming language [19]. The relative proportions of Likert scale responses were calculated and goodness of fit tests were performed for each of the questions.

The study included additional guideline-based focus groups of up to 90 min in length. Following the data collection phase, the recorded interviews underwent meticulous transcription, ensuring accuracy and completeness of the gathered information. The subsequent analysis employed the qualitative content analysis method [20]. This approach enabled a systematic exploration of the data, facilitating a nuanced understanding of the participants' perspectives. The derivation of deductive overarching categories was grounded in both empirical findings from the project's progression and the interview guideline.

# 3 Methodology

## 3.1 Pre-test

Before the platform went live for the first test-phase with external users, a pre-test was conducted with the focus on the usability of the evaluation questionnaire. However, the pre-test shows some interesting results regarding the problem of progress indicators. Prior to the test, the minimal viable product was extended and comprised three learning units from different modules, the progress bar from the LearnR theme, the Game tool, the learning unit chooser ISy Metaselect and a pre-defined learning path visualized by Learning Plans Progress X Version as described in Sect. 1.2.

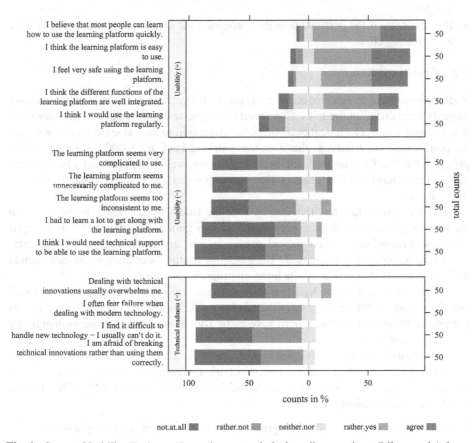

**Fig. 1.** System Usability Scale results and some technical readiness ratings (Likert-scale) from the pre-test. (-) marked ratings have a positive meaning.

The pre-test was conducted with nursing students (n = 30) from the University of Osnabrück. The aim was to test the initial learning content with regard to the content itself and the media-didactic implementation as well as the accuracy of the learning content and learning control tasks. In addition, feedback was obtained on learning on the platform in general.

Students were introduced to the platform and had the task of learning on the platform and filling out the evaluation form (see Sect. 2). The additional qualitative data collection was carried out after a week of testing.

50 questionnaires were returned, because some of the students evaluated the platform twice. For all usability ratings there was a clear more than chance trend (in summary: $\chi^2$ (4, n = 50) > 26.2, p < 0.001) for positive answers (see Fig. 1). The same is true for technical readiness. The most important result for this study from the qualitative data collections is following observation:

- A lot of back and forth clicking [both in terms of finding the content and within the nuggets].
- It is desirable if the percentage in the [progress] bar is constantly updated, can have a motivating effect.

### 3.2 First Test-Phase

The first test-phase was carried out after the pre-test. The platform contained five learning nuggets from different modules. Compared to the pre-test, the evaluation questionnaire was revised. From a technical point of view, navigation to the same destinations within the platform was restricted, so that even less 'clicking back and forth' was required. The progress bar itself has not been changed, but the interval of the platform's background update (cron) has been shortened, on the assumption that the progress should be updated more quickly.

The most important research question for the study, which was to be answered in the first test-phase, was: What experiences do nurses gain when using the Onlinecampus Pflege with regard to the technological, media-didactic and content-related implementation of the learning nuggets offered? The guideline for the focus groups does not include a direct question that addresses the learning progress indicators.

As reported in [21] the trial period had a duration of 10 weeks and was carried out with a total of 90 participants of the target group. The evaluation questionnaire was completed by 38 users. Focus groups were carried out with seven participants in digitally supported interviews.

The learning platform was rated significant (p < 0.001), "easy" to use (88%) and easy to learn (81%) [21]. Again, more information in respect to the current study gave the focus group results. It's mentioned in the derived deductive category of framework conditions and sustainability:

- Embed the score ranking and progress bar more prominently on the platform.

In conclusion, the results of the pre-test and the first test-phase confirmed that the use of the Moodle platform in the chosen form is suitable for offering an online self-learning course. The compact form of the learning units was also well received. The design of the user interface was also highlighted as positive. However, a major problem for an optimal user experience was found in the indicators of learning progress, although or precisely because the participants show a high willingness to use technology.

### 3.3 Analyses of the Progress Indicators

In the first step the operating principles of the existent progress indicators in the Moodle instance were analyzed starting with the indicators in the basic Moodle followed from the analyses of additionally added learning progress indicators in the developed Moodle instance.

**Learning Progress Indicators in Basic Moodle LMS.** All courses a user has enrolled in are displayed in the user's dashboard, a front page for the user where learning units can be selected, and other user-dependent information is visible and accessible. Each of these courses is visualized as a course image with a progress bar indicating the learning progress within the course. This progress bar is updated each time the user returns to the dashboard.

Within a course an optional toggleable course progress sidebar displays all activities in a course visualized as a table of content, where the user can access each of the activities via mouse click. If there was an activity completed it is highlighted. This table of content is updated whenever the page reloads and for manually marked completions it is updated in real time. This sidebar is not part of the Moodle instance but was included in the analyses.

The course activity information is visualized for activities that need to meet defined criteria and provides various information about the completion status of the activity. As the requirements are met, both the color and the information change to indicate that all requirements have been met and the activity is complete. The activity information is updated after a page refresh.

The gradebook displays the grade of the user as a cumulative grade or individual grades for specific activities. It is accessible by the user from within a course to view the course grades but also from the user's profile menu in the header of each page. The gradebook opens a new page.

**Additionally Added Learning Progress Indicators.** The Learning Plan Progress displays a vertical line connecting the steps of the learning path, from where the associated courses can be selected. It highlights already completed learning units and a completed learning path is collapsed and highlighted. The Learning Plan Progress is updated when the user completes a course and gets back to the dashboard.

The course format Buttonsx offers buttons for the navigation that implicitly indicate the upcoming and already attended learning units within the course as far as the user visits the course section in chronological order. However, it is a navigation bar and thus highlights the current section only.

The LearnR progress bar is a traditional progress bar that is visualized as horizontal bar with colored progress indicator and the written information about the percentage of task completion. In accordance to [22] a progress indicator that increases the user experience. Somewhat surprisingly, the progress bar doesn't appear until the user achieved some progress. The progress bar itself is updated after a page refresh.

The Game competition tool visualizes the user's progress in comparison to other users by a score, a level and a ranking. For the individual learning progress within the current level a progress bar is displayed along the information on how much score points are missing to reach the next level. Levels depend on different scores set by the course creator depending on the effort required for each learning activity. All information given by the learning progress indicator updates after the page is reloaded.

**Problem Detection.** The previous section listed many of the predefined learning progress indicators used in the Moodle instance. So it is obvious that they are not missing. All of them visualize the kind of progress that users require in the evaluation. It is not clear whether the Learning Plan Progress met the users' needs as it was not used by the participants in the tests.

It is also obvious from the last section that all the progress indicators update their status after a page reload. Only manually completion is detected in real time and updates at least the sidebar's table of content. As of Sect. 1.2, manual completion is used in the Moodle instance discussed here for all knowledge acquisition but not for learning assessments. Learning assessments are completed rule based and the content is H5P activities.

It follows from the course design described in Sect. 1.1 that page reloads in Moodle are frequent. For example, to complete an activity, learners will open an activity via a link from the table of contents sidebar or the course content page, complete it and then return to the course page. The page will reload, and the activity information and the table of contents sidebar will be updated so that learners can track their progress through the course. After completing the course or selecting a different course, learners access their dashboards via a link that reloads the page. All progress indicators will be updated. The same applies to access to the grade book.

While the latter is also true in the course design for the Moodle instance described in Sect. 1.2, in the former active learning scenario within the course, the page does not reload. As the course is designed for minimal navigation, all activities are embedded in the course page, so there is no jumping back to the course page and an associated reloading of the page. As a result, no learning progress indicator, other than the table of contents in the sidebar for manually completed activities, is updated live. Even the course format ButtonsX is JavaScript based and does not reload any content.

On the one hand, due to the brevity of the learning units, it was not expected that users would recognize the missing updates and interpret the course progress information given as the last accessed progress each time they visit the course to inform them of how much work was still to be done. On the other hand, if there was a progress indicator, it should visualize the progress made.

Although not all learning progress indicator that are available for Moodle (e.g. a block plugin Progress Bar [23]) were tested, it is assumed that the same problem will appear with any of them. Although the Moodle development framework offers a "an adhoc reactive library that can be used to implement small reactive applications on any Moodle page" [24] it is hardly used in external plugins. The table of contents sidebar as progress indicator is a new feature since Moodle 4. The sidebar registers reactive instances that are mutated when a manual completion toggled event is dispatched. In any case, neither there are reactive instances in any of the additionally added progress indicators nor in the user interface for activity information provided by the Moodle core.

The obvious problem is the course design used in the developed Moodle instance. As of Sects. 3.1 and 3.2, the usability of the platform was rated positively and, apart from the learning progress indicators, the platform meets the requirements of the target group. Therefore, a modification of the course design was not the preferred solution. Due to the positive evaluation of the course design, a solution for a live status update of all used learning progress indicators was developed, as presented in the next chapter.

### 3.4 Development of the Moodle Plugin Live Course Progress UI Updates

**Preliminary Considerations.** Prior to the development of a new Moodle plugin, the use of the reactive library of Moodle for all the indicators was discussed. The sidebar successfully uses the reactive library for manual completion, so this is a proof of concept that thus could also be applied to other progress indicator user interfaces. This solution would have required further development of all progress indicators used in the Moodle instance so far. The ButtonsX course design, the LearnR theme, the Game plugin and the activity information would have required further development. The table of contents sidebar was out of view because it was not activated in the course design except for the analyses in Sect. 3.3. This solution would be very far-reaching, as it would affect externally developed plugins and the Moodle core and would also limit further development of the Moodle instance to these indicators, or any other indicators would have to be updated in the same way. Furthermore, it is not clear how Moodle's reactive library can support a client-sided data stream for the rule-based completion data that's mutation happens somewhere in the communication between web services and the database. For manual completion the mutation is given by the user's interactions. If it is marked complete, it is completed. This requires no additional calculation logic.

Since most of the progress indicators in Moodle and in external Moodle plugins do not provide reactive instances, a more flexible solution for all these was seen in the development of a plugin that would allow any learning progress indicator or even other potentially reactive instances in a Moodle course page to be updated in real time without reloading the page. Course progress indicators need to be updated whenever an activity is completed.

The tasks of such a plugin are to listen to events that are triggered by the system whenever a course progress is modified and update the different user interfaces. In more detail listeners need to be implemented for the activity completion events. Each of the user interfaces need to be detected in the DOM and rewritten with the updated progress information. These tasks were implemented in the new Moodle plugin Live Course Progress UI Updates [25].

**Implementation.** Moodle distinguishes between manual completion of activities and completion rules (see Sect. 1.1). The latter are used, at least in the Moodle instance in Sect. 1.2, for activities from the HTML5 package (H5P) for learning assessments. For knowledge acquisition, however, manual completion is used.

Moodle triggers an event for manual completion toggled, but not when completion rules are met. But H5P activities send xAPI statements via the H5P dispatcher from the H5P DOM element. Not all H5P activities return the same statements. Some provide a completion attribute, others do not. However, all xAPI statements return a score attribute. Not all scores necessarily meet the activity completion criterions. Thus, at this point it is not clear if there was any progress that needs to be visualized in the progress indicators. The Moodle core provides web services for the communication between the server-side php web page, the database and the client-side JavaScript functions. However, several useful web services for course completion information are not accessible via AJAX. This means, for example, that it is not possible to get the completion status of an element via AJAX, even though it is already implemented as a web service.

As a solution the plugin adds listeners for both the manual completion toggled event and the H5P dispatcher for xAPI messages with a score attribute, and dispatches a single event itself, with no control over whether the item's completion status has really changed. However, the Moodle instances database is updated after an activity has been completed, so the database data is the most trustworthy.

For each progress indicator used so far in the Moodle instance within a course, web services have been developed and added by the plugin, which call the HTML renderer function of the corresponding plugin for the progress indicator or the whole user interface were necessary. Whenever the single custom event is dispatched, these web services are called, the DOM elements of the indicators are replaced with the new rendered HTML elements, which are rebuilt with the new trusted information from the database.

**Extensibility.** To extend the plugin for other user interfaces that need an update after some activity completion, a new web service needs to be added to the plugin, and the call to that function just needs to be added to the custom event listener. Or plugins can listen to the dispatched custom event and implement their own routine to rewrite the information of the specific DOM element.

### 3.5 Second Test-Phase

The second test-phase took place over three months, half a year after the first with overall 480 users on the platform. The platform provided 18 learning nuggets. Predefined learning paths were added and most important for the current study the Moodle plugin Live Course Progress UI Updates extended the Moodle instance to update the learning progress indicators as demanded by the participants of the first test-phase. The evaluation questionnaire was completed by only 15 users. The learning platform was rated as significant, "save to use" (73%, $\chi^2$ (4, n = 15) = 18, p < 0.01) and "easy to learn" (67%, $\chi^2$ (4, n = 15) = 18, p < 0.01). In general, the same trends as in the pre-test were recognizable, but without reaching statistical relevance.

For the second test-phase the guidelines have been supplemented with the question that addresses the learning progress indicators: How did you perceive the technical functions on the learning platform (e.g. learning paths, learning progress indicators, etc.)? 13 focus groups collected quantitative data with 127 participants. The analyses of the data are still pending. However, there are first impressions from the focus groups. The deductive overarching category technical aspects was derivated from the data. It showed that: Those who have seen the progress indicators, find the indicators an incentive. Some mentioned:

- "I went for the question mark. And there I somehow had over 70 %. And there was still a little bit missing before I would have had my first success, that was there".
- "No, I think I checked, they were right. I still had 13 out of 19 points or something like that. And then I was still kind of at zero percent, I don't know. (laughs)"

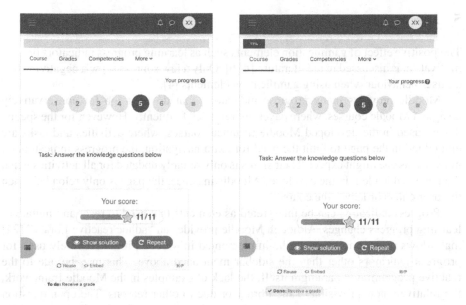

**Fig. 2.** A H5P activity that is scored and completed by the user in the developed and evaluated Moodle instance from the first test-phase (left) with missing updates of the progress indicators (the progressbar at the top and the activity information below the H5P element) and from the second test-phase in (right) with updated progress indicators.

## 4 Results

The Moodle LMS is a suitable solution for a learning platform for the acquisition of digital skills for professional nurses. The special course design in the Moodle instance with less navigation effort meets the requirements of the diverse and special target group. However, the design reduces the page reload frequency. Not all learning progress indicators in Moodle refresh their status without a page reload. Thus, the advantages of such progress indicators are not perceivable in the special course design with less navigation effort like the evaluations in the pre-test and the first test-phase showed. The solution to this problem was to develop a Moodle plugin, Live Course Progress UI Updates. The plugin updates all progress indicators whenever progress is made within a course without reloading the page. Figure 2 shows an example with a progress bar and the activity information of the difference user experience. Without the use of the new plugin the user does not get information about their success. The information section is not updated and still informs about the to do instead of the success done. The progress bar does not show any progress as well. With the use of the plugin both elements are modified and indicate the learning progress.

The preliminary results of the second test-phase suggest a positive effect on the user experience. Some problems still seem to exist. However, these cannot be resolved with the Live Course Progress UI updates.

# 5 Discussion

The positive effect of gamification elements such as learning progress indicators on user motivation is discussed in the literature [4–6]. Only a few sources show a negative effect on user behaviour when using gamification elements [4].

Moodle provides many progress indicators, that do their job for conservatively designed Moodle courses, where pages are reloaded frequently. However, for the special design used in the developed Moodle instance courses, where activities and tasks are embedded in the page to limit the need for extra navigation, the progress indicators do not work as one might expect. Their status is only reliably updated for all activities when the page is reloaded. In the developed Moodle instance, the page is only reloaded when the user enters or leaves the course.

Progress indicators can be interpreted as elements that need to react and mutate as learning progress changes. Although Moodle provides an "adhoc reactive library" [24] that allows reactive instances to be implemented in Moodle, it is not widely used for progress indicators other than the sidebar mentioned above. This may be due to the reactive programming paradigm itself, the lack of examples in the Moodle framework, the relatively new provision of the library or due to other reasons. The open question of how to implement a data stream for the reactive instances for the rule based course progress in the Moodle framework was one of the reasons why this approach was not followed here. However, if there are newer plugins that use reactive instances, there are also older plugins that should be given the functionality to update whenever the course progress has changed. For this reason, the Moodle Live Course Progress UI Updates plugin has been developed (Sect. 3.4).

The advantage of the plugin is that it is independent of any theme, course design or course format. Furthermore, no developments on existing plugins are necessary. The plugin replaces the DOM elements. All the plugin needs to update a DOM element is a web service that calls the function that renders the HTML of the progress indicator DOM element. For existing plugins, the renderer functions are more or less usable for a minimal replacement of DOM elements. In the case of the LearnR theme progress bar, the progress bar is rendered individually and can be replaced with the effort of replacing the entire progress bar. A more minimal effort was to replace or modify the progress bar width value, but there is no renderer for this single element, nor a unique DOM identifier. The same applies to the Game tool and the activity information for rule based completed activities at least for the H5P activities used in the Moodle instance discussed here. A single renderer is provided for the entire Game tool, so it is replaced as a whole. A better way would have been to update the values for each score, level, rank and level progress. To do this, the calculation logic would have to be the target of the web service, the individual DOM elements would have to be found, and the individual values would have to be modified. This is all done by the renderer itself and was therefore considered less efficient and more error-prone than simply replacing the whole DOM element rendered by the native function.

Updating values of DOM elements only, such as progress bar widths, score, level or rank numbers results in a smoother transition than updating the whole element. A smoother transition results in a better user experience. However, if no DOM identifier is available or the computational logic is difficult to isolate, then replacing the entire element using the native functions is the only reliable option.

Experience in the development of this plugin has shown how important it would be for each potentially modifiable element to have a unique identifier in order to provide an interface for interoperability with update functions. This is not a new insight, but therefore even more surprising that accessing different DOM elements was more difficult than expected, even though these elements are predestined for mutations.

The solution of the plugin seems simple and it was expected that such a solution already exists. However, as discussed above, there is no need for this functionality in traditional course design. Furthermore, the Moodle implementation provides many of the necessary interfaces and frameworks, such as events and the ability to use web services. However, the minimal requirements for updating existing DOM elements via JavaScript for rule-based activity completion are hampered by the lack of events that trigger the completion actions at least for H5P activities or the lack of AJAX availability for some of the web services that are provided and are useful for the task of getting information about activity completion. Due to the taboo on modifying the Moodle core implementation, Live Course Progress UI Updates uses other routines to make it work.

Moodle core updates should be taken into account for ease of access. There may be some security reasons for the necessary modifications to the core code, which are not covered at this point. Until then, the Live Course Progress UI Updates will do the job of refreshing the progress indicators. The biggest weakness of the plugin is the renderers called by the web services. Whenever these are changed, the web service needs to be rewritten.

Although not all requirements for the best user experience can be met automatically by the plugin, it does update the progress indicators and this is what the user asked for in the evaluation. The preliminary results of the second test-phase do not suggest that there are any problems with the missing smoothness in the dynamics of the progress indicators. There is no explicit user demand for progress indicators detected anymore. Nevertheless, some problems with the indicators can be derived from the statements of the focus group participants of the last test-phase. These problems can be traced back to setting errors in the individual progress indicators like the points to reach in the Game tool or the H5P activities.

## 6 Conclusion and Outlook

Due to a specific course design for the Moodle instance Onlinecampus Nursing, which meets the target group's need for less navigation effort and which is rated as highly usable by the users, the learning progress indicators are not updated as expected.

Although Moodle provides many of these indicators that work for the traditional Moodle course design and outside of a course, users require live updates of these indicators within a course in the special course design. The literature supports the positive impact of learning progress indicators. In order to provide the best user experience, the Moodle plugin has been developed to enable real-time updates of learning progress indicators within the given framework, although the core Moodle implementation does not provide the simplest way of doing this. The plugin is self-contained and extensible. This means that older Moodle plugins that provide learning progress indicators, or any page elements that need to be updated after an activity has been completed, can be updated via the plugin with less implementation effort. New plugins can try to use Moodle's reactive library to implement reactive elements for the best user experience. At least plugins should be implemented using unique identifiers and easily callable isolated routines for potentially mutating values in the DOM.

The remaining problems with the progress indicators in the Moodle instance will be focused on in the next test-phase. The settings of the activities and progress indicators will be reviewed and corrected accordingly. This is a prerequisite for the updated progress indicators to really show the correct learning progress. Only then does it make sense to use these elements.

**Acknowledgments.** This study was funded by Federal Ministry of Education and Research funding guideline INVITE (grant number 21INVI09).

**Disclosure of Interests.**   The author has no competing interests to declare that are relevant to the content of this article.

# References

1. Moodle Homepage. https://moodle.org/. Accessed 15 July 2023
2. Wulff, S., Borcherding, G., Pengel, J., Meißner, A., Hülsken-Giesler, M.: Onlinecampus Pflege: Für kompetenten Umgang mit digitalen Technologien in der beruflichen Pflege qualifizieren. Zeitschrift Sozialmanagement **20**(1), 131–138 (2022)
3. Borcherding, G., Hülsken-Giesler, M., Meißner, A.: Digitale Kompetenzen erwerben. Pflegezeitschrift **74**, 38–41 (2021). https://doi.org/10.1007/s41906-021-1145-0
4. Mustafa, A.S., Karimi, K.: Enhancing gamified online learning user experience (UX): a systematic literature review of recent trends. Hum.-Comput. Interact. Beyond-Part I 74–99 (2021). https://doi.org/10.2174/9789814998819121010007
5. Conrad, F.G., Couper, M.P., Tourangeau, R., Peytchev, A.: The impact of progress indicators on task completion. Interact. Comput. **22**(5), 417–427 (2010). https://doi.org/10.1016/j.intcom.2010.03.001
6. Hanus, M.D., Fox, J.: Assessing the effects of gamification in the classroom: a longitudinal study on intrinsic motivation, social comparison, satisfaction, effort, and academic performance. Comput. Educ. **80**, 152–161 (2015)
7. H5P Homepage. https://www.h5p.org. Accessed 15 July 2023
8. ISy Metaselect Homepage. https://github.com/ild-thl/moodle-block_isymetaselect. Accessed 15 July 2023
9. ISy Meta Homepage https://github.com/ild-thl/moodle-local_isymeta. Accessed 15 July 2023
10. Learning Plan Progress X Version Homepage. https://github.com/tinjohn/moodle-block_lpprogressx. Accessed 15 July 2023
11. Learning Plan Progress Homepage. https://moodle.org/plugins/block_lpprogress. Accessed 15 July 2023
12. John, T.: tinjohn/moodle-format_buttonsx: Buttonsx - an evolution of the Buttons course format for Moodle (rv1.0.0). Zenodo (2022). https://doi.org/10.5281/zenodo.10523527
13. Buttons Hompage. https://moodle.org/plugins/format_buttons. Accessed 15 July 2023
14. LearnR Hompage. https://moodle.org/plugins/theme_learnr. Accessed 15 July 2023

15. Game Hompage. https://moodle.org/plugins/block_game. Accessed 15 July 2023
16. Brooke, J.: SUS: a "quick and dirty" usability scale. In: Jordan, P.W., Thomas, B., Weerd-meester, B.A., McClelland, A.L. (eds.) Usability Evaluation in Industry. Taylor and Francis, London (1996)
17. Neyer, F., Felber, J., Gebhardt, C.: Entwicklung und validierung einer kurzskala zur erfassung von technikbereitschaft. Diagnostica **58**, 87–99 (2012). https://doi.org/10.1026/0012-1924/a000067
18. SociSurvey: Online Survey Tool Hompage. https://www.socisurvey.com/. Accessed 15 July 2023
19. R Core Team: R: A language and environment for statistical computing. R Foundation for Statistical Computing, Vienna, Austria (2021)
20. Mayring, P., Fenzl, T.: Qualitative Inhaltsanalyse. In: Baur, N., Blasius, J. (eds.) Handbuch Methoden der empirischen Sozialforschung, pp. 633–648. Springer, Wiesbaden (2019). https://doi.org/10.1007/978-3-658-21308-4_42
21. Möller, A.L., et al.: Gute Pflege mit digitaler Unterstützung ermöglichen – das Weiterbildungsangebot für digitale Kompetenzen in der beruflichen Pflege. In: Boll, S., et al. (eds.) Zukunft der Pflege. Tagungsband der 6. Clusterkonferenz 2023: Mit Pflegeinnovationen die Zukunft gestalten – menschlich, professionell, digital, Oldenburg, Germany, pp. 39–43 (2023)
22. Li, Y., Liu, C., Ji, M., You, X.: Shape of progress bar effect on subjective evaluation, duration perception and physiological reaction. Int. J. Industr. Ergon. **81**, 103031 (2021). https://doi.org/10.1016/j.ergon.2020.103031
23. Progress Bar Hompage. https://moodle.org/plugins/block_progress. Accessed 15 July 2023
24. Moodle Reactive Library Homepage. https://moodledev.io/docs/guides/javascript/reactive. Accessed 15 July 2023
25. John, T.: tinjohn/moodle-local_livecoprogressuiups: live course progress UI updates for moodle (rv1.0.0). Zenodo (2023). https://doi.org/10.5281/zenodo.10523027

# Towards SDGR-Compliant Cross-Border Education Services

Tomaž Klobučar[✉]

Jožef Stefan Institute, Ljubljana, Slovenia
klobucar@e5.ijs.si

**Abstract.** Learners face various challenges when accessing online cross-border education services, e.g. when enrolling at foreign universities or applying for scholarships abroad. Challenges include the non-recognition of identification means and difficulties in providing and validating paper evidence. The EU project DE4A has addressed these challenges by implementing and validating the once-only principle across borders in the context of the European Union. This paper describes the infrastructure developed, the educational services improved and integrated into the infrastructure, the user experiences of the students from Portugal, Slovenia, and Spain who used these services, and various lessons learnt from the analysis, design, customisation, integration, and testing. Students appreciated the duration of the improved procedures, the control in managing their own credentials, the security and privacy protection, and the effort required. The improved procedures also benefit educational institutions, which can save considerable time in processing student information, particularly in the validation of higher education diplomas, by obtaining accurate and reliable student data in electronic format. Collaboration between several institutions from Portugal, Slovenia, and Spain has shown that the secure, high-quality, and user-centric cross-border exchange of evidence for online higher education procedures brings tangible benefits that will greatly facilitate student mobility in Europe and reduce the administrative burden.

**Keywords:** Cross-border education service · Single Digital Gateway Regulation · DE4A

## 1 Introduction

Learners face various challenges when accessing online cross-border services. First, their national identification means and study achievements are not always recognised as valid abroad. In addition, educational service providers often require users to provide a set of paper evidence that already exists in domestic or foreign authentic sources, for example higher education diplomas. A better user experience can be achieved in these cases by implementing a once-only principle [1], which aims to ensure that learners provide the required information only once and that authorities can share this information with each other in subsequent procedures, taking into account the protection of personal data and with the consent of the individuals concerned. The once-only principle also benefits the authorities, as the evidence required for the procedures comes from trustworthy sources,

© The Author(s), under exclusive license to Springer Nature Switzerland AG 2024
P. Zaphiris and A. Ioannou (Eds.): HCII 2024, LNCS 14723, pp. 170–181, 2024.
https://doi.org/10.1007/978-3-031-61685-3_13

usually in electronic form, which is easier to process. While this principle is relatively easy to ensure at national level, its implementation across borders remains a challenge.

This paper focuses on the context of the European Union and the Single Digital Gateway Regulation (SDGR) [2]. Under the SDGR, all EU Member States were required to establish an EU-wide technical system for the cross-border automated exchange of evidence and the application of the once-only principle by the end of 2023. The SDGR lists a number of procedures that cross-border users must be able to access fully online if these procedures are already online for domestic users in a Member State in areas such as studying, working, moving, retiring, or starting a business [2]. In the area of studying, these procedures are (1) applying for funding for tertiary education, such as scholarships and loans, from a public body or institution, (2) submitting a first application for admission to a public higher education institution, and (3) applying for academic recognition of diplomas, certificates or other evidence of studies or training.

For the past few years, the European Commission and the Member States have been working on a technical system for the SDGR compliant cross-border exchange of evidence. Evidence is defined here as any document or data required by a competent authority, e.g. ministries or universities, to prove facts or compliance with the requirements of the above mentioned procedures [2]. This paper describes how the EU project DE4A (Digital Europe for All; https://www.de4a.eu) enabled and validated the implementation of the once-only principle across borders in the higher education domain and improved the experience of the learners using cross-border education services, such as enrolment to foreign universities. Various approaches to enable the once-only principle have been designed, implemented, and validated within the DE4A [3]. These approaches, which are more user-centric and privacy-friendly than previous attempts, such as in [4], differ in the role of the user, the interaction patterns, the location of the evidence preview and consent to cross-border transmission and use of educational data, and the technology for data exchange. Implementing and piloting different approaches on a large scale was an important step towards a common solution that meets the SDGR requirements and the needs of the Member States, ensures the security and privacy of the users, and provides a satisfactory user experience.

The structure of the paper is as follows. In Sect. 2, use cases and a technical system for the provision of cross-border services and the exchange of evidence are presented, while Sect. 3 gives an example of an education service that was integrated with the system. User experience of the students validating the services is analysed in Sect. 4, and the lessons learnt are summarized in Sect. 5.

## 2 Use Cases and Once-Only Technical System

### 2.1 Use Cases

In the education domain, the project focused on higher education students with virtual or physical mobility needs in the European Higher Education Area. By piloting three use cases (UC#1 - Application to public higher education, UC#2 - Applying for a study grant, and UC#3 - Diploma recognition) it aimed to validate processes/procedures (c.f. Annex II of SDGR [2]) for students from the three participating Member States (Portugal,

Slovenia, and Spain) for registration to higher education abroad and eventually applying for a student grant as well as for studies recognition [5]:

- UC#1: The first use case focused on the procedure for applying for admission to public higher education institutions abroad. This procedure corresponds to the "Submitting an initial application for admission to public tertiary education institution" procedure from Annex II of the SDGR [2]. Portugal, Slovenia, and Spain were involved in this use case. Portugal and Slovenia implemented applications to both Bachelor and Master programmes, while Spain only to Master programmes because enrolment in Bachelor programmes is a matter of regional governments.
- UC#2: The second use case focused on the procedure of applying for a study grant abroad. This procedure corresponds to the "Applying for a tertiary education study financing, such as study grants and loans from a public body or institution" procedure from Annex II of the SDGR [2]. Slovenia and Spain participated in this use case: Slovenia as service provider (data consumer) and Spain as data provider.
- UC#3: The third case focused on diploma recognition. This procedure corresponds to the "Requesting academic recognition of diplomas, certificates or other proof of studies or courses" procedure from Annex II of the SDGR [2]. Portugal and Slovenia were involved in this use case as issuers and verifiers of higher education diplomas in the form of verifiable credentials, and Spain only as issuer of verifiable credentials.

## 2.2 Interaction Patterns

As mentioned in the introduction, various approaches for enabling the once-only principle, represented by interaction patterns, were designed, implemented, and validated within the DE4A [3]. Two of them are relevant for the present work: the user-supported intermediation pattern (validated in UC#1 and UC#2) and the supported user-managed access pattern (validated in UC#3) [3]. In both cases, a learner interacts directly with an educational service provider and a trusted source of educational data. The difference between the two approaches lies in the way evidence is transferred to a service provider. In the first case, learners preview their evidence at the authentic source of evidence and approve direct cross-border transfer from the source to the service provider. In the second case, learners download their evidence to the digital wallet and submit the evidence to the service providers by themselves, i.e., there is no direct interaction between the data and the service providers.

## 2.3 Canonical Evidence

The concept of canonical evidence was introduced to ensure cross-border data interoperability between data consumers and data providers and compliance with the legal requirements of the selected procedures [6]. As there is no yet a standardised electronic representation of evidence for specific use cases agreed upon by all EU member states and the results of the Deloitte study showed that there is little overlap in the attributes that compose academic evidence in the different Member States [7], we first identified the evidence that is required by the participating service providers (data consumers) and can be provided by the data providers within the project, and defined data models for this evidence, largely based on the EDCI data model [8].

Four types of canonical evidence were defined for the services in the higher education domain. The first type (higher education diploma) proves that an individual has obtained a higher education diploma, while the second type (secondary education completion) proves that an individual has completed secondary education [9]. These canonical evidences were primarily used for enrolment in the Master or Bachelor programmes in UC#1. The other two canonical evidence types are related to UC#2 and define non-academic information needed for the purposes of awarding study grants: large family certificate and disability certificate [9]. The large family certificate proves that a student is a member of a large family, while the disability certificate proves that the student has a specific disability. Initially, other evidence types were also considered for piloting this use case, such as the income of the student's family, but it was too difficult to provide this data in all participating countries during the project period.

## 2.4 Infrastructure

In this section, an infrastructure that enables direct interaction between the service and the data providers (user-supported intermediation interaction pattern) is presented. Among the various approaches piloted in the project, this is the closest to that agreed in the latest version of the EU technical design documents of the once-only technical system [10]. The implemented system (see Fig. 1) includes education service providers (data consumers), authentic sources of educational evidence (data providers), identity providers and their authentication Services (AS in Fig. 1), eIDAS [11] nodes for cross-border authentication, and a technical system for the evidence transfer across borders.

**eIDAS Infrastructure.** The eIDAS infrastructure is used for authenticating individuals requesting education services. It consists of a number of interconnected national eIDAS nodes that can either request or provide cross-border authentication. Within DE4A, a preproduction eIDAS infrastructure was used as not all Member States, e.g. Slovenia, had notified their identification scheme in time.

**Data Consumers.** Data consumers in the context of the project are institutions that provide public services. In the higher education domain these can be universities and other higher education institutions, ministries, or regional governments. Table 1 shows the data consumers from the higher education domain that participated in the DE4A project, the use cases in which they were involved, and the type of procedures that were validated.

**Data Providers.** Data providers are institutions that manage data that go beyond the minimum identification data and provide evidence on academic achievements, such as certificate of completion of secondary education or higher education diploma, and non-academic attributes. Here too, the data providers may be universities and other higher education institutions, ministries, or regional governments. Table 2 shows the data providers from the higher education domain that participated in the DE4A project, the use cases they were involved in, and the type of evidence they provided.

In Slovenia, the eVŠ system at the Ministry of Education, Science and Sport of the Republic of Slovenia contains information about all students studying or who have studied at one of the Slovenian higher education institutions (HEI). HEIs feed the eVŠ

**Table 1.** Data consumers

| Institution | Use case | Procedure type |
|---|---|---|
| Universitat Jaume I, Spain | UC#1 (Master programmes) | Real procedure in production |
| INESC-ID, Portugal | UC#1 (Bachelor and Master programmes), UC#3 | Simulated procedure |
| Ministry of Education, Science and Sport, Slovenia | UC#1 (Bachelor and Master programmes), UC#3 | Real procedure in preproduction |
| Jozef Stefan Institute, Slovenia | UC#2 | Simulated procedure |

**Table 2.** Data providers

| Institution | Use case | Evidence type |
|---|---|---|
| SGAD, Spain | UC#1, UC#2, UC#3 | Higher education diploma (real), secondary education diploma (test), large family certificate (test), disability certificate (test) |
| INESC-ID, Portugal | UC#1, UC#2, UC#3 | Higher education diploma (real) |
| Ministry of Education, Science and Sport, Slovenia | UC#1, UC#3 | Higher education diploma (real) |

system with information on study programmes, finished studies and obtained degrees, students who quit the programme, achieved ECTS for the past year, etc. Additional details about temporary achievements during a school year, e.g. marks at exams, are currently available only in the university information systems. In the eVŠ system, the data about students can be accessed over a WSDL-defined web service. The service allows fine-grained access control (entity and attribute based) to be able to define what data an entity has access to and for what purpose.

In DE4A, the eVŠ service in preproduction has been integrated through the Slovenian national system Tray and the central Preview component into the DE4A infrastructure. The service provided real data (higher education degree diplomas) only for preselected students who signed a GDPR form and were using real eIDs.

**Once-Only Technical System.** A system for cross-border evidence transfer, where there is direct interaction between data providers and consumers, is based on an eDelivery network and consists of several components, such as connector and IAL/SMP [12], as shown in Fig. 1.

An evidence transfer system is based on eDelivery [13], an EU building block that helps institutions exchanging data via AS4 access points, based on the AS4 messaging protocol [14]. To help service providers and data sources with sending requests for evidence or responses over an eDelivery network a DE4A Connector was developed in the DE4A project that integrates an AS4 access point [12]. The connector also obtains the message routing information, by exchanging information with external components such as the Central IAL (Issuing Authority Locator) and the SMP (Service Metadata Publisher). In the project, each country set up its own central DE4A connector and all service and data providers exchanged data through their national connectors.

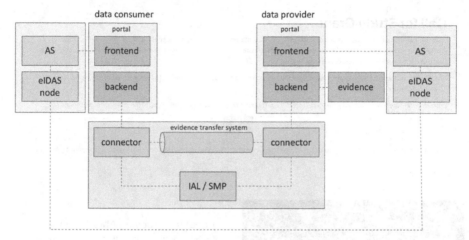

**Fig. 1.** DE4A infrastructure for cross-border services

# 3 Cross-Border Application for Study Grants

One of the education services integrated with the DE4A infrastructure is presented in more detail here. The Jozef Stefan Institute is the biggest research institute in Slovenia. As part of the DE4A project, we have set up a preproduction service where foreign students can apply for study grants. Students from countries participating in DE4A can explicitly request that their diplomas, large family evidence, or disability evidence are securely retrieved from the official repository in the country in which they completed their undergraduate studies or the country in which they reside. The following user journey shows how the portal and the DE4A infrastructure are used for cross-border applications for study grants.

Anna is a Spanish citizen who has just enrolled in the Doctoral programme in computer science at the Jozef Stefan International Postgraduate School in Slovenia and will conduct her research at the Jozef Stefan Institute. She has completed her Master studies at the Universitat Jaume I in Spain. Before starting her studies in autumn, she would like to apply for a Slovenian study grant for foreign EU students to finance her tuition fees and living expenses in Slovenia.

She visits the grants portal (Fig. 2) with information on several calls for study grants, where STEM students from Portugal and Spain who are studying or will study at one of the higher education institutions in Slovenia and conduct their research work at the Institute can apply for a grant. The grants available are both merit and social–based, meaning that the criteria for selecting applicants to receive grants include previous academic performance and the social situation of the applicants. The calls for grants therefore require various combinations of academic and non-academic evidence (higher education diploma, large family evidence, disability evidence) to be submitted.

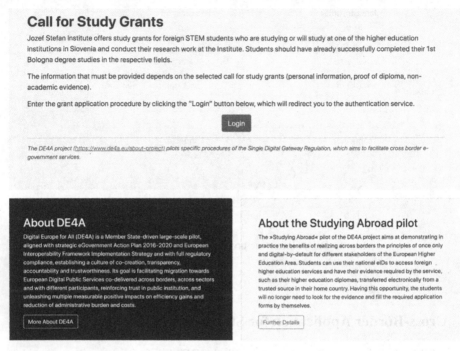

**Fig. 2.** Grant application service

Anna authenticates herself using the Spanish notified eIDAS identification scheme. After successful authentication, she is presented with a list of available calls for study grants. For each call, the evidence types that must be provided as part of the application are displayed.

Once she has selected the desired call, Anna is given a choice to use a DE4A technical system for the automatic transfer of the required evidence from Spain to Slovenia (Fig. 3).

After selecting an authentic evidence source for her evidence and explicitly agreeing to use the DE4A technical system, she is redirected to a national authentic source in Spain. There she authenticates herself again and selects which evidence she wants to be sent across the border. Before the exchange takes place, she has the opportunity to preview the evidence, e.g. the higher education diploma and the large family certificate. The content of the selected evidence is displayed so that Anna can check the validity of the information in the evidence. Once she agrees with the transfer, the evidence is sent directly from the data source in Spain to the grant service in Slovenia, and she is redirected back to the service provider.

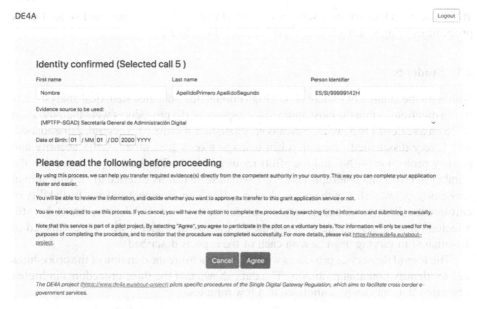

**Fig. 3.**  Grant application service - Explicit request

The data consumer checks the completeness of the data and the validity of the evidence. If the application form is valid, it returns the acknowledgement of receipt of such application. Anna is later informed that her grant application has been approved.

## 4  User Experience

The final infrastructure and the integrated data consumers and data providers within the higher education domain (see Tables 1 and 2) were validated from October 2022 to March 2023 by 104 students: 45 from Spain, 30 from Slovenia, and 29 from Portugal. The grant application service in Slovenia (Use case 2) was used by 28 students, 20 from Spain and 8 from Portugal. In addition, 38 students used the enrolment services in Portugal, Spain, and Slovenia (Use case 1), and 38 student issuance and validation of higher education diplomas in the form of verifiable credentials (Use case 3). Before using the services, students were provided with participation guidelines, which included instructions on how to use the services and recordings of the procedures. The participation guidelines were published on the pilot microsite (https://www.de4a.eu/studyinga broadpilot). Depending on the use case and Member State, students used either real or test identities and real or test academic evidence. After using the service, every student completed an online questionnaire and provided feedback and estimated satisfaction with the effort required, the clarity, simplicity and duration of the procedure, the number of errors and interruptions, language, communication, security and privacy protection, control in managing education credentials, and the overall experience. In addition, university administration staff in the three participating Member States was interviewed to collect their experience with the implemented procedures from the university's point of view. The main focus of the interviews was to obtain feedback on the benefits that DE4A procedures bring to universities, especially the time savings.

## 4.1 Students

Although the number of students is not high enough for a detailed statistical analysis, it is worth mentioning that the most appreciated aspects of the procedures were their duration (4.26 on a scale of 1 to 5, where 5 means very satisfied, 4 satisfied, 3 neutral, 2 dissatisfied, and 1 very dissatisfied), the control in managing own credentials (4.16), security and privacy protection (4.09), and the effort required (4.02). The least appreciated was the number of errors and interruptions (3.52), which were mainly external to the educational services (e.g. instability of the preproduction eIDAS environment and nonavailability of enrolment calls at participating institutions during the whole validation period), but still affected the services. Figure 4 shows the proportion of students who were satisfied or dissatisfied to varying degrees with each of the aspects described.

The logs of the service providers were used to measure the duration of the procedures and to identify potential problems. The data shows that the three procedures in higher education domain can be completed in a few minutes.

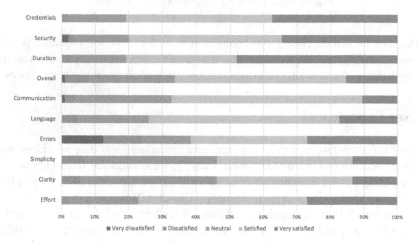

**Fig. 4.** Share of satisfied students per aspect

## 4.2 University Administration

The improved online procedures in the higher education domain also benefit universities and their administration. When foreign students use educational cross-border services in Slovenia, student offices need to validate their diplomas. At this stage, they first search for the contact details of a relevant institution in the particular country and then prepare and submit a diploma validation request. This takes about 30 min per student. It is often difficult for them to find the information on where they need to send a request. In the case of some countries, for example, no contact information is available, and the request must be entered into a special portal. Sometimes, it can take a week before they receive information about the authenticity and validity of the diploma or they do not receive any response at all. The new procedure thus saves at least 30 min of work per foreign student and ensures that the information about the validity of the diploma is always available from a trusted source.

The student office staff at Slovenian universities must also respond to requests from foreign universities to validate the diplomas of Slovenian students using the service abroad. In the case of enrolment for the third Bologna degree, this is done at the university level. For other degrees, an application is forwarded to the relevant faculty, for example. In these cases, it currently takes between 10 and 15 min to complete the form in English and submit it to the foreign institution, which is not necessary anymore with the new procedure.

## 5  Lessons Learnt

In this section, various lessons learnt from the analysis, design, customisation, integration, and testing phases are gathered. Advice is also provided to other educational institutions that will face the mandatory integration of their services with the once-only technical system in the near future.

### 5.1  Analysis and Design

**Evidence.** Semantic interoperability in education is still an issue. Within the project, it was not easy to find a common denominator for academic evidence from the three Member States, as some of the data required by one Member State was not available in another Member State. This problem will only increase when the same is done for the entire European Union. The SDG semantic working group is currently working on the harmonization of evidence in various domains across the EU, including higher education. One issue here is the completeness of data as this is crucial for reducing the burden of processing evidence. If data is missing from the evidence, other channels must be used to retrieve this data.

The challenge is even greater for the non-academic evidence required for the study grant application procedure. Member States are not yet prepared to make such evidence available across borders and the problem becomes greater the more sensitive the data is, such as in the case of evidence of disability or financial information of applicants and their families.

**Multiple Evidence Cases.** Calls for applications for study grants usually ask for different types of evidence, both academic and non-academic. If an authentic source or a national technical system with a centralised preview can provide multiple types of evidence at once, a single request for multiple evidence types can reduce the complexity of the procedure. The DE4A interaction patterns and data models have been designed to allow such requests.

**Clarity and Simplicity of Procedures**
Different cross-border procedures in the higher education domain vary in complexity. Particular attention should be paid to their clarity and simplicity.

### 5.2 Customization, Integration, and Testing

The lessons learnt in the customisation, integration, and testing phase mainly relate to the usefulness of the common components, the documentation, and the collaboration between different entities.

**Integration of Data Consumers and Data Providers**
The concept of a DE4A connector with an integrated AS4 gateway enabled easier integration of data and services providers and cross-border evidence exchange. It is also useful for educational institutions to have access to a test environment or playground where they can test first their integration with common components. Nevertheless, educational institutions planning to integrate their services and data sources with a once-only technical system should not underestimate the integration effort and start preparing their cross-border procedures for integration with national common components.

**Interoperability Testing**
Connectathons, involving developers from all pilot partners, have been beneficial for connectivity and cross-border interoperability between data and service providers. Sharing information about current key technical configurations was of paramount importance, as end-to-end connectivity is entirely dependent on these configurations being implemented correctly. Interoperability testing also requires easy access to the test credentials of sample test participants with various test evidence.

**eIDAS-Based Authentication**
During the pilot, it was found that students typically did not have their eIDAS-based authentication means, e.g. citizen cards, activated for cross-border eIDAS authentication.

## 6 Conclusion

The SDG Regulation and the technical system for its implementation enable the realisation of the once-only principle and secure and seamless cross-border electronic transactions between businesses, organisations, citizens, and public authorities in a variety of areas. In this article, we have shown how the EU project DE4A addressed the problem of implementing and validating a technical system through a pilot in the higher education domain. The collaboration between several institutions from Portugal, Slovenia, and Spain in the DE4A project has proven tangible benefits from the secure, high-quality, and user-centric cross-border exchange of evidence for online higher education procedures that will greatly facilitate student mobility in Europe and reduce the administrative burden.

**Acknowledgments.** The work was supported by the European Commission through the DE4A (Digital Europe for All) project, no. 870635. The author would like to acknowledge the contributions from the project consortium, with special mention of the Studying abroad pilot in the work package 4 – Cross-border pilots for citizens and business and evaluation.

# References

1. Kalvet, T., Toots, M., van Veenstra, A.F., Krimmer, R.: Cross-border e-government services in Europe: expected benefits, barriers and drivers of the once-only principle. In: ICEGOV'18 Proceedings of the 11th International Conference on Theory and Practice of Electronic Governance, pp. 69–72 (2018)
2. European Union: Regulation (EU) 2018/1724 of the European Parliament and of the Council of 2 October 2018 establishing a single digital gateway to provide access to information, to procedures and to assistance and problem-solving services and amending Regulation (EU) No 1024/2012 (2018)
3. Bielowski, A., et al.: D2.7 Interoperability architecture for cross-border procedures and evidence exchange in light of the single digital gateway regulation. DE4A deliverable D2.7 (2022). https://www.de4a.eu/project-deliverables
4. Schmidt, C., Krimmer, R.: How to implement the European digital single market: identifying the catalyst for digital transformation. J. Eur. Integr. **44**(1), 59–80 (2022)
5. Klobučar, T., et al.: D4.4 studying abroad – final running phase. DE4A deliverable D4.4 (2023). https://www.de4a.eu/project-deliverables
6. Karunaratne, T., Kontopoulos, E., Konstantinidis, I., Guzmán Carbonell, A.R.: A canonical evidence-based approach for semantic interoperability in cross-border and cross-domain e-government services. In: Proceedings of ICEGOV 2022 (15th International Conference on Theory and Practice of Electronic Governance), pp. 1–9 (2022)
7. Deloitte: D04.01 – Final Report - Study on Data Mapping for the cross border application of the Once-Only technical system SDG (2020)
8. Europass Digital Credentials Infrastructure. https://europa.eu/europass/en/europass-tools/european-digital-credentials. Accessed 01 Feb 2024
9. Karunaratne, T., Kontopoulos, E.: Supporting learning mobility with student data harmonisation: a European perspective. In: Proceedings of ECEL 2022 (21st European Conference on e-Learning), pp. 156–164 (2022)
10. Technical design documents, v1.0.0 (2023). https://ec.europa.eu/digital-building-blocks/sites/display/OOTS/Technical+Design+Documents. Accessed 01 Feb 2024
11. European Union: Regulation (EU) No 910/2014 of the European Parliament and of the Council of 23 July 2014 on electronic identification and trust services for electronic transactions in the internal market and repealing Directive 1999/93/EC (2014)
12. Ferrero Merchán, J., Berdón Hinojosa, H., Helger, P., Moreno Alcázar, E.: D5.6 final release of DE4A common components. DE4A deliverable D5.6 (2023). https://www.de4a.eu/project-deliverables
13. European Commission: eDelivery. https://joinup.ec.europa.eu/collection/digital-building-blocks/solution/edelivery/about. Accessed 01 Feb 2024
14. OASIS: AS4 profile of ebMS 3.0 version 1.0, OASIS standard (2013)

# Teachers' Perspective on the Implementation of GDPR in Schools – A Design-Oriented Case Study

Emanuela Marchetti[1](✉) [iD], Andrea Valente[1] [iD], Claus Witfelt[2] [iD],
Daniel Amo-Filva[3] [iD], Alicia Garcia-Holgado[4] [iD], Lucia Garcia-Holgado[4] [iD],
Elisabetta Vidotto[5], Maria Elena Garzotto[6] [iD], Francisco José García-Peñalvo[4] [iD],
David Fonseca Escudero[3] [iD], Tihomir Orehovacki[7] [iD], Marjan Krasna[8] [iD],
Igor Pesek[8] [iD], Ivana Ruzic[9] [iD], Karim Elia Fraoua[10] [iD], and Fernando Moreira[11] [iD]

[1] University of Southern Denmark, Kolding, Denmark
{emanuela,aval}@sdu.dk
[2] Oerestad Gymnasium, Copenhagen, Denmark
[3] La Salle, Ramon Llull University, Barcelona, Spain
{daniel.amo,fonsi}@salle.url.edu
[4] University of Salamanca, Salamanca, Spain
{aliciagh,luciagh,fgarcia}@usal.es
[5] Arborio Comprehensive School, Arborio, Italy
elisabetta.vidotto.d@icarborio.edu.it
[6] I.I.S. Eugenio Bona, Biella, Italy
mariaelena.71@iisbona.edu.it
[7] Juraj Dobrila University of Pula, Pula, Croatia
tihomir.orehovacki@unipu.hr
[8] University of Maribor, Maribor, Slovenia
{marjan.krasna,igor.pesek}@um.si
[9] Primary School Čakovec, Čakovec, Croatia
[10] Gustave Eiffel University, Champs-sur-Marne, France
karim.fraoua@univ-eiffel.fr
[11] Universidade Portucalense, Porto, Portugal
fmoreira@uportu.pt

**Abstract.** In this paper, we are interested in investigating how the introduction of GDPR has affected the teachers, with respect to how the new rules have altered their practices, which issues or challenges they have experienced, and which strategies they have developed to overcome such issues. Proceeding from an ecological perspective, we look at schools as complex ecologies, in which every change, happening at various scales and involvement levels, affects each actor in specific ways and at different degrees, altering their practices and mutual relations. Activity theory is also used, as a critical lens to look at teachers' practices that have been disrupted by the increasing digitalization of schools. In our data collection, we adopted a user-centered design methodology, supported by ethnomethodology and co-design workshops in situ and online. According to our data teachers are experiencing pressure with respect to three main aspects: educating themselves and their students about GDPR and use of Social Media (SoMe) platforms, which are

P. Zaphiris and A. Ioannou (Eds.): HCII 2024, LNCS 14723, pp. 182–199, 2024.
https://doi.org/10.1007/978-3-031-61685-3_14

designed to facilitate data sharing on a global scale; how to handle students' data avoiding leaks or potential conflicts, and finally the expansion of the boundaries of the school ecology. This last aspect appears of critical relevance, as the increasing digitalization of education and the spread use of SoMe platforms, has compromised the locality of the school as an ecology, leading to increasing uncertainty and lack of overview on the actions undertaken by its actors.

**Keywords:** GCPR · School Ecology · User-Centered Design · Teaching

# 1  Introduction

General Data Protection Regulation (GDPR) consists of a series or norms on data security and protection. It was emanated on May 2018 by the EU and it is presented as the "toughest" corpus of rules in data protection (https://gdpr.eu/what-is-gdpr/?cn-reload ed=1 – 11/12/23). GDPR targets any organizations collecting data from citizens, to signal the EU's strict position on data privacy and security, hence encouraging citizens to feel safe, while engaging in various practices on the Internet and SoMe platforms. GDPR norms are aimed at providing guidelines to private and public organizations, who handle digital data about citizens [1, 2], while attempting at providing citizens with a sense of security when dealing online transactions.

This study focuses especially on the teachers' perspective on the implementation of GDPR in the schools and has multiple aims:

- Investigating how the implementation of GDPR in schools has affected teachers,
- Enabling teachers to gain new knowledge and evaluate their current knowledge on GDPR,
- Identify requirements to develop a digital tool that could foster understanding on GDPR regulations and implications.

Our study suggests that GDPR regulations has been challenging for teachers, assuming knowledge about digital platforms that does not belong to the core of their teaching and learning practice, and are permeating secondary actions, which teachers typically handle more or less unconsciously while performing tasks related to grading and evaluating students and exchanging information with other teachers. Moreover, students can share inappropriate data about teachers and other students, causing additional issues to the teachers, even when outside of the school, far from the custody of the teachers, yet forcing them to take action.

In this respect, we propose an ecological perspective, leveraging activity theory, analyzing teachers experience with integrating GDPR in the school, to highlight the many subtleties related to the responsibilities assigned to teachers in relation to the integration of GDPR inside the school.

## 2 Data Protection in the Schools

Since the past 10 years teachers are experiencing a tension in their ecology [1, 2], as schools are experiencing a rapid evolution in their digitalization and use of ICT tools. Moreover, in relation to Covid-19 [1, 12] teachers have been pushed to use digital platforms in gathering and exchanging students' data, but on the other hand, they have to be careful about the data they share about the students and how they share them. An increasing pressure on schools to digitalize their practice was pushed by IT companies and research, showing how use of Artificial Intelligence, Machine Learning, and Learning Analytics could enhance improve teaching and learning practices, and facilitate form of personalized learning [1, 22]. Hence use of digital platforms has become a requirement for teachers, most critically during Covid-19 lockdowns, during which digital remote working and learning practices were the only feasible alternatives to face-to-face practices, causing a disruptive technological innovation in schools and society as a whole [11]. This innovation took place amid multiple emergent issues, such as: securing access to all the students in spite of their access to adequate IT infrastructure and Internet connection from home [10–12]. Students experienced issues in relation to lack of connection with teachers and their classmates, the last one leading to a sense of boredom, isolation and lack of engagement all together [11]. The teachers, however, were challenged in keeping the attention of their students, trying to balance individual and collaborative engagement for their students, hence being pushed to adopt new digital platforms which were not familiar to them. As pointed out by Petterson [18] this sudden digitalization acted as a transformative force at multiple organizational levels, challenging schools to rethink their pedagogical and organizational practices. Unfortunately, according to Petterson [18] only few studies have analyzed the digitalization of schools from a multilevel organizational perspective, and this is in fact one of the goals from our studies. In general, it has been discussed how digital transformation in schools is often led on a small scale, by individual enthusiasts, who put their knowledge at disposal of their colleagues [18]. This is something that emerged during our studies, as teachers were increasingly required to digitally share teaching material to their students, to store documents and records about students on the provided digital platform, and conduct online teaching and meetings, so it also increased the risk of data leaks [10, 12]. Hence the teachers were more proficient in IT, provided assistance for their colleagues in case of doubts and establishing protocols on the fly.

Moreover, with the increased use of digital platforms, a privatization of practices related to storing and sharing of the students' data occurred [1, 22]. Practices that took place in analogue forms, as teachers were entering grades and evaluation on a paper register, turned into digitalized practices, involving platforms provided by IT companies and defined by complex interplay between technical architectures, business models, and mass user activity [22]. This process of privatization forced schools to rely upon private companies for data protection, turning practices that were once local and intrinsically safe into globalized potentially unsafe practices [17, 22], introducing risks of data leaks, manipulation, and unauthorized access [1, 2]. Hence security has become a main concern, defined as the extent to which unauthorized access and use of data is prevented by an application. Two dimensions appear as critical in security: integrity, which refers to the degree of trustworthiness of the users' data, and confidentiality, which refers to the extent to which data can be accessed by users without authorization [1, 2].

In order to make sense of these emerging issues from the teachers' perspective, this study leverages theories such as digital ecologies and activity theory to analyze how the introduction of GDPR norms have affected teachers' practice. Setting an ecological framework enables us to evaluate the impact of GDPR rules from a systemic perspective, looking at teachers as actors in an institutional setting. Activity theory can enable us to provide conceptual tools, to discuss how individual teachers have experienced the imposition of rules, which are not central to teaching practices or content, but rather to collateral aspects of the digitalization of their teaching practice.

## 2.1 An Ecological Perspective on GDPR in the Schools

This study is grounded on an ecological perspective on technologically supported practice, to properly address the issues experienced by teachers and students, when dealing with the hidden risks embodied in sharing practices within SoMe platforms, and their reception of GDPR norms within the school as an ecology for learning and social interaction.

We understand ecology as a "system of people, practices, values, and technologies" on a local context [17]. The term ecology is understood as a biological metaphor [19], to point out at how any context of practice, can be compared to a natural niche, in which multiple species are interacting more or less directly with each other, through different resources and tools that are available in their ecology. Ecologies can be contexts for professional practice as well as cultural institutions, such as schools or library [17]. The actors participating in an ecology are seen as if they were species within the natural environment, each with their own goals and yet intertwined with each other so that any change introduced in the ecology, will affect each species involved.

Nardi and O'Day [17] argue that a metaphor of ecology could "foster thought and discussion" and the ecology as a metaphor provides a lively image, suggesting properties and relations that can be found in technological environments. A main contribution to the technological discourse, is the notion that any change or transformation related to the introduction of new technologies, will end up affecting all the actors involved in the ecology, and their respective practices and relations.

Enquist [9] proposes the notion of distributed self, to investigate how artefacts are included when studying an individual person. From the perspective of the distributed self, the individual is caught in a "snapshot" representing the actors in their network, including their tools and practices. Technologies are seen as tools to perform a practice and reach a goal within a practice.

Similarly, Kumar et al. [13] propose an ecological framework [7, 8] to investigate the issue of data protection in schools. Data protection is seen by Kumar et al. [13] as a complex issue, demanding for a multilayered understanding of its local and global spheres regarding the experiences of the students. Kumar et al. distinguish between a series of layers such as: a microsystem, which deals with specific activities occurring in the classroom; a mesosystem, which refers to the broader sphere of the classroom, the neighborhood, and community settings; an exosystems, defined by social structures that influence microsystems in which students interact like the school or district policies. The macrosystem is defined by the overarching institutions of culture or subcultures, such as laws and social trends, permeating the micro, meso and exostystems. The chronosystem refers instead to changes overtime that can affect "individuals, environments, and the relations between them" [13].

Taking inspiration from the mentioned theories, we look at schools as complex ecologies, in which every change, being at the micro (inner circle) or exosystem (societal circle), affects each actor in specific ways and at different degrees, altering their practices and mutual relations. In the context of this paper, we are specifically interested in investigating how the introduction of GDPR norms and regulations has affected the teachers, with respect to: how the new rules have altered their teaching practices, which issues or challenges they have experienced, and which strategies they have developed to overcome such issues.

## 2.2 Activity Theory and GDPR

In the previous section we have established an ecological framework to analyze how GDPR has been introduced within the ecologies of schools, this section is presenting activity theory as a critical lens to zoom in the teachers' practices that have been disrupted by the increasing digitalization of schools.

Activity theory aims at studying how people engage in their own practices through the use of their tools, and the relationships among people, their tools and the practices [7, 18].

Engeström [7, 8], introduces activity theory together with the concept of expansive learning, as "approaches to studying the complexities and contradictions in authentic workplace environments". Individuals constantly negotiate how to manage their attention and their use of tools. Moreover, we identify a fragmentation in relation to how the rapid digitalization of schools and the consequent integration of GDPR rules are challenging school practices, in connection to complex societal changes such as: broader use of SoMe platforms among young people, digitalization of work practice associated to the need for any professional to develop IT skills, and recent lockdown practices enforcing distant education.

According to the core principles of activity theory [3, 15], human practice is segmented in a series of three hierarchical levels: the first being "activity" which defines the main practice people are engaged in and on which people are focused consciously and purposefully. An activity is generally aimed at "satisfying a need" by mean of a "material or ideal" object [3], and it coincides with the purpose of the individual engaging in the whole activity. The second level is called "action" and defines a level of practice which supports the main practice, and which people perform with less conscious attention. The level of activity and its purpose determines which actions the individual is going to undertake, to achieve the defined goal, which should match the outcome of the activity itself. The last level is called "operation" and refers to the level of practice, in which people engage almost automatically. Operations are triggered in an individual by the conditions of the actions, such as the material contingencies, in this sense operations are performed automatically and lack a specific purpose, other than facilitating the necessary actions to fulfill the purpose of the activity [3, 15].

The hierarchy between the different levels is not fixed, for instance, an action can become an operation through forms of automation/internalization, and an operation can become an action through conceptualization in breakdown situations [3]. For instance, within the activity of writing an email, typing can be seen as the action and moving fingers to press the key as the operation, each of this level requiring progressively less conscious focus. But when typing a password, an individual might breakdown and focus attentively on the sequence of the keys to press, to avoid mistakes.

Petterson proposes to apply activity theory to the digitalization of schools, through the CHAT framework [7, 15], which focuses on the formation and development of "object-oriented activities" [18]. Within the CHAT framework, activities are analyzed in a three-way interaction involving a subject, an object and mediating tools [18]. Objects and tools define the core of the activity, as in the case of writing an email, the whole activity would make sense without a computer connected to the Internet. Objects and tools become sense makers for our activities, defining what we do and to the point that any transformation of human action is driven by tools. This three-way interaction is in turn affected by three main forces, such as: rules directing the activity, a community in which the activity is conducted, and the division of labor among actors in the activity [7].

Looking at the integration of GDPR norms within schools, we notice that as teachers utilize digital platforms to register students' data, their focus is placed on writing the data correctly, not on how digital platforms work beneath the visible interface. The technicality of using specific platforms and how to enter the data, belong to the levels of actions and operations, which are by definition performed with decreasing intentionality. Moreover, as digital platforms are inherently complex [1, 10, 22], data protection is linked to "black boxing" [18], a known issue in the use of digital platforms. Black boxing deals with the hidden functionalities of digital technologies and algorithms, which are mostly accessible to experts, therefore, hence it is impossible for the teachers to be aware of how exactly the data are being stored and protected.

Moreover, applying the CHAT framework to our case, it emerges data represent the objects to be created and handled, previously on paper and more recently in a digital form through specific tools, which could be officially provided by the school. Data about the students are the object defining all the activities and use of tools related to data protection, and the implementation of GDPR rules. As soon as digital data is created, starting from didactic material to the assignments and evaluations, the risk of data leaks emerges from the opaque functionalities of the provided tools-platforms and the interrelations between the different actors involved. A paradox can be identified in relation to the rules applied to the digitalization of schools, as the increasing digitalization of the school, enforced by the pandemic, has increased the risk of data leaks and imposed more constraints on the teachers, who are responsible for creating and sharing digital data about the students, but also of protecting these data, utilizing black boxed platforms, which increase risks in data leaks.

## 3  Method

This study has been conducted as a research-through-design process, in which teachers and students have been involved in designing an app aimed at fostering a dialogue and awareness on GDPR norms and risks with data sharing on SoMe platforms. By research through design, we mean a research process that aims at gaining new knowledge, involving the target group in the conception of an artefact [6, 23]. In our view, the design process provided room for concretizing a discussion that could be felt as too abstract or distant from the daily engagement of the participants. For instance, inviting participants to sketch a mock-up or comment on the features of a given one, enables the participants to engage within a delimited negotiation room, centered around the mock-up and which functionalities it could unlock for the participants and their ecologies. Hence the newly introduced mock-up provides a temporary ecology, linking participating actors in reimagining their future lives, if the artefact will come into function with which features it would be better supporting the actors. In this way, both groups can reflect on which issues or doubts should be addressed in an app regarding data security, to be more useful to them.

We adopted a user-centred design methodology [20], supported by ethnomethodology and co-design workshops in situ and online, and we attempted as much as possible to incorporate a participatory design mind-set [4, 20]. During these workshops, templates were provided to support group discussions among the participants, teachers or students. The templates involved three main questions about their experience with SoMe and data security, such as: the most used platforms, if they received official training from the school and how, which challenges they had to face and which strategies they have eventually adopted to avoid issues. The two final questions were conceived to enable us to collect personal stories or anecdotes, that we could use as cases to enrich our design process. The design process was conducted through a series of design iterations; the third iteration is currently underway (Table 1).

The first iteration involved 3 classes of students and teachers from Oerestad gymnasium in Copenhagen, where we conducted a series of workshops, introducing students to GDPR and in discussing their use of SoMe. The students also interviewed their teachers, created a series of prototypes, which resulted in the forms of quiz for self-evaluation targeted students of their age (17–19 years old). At the same time, 2 groups of master students from our design and information technology programme at the University of Southern Denmark conducted inquiries with local school of data security for their semester project and produced a couple of simple prototypes.

In the second iteration, another class from Oerestad gymnasium took over the development of the prototypes. These students collected data from each other, interviewing their teachers and participating in events involving IT staff to be introduced formally to GDPR. The resulting prototypes had the form of apps embodying self-evaluation quizzes on GDPR, when a wrong answer was given explanations on the norms was displayed. A series of playful themes were explored, including animals and colourful layouts resembling SoMe platforms (Fig. 1).

Moreover, one of the researchers, who is a computer science teacher from the gymnasium conducted one in-depth workshop with the teachers from the gymnasium, to provide updated knowledge to the other teachers and exchange experiences with them.

**Table 1.** Overview of design iterations.

| Iterations | Schools Involved | Outcome |
|---|---|---|
| 1st Iteration-Spring 2023 | Oerestad Gymnasium, Copenhagen (DK) Syddansk University Students (DK) | Preliminary data: 7 initial sketchy prototypes and data from local schools point |
| 2nd Iteration – Winter 2023 | Oerestad Gymnasium Copenhagen (DK) Arborio Comprehensive School, Arborio (It) – 3 classess and 10 teachers I.I.S. Eugenio Bona, Biella (It) – 2 classes and 6 teachers | Second turn of data collection: 5 prototypes from Oerestad gymnasium, tested with teachers and students at the two Italian school |
| 3rd Iteration – Spring 2024 | Syddansk University Students (DK) from engineering and design, Oerestad Gymnasium, Copenhagen (DK), Arborio Comprehensive School, Arborio (IT), I.I.S. Eugenio Bona, Biella (IT) | Starting now – SDU students will develop further an app or simulation, based on the data from the previous iterations |

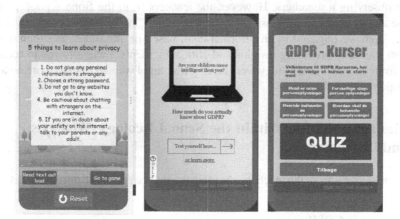

**Fig. 1.** Screenshots of the three prototypes created by Oerestad Gymnasium students and tested with the Italian schools.

The students from Oerestad created a series of quizzes for Three of the students' prototypes were selected for testing, and a series of workshops were conducted with two Italian schools: three junior high school classes from Arborio Comprehensive school, located in the province of Vercelli, and two high school classes from Bona Institute, a commercial high school in the province of Biella. Both schools were interesting for us, as the teachers wished support to run modules on data security targeted at their students, but also to keep their own knowledge up to date. The involvement of these schools enabled us to use the SPADATAS project as a concrete platform for sharing knowledge across Europe on data fragility and the implementation of GDPR in schools. In this sense the project itself, allowed for the creation of a transnational design space, in which the prototypes acted as mediational means [23] to foster a conversation and sharing of experiences across Europe.

In our data collection, we tried to be compliant with GDPR norms avoiding unnecessary data leaks, hence we did not record any of the workshops, relying upon traditional ethnographic data gathering techniques, such as annotations and ethnographic drawings [5, 16]. Quick sketches were taken during the workshops with black ink, to capture the mood generated by the discussion on GDPR, which were digitalized and polished to provide a clear documentation of the workshops. Moreover, for the scope of the project it was not our focus to collect demographic or sensitive data on the participants, we were rather interested in gathering insights on how different actors in the school ecology related to GDPR norms and concrete cases experienced by them. We transcribed these experiences as self-reported critical incidents, illustrating their challenges with the implementation of GDPR norms in the school. The format of the workshop needed to be adapted to the teachers' needs, the teachers from Arborio liked to have time on their own to answer the questions and evaluating the prototypes in pairs, and the whole workshops lasted for circa 45 min and was conducted in the afternoon after a long day, as it was hard to find a better time in their schedule. When the templates were used, our analysis focused on the notes provided by the participants on the templates and from notes taken by the observing researchers. However, the teachers from the Bona school, preferred to have an informal chat because as one teacher said: "We have always so many forms to fill…", so we engaged in an informal chat, based on the three questions from the template, verbally providing insights and critical incidents. I was allowed to record the audio from the interview, as they were talking fast, and I wanted to make sure no to miss any important detail.

## 4 Managing GDPR Within the School Ecology: Analysis and Discussion

Based on accounts from the teachers, the main themes that emerged during the discussion were:

1. Education in GDPR
2. Handling data about the students
3. Intersecting ecologies

The first theme, "education in GDPR" constitutes the main issue and goal to be tackled by the teachers: they need both to get educated about how to prevent data leaks, and to educate their students about GDPR. In the terms of activity theory, the second theme deals with the object defining the scope of the activities related to the digitalization of the school and data protection [7, 18], hence constituting the goal and main focus [3] of the implementation of GDPR in schools. Finally, the third theme that emerged through the workshops, points at a need to articulate the teachers' perception of loss of locality of the school ecology [10, 13, 17].

In the next sections, these themes will be discussed based on the data from the workshops, supported by a series of critical incidents reported by the teachers, to illustrate the teachers' experiences, the challenges they are facing, and the strategies they have developed to avoiding data leaks.

## 4.1 Education in GDPR

A difference that emerged among the teachers was the presence of official training in implementing GDPR for teachers. In Denmark schools received official courses from the administration, to secure a minimum level of awareness and conformity to the norms. For instance, at Oerestad gymnasium an extensive online course was purchased from a company; new modules are available to employees each year, to keep them updated in IT-security and data privacy. These courses are described by one of the teacher and co-author as: "well done, but quite traditional and not very popular among teachers". These courses seem to be developed in general for organizations to feel safe regarding respecting the laws, but are seen as lacking concrete guidelines addressing the teachers' needs. A Danish teacher confessed to have missed the courses, but believes to have things under control, saying that: "if I take pictures from excursion, I ask the students before I publish them on the class website (…) on my computer I have lot of former assignments with grades and names. If I use them as examples, I remove all sensitive data". Another Danish teacher believes that in teaching creative subjects, privacy is not a big issue, but said that "we should pay more attention to this and I am very interested". However, when teaching music, students record themselves working on polishing their performance, and since "recording and performing is a big part of our work, so we should pay attention to the new rules". These quotes seem to report a sense of security in how to handle the situation, but also a heightened awareness to tread more carefully than in the past.

The teachers from both Italian schools did not receive official training and relied heavily on self-education. A teacher from Arborio (and co-author) said to have used time on her own to find resources online and educate herself on the issue. Her main concerns were to be more educated on the subject, but also how to address her students as they "share pictures and videos that are borderline!" be it images of themselves or their friends, especially girls "exposing" themselves on SoMe platforms like Tiktok. Other teachers reported to have tried to follow some courses, but that most courses in IT for teachers focus on digital pedagogy or use of specific tools, and not so much on GDPR. Two teachers from Bona said that they received training from a previous job or from another employer. One of these teachers was appointed by the others as a possible expert in the group, and the others said giggling: "So we can ask you!". The two teachers said that their training was helpful, but at times created issues as they felt that they missed more school-specific guidelines. Another teacher said that she finds helpful to follow an international podcast on GDPR and cybersecurity.

Interestingly, teachers from both countries said to feel the need for more concreteness and appropriateness of training to actual cases. At Oerestad it was reported that: "Many colleagues didn't recall that they have participated in the online courses – or their content" and one of the interviewed teachers did not show particular interest for the official course.

Another teacher said that "I was aware about GDPR, but didn't pay much attention to it, but projects like SPADATAS and the courses at Oerestad Gymnasium directed my attention towards these very important topics". As a result, this teacher said to pay more attention while taking pictures and videos, or when asking the students to use some kind of SoMe platform for an assignment.

The teachers from Denmark and Italy reported that IT staff was available for questions and provided a safety protocol, such as use of passwords for shared computers, logging out and history cleaning up procedures, to prevent that students could access data about their classmates. Moreover, the teachers are required to use only the official platforms for file sharing and online meetings, with related issues regarding usability and individually preferred platforms. A strategy of peer-learning has emerged, in which teachers with a stronger IT background act as referents for their colleagues. One of the teachers from Bona was regarded as a potential referent, and at Oerestad the IT teacher participating in the project took charge of the situation and produced "a purely online course, which I send out to a lot of collages and students as an example, with games, quizzes etc." (Fig. 2).

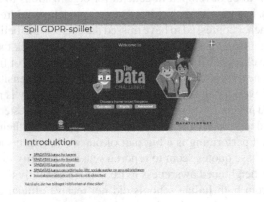

**Fig. 2.** Start page of the course created by Oerestad Gymnasium IT teacher - https://clauswitfelt. github.io/privacy/ (last seen on 12-02-24).

The students were involved in creating courses and apps and videos (Fig. 3), included the prototypes tested by the Italian schools, which were also sent to their former compulsory schools. These newly created resources added value from the teachers' perspective, as they were built on concrete cases and addressed different target groups like teachers, students, and parents. Short meetings were conducted around the online course, supported by slide presentations and a more "theoretical course" about the European Privacy Act, European AI act for social science teachers. Similarly, the analysis of the Italian teachers of the prototypes, pointed at the need for specific guidelines and with an adequate tone of voice that could be attractive to teenagers.

## 4.2  Data About Students

Teachers deal with GDPR when creating and handling data about the students, at times it might be personal data, such as their names, grades and difficulty with a subject,

**Fig. 3.** IT staff speaking at a data security seminar at Oerestad Gymnasium.

or even sensitive data, regarding diagnoses or difficulties related to their sociocultural background. However, the need for teachers to keep protected data about students is not new, as it deals with any practitioner's professional ethics and confidentiality oath [21]. Specific situations might require practitioners to breach the confidentiality oath, for instance in discussing a case with family members, especially if it is in the interest of the client [21]. The same can be said for teachers, they were never allowed to discuss grades or personal matters about their students, a part when discussing the students' performance with their colleagues and with the students' parents to provide adequate support. In this sense, it is not new to teachers to keep their students anonymous and their personal information secret, as reported by a teacher from Oerestad: "I also tell my students about it. We have tough guidelines about this, for instance, that students can use an anonymous mail for logging into platforms on the internet, without giving away personal information". On the other hand, a teacher from Oerestad reported a critical incident in which "some students wanted to video-record me and students shocking some other students with a test, in order to analyze it for a psychology project. I told them, that this was not ethically ok, nor in order with general rules of GDPR and privacy".

Howcver, current circumstances have challenged established confidentiality practices within schools, as teachers are required to handle data about their students through digital platforms, embedded with specific affordances aimed at seamlessly sharing texts, images, and videos, locally as well as globally. Recent experiences with lock-down have pushed further the digitalization of school ecologies, forcing teachers to experiment without proper training, in Denmark as in Italy [12]. As previously mentioned, teachers have been encouraged to pay attention to aspects of their practices that are technologically black-boxed [14] and that refers to less-conscious actions and operations [3]. The combination of these factors can lead to mistakes, for instance it was reported by Arborio teachers that they have forgotten to log off from shared computers, as their attention was captured by other occurrences such as: students arguing or calling for help, or colleagues engaging in casual conversations. Moreover, multiple platforms are being tried over time by the schools in both countries and updated utilities are being integrated together with new data security procedures. These shifts constitute a factor of additional pressure, as expressed by a few teachers, who defined these platforms are "unstable", because "as soon as you learn them, you have to relearn them again, and then a totally new one is added to your plate!", a form of perceived unreliability.

Other colleagues' actions have been reported as a potential issue as well, an Italian teacher reported a critical incident in which data about a student were shared by a colleague to the other teachers, without consent. This put the teacher in a difficult situation as it was not clear how this colleague could have acquired these data and how to react against this person. In terms of design requirements for an app targeting schools, this incident points at the need to address legal implications and strategies for student or teachers to protect themselves, also after an infraction has occurred at their expenses. The teacher in this incident was thinking of asking the IT staff but refrained from it, to avoid conflicts. In response to this issue, this teacher resolved to write notes on paper and then insert them in the platform from home.

## 4.3  Intersecting Ecologies

The most complicated issue with implementing GDPR rules, emerged from the lack of clear boundaries within the school ecology. The teachers argued that they feel a responsibility in educating their students to protect their data. Students are seen as erratic actors, causing unexpected infractions with consequences for the teachers, with or even without bad intentions. Interestingly, several Danish teachers reported not to think too much about GDPR in their teaching, but to be more concerned about their children, however, they have reported the need to address guidelines for sharing of videos or images from the classroom to public platforms. In this respect, feedback on the prototypes focused on the need of addressing the risks of reckless sharing of videos and images among teenagers, including implications over a long-time span.

A teacher from Oerestad said to be more concerned about GDPR from an administrative perspective as "there are a lot of problems", such as seeing "a lot of data about students, and I pay a lot of attention to where I leave resumes of meeting etc.". A couple of critical accidents provided by teachers from both Italian schools, referred to the issue of students' irresponsible sharing of data online. In one school a student has shared denigratory comments about a teacher on a public SoMe platform. The post was found by the teachers and was discussed in a meeting among teachers and parents. In the other incident, a student shared a video showing a classmate cleaning the classroom, after having inadvertently poured hot chocolate on the floor. The incident was described by the teacher during our workshop as an "innocent" occurrence, the student in the video acted out and laughed at the occurrence with the other classmates, not showing any signs of distress. According to the teacher, the students posted the video on a public SoMe platform and it "was seen and reshared on (the platform) and then the mother of that student saw it, and she was angry because she thought that her kid was bullied". The mother contacted the teachers for a meeting in which she accused the teachers of not taking care of bullying in the classroom. The incident resulted in disciplinary measures against the students who shared the video, who could not understand what the problem was, as well as the student displayed in the video.

Both incidents deal with content being irresponsibly shared on public platforms by students, who were not aware of the potential consequences, which spread beyond the school ecology. In this respect, the teachers complained about lack of contact with the students' families, especially with those who are struggling in school and are at risk of reckless behavior. We see these incidents are related to how the digitalization of the schools have challenged the locality of the school ecology. Nardi and O'Day [17] argue that ecologies are local and should have boundaries that are easy to identify for the actors, and within this locality tools and practices acquire specific social meaning among the actors. The school ecology provides a framework for negotiation of meaning within the actors, including how protected they can be by rules and practices. The use of digital platforms, has compromised the locality of the school ecology, making its boundaries harder to identify for the actors. In this sense, actors are lacking an overview of the meaning that their actions could acquire, when exposed at the margin of their ecology. Both the ill-intended and the innocent incidents have caused unexpected consequences for the students, who were focusing the local meaning of the content they shared, especially in the second incident which was not motivated by hurtful motives. A teacher pointed out at the uncertainty of the school ecology, in connection to when and where data protection practices enforced by the school lose value and effect. This teacher was asking if students' data are not protected when for instance: "I am sending information from my official email to the families' email, but they maybe have Gmail, am I compromising the students' data?" The Italian teachers also said that other schools in the region have been provided with an email account hosted by the school platform, to keep the communication safe. It was reported also that during lockdown the teachers have made groups on public SoMe platforms to reach each other for emergencies. But since GDPR rules have been introduced, they have stopped using those platforms for actual communication, they only use public platforms to send warnings to each other, but then conduct the actual communication through the institutional channels. This approach is similar to the national strategy implemented in Denmark, in which families get a notification in their personal email, but to access the actual communication they have to log in into the national IT platform. In terms of design requirements, these incidents point at the need to address what can happen when data leave protected platforms, on the boundaries between school and outside ecologies, especially regarding videos and pictures should be prioritized, as the students seem to be unaware of the legal implications.

## 5 Discussion

During our study, it emerged how the implementation of GDPR is a consequence of the increasing digitalization of the school as an ecology, challenging this ecology to address societal changes led by the digitalization of a variety of social and economic practices. Teachers appear as unique actors in this ecology, because their role require them to on the boundaries between the school ecology, and not only regarding digitalization, being responsible for:

1. Educating themselves in any societal change so to adopt an ethical professional conduct,
2. Fostering an awareness in the students about societal change, to prepare them to be active citizens of their society.

This means that teachers must be updated on new occurring issues and rules, to adapt their professional practice, and at the same time teach their students about the new rules and issues, from the students' point of view. In the specific case of our study, creating and sharing data, is literally placing teachers and their students on the boundary of the school ecology, as through digital platforms data escape the meaning making sphere of the ecology, as well as the established protection protocol, putting at risk of legal repercussions all actors. In this sense, we look at teachers as complex actors within the school ecology [17, 19], in which whatever societal change is being brought to the school, it will critically affect them and their practice. Collegial discussion represents a precious practice within the mesosystem of the ecology [13], offering room for value negotiation, knowledge exchange, and generation of new practices. This has implications for expanding the role of specific more experienced teachers, who find themselves, in many cases willingly acting as mentors for their colleagues [18], as confirmed by our study. From the perspective of the distributed self (Enquist) regarding GDPR in the school, teachers as individual actors are caught in a snapshot playing multiple roles: educating themselves, their students and sometimes also their colleagues.

Inconsistencies are introduced within established safety protocols and practices from the exosystem to the microsystem of the school ecology, as sharing of information by default does not only take place through the official platforms, for instance through families' email accounts. In this respect, Petterson [18] argues that a large-scale coordinated transformation would be needed to manage the digitalization of the school. However, we find a tension between this statement and our result: in Denmark an exosystem strategy was attempted, centrally coordinated by the school and the government, and at national level schools can only communicate to families through nationally protected platforms; however, teachers are still missing guidelines addressing the specificity of their ecology. Through our comparison between Italian and Danish cases, we find that societal changes like the digitalization of schools and the implementation of GDPR rules must be negotiated among micro- and exosystem to make sense for the actors of the multiple ecologies affected. In the case of the Danish school, the course was found valuable but too general, addressing organizations, rather than schools in specific. In the Italian cases, an exosystem strategy was missing, beside the GDPR norms, and this led teachers to learn on their own, facing occurring incidents. Despite these differences, in both cases collegiality enables teachers to reshape their ecology, contributing on how each school can appropriate new rules matching their specific organizational values and routines. A large-scale strategy is needed to provide solid grounding for collegiality to construct a negotiation room, about what to incorporate and what to reshape, to fit the ecology, as no global input could consistently fit each specific school.

Moreover, from an activity theory perspective, since GDPR address actions and operations lacking specific purposes [3, 7], teachers cannot articulate openly their concerned or goals, as it is not their primary focus. However, teachers can become aware of their concerns by experiences honing on their collegiality, as shown by the collected critical incidents. Hence, it is unavoidable that large-scale strategies cannot by definition address the complexity of the integration of GDPR in schools, on the other hand it is desirable that a large-scale strategy would provide extra resources to innovate in the microsystem.

This is the goal of the SPADATAS project, aiming at supporting teachers at the microsystem to get in touch with each other, exchanging knowledge and strategies, hence gaining a broader overview on the expanding boundaries of school ecologies. The teachers we interacted with stated that they were happy to be part of the project, as they felt that they needed additional support in learning to apply the GDPR rules to their daily practice.

In this expansion of the school boundaries, the students emerge as unpredictable actors, especially when sharing visual material on their personal SoMe accounts, which might refer to their classmates or other teachers (as in the critical incidents previously discussed). Students' actions might expose classmates or teachers in improper ways, resulting in leaks of personal or sensitive information about themselves or their classmates. From the perspective of the distributed self [9], each student acts on transformative platforms crossing multiple ecologies, delivering messages with unpredictable meaning and consequences. This has consequences for the role and responsibilities of the teachers, who are kept accountable for the conduct of their students when they share potentially inappropriate contents related to the school, even when the sharing happens outside the school. From an activity theory perspective, students are affected by black boxing too, and having to focus on semi-automatic actions such as clicking and swapping on their phone, to share visual content to their friends and classmates. Hence, we identify a need for an interdisciplinary discourse on the digitalization and GDPR integration in schools, as school-confined ecologies have transformed into interconnected networks, with open boundaries.

## 6  Conclusion

In this study we have addressed the integration of GDPR in European schools, comparing cases from a Danish and two Italian secondary schools. We engaged in a research-through-design investigation, which led to uncover broader perspectives on our research focus. In the start of the study, we found how teachers and students were affected in interconnected by different ways, therefore, we decided to analyze in depth their issues and needs, and this study presents our current findings on the teachers' perspective.

Digging further into the integration of GDPR, which seemed at first sight an additional burden on the teachers' shoulders, we discovered a more complex pictures, connected to the increasing digitalization of European schools. Three main aspects emerged in relation to how the teachers are experiencing the integration of the new norms: a need to educate themselves and their students, doubts about how to follow the norms when handling students' data, and difficulties in making sense of how digital platforms are challenging the boundaries of the school. The combination of the data sharing affordances provided by digital platforms and the obligation to use these platforms, has pushed teachers into a paradox, in which they cannot avoid creating and sharing digital data about their students.

The main issue has been identified in the difficulty teachers and especially students experience in making sense of the expanding boundaries of the school ecology, which is being transformed into a networked system with open boundaries. Teachers and their collegial practices have emerged as meaningful local practices, enabling teachers to find their way around the application of GDPR and the risks of data leaks. In particular, the teachers have emphasized a need to foster awareness in their students regarding the unpredictable consequences of sharing videos and images displaying themselves and their classmates to public platforms, which elude institutional protection. This need will be approached in our next design iteration, which will focus on how a digital app could contribute to foster a dialogue between teachers and students on the sharing of visual content, on the global dimensions of the contemporary networked school ecology.

# References

1. Amo-Filvà, D., et al.: Security and privacy in academic data management at schools: SPA-DATAS project. In: Zaphiris, P., Ioannou, A. (eds.) HCII 2023, Part I. LNCS, vol. 14040, pp. 3–16. Springer, Cham (2023). https://doi.org/10.1007/978-3-031-34411-4_1
2. Amo-Filvà, D., et al.: Open educational resources to enhance students' data protection in schools (2022)
3. Bertelsen, O.W., Bødker, S.: Activity Theory. HCI Models, Theories, and Frameworks: Toward a Multidisciplinary Science, pp. 291–324 (2003)
4. Björgvinsson, E., Ehn, P., Hillgren, P.A.: Participatory design and "democratizing innovation". In: Proceedings of the 11th Biennial Participatory Design Conference, pp. 41–50 (2010)
5. Causey, A.: Drawn to See: Drawing as an Ethnographic Method. University of Toronto Press (2017)
6. Cross, N.: Designerly ways of knowing. Des. Stud. **3**(4), 221–227 (1982)
7. Engeström, Y.: Activity theory and individual and social transformation. Perspect. Act. Theory **19**(38), 19–30 (1999)
8. Engeström, Y., Pyörälä, E.: Using activity theory to transform medical work and learning. Med. Teach. **43**(1), 7–13 (2021)
9. Enquist, H.: A socio-material ecology of the distributed self. Des. Philos. Pap. **6**(2), 123–140 (2008)
10. Foster, C.A.: Your home, the new classroom: how public-school zoom use encroaches into family privacy. J. High Tech Law **22**(131), 131–175 (2021)
11. Garcia-Morales, V., Garrido-Moreno, A., Martin-Rojas, R.: The transformation of higher education after the COVID disruption: emerging challenges in an online learning scenario. Front. Psychol. **12**, 616059 (2021)
12. Garzotto, M.E., Marchetti, E.: Distant yet personal: equality in distant education during Covid-19 lockdown in Italy. Aktualitet **15**(3), 40–51 (2021)
13. Kumar, P.C., Chetty, M., Clegg, T.L., Vitak, J.: Privacy and security considerations for digital technology use in elementary schools. In: Proceedings of the 2019 CHI Conference on Human Factors in Computing Systems, pp. 1–13 (2019)
14. Lakkaraju, H., Bastani, O.: "How do I fool you?": manipulating user trust via misleading black box explanations. In: AIES 2020, New York, NY, USA, pp. 79–85 (2020)
15. Leont'ev, A.N.: Activity, Consciousness, and Personality. Prentice-Hall, Englewood Cliffs (1978)
16. Marchetti, E.: At observere gennem dine hænder: tegning som etnografisk praksis. In: Grønning, A., Enemark Lundtofte, T., Kampmann Walther, B. (eds.) Medievidenskab - Metoder og Teorier, pp. 83–97. Syddansk Universitetsforlag, Odnse (2022)
17. Nardi, B.A., O'Day, V.: Information Ecologies: Using Technology with Heart. MIT Press (2000)
18. Pettersson, F.: Understanding digitalization and educational change in school by means of activity theory and the levels of learning concept. Educ. Inf. Technol. **26**(1), 187–204 (2020)

19. Raptis, D., Kjeldskov, J., Skov, M.B., Paay, J.: What is a digital ecology? Theoretical foundations and a unified definition. Aust. J. Intell. Inf. Process. Syst. **13**(4), 5 (2014)
20. Sanders, E.B.N.: From user-centered to participatory design approaches. design and the social sciences. In: Frascara, J. (ed.) Taylor & Francis Books Limited (2002)
21. Starr, W.C.: Ethical theory, confidentiality, and professional ethics. Metaphilosophy **15**(2), 129–140 (1984)
22. Van Dijck, J., Poell, T.: Social media platforms and education. SAGE Handb. Soc. Media 579–591 (2018)
23. Zimmerman, J., Forlizzi, J.: Research through design in HCI. In: Olson, J., Kellogg, W. (eds.) Ways of Knowing in HCI, pp. 167–189. Springer, New York (2014). https://doi.org/10.1007/978-1-4939-0378-8_8

# A Communication Support System
# for Japanese Language Learners Using
# Code-Mixing

Mondheera Pituxcoosuvarn[✉][iD], Yohei Murakami[iD], and Shinnosuke Yamada

Ritsumeikan University, 1-1-1 Noji-Higashi, Kusatsu, Shiga 525-8577, Japan
mond-p@fc.ritsumei.ac.jp

**Abstract.** Machine translation (MT) has become a cornerstone in intercultural communication, facilitating the translation of native languages.
However, for foreign language learners, emphasizing language practice
in the target language is crucial. This paper introduces a communication tool designed to enable interactions between native Japanese speakers and novice non-native speakers, aiming to maintain language practice opportunities while ensuring effective communication. The system
supports text-based chat, employing a code-mixing machine translation
(CMMT), enabling conversations between native Japanese speakers and
non-native learners. Through this code-mixing approach, our system provides a practical tool for language learners, fostering realistic and utili-
tarian language practice in diverse communication scenarios within the
Japanese language. This design bridges the gap between language learning and effective communication, acknowledging the significance of linguistic practice in enhancing the proficiency of non-native speakers.

**Keywords:** Computer supported collaborative work · Intercultural
collaboration · Language learning

## 1   Introduction

In an increasingly interconnected world, people recognize the necessity of overcoming language barriers to engage in meaningful communication. To address
this, individuals turn to foreign language education as a means of acquiring linguistic proficiency. The pursuit of language learning not only facilitates effective
communication but also fosters a deeper understanding of diverse cultures. As
individuals invest in the acquisition of foreign language skills, they enhance their
ability to engage in cross-cultural dialogues, bridging gaps and fostering global
understanding.

The influx of foreigners into Japan for various reasons has prompted a surge
in the demand for Japanese language acquisition. Whether driven by professional opportunities, academic pursuits, or cultural exploration, these individuals strive to gain proficiency in Japanese. Scientific research emphasizes the

© The Author(s), under exclusive license to Springer Nature Switzerland AG 2024
P. Zaphiris and A. Ioannou (Eds.): HCII 2024, LNCS 14723, pp. 200–210, 2024.
https://doi.org/10.1007/978-3-031-61685-3_15

cognitive benefits associated with bilingualism, suggesting that acquiring a new language can enhance cognitive flexibility, problem-solving skills, and even delay the onset of cognitive decline. Therefore, the endeavor to learn Japanese extends beyond mere linguistic acquisition, offering individuals a cognitive advantage and a deeper integration into Japanese society.

In the contemporary landscape of language learning, machine translation (MT) emerges as a viable option to navigate linguistic challenges. However, reliance on MT comes with its own set of limitations, particularly in the context of skill development. While MT provides a quick and efficient means of understanding foreign languages, it deprives language learners of the essential practice required for skill refinement. Effective language acquisition involves active engagement with the language, including speaking, listening, and comprehension exercises, which MT alone cannot adequately address. Thus, while MT may serve as a valuable tool for certain tasks, it cannot replace the nuanced learning experiences that come from direct interaction and practice in acquiring a foreign language.

Moreover, relying solely on the communication skills of language learners may prove insufficient, as the effectiveness of communication is intricately tied to the proficiency level attained. The challenges intensify when considering the demands of specific contexts, such as the workplace, where communication often involves intricate and nuanced interactions. For instance, if a foreigner is required to utilize the Japanese language in a professional setting characterized by complex communication requirements, individuals with language proficiency levels significantly below native fluency may encounter considerable difficulties. The intricacies of workplace communication necessitate a nuanced command of the language, encompassing not only basic conversational abilities but also a deep understanding of specialized vocabulary and professional etiquette. In such environments, a substantial gap between the learner's proficiency level and the demands of the professional context may impede effective communication and integration into the Japanese-based professional milieu.

The demand for a tool that seamlessly facilitates communication while preserving the opportunity for language practice is evident in today's multilingual landscape. Such a tool is crucial for individuals seeking to engage in effective conversations across language barriers without compromising the valuable practice needed for language enhancement. Striking a balance between fluid communication and ongoing language skill development is essential for fostering meaningful interactions in diverse linguistic contexts.

This paper propose a tool focusing on employing code-mixing strategies to develop a chat system aimed at facilitating communication between Japanese speakers and foreigners possessing a basic understanding of the Japanese language. Code-mixing, a linguistic phenomenon characterized by the integration of two or more languages within a single communicative context, serves as a strategic tool in multilingual discourse [7]. Particularly advantageous in the context of foreign language learning, this approach not only fosters communication but also provides individuals with an opportunity to practice and enhance their Japanese language skills [10]. Our system seamlessly integrates code-mixing into chat platforms, presenting Japanese text with challenging words substituted by English, Chinese, or other native languages, depending on the non-native speaker's proficiency level.

## 2   Related Work

The term "language contact," as introduced by Thomason [8], delineates environments where two or more languages coexist, leading to linguistic phenomena like "code-switching" and "code-mixing." Code-switching, as meticulously defined by Holmes [4], involves a conscious and deliberate choice guided by specific motivations, contextual cues, and the dynamics of the relationship between speakers and their interlocutors. In contrast, code-mixing, according to Holmes, transpires without a predetermined pattern or explicit motivation. Bokamba's exploration [1] delves into code-mixing by examining how lexical elements, such as prefixes and suffixes, are intricately intertwined in this linguistic phenomenon.

Gardner-Chloros [3] characterizes "code-switching" as the practice of bilinguals or multilinguals seamlessly interweaving several languages or dialects within the same sentence or conversation. Both "code-switching" and "code-mixing" share the fundamental concept of alternating between multiple languages within a single conversation, a notion underscored by Myers-Scotton [5] and Valdes-Fallis [9]. While prior research predominantly focused on bilingual children, examining their use of code-switching as a means to compensate for vocabulary gaps, this study takes a departure. It accentuates how speakers employ code-mixing not merely as a compensatory linguistic tool but as a deliberate strategy to address their own vocabulary limitations.

Fujimura's study [2] provides additional insights, revealing that code-mixing serves a distinct purpose in emphasizing the intended message, especially within close relationships. This perspective presupposes a shared linguistic context, where the interlocutors are presumed to comprehend the multiple languages used. Unlike earlier research that primarily viewed code-switching and code-mixing through the lens of vocabulary enhancement and comprehension, this study underscores the nuanced motivations behind code-mixing, portraying it as a dynamic linguistic practice employed for expressive emphasis and communicative purposes within specific social dynamics.

## 3   Code-Mixing Machine Translation

In the context of cross-cultural communication, challenges arise during initial encounters or in situations where the language proficiency of the interlocutor is uncertain, potentially leading to communication discrepancies. Our research focuses on leveraging code-mixing within a chat environment to address these challenges systematically. Through the customization of code-mixing settings in a chat room, our objective is to optimize communication with non-native speakers by mitigating vocabulary limitations. Inspired by the linguistic adaptation observed in infants exposed to multiple languages, our system emulates the strategic use of code-mixing to facilitate seamless interactions in diverse linguistic contexts.

To empirically demonstrate the efficacy of our system, Fig. 2 elucidates the processing pipeline and presents a concrete example of code-mixing application. In this scenario, a native Japanese user inputs a sentence in Japanese, triggering the system to dynamically translate the entire message into a code-mixed format. Subsequently, a non-native Japanese user can comprehend the original sentence, with challenging words replaced by equivalents from another language, such as English. This algorithmic approach serves as a pragmatic solution for real-time cross-linguistic communication, offering a computationally-driven means to navigate language barriers in interactive conversational settings.

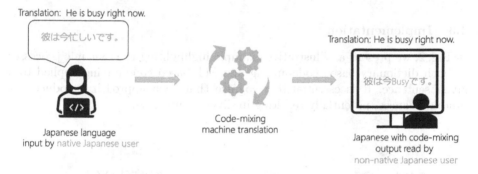

**Fig. 1.** An illustration of how a message can undergo code-mixing through the utilization of CMMT.

## 4   Code-Mixing Method

In the development of our language learning tool, we have implemented two distinct code-mixing strategies to enhance the user experience. These strategies leverage vocabulary lists based on proficiency levels, with a focus on the Japanese Language Proficiency Test (JLPT) levels ranging from N5 (lowest) to N1 (highest). Proficiency levels are benchmarked against the JLPT, ensuring alignment with recognized language standards. Learners can customize their experience by selecting their proficiency level, allowing the tool to tailor the code-mixing approach accordingly.

### 4.1   Dictionary-Based Code-Mixing

To facilitate vocabulary learning, we created dictionaries corresponding to each proficiency level. These dictionaries serve as a comprehensive resource for words relevant to learners at different stages of proficiency. The process begins with the tokenization of the input sentence, breaking it down into individual words or tokens. Subsequently, we selectively substitute only the words that correspond to a higher proficiency level. This ensures that learners encounter and engage with more advanced vocabulary while maintaining overall comprehension.

### 4.2 Machine Translation (MT) Based Code-Mixing

Our second strategy involves the use of machine translation to introduce a foreign language element into the learning process. The initial step is the translation of the sentence into the foreign language of choice. Following translation, words that the user is expected to know, considering their current and lower proficiency levels, are replaced with their Japanese equivalents. The resulting sentence structure reflects the translated language, providing a context-rich learning experience.

### 4.3 Implementation

In Fig. 2, we present an illustrative example highlighting the dynamic processes of both dictionary-based code-mixing and MT-based code-mixing applied to a given sentence. It is essential to recognize that each approach introduces its unique nuances, potentially resulting in diverse outcomes.

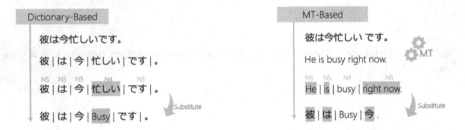

**Fig. 2.** An example of a sentence undergoing the processes of dictionary-based code-mixing and MT-based code-mixing.

Table 1 illustrates word substitution patterns corresponding to each JLPT level and two distinct strategies-dictionary-based and machine translation-based. The first column categorizes the Japanese Language Proficiency Test (JLPT) levels, ranging from N1 (highest) to N5 (lowest). The second and third columns delineate the levels of words that undergo substitution in each strategy. Notably, the N0 category encompasses particularly challenging words and technical terms that do not fall within the vocabulary data range of N1 to N5.

**Table 1.** Word substitution for each JLPT Level and strategy.

| JLPT Level | Dictionary-Based Substitution | MT-Based Substitution |
|---|---|---|
| N1 (Highest) | N0 | N1, N2, N3, N4, N5 |
| N2 | N0, N1 | N2, N3, N4, N5 |
| N3 | N0, N1, N2 | N3, N4, N5 |
| N4 | N0, N1, N2, N3 | N4, N5 |
| N5 (Lowest) | N0, N1, N2, N3, N4 | N5 |

### 4.4 Preliminary Experiment

Previously, we conducted an experiment to explore two code-mixing strategies and determine their suitability for learners at N1 and N2 proficiency levels [6]. Our focus was on assessing the effectiveness of both dictionary-based and MT-based code-mixing strategies among N1 and N2 learners using a taboo game as a tool to evaluate message comprehension. The participants in the study were seven non-native Japanese speakers, categorized based on their proficiency in Japanese.

The results revealed that the dictionary-based substitution strategy produced an average correct response rate of 0.4 for N2 learners. In contrast, this strategy exhibited a notably higher average correct response rate of 0.73 for N1 learners.

These findings indicate that, at the N2 level, the MT-based substitution strategy outperforms the dictionary-based substitution strategy. Conversely, at the N1 level, the dictionary-based substitution strategy yields better results (Table 2).

**Table 2.** Average Percentage of Correct Responses in Taboo Games for Each Strategy, Categorized by Japanese Language Proficiency Level

| Strategy/Participant Level | JLPT N1 | JLPT N2 |
|---|---|---|
| Dictionary-based substitution | 0.73 | 0.40 |
| Machine translation-based substitution | 0.63 | 0.70 |

Building on the findings of the preliminary experiment, the system recommends employing dictionary-based substitution for N1-level users and MT-based substitution for those at N2 and lower proficiency levels.

## 5 Design Proposal

### 5.1 System Architecture

Figure 3 illustrates the interaction between the user and the system, focusing on code-mixing communication between a native Japanese speaker and a non-native speaker with English as their mother tongue. Initially, the non-native Japanese speaker shares their Japanese language proficiency with the system.

When a message is sent by the native Japanese speaker, the system employs a dictionary-based code-mixing strategy for individuals with N1 proficiency, while those with N2 proficiency or lower will experience the MT-Base code-mixing strategy. The resulting output message will be in code-mixed Japanese. However, depending on the message's complexity and the non-native speaker's skill level, the output message may also be in Japanese only.

Upon receipt of a message from the non-native speaker, the system initiates a screening process to assess the linguistic content. If the message is identified as code-mixed Japanese, it undergoes translation into Japanese using a dictionary substitution approach, chosen for its simplicity in this particular version.

In instances where the message is in a language other than Japanese, such as English, the system activates machine translation, transforming the content into Japanese for the convenience of the native Japanese speaker.

For messages originally composed in Japanese, the system presents the content as is, without translation. This multi-tiered approach ensures effective communication between native Japanese speakers and non-native speakers, adapting the translation strategy based on the language complexity and origin of the messages.

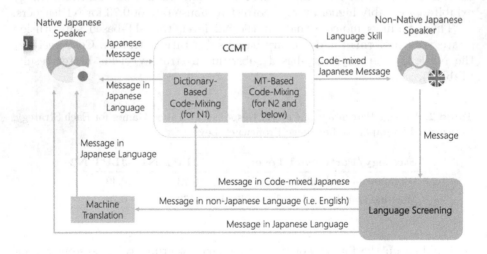

**Fig. 3.** The architecture of the proposed system.

## 5.2   User Interface Design

This section presents proposed design interfaces for the communication tool. The figures in this section depict mobile application mockups; however, the design is versatile and can also be implemented for use on the web as an application.

**Language Selection.** Upon logging in, users gain the ability to adjust their language settings within the interface. The language settings section provides options for selecting both the user's preferred language and the language they are currently learning. Additionally, a checkbox is available for users interested in receiving code-mixed messages. Upon checking this box, a dropdown menu for language level selection becomes visible, allowing users to specify their proficiency level and tailor the communication tool to their language learning needs. This intuitive and customizable feature is proposed to enhances the user experience by accommodating individual language preferences and learning goals (Fig. 4).

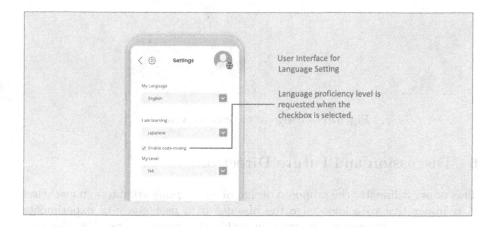

**Fig. 4.** The design of the language selection page.

Even when the user selects their preferred language, the application will automatically examine their messages. For instance, if English is chosen as the language, but the message contains Japanese words, the system will promptly identify and translate those Japanese words into the recipient's language, in this case, Japanese.

**Chat User Interface.** The chat interface is intentionally designed to be intuitive and user-friendly, resembling a typical chat system. What sets it apart is that users can choose their preferred language, allowing them to both compose and read messages in their language of choice. Simultaneously, the system seamlessly translates messages into other languages, ensuring effective communication among users with diverse language preferences. An added feature from the language setting allows users to opt for code-mixed messages, where, if selected, they will see messages with code-mixing, presenting a dynamic and personalized language experience within the familiar chat environment.

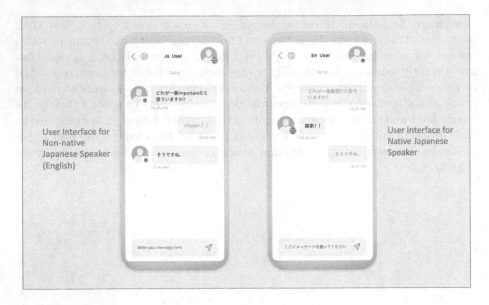

**Fig. 5.** The design of the chat user interface.

# 6    Discussion and Future Direction

This paper delineates the proposed design of a communication tool; nonetheless, it is imperative to acknowledge the absence of a user study or experimentation regarding the system's interaction within the current scope. A forthcoming endeavor is envisaged to conduct a comprehensive experiment aimed at scrutinizing the nuances of user interactions with the system. This prospective research initiative is anticipated to yield valuable insights into user experiences and preferences, thereby facilitating the refinement and augmentation of the proposed communication tool.

## 6.1    Influence of Chinese-Origin Character

It's crucial to highlight that our investigation solely engaged native Chinese speakers, preventing us from conducting comparative experiments to gauge the influence of Chinese characters on the outcomes. Due to the common characters shared between Chinese and Japanese, some Japanese Kanji (Chinese-origin characters) might be understood by Chinese readers without requiring substitution or translation. It's essential to acknowledge that the impact could vary when dealing with language pairs such as Japanese-English or Japanese and other languages.

   In addition, Japanese learners with a Chinese language background might encounter confusion with homographic characters that have different meanings and pronunciations. For instance, the Kanji character "行" is pronounced as "xíng" in Mandarin Chinese, meaning "to go" or "to travel." In Japanese, the same character can be pronounced as "kou" or "gyou," with meanings ranging from "to go" to "line" or "row." This overlap in characters with diverse linguistic interpretations underscores the potential for misunderstanding and emphasizes the importance of distinguishing context and pronunciation nuances for accurate comprehension in language learning.

## 6.2 Hiragana Usage

Hiragana and Kanji form integral components of the Japanese writing system. Hiragana, a syllabic script with 46 characters, is primarily used for native Japanese words, grammatical elements, and verb conjugations. Considering the incorporation of both scripts, particularly in language learning, it is crucial to tailor the approach based on the learner's proficiency level. This consideration is especially pertinent for learners from diverse language backgrounds, such as English speakers, where utilizing Hiragana may be more accessible. Therefore, adopting a strategic approach to determine when to use Hiragana or Kanji characters can benefit learners at different proficiency stages. Future experiments may involve exploring code mixing with Hiragana for Kanji separately, tailored to each proficiency level, to enhance language learning experiences.

## 7   Conclusion

In conclusion, this paper underscores the critical role of effective communication in an increasingly interconnected world, emphasizing the significance of overcoming language barriers through foreign language education. The surge in demand for Japanese language acquisition, driven by diverse motivations, underscores the cognitive and societal benefits associated with bilingualism. While machine translation (MT) offers a quick solution to linguistic challenges, it falls short in addressing the nuanced learning experiences essential for skill development. The complexities of workplace communication further highlight the importance of achieving a nuanced command of the language.

Recognizing the need for a tool that bridges the gap between communication and language practice, this paper proposes a chat system employing code-mixing strategies. Code-mixing, as a linguistic phenomenon, proves advantageous in multilingual discourse and is particularly beneficial for foreign language learning. Our system integrates code-mixing into chat platforms, facilitating communication between native Japanese speakers and non-native learners. By seamlessly substituting challenging words with translations in English, Chinese, or other native languages, the tool provides users with valuable language practice opportunities. This innovative approach aims to strike a balance between fluid communication and ongoing language skill development, offering a promising avenue for meaningful interactions across linguistic contexts. Future endeavors will involve conducting user studies and experiments to evaluate the system's effectiveness in enhancing language proficiency and fostering cross-cultural communication.

**Acknowledgments.** This research was partially supported by a Grant-in-Aid for Scientific Research (A) (17H00759, 2017–2020), a Grant-in-Aid for Scientific Research (B) (21H03561,2021–2024) and a Grant-in-Aid for Early-Career Scientists (21K17794,2021–2024) from the Japan Society for the Promotion of Science (JSPS).

**Disclosure of Interests.** The authors have no competing interests to declare that are relevant to the content of this article.

# References

1. Bokamba, E.: Are there syntactic constraints on code-mixing? World Engl. **8**(3), 277–292 (1989)
2. Fujimura, K.: The necessity of "code-switching" and "code-mixing" in bilingual discourse: the case of Japanese speakers in the UK. Bull. Yasuda Women's Univ. **41**, 23–32 (2013). (in Japanese)
3. Gardner-Chloros, P.: Code-Switching. Cambridge University Press, Cambridge (2009)
4. Holmes, J.: An Introduction to Sociolinguistics, 3rd edn. Longman, Essex (2008)
5. Myers-Scotton, C.: Social Motivations for Codeswitching: Evidence from Africa. Oxford University Press, Oxford (1993)
6. Pituxcoosuvarn, M., Murakami, Y., Yamada, S.: Code-mixing strategies for computer mediated communication with non-native speakers. In: Proceedings of the 13th International Conference on Advances in Information Technology. IAIT 2023, Association for Computing Machinery, New York, NY, USA (2023). https://doi.org/10.1145/3628454.3631155, https://doi.org/10.1145/3628454.3631155
7. Tay, M.W.: Code switching and code mixing as a communicative strategy in multilingual discourse. World Engl. **8**(3), 407–417 (1989)
8. Thomason, S.: Language Contact. Edinburgh University Press, Edinburgh (2001)
9. Valdes-Fallis, G.: Code-switching among bilingual Mexican-American women: towards an understanding of sex-related language alternation. Int. J. Sociol. Lang. **17**, 65–72 (1977)
10. Waris, A.M.: Code switching and mixing (communication in learning language). J. Dakwah Tabligh **13**(1), 123–135 (2012)

# A Study on Sensors in Higher Education

Sarthak Sengupta[1] (ID), Anindya Bose[2] (ID), Fernando Moreira[3](✉) (ID),
David Fonseca Escudero[4] (ID), Francisco José García-Peñalvo[5] (ID),
and Cesar Collazos[6] (ID)

[1] IIHMR University, Jaipur, India
[2] 6th Generation of Computing, London, UK
[3] REMIT, IJP, Universidade Portucalense, Porto & IEETA,
Universidade de Aveiro, Aveiro, Portugal
fmoreira@upt.pt
[4] Department Architecture La Salle, Universitat Ramon Llull, Barcelona, Spain
david.fonseca@salle.url.edu
[5] Departamento de Informática y Automática, Universidad de Salamanca, Salamaca, Spain
fgarcia@usal.es
[6] Departamento de Sistemas, Universidad del Cauca, Popayan, Colombia
ccollazo@unicauca.edu.co

**Abstract.** The Coronavirus crisis affected the higher education system drastically. A rapid surge in the usage of sensors and wearable technologies was observed. So, a need to pursue further research on the implementation of sensors in higher education institutions has been witnessed. This research study revolves around exploring the relevant research studies on sensors and higher education. The study found that a notable number of global research studies have been pursued on sensors but very few were relevant to the context of higher education institutions. It was also observed that the number of relevant research studies on the topics increased during and after the COVID-19 pandemic. It was also observed that most of the relevant research studies were published by developed countries like the USA, China, and England but negligible studies were performed by other countries. So, this study can pave the foundation to formulate novel approaches in the strategic implementation of sensors in higher education institutions across the world.

**Keywords:** Sensors · Higher education · wearable technologies · bibliometric analysis · Coronavirus crisis

## 1 Introduction

Nowadays, a significant rise in the usage of sensors in higher education institutions has been witnessed. Wearable technologies have been used for many years by embedding on various devices like calculator watches, shoes, Walkman, hearing aids, pagers, Bluetooth headsets, smartphones, Fitbit, eyeglasses, smart watches, etc. [1] Sensors have been instrumental in detecting patterns for enhancing the performance of students [2].

P. Zaphiris and A. Ioannou (Eds.): HCII 2024, LNCS 14723, pp. 211–221, 2024.
https://doi.org/10.1007/978-3-031-61685-3_16

The monitoring of learning capabilities has been experimented with biometric devices also [3]. Moreover, a pressing need to implement wearable sensors in higher education institutions has been witnessed especially after the Coronavirus crisis because many students, teachers, and other people in various institutes were facing health issues while attending to their duties on campus.

Proper evaluation of the implementation of sensors for educational purposes are essential requirement for higher education institutions. Real-time monitoring with sensors can be an effective mechanism for evaluating the stakeholders and it can be an efficient method for understanding the health status of them. It is essential to investigate the viability of such sensors and their adoption in various higher education institutions. Therefore, the main objective of this research study is to conduct a bibliometric analysis on sensors and higher education for exploring relevant research studies across the world.

The research study has been divided into various sub-sections. The next section discusses the literature review regarding relevant research articles on the domain. The methodology was also discussed later. After that, the analysis and findings were discussed. Last but not the least, the conclusions were discussed.

## 2    Literature Review

A rigorous review of relevant literature was thoroughly explored accordingly. Leading research databases were meticulously searched to extract relevant articles on sensors and higher education. So, this research study was mainly dependent on secondary data.

A sensor can be defined as a device that can transmit a resulting impulse. For example, sensors can be useful for the measurements or operation of a control, in response to a physical stimulus, such as heat, light, sound, pressure, magnetism, or a specific motion. Conventional learning settings generally offer greater chances for improvement of interactions through the usage of sensor technology. A sensor can allow the real-time sharing of various kinds of essential information that bridges the gap between digital and physical surroundings. Nowadays, it is becoming increasingly simpler to incorporate common items with sensors, such as doors, lights, laptops, mobile phones, etc., into the digital environment. The ability of such systems in gathering and interpreting sensor-related data holds great promise as well as potential for e-learning applications which are primarily aimed at removing the obstacles brought due to learning in a digital setting. For instance, learner activity, emotion, posture, and movement patterns can be identified through sensor-based data analysis [4, 5]. This data can be utilized further for personalization in context-aware adaptive learning [6].

The software and tools can be used for recording daily activity records, following users' online preferences and activities, along with monitoring other non-physical stimuli that may be deemed sensing. In this research study, various definitions of sensors were also reviewed based on virtual and physical stimuli that are utilized for measuring or tracking an item or its features. A sensor can be a software program or a device. The standardization of learning systems with the assistance of sensors can be made possible by the availability of a reference model that can explicitly recognize its capabilities and presence in a learning system. According to a relevant research study [7], a reference model has been elaborated basically as an abstract framework for understanding the significant relationships among the entities of some particular environment. While modeling a class of problems, such domain-specific ontology helps in enabling a shared understanding of the items and their interactions accordingly. Therefore, a reference model offers a taxonomy of concepts that can be useful for the identification of common functional system elements, recording data flow, comparing systems, and connections between these elements. Therefore, the key components of such sensors-based learning systems can be found using a reference model, which can also establish the design standard for these systems.

It was also observed that the COVID-19 pandemic has affected the health and immunity of people drastically. Continuous monitoring of the internal stakeholders' health in higher education institutions is the need of the hour. The internal stakeholders of higher education institutions include students, faculties, teachers, staff, administrative officers, etc. [8] So nowadays, portable, and miniaturized sensors are becoming a need in our everyday lives. Thanks to technological advancements, these devices allow humans to easily interface and communicate with machines and computers. Users can engage in a variety of activities through this interaction using interfaces like a desktop computer, smartphone, touch- or gesture-based system, or more sophisticated technologies like augmented reality (AR) and virtual reality (VR) [9, 10].

A wearable gadget like a wristwatch in the early twenty-first century was less of a tool for facilitating human–computer connection and more of an industrial design. Tiny digital devices made to be worn on the human body are known as wearable technology [11, 12]. Wireless connectivity can be included in them to easily access and exchange contextually relevant data [13]. A growing number of applications, such as health monitoring [14, 15], gesture detection [16–18], entertainment [19], gaming [20], and fashion [21], use wearable technology. Wearable technology has been utilized in education more recently [22–24]. According to recent studies, wearable sensors are used by educators to enhance the quality of their instruction, and students can use these sensors to increase interaction and participation in the classroom [25, 26]. Wearables have the potential to significantly impact learning and education because of their imperceptibility and direct touch with the human body [27, 28]. The capability of wearable sensors has greatly advanced, becoming more practical, user-friendly, and real-time performing [29]. The development of wearable technology for education was previously the focus of a separate scientific conference [30]. Nonetheless, the pre-university learner experiences were the primary focus of most reported contributions. Thus, the purpose of this research study is to evaluate wearable technologies for learning in additional detail and to concentrate on their application in a higher education setting.

One of the earliest applications of wearable technology in education was VR headsets, especially for teaching abstract courses like geometry and mathematics [27, 31]. The literature claims that this kind of VR technology accelerated the growth of collaborative and immersive learning in the classroom [32]. Furthermore, a lot of research has been done on augmented reality (AR) and extended reality (XR) for educational reasons [33–35]. Additionally, as wearable technology has become more widely employed in education, virtual field excursions have been made possible by digitally enhancing physical activities [36]. By eschewing the traditional understanding of information technology and education and redefining technology and information as a "digital augmentation of physical activities," this work highlights the advantages of collaborative exploration and discovery, where data collection and learning reflection are done in tandem. Other wearables, such as head-mounted displays, are also available to view historical events and improve learning by allowing users to experience and feel history as reality [37]. Therefore, the research indicates that the use of wearable technology in the classroom has benefited student learning [38–40]. Benefits were shown across a broad range of disciplines and age ranges, including K–12 education and postsecondary education. According to recent K–12 research, students' reduced self-worth assessments and concerns about their health and safety are the main drawbacks of wearing wearable technology [41]. Moreover, the importance of portable biosensors [42] has increased especially during the COVID-19 pandemic [43]. Therefore, the rigorous review of relevant literature helped in understanding various aspects of sensors in higher education institutions.

## 3   Methodology

The study is primarily based on secondary data. The data was collected from leading research databases like Web of Science (WoS), Emerald, Scopus, IEEEXplore, Springer-Nature, etc. Relevant studies in the domain were explored. Bibliometric analysis was performed accordingly. The research team of subject matter experts brainstormed together to decide the set of relevant keywords needed for the extraction of required data to perform further analysis.

The research gap found while performing the rigorous review of the literature was that negligible studies have been done in the areas of sensors and higher education. So, the research objective was formulated accordingly. The objective of this research study is to explore the global research studies on sensors and higher education.

## 4   Analysis and Findings

The relevant review of the literature helped in understanding various aspects of sensors in higher education. The bibliometric analysis was performed in this sub-section with the assistance of a secondary dataset collected from the Clarivate Analytics' Web of Science (WoS) research database. It is considered a major research database globally for performing such analysis [44–46]. All the relevant research articles provided in the extracted dataset from WoS were thoroughly explored. So, the search keywords namely sensors and higher education were finalized accordingly. The relevant research studies and research team were also instrumental in fixing these keywords for data extraction purposes. Therefore, the search criteria included two keywords mentioned above along with the AND Boolean gate or operator to extract the intersection set, i.e., the research articles consisting of both the keywords namely sensors and higher education. Moreover, the "Topic" search option was selected to consider the research articles on those relevant topics in the Web of Science core collection. Therefore, a total number of 112 research publications were shortlisted for further analysis and results were found eventually.

Figure 1 provides the bar chart regarding the years versus the number of research publications in that corresponding year. The bar chart provided the year-wise number of research publications in descending order, i.e., the horizontal X-axis provided the years whereas the vertical Y-axis provided the number of research publications in that particular year. In Fig. 1 it can be observed that the years 2022, 2023, and 2021 published the highest number of relevant research studies on sensors and higher education. There is a saying which can be quoted that "necessity is the mother of invention". The time span between the years 2021 to 2023 marks the era of the Coronavirus crisis which pushed the need for sensors in higher education institutions. Figure 2 provides the treemap chart regarding research categories based on the Web of Science platform. Here it can be observed that the engineering category comprised the maximum number of research studies on sensors and higher education followed by categories namely computer science, education educational research, etc.

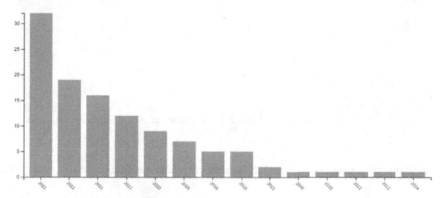

**Fig. 1.** Bar chart regarding years V/S no. of research publication in descending order

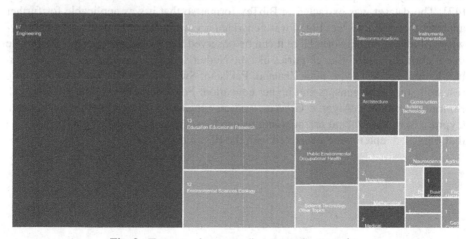

**Fig. 2.** Treemap chart regarding research categories

Figure 3 depicts the bar chart regarding the country versus the number of research publications by that country. The bar chart provided the country-wise numbers of research publications in descending order, i.e., the horizontal X-axis provided the countries whereas the vertical Y-axis provided the number of research publications by that particular country. It can be observed in Fig. 3 that China, England, and the United States of America (USA) are leading the list regarding the highest number of research publications on sensors and higher education. So, the collaborative research team comprising authors from India, Portugal, Spain, and Colombia attempted to pursue this research study and contribute to the relevant domain gradually. Moreover, please note that Figs. 1, 2, and 3 were generated with the help of the Web of Science platform.

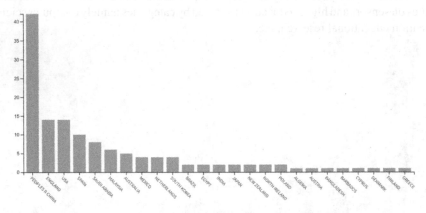

**Fig. 3.** Bar chart regarding Countries V/S Number of research publications in descending order

Subsequently, the WoS dataset was inputted into the R-Studio software and bibliometric analysis was performed with the help of the Bibliometrix package accordingly [47]. The dataset was extracted in BibTex format so that it was applicable for further analysis by the R tool. So, Fig. 4 was generated accordingly which depicts the country-wise collaboration network. Here it can be observed that China is playing a major role in collaborating with other countries like the Netherlands, United Kingdom, Saudi Arabia, Korea, Japan, Egypt, New Zealand, Pakistan, Sweden, and Barbados for pursuing research studies on sensors and higher education. Few countries like the United Arab Emirates, Denmark, Algeria, Greece, Tunisia, Singapore, Hungary, Brazil, Morocco, Cyprus, Italy, and Poland are pursuing research on this area on their own. Please note that Figs. 4, 5, and 6 were generated with the RStudio tool.

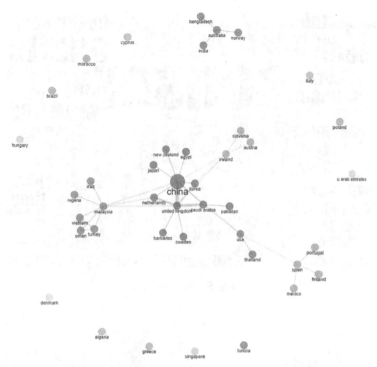

**Fig. 4.** Country-wise collaboration network

Figure 5 provided below depicts the word cloud. In this figure, the size of the word is directly proportional to the frequency of usage of that keyword in the relevant research studies. Here it can be observed that the words namely impact, sensor, design, and system are essential keywords because of their larger size.

The thematic evolution has been provided in Fig. 6. The thematic evolution is very useful in detecting conceptual sub-domains [48]. In Fig. 6 it can be seen that two cutting years were selected as 2019 and 2021. This was done to check the sub-domains or relevant themes being pondered upon before, during, and after the COVID-19 pandemic. It can be observed that before the pandemic, i.e., till the year 2019, the sub-domain namely reliability came up. But during the pandemic, i.e., after the year 2019 to 2021, other themes or sub-domains were observed like students, internet, system, adults, and higher-education. Moreover, after the pandemic, i.e., after 2021 till the present, the sub-domains or themes are internet and design. Therefore, it can be observed that the sub-domains changed substantially before and during the pandemic but not much change was witnessed after the pandemic. Therefore, the bibliometric analysis helped in understanding the relevant research studies being published across the world on sensors and higher education.

**Fig. 5.** Word cloud

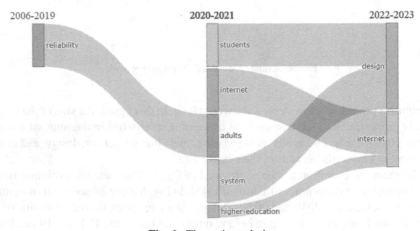

**Fig. 6.** Thematic evolution

## 5   Conclusion

The COVID-19 pandemic drastically affected the educational system across the world [49]. So, a rampant need to improvise the educational system with the help of sensors can be an instrumental strategy for the overall growth and development of stakeholders in higher education institutions. This study observed that a notable number of global research studies have been pursued on sensors but very few were relevant to the context of higher education institutions. It was also observed that the number of relevant research studies on sensors and higher education increased during and after the Coronavirus crisis.

This research study also found that most of the relevant research studies were published by developed countries like the USA, China, England, and Spain but negligible studies were performed by other countries like India, Portugal, and Colombia. Therefore, this research study concluded that a significant rise in relevant research studies is needed to achieve the new normal for coping up after the Coronavirus crisis. Moreover, it was also observed that the global fraternity of researchers upgraded their sub-domains and themes of research fields during and after the Coronavirus crisis accordingly.

The after-effects of the COVID-19 pandemic can be combatted with the help of the efficient implementation of effective sensors in higher education institutions. This research study can pave the foundation for moving ahead with future research directions regarding sensors for higher educational development. Moreover, various relevant studies explored while performing the rigorous review of the literature have also provided further scope of research on approaches for sensor fusion [50], ambient sensors [51], tracking sensors [52], and robotic sensors [53] for educational purposes [54, 55]. So, this present research study can help in building novel approaches for implementing sensors in higher education institutions in various countries across the world.

**Acknowledgements.** This work was supported by the FCT – Fundação para a Ciência e a Tecnologia, I.P. [Project UIDB/05105/2020].

# References

1. Khosravi, S, Bailey, S.G., Parvizi, H., Ghannam, R.: Wearable sensors for learning enhancement in higher education. Sensors **22**(19), 7633 (2022)
2. Gonzalez Crespo, R., Burgos, D.: Advanced sensors technology in education. Sensors **19**(19), 4155 (2019)
3. Ferreira, C.P., González, C.S.G., Moreira, F.: Learning monitoring model with biometric devices for business simulation games: PBP methodology. In: 2023 18th Iberian Conference on Information Systems and Technologies (CISTI), Aveiro, Portugal, pp. 1–6 (2023)
4. Brunelli, D., Farella, E., Rocchi, L., Dozza, M., Chiari, L., Benini, L.: Bio-feedback system for rehabilitation based on a wireless body area network. In: Fourth Annual IEEE International Conference on Pervasive Computing and Communications Workshops (PERCOMW'06), pp. 527–531 (2006)
5. Lara, O.D., Labrador, M.A.: A survey on human activity recognition using wearable sensors. IEEE Commun. Surv. Tutor. **15**, 1192–1209 (2013)
6. Zimmermann, A., Specht, M., Lorenz, A.: Personalization and context management. User Model. User-Adapted Interact. **15**, 275–302 (2005)
7. Mackenzie, C.M., Mccabe, F., Brown, P.F., Net, P., Metz, R., Hamilton, A.: Reference Model for Service Oriented Architecture 1.0 (2006)
8. Sengupta, S., Vaish, A.: A study on social media and higher education during the COVID-19 pandemic. Univ. Access Inf. Soc. (2023)
9. Chan, J.C., Leung, H., Tang, J.K., Komura, T.: A virtual reality dance training system using motion capture technology. IEEE Trans. Learn. Technol. **4**, 187–195 (2010)
10. Santos, M.E.C., Chen, A., Taketomi, T., Yamamoto, G., Miyazaki, J., Kato, H.: Augmented reality learning experiences: survey of prototype design and evaluation. IEEE Trans. Learn. Technol. **7**, 38–56 (2013)
11. Kim, J., Campbell, A.S., de Ávila, B.E.F., Wang, J.: Wearable biosensors for healthcare monitoring. Nat. Biotechnol. **37**, 389–406 (2019)

12. Imran, M.A., Ghannam, R., Abbasi, Q.H.: Engineering and Technology for Healthcare. John Wiley & Sons, Hoboken, NJ, USA (2020)
13. Liang, X., et al.: Fusion of wearable and contactless sensors for intelligent gesture recognition. Adv. Intell. Syst. **1**, 1900088 (2019)
14. Moin, A., et al.: A wearable biosensing system with in-sensor adaptive machine learning for hand gesture recognition. Nat. Electron. **4**, 54–63 (2021)
15. Yuan, M., et al.: Electronic contact lens: a platform for wireless health monitoring applications. Adv. Intell. Syst. **2**, 1900190 (2020)
16. Liang, X., Ghannam, R., Heidari, H.: Wrist-worn gesture sensing with wearable intelligence. IEEE Sens. J. **19**, 1082–1090 (2019)
17. Tanwear, A., et al.: Spintronic sensors based on magnetic tunnel junctions for wireless eye movement gesture control. IEEE Trans. Biomed. Circuits Syst. **14**, 1299–1310 (2020)
18. Tanwear, A., et al.: Spintronic eyeblink gesture sensor with wearable interface system. IEEE Trans. Biomed. Circuits Syst. **1**, 1–14 (2022)
19. Page, T.: A forecast of the adoption of wearable technology. Int. J. Technol. Diffus. **6**, 12–29 (2015)
20. Lindberg, R., Seo, J., Laine, T.H.: Enhancing physical education with exergames and wearable technology. IEEE Trans. Learn. Technol. **9**, 328–341 (2016)
21. McCann, J., Bryson, D.: Smart Clothes and Wearable Technology. Elsevier, Amsterdam, The Netherlands (2009)
22. Ferrier, B., Lee, J., Mbuli, A., James, D.A.: Translational applications of wearable sensors in education: implementation and efficacy. Sensors **22**, 1675 (2022)
23. Almusawi, H.A., Durugbo, C.M., Bugawa, A.M.: Wearable technology in education: a systematic review. IEEE Trans. Learn. Technol. **14**, 540–554 (2021)
24. Liang, J.M., Su, W.C., Chen, Y.L., Wu, S.L., Chen, J.J.: Smart interactive education system based on wearable devices. Sensors **19**, 3260 (2019)
25. Gao, W., Wei, T., Huang, H., Chen, X., Li, Q.: Toward a systematic survey on wearable computing for education applications. IEEE Internet Things J. **9**, 12901–12915 (2022)
26. Matteucci, I.: Wearable technologies as learning engines: evaluations and perspectives. Ital. J. Sociol. Educ. **13**, 161–179 (2021)
27. Bower, M., Sturman, D., Alvarez, V.: Perceived utility and feasibility of wearable technologies in higher education. In: Proceedings of the World Conference on Mobile and Contextual Learning, Shanghai, China, pp. 47–56, 13–15 June 2016
28. Ahmed, M.D., Leung, W.C.W.: Using wearable devices to enhance quality of physical education for students. Strategies **34**, 54–56 (2021)
29. Qu, X., Wang, J., Miao, R.: Wearable technology and its application in education. Res. Dev. Sci. Technol. **6**, 135–144 (2022)
30. Lee, M.J.W.: Guest editorial: special section on learning through wearable technologies and the internet of things. IEEE Trans. Learn. Technol. **9**, 301–303 (2016)
31. Kaufmann, H., Schmalstieg, D., Wagner, M.: Construct3D: a virtual reality application for mathematics and geometry education. Educ. Inf. Technol. **5**, 263–276 (2000)
32. Colella, V.: Participatory simulations: building collaborative understanding through immersive dynamic modeling. J. Learn. Sci. **9**, 471–500 (2000)
33. Iop, A., et al.: Extended reality in neurosurgical education: a systematic review. Sensors **22**, 6067 (2022)
34. Wang, J., Qi, Y.: A multi-user collaborative AR system for industrial applications. Sensors **22**, 1319 (2022)
35. Yildiz, E.P.: Augmented reality research and applications in education. In Augmented Reality and Its Application. IntechOpen, London, UK (2021)

36. Rogers, Y., et al.: Learning through Digitally-Augmented Physical Experiences: Reflections on the Ambient Wood Project; Working Paper; University of Southampton, Southampton, UK (2002)
37. Nakasugi, H., Yamauchi, Y.: Past viewer: development of wearable learning system for history education. In: Proceedings of the International Conference on Computers in Education, Washington, DC, USA, pp. 1311–1312, 2–6 December 2002
38. Camacho, V.L., de la Guía, E., Olivares, T., Flores, M.J., Orozco-Barbosa, L.: Data capture and multimodal learning analytics focused on engagement with a new wearable IoT approach. IEEE Trans. Learn. Technol. **13**, 704–717 (2020)
39. Ngai, G., Chan, S.C.F., Cheung, J.C.Y., Lau, W.W.Y.: Deploying a wearable computing platform for computing education. IEEE Trans. Learn. Technol. **3**, 45–55 (2010)
40. Teitelbaum, D., et al.: Use of wearable point-of-view live streaming technology for virtual physical exam skills training. Can. Med. Educ. J. **13**, 64–66 (2022)
41. Jovanovic, P., Kay, R.: Examining the use of wearable technologies for K-12 Students: a systematic review of the literature. J. Digit. Life Learn. **1**, 56–67 (2021)
42. Bose, A., Sengupta, S.: Fabrication and characterization of pillar interdigitated electrode for blood glucose sensing. Sens. Rev. **41**(2), 200–207 (2021)
43. Mobed, A., Shafigh, E.S.: Biosensors promising bio-device for pandemic screening COVID-19. Microchem. J. **164** (2021)
44. Sengupta, S., Vaish, A.: A study on social networking platforms in higher education institutions. Acad. Market. Stud. J. **26**(3) (2022)
45. Abramo, G., D'Angelo, C.A.: An assessment of the first scientific habilitation for university appointments in Italy. Econ. Polit. **32**, 329–357 (2015)
46. Conde, M.Á., Fonseca, D.: Information society skills: is knowledge accessible for all? Part I. Univ. Access Inf. Soc. **17**, 223–227 (2018)
47. Aria, M., Cuccurullo, C.: Bibliometrix: an R-tool for comprehensive science mapping analysis. J. Informet. **11**(4), 959–975 (2017)
48. Chen, X., Lun, Y., Yan, J., et al.: Discovering thematic change and evolution of utilizing social media for healthcare research. BMC Med. Inform. Decis. Mak. **19**, 50 (2019)
49. García-Peñalvo, F.J., Corell, A., Abella-García, V., Grande, M.: Online assessment in higher education in times of COVID-19. Educ. Knowl. Soc. (EKS) 21, 26 (2020)
50. Marcos-Pablos, S., Lobato, F., García-Peñalvo, F.J.: Integrating emotion recognition tools for developing emotionally intelligent agents. Int. J. Interact. Multimed. Artif. Intell. **7**(6), 69–76 (2022)
51. Marcos-Pablos, S., García-Peñalvo, F.J.: Technological ecosystems in care and assistance: a systematic literature review. Sensors **19**(3), Article 708 (2019)
52. Cavalcanti, J., Valls, V., Contero, M., Fonseca, D.: Gamification and hazard communication in virtual reality: a qualitative study. Sensors **21**(14), 4663 (2021)
53. Amo, D., Fox, P., Fonseca, D., Poyatos, C.: Systematic review on which analytics and learning methodologies are applied in primary and secondary education in the learning of robotics sensors. Sensors **21**(1), 153 (2021)
54. Marcos-Pablos, S., García-Peñalvo, F.J.: More than surgical tools: a systematic review of robots as didactic tools for the education of professionals in health sciences. Adv. Health Sci. Educ. **27**(4), 1139–1176 (2022)
55. Pou, A.V., Canaleta, X., Fonseca, D.: Computational thinking and educational robotics integrated into project-based learning. Sensors **22**(10), 3746 (2022)

# Hybrid Spaces in Higher Education:
# A Comprehensive Guide to Pedagogical, Space and Technology Design

Robin Støckert[ID] and Veruska De Caro-Barek[✉][ID]

Norwegian University of Science and Technology, Trondheim, Norway
{robin.stockert,veruska.de.caro}@ntnu.no

**Abstract.** With this case report article, we hope to provide an overview of many important factors that positively impact or hinder the development and activities within hybrid spaces in higher education. Our findings gravitate around an exploratory case study on a unique shared physical/hybrid space called the "The Portal," designed to host a joint international master program connecting the two largest universities in Norway. The origin of our research comes from a cross-university physical/hybrid space. However, any of our findings will also fit other similar solutions described as physical/hybrid/online cross-campus, multi-campus, or distributed spaces for teaching and learning. This paper contains selected research and gathered experiences from 2016–2024 within the SALTO research program, designing hybrid learning environments/spaces and finding the appropriate technical and pedagogical approaches focusing on the learning/teaching experience.

**Keywords:** Hybrid · Pedagogy. Space · Technology

## 1 Introduction

Many factors influence strategic decisions and governance within Higher Education Institutions (HEI). Role, responsibilities, purpose, governance, and inertia are all critical issues that need to be considered in the modernization [1, 2, 3] of universities to accommodate international and national strategies and governmental reforms in a complex and ever faster-developing world. At the global level, we find the visions of the United Nations Sustainable Development Goals (SDG) with an overall aim to end poverty, protect the planet, and ensure prosperity for all by 2030 [4]. SDG4 aims to ensure equal access to affordable and quality technical, vocational, and tertiary education, including University. "A commitment to ensure access to inclusive and equitable quality education and promote lifelong learning for all."

The Education 2030 Framework for Action, which UNESCO leads, guides the ICT implementation of these ambitious goals and commitments. As for HE recommendations in education policies and masterplans: "ICT should enhance the quality, efficiency, and

P. Zaphiris and A. Ioannou (Eds.): HCII 2024, LNCS 14723, pp. 222–240, 2024.
https://doi.org/10.1007/978-3-031-61685-3_17

accessibility of higher education through its applications in various teaching and learning situations.... In particular, technology-enhanced classroom teaching, distributed learning, and blended learning can improve the quality of HE programs."

One goal and objective is to expand access to HE and develop an eco-system containing flexible (anytime and anywhere) distance education. Overall, the UNESCO guidelines [5] provide a holistic examination of ICT's roles in strengthening practical provision and administration and the three traditional missions of a university: teaching, research, and service.

Furthermore, giving access to ICT-based resources regardless of time and various learning spaces provides more flexibility for remote students, students with extra work, and students with families. Many of these activities align with the UNESCO ICT guidelines. According to the EU's European strategy for Universities [6] from 2022, the digital transition gives universities a fundamental role in equipping students and researchers for a future based on hybrid solutions, representing a good balance between physical presence and digital tools. Furthermore, the strategy aims to "reinforce transnational cooperation between universities to strengthen their capacities to equip young people, lifelong learners, and researchers with the right competences and skills."

Several interpretations and suggestions exist on how Universities can adapt to the SDGs [7, 8]. For teaching, two categories [9] can describe the approaches aligning Universities with SDG. The first category is teaching SDG, and the second is applying SDG as a pedagogical means within teaching itself, focusing on teaching quality based on numerous factors like peer or student feedback and transparent learning outcomes to suit individual educational trajectories by optimizing the curriculum's design, structure, and experienced usefulness. Put a focus on students' well-being/mental health and sense of trust and belonging. Providing the students with meaningful but complex tasks to solve as a group may increase their autonomy, innovation, and motivation.

Hence, the former role of the University as a developer of students' professional skills and competencies toward an academic degree to secure a future job is outdated.

There is a need to integrate 21st-century skills [10] and competencies into the University education. Enabling and preparing the students [11] for a future workplace requires collaborating and communicating, doing complex problem-solving within cross-disciplinary teams, extending digital skills, adapting to a rapidly changing, interconnected world, and taking social and civic responsibility.

To ensure lifelong learning, the University must be able [12] to deliver flexibility, easy access, and multi-format educational activities and resources adapted to students in various phases and places in life. In principle, the University must deliver a sustainable expansion [13] to be accessible and provide services and resources across the physical, hybrid, and online learning environment [14] as described in "Universities without walls - A vision for 2030" made by the European University Association) [15].

The mentioned visions and approaches toward 2030 contain many pitfalls, promises, and perils at risk globally, internationally, and nationally. On a global scale, we face impacts from climate, energy, and demographic changes, and on an international scale, we experience political, societal, and security issues, causing latency and recalibration of milestones and progress. In Europe, many HEI institutions face lower student enrollment and increased operational and maintenance costs, funding uncertainty, resignation and mitigation of leadership and staff, and the demand for increased ICT security and privacy threats [16].

According to the 2023 UN SDG report, the progress toward quality education is slower than expected, and COVID-19 has had a substantial negative impact on education, causing learning losses in four out of five of the 104 countries studied in the report. Factors slowing down the progress vary across regions, and "access" to education is far from universal. Barriers described in the report concern lack of essential services and infrastructure, access to computers and the internet. Furthermore, limited user skills in Information and Communication Technology (ICT) hinder universal and meaningful connectivity, communication, collaboration, problem-solving, and content creation [17].

Hybrid and blended learning do not have one general and agreed-upon definition. [18–21] and is often used to describe various learning modalities in time and space, where students' and teachers' locations and related activities can be a mix of various learning environments and interactions with the help of digital technology.

Meanwhile, our solution and research build on a specific setup between the two universities. The SALTO and MCT approach described in this paper coincides with many of the above strategies and visions concerning collaboration between universities, administration, researchers, teachers, and students, hybrid and blended learning approaches, easy access and sharing of resources, a focus on ICT skills and infrastructure, and caretaking the human factor.

For our development, pedagogy, space, and technology were the principal design elements [22], and students and teachers were the users, representing the human factor in the equation. In addition, we had audiovisual(AV) and IT(Information Technology) support in the design and implementation phase and administrative support at both universities running the master's program.

In our case, we define hybrid as a shared physical-virtual workspace between two Universities, with a design and technologies facilitating and enabling various types of communication, collaboration, and interaction. In addition, the mediating technology enables synchronous/asynchronous sharing of resources and activities between the universities and external users. For MCT, the focus was to design and optimize an "always-on" shared physical-virtual workspace to enable a more natural and spontaneous human interaction without starting a Teams or Zoom conference.

We define blended learning in this setting (learning environment) as taking various approaches and using the appropriate digital tools in the learning process.

## 2   Background and Context

The backdrop and starting point go back to 2018, when the two largest universities in Norway, NTNU (Norwegian University of Science and Technology and UiO (University of Oslo) started a joint international Master's program in Music, Communication and Technology. (MCT).

The learning environment of MCT originates from a shared space called "the Portal" designed for students' active learning and sharing of resources between the two universities located more than 500 km apart. "The Portal" is a shared physical-virtual workspace with a design and technologies facilitating and enabling various types of realtime communication, collaboration, and interaction. MCT got support from a rector-supported development program to investigate and develop solutions for "Student Active Learning in a Two-campus Organization" (SALTO), using MCT and the Portal as the testbed and environment for the research and development.

Our findings and previously published papers indicate that the planning, development, and use of a cross-university learning space are difficult to orchestrate with various stakeholders. Factors like university cultures, related governmental or local university strategies, and many practical, pedagogical, technical, economic, and organizational elements influence the process's different stages and timing. Hence, anchoring the process within the University and developing a shared understanding between various stakeholders in developing the hybrid learning environment and the Master's program is crucial.

## 2.1 MCT

When the International Master's program in Music, Communication, and Technology (MCT) launched in the autumn of 2018, it was the first cross-disciplinary/campus/University program in Norway, a collaboration project between the two most prominent universities, NTNU( Norwegian University of Science and Technology and UiO(University of Oslo).

The basic idea came from Alexander Refsum Jensenius (UiO) in 2016 to formalize a long cooperation between the Music Technology Department at NTNU, doing work and research within sound processing, production, and performance, and the Music Science Department at UiO, researching sound, movement, and machine learning. Combining these resources and knowledge and providing international students with various backgrounds, a plethora of workshops, and topics like physiology, machine learning, acoustics, informatics, and entrepreneurship was the core idea of MCT [23].

The Portal was the shared physical/hybrid space for all activities, where students from both locations should work in groups, collaborate, and simultaneously develop their learning environment [24] with the teachers to become "technological humanists". In addition, the Portal's 24/7 "always on" concept would enhance the sense of co-presence [25] and facilitate a natural flow of information and social interaction between the participants, with a precise aim to reduce the one-way transmission from the teacher as the "Sage on the stage" lecturing to students across the Portal. In other words, scaffold students and teachers to design a shared stage where they perform together and the teacher sometimes can take the role of "guide on the side".

Other circumstances supporting MCT's establishment were political signals from the Ministry of Knowledge, the structural reform within higher education, and the merger between three University colleges and NTNU in 2016. The merger introduced challenges on many levels and exposed a political and practical field of needed research and development to find reasonable cross-campus/distributed solutions within HE.

## 2.2 SALTO

In 2017, MCT got support from a rector-supported development program to investigate and develop solutions for "Student Active Learning in a Two-campus Organization" (SALTO), using MCT and the Portal as the testbed and environment for research and development.

The SALTO project was a part of the NTNU Teaching Excellence initiative, an integrated and wide-ranging initiative aimed at helping NTNU achieve its goal of providing high-quality education at a high international level.

The initiative comprises a portfolio of development measures to strengthen teaching skills by developing innovative teaching, learning, and assessment practices. The measures aim to improve students' learning outcomes.

During the project period, SALTO first engaged in the physical and hybrid design of the shared learning space (Portal), finding the most relevant architectural, organizational, and technological solutions to support the planned pedagogical activities between the Universities. [26] The pedagogical approach focused on flipped and collaborative learning through short but intensive workshops and minor internal projects, sometimes with external participants and partners.

Secondly, SALTO focused on the students' and teachers' voices concerning their experiences related to teaching and learning activities at MCT and let them tell their version of the story. We examined the factors that impact the dynamics and human interaction within the Portal and MCT, for instance, ownership, motivation, innovational approaches, teamwork, and trust. For more information about SALTO visit the web pages [27].

## 2.3 The Portal

The Portal is the working title of the design and functionality of a shared physical/hybrid workspace between UiO and NTNU, facilitating "student active learning" and focusing on communication, collaboration, and interaction. The starting point was to modify and extend the PST Framework for a cross-campus setting.

Hence, the concept idea consists of two identical/symmetrical/mirrored physical rooms, one at each University. Various technologies connect these physical rooms(shared space) and the applied pedagogy and related activities are mediated through this technology. See Fig. 1.

These rooms are interconnected(networked) by various layers of technology to facilitate the feeling of being in "one common shared room/space". The primary system for audiovisual communication should always be "on" and create the feeling of looking through the mirror/glass and seeing the other side without setting up a conference call. There is a focus on real-time synchronous activities, meaning that the audiovisual latency between the interconnected physical rooms (500 km apart) is so tiny that the students can perform and play music together, even though they are in different physical locations. The strive toward low latency was to preserve natural human communication and micro-signaling [28] in dialogue and interaction, which is often lost or reduced through the use of general conference systems with various artifacts concerning video and audio quality due to compression, latency, network issues, end equipment, and other non-controllable "features".

However, the many layers of technology in the Portal also support general videoconference systems like old hardware Polycom units and software like Teams. Zoom rooms at each end of the Portal, with additional Zoom client software running on any device, were the preferred solution and had many options for live-switching USB equipment like cameras and microphones. Zoom provides excellent flexibility in sharing desktops, extra cameras, and sound sources. These features were practical in projects where students could use their mobile as an extra video source input to the Zoom room conference—for instance, sharing a close-up of their print board and components with their device (phone, tablet). In addition, Zoom offered features to analyze and work with audiovisual compression versus bandwidth, High-quality audio, test various equipment, and pedagogical tools like breakout rooms. Many of these features came in handy during COVID-19, when the students had to stay home in their own country, and all activity moved online. Zoom was stable and running on almost any device and operating system, even if the bandwidth was unstable when connecting students from Ecuador in the west to China in the east.

The physical endpoints of the Portal are in themselves a stage/BlackBox, which can be rigged/re-configured for different learning scenarios. As with a standard stage for a concert or theatrical performance, various technologies are available and used to create a connection, enhance, amplify, and transmit the event/performance to an audience, whether close to the stage, sitting in the back, looking at large screens on the stage or watching the streaming or recorded (often edited) version from a remote location. The total experience and the feeling of a successful event/performance depend on the performer and the content, the mediating technology (technicians, producers), and the audience.

In other words, the endpoints of the Portal contain people working on stage, behind the stage, and acting as audiences simultaneously. However, the Portal has the extraordinary dimension of enabling interaction, collaboration, and shared activities across the distance between all event participants. As with any theatrical performance, we must set the stage with the right props to create a context or scenario related to the performance. In the Portal, the students and teachers work together to find the best scenarios and the optimal mediating technology to enhance and share the learning and teaching performance/experience. In context, the efficiency of the pedagogy approach/related activities relies on the degree of adaption of the learning scenario and physical/hybrid/online environment to optimize students' learning experience [29].

The physical implementation of the Portal concept idea with the mirrored rooms introduced challenges for NTNU. Uio already had a Portal room, but NTNU had to design and build it from scratch, delaying the planned symmetrical activities between the universities within MCT.

The good thing about this delay was that NTNU could design a complete eco-system around the Portal mirrored room by adding smaller group rooms and a social zone. Plan the interplay between the technical infrastructure, network, acoustics, HVAC, lighting, furniture, ceiling truss systems for lights, cameras, sensor systems, and multichannel speaker setups. The Portal eco-system had a dedicated HVAC system with sensors controlling the air quality and the temperature. General lighting was daylight LED since the main Portal room had no windows to prevent unwanted incoming outside light and control acoustic reflection from hard surfaces.

The complete architectural design and focus on small but essential details provided a solution that completely controlled the environment and enabled re-configuring and adapting to various teaching and learning scenarios [30]. For instance, beamforming microphones could track voices without acoustic challenges like reverberation and standing waves in the room. Placing and using extra lighting provided high-quality surroundings for video cameras to deliver crisp quality, depth, and clarity. Furthermore, the Portal's holistic design, ergonomics, architectural aspects, and functionality can contribute to cultivating the multidimensional "wellness" experience in a physical/hybrid setting and the transitions between them for all participants [14].

## 2.4 Expanding the PST Framework

The digital revolution of the past century has moved us from the Fourth Industrial Revolution (4IR) [31], described by a convergence of technologies that blurs the boundaries between the physical, digital, and biological realms toward a holistic shift that integrates technology, ethics, and humanity, shaping the future of work and society (5IR).

Likewise, we observe that the boundaries of physical/hybrid/online/virtual spaces are becoming more transparent and permeable within HE. As a natural consequence, new opportunities and pitfalls appear. First, it gives students more flexibility and the possibility to study anywhere, anytime, and in any format. However, it simultaneously introduces fragmentation in students' learning experience by distributing activities, (social) interactions, resources, and lectures over time and space. This fragmentation puts pressure on the teachers and administration to deliver many services to the students and simultaneously "promote connected learning- to help students (re)connect what they are learning: ideas to ideas, principles to problems, theory to practice…" [32] Furthermore, to create (in)formal spaces where students can work together, feel safe, interact, and be social.

There are, however, many definitions of place and space and their interrelations, but in our case, we would like to define the relation of "space" and "place" as the former being more abstract or extensive than the latter [32].

Twenty years ago, Diana Oblinger wrote about leading the transition from classrooms to learning spaces [33], claiming that "Good learning space design can support each institution's mission of enabling student learning. In fact, the convergence of technology, pedagogy, and space can lead to exciting new models of campus interaction." These ideas were taken further by Radcliffe's PST framework [34] in 2008. Here, the focus was mainly on the range of physical places for learning (Place for Learning -Spectrum exploring the relationships between various spaces, people, and learning modality.), where "Pedagogy seems to be the logical element to consider first, then space and finally technology. "However, this does not suggest a hierarchy or value pedagogy over space or technology. Rather, it is a recommended place to enter the pedagogy-space-technology loop in order to go through an iterative process".

Manciaracina [35] claims that the presence of the users seems missing in the PST framework. Pushing forward that in a learning environment, the users are players, actors, directors, facilitators and sources of resistance, students and teachers, learners and tutors. They should be a significant element of the framework and equally connected and related to the other parts, creating new design dynamics and a sense of cognitive, social, and teaching presence [36–38].

The missing link in the PST framework that glues everything together is indeed human interaction, or the human factor (Fig. 1.), as we call this element that accounts for the interaction between students and educators, students and students, educators and educators, and how this interaction concretizes itself in collaborative teaching and learning practices" [39].

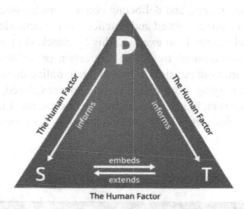

**Fig. 1.** PST Framework modified with the Human Factor

In order to use the PST framework for MCT with a focus on active learning in a new type of cross-university shared learning space (The Portal), some modifications were necessary (Fig. 2.). First, we focused on making the boundary between the Portal endpoints transparent to enable a natural human interaction (sense of co-presence) [25, 40, 41] and flow of resources. Various types of applied technology interconnect the Portal's physical endpoints and create a shared/hybrid space by mediating communication, collaboration, and interaction, preparing an environment/eco-system conducive to active learning.

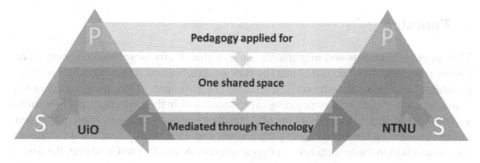

**Fig. 2.** Extended PST Framework

Secondly, we defined pedagogy not only as a starting point to enter the framework iterative process but as the most crucial component in the PST framework. The main pedagogical building blocks are student active learning, flipped learning, and peer learning. The iterative process also runs within the pedagogical element as a fast feedback loop between the students and the teachers to ensure an adaptive approach toward teaching and learning and the evolution of their shared learning space. It facilitates students to acquire and create new knowledge that scaffolds their needs and interests, boosting their engagement and intrinsic motivation. [41] enveloped by students' active and social learning in a continuum between physical, hybrid, and online learning environments. The continuum builds on "educator presence in online settings, interactions between students, teachers, and content, and deliberate connections between online and offline activities and between campus-related and practice-related activities." [29].

A proposed model (Table 1) to examine this by Støckert et al. (2020) [14] starts with three levels of synchronous (real-time) education or collaborative practices, all spread over a continuum from physical to hybrid, up to online domains. The framework holds nine situations ranging from pretty mature to unexplored, which raises many questions that need answers. In our case, finding the most critical factors impacting the learning/teaching experience moving between the various scenarios in the framework is interesting.

**Table 1.** Education Spaces Framework

| Education Spaces Framework | Physical | Hybrid | Online |
|---|---|---|---|
| Frontal Pedagogy (FP) | A | D | G |
| Participatory Practice (PP) | B | E | H |
| Joint Problem Solving (JPS) | C | F | J |

## 3   Educators

The conceptual visions and implementation of a shared cross-campus/university learning environment often become blurred by various stakeholders within the administrative, economic, and strategic sections of the University structures. They focus on economic convenience and stable old structures and processes within the University, not innovation and new ideas. Hence, examining the MCT teacher's pedagogical vision and implementation experiences toward designing the content and the learning space and facilitating the student within these scenarios is of great interest. According to Goodyear, the design of learning spaces is challenging and under-researched.

As a guide for our research [42] approach, examining this process, we asked: "What elements do educators in a hybrid cross-campus learning environment identify as essential for providing a supportive learning experience for students?".

## 3.1 Flexibility

The first essential finding was flexibility, which starts with the structure and planning of the whole master's program, with various topics and small workshops/projects running throughout the whole semester. The students had various backgrounds/interests and previous education. Hence, the educators indicated that they provided options for the students to choose learning activities and topics linked to their prior learning experiences/interests or to choose an area that was new to them, empowering the students to take control of their learning [43] and work on their 21st-century skill within their group, consisting of members from both physical locations.

Furthermore, providing the students with the choice of finding/making the right digital tools for the tasks and how to co-configure [44] their learning space (Portal) to collaboratively (cross-university groups) solve authentic tasks, hands-on challenges and real-world (wicked) problems [45].

In general hybrid terms, flexibility usually describes the choice between attending a physical lecture or watching it online in real-time or later if that is more convenient.

## 3.2 Trust and the Human Element/Factor

The second important finding was "trust and the human element/factor". The findings highlighted the importance of trust development through collaborative online teamwork within an environment where students felt safe and supported and could contribute to the learning process.

First of all, every new student at MCT got an introduction workshop/course based on EiT (Experts in Teams) [46] an NTNU signature course, to give them a broader perspective on their academic competence and to train them in giving and receiving constructive feedback. Furthermore, to establish an understanding of the prerequisites for good interdisciplinary collaboration experience and taking advantage of the skills in an interdisciplinary team. The course contains exercises to build trust between the participants and methods to reflect on the group processes adapted to working in a physical/hybrid environment like the Portal. [47] Furthermore, to establish a common understanding among educators and students about the transparency of assessment with courses, workshops, and projects. In addition, define a common understanding of netiquette (ground rules for communication, collaboration and interaction mediated by technology), for all participants in the Portal.

In retrospect, establishing groups from day one was good for developing trust and solid groups and friendships. Within these groups and between groups, students established their own "digital corridors" where they could meet before or after sessions to clarify, discuss, or socialize. Small groups (4–5), enable a more natural flow of communication, interaction, and collaboration dynamics, causing a higher sense of social presence and a shared safe space before they start to get familiar with the whole class and the various learning environments they will encounter.

### 3.3 Motivation and Engagement

The educators provided a variety of authentic activities/workshops/projects attempting to drive student motivation [48] and engagement. Giving the students a choice increases their engagement and intrinsic motivation to participate actively in the Portal learning environment.

### 3.4 Ownership

Many of the already mentioned factors contribute to ownership [49]. However, educators pinpointed the following factors important in developing student ownership: Establishing good communication, social interaction, engagement, self-directed and -regulated learning, and regular reflective practice. At the same time, developing a shared understanding and teacher ownership toward the MCT program's design and the constant revisions and transformation of the applied pedagogy and content was crucial.

Teacher ownership is often referred to "as a key factor in the success, or failure, of an improvement effort" [50].

## 4 Students

Our research explores how our students at MCT experience their learning space (Portal) as an arena for student active learning and collaboration [39] and identifies the elements that most likely would impact the student's motivation and ownership [51].

### 4.1 Motivation and Ownership

The students identified motivation and ownership as essential elements in the MCT program and mentioned three themes that could facilitate and scaffold them: Autonomy, the importance of peer learning, and finally, good communication and social bonding. Students need the freedom to select projects that align with their interests and facilitate knowledge growth. Peer learning is highly valued but requires time to overcome challenges such as language, cultural differences, and skill gaps. Effective communication and social bonding within groups are crucial for maximizing the benefits of peer learning. The technology enables successful peer learning and group bonding in a cross-campus setting. Interestingly, the students did not associate assessment with motivation or ownership.

### 4.2 Collaboration

From the student viewpoint, the key factors promoting collaborative learning include focusing on their learning preferences (like personal interests), encouraging participation and choice, and facilitating cooperation and personal relationship development among team members.

In other words, The Portal delivers a supportive learning environment, providing relevant learning activities based on students' interests and previous knowledge working with team-based/hands-on projects, taking advantage of the diversity of competencies in the group, strong group union, and student involvement that promote a shared sense of ownership.

Feedback from students underscores the importance and value of a shared collaborative learning experience with their educators and a sense of ownership that emerges from working together. They collectively appreciated the efforts made by educators in customizing the learning activities to align with students' interests and prior knowledge. Interestingly, these statements coincide with the educator's statements.

In the cross-campus setting of Portal, the availability of teachers on-site (both physical locations), combined with teaching expertise from both within and outside the campus, is essential for effective teaching and learning design, especially in practical or hands-on learning settings that enhance the student's learning process.

At the same time, several factors harmed collaborative learning: Students' uneven levels of competence, unclear distribution of responsibilities among students and between students and educators, too many tasks, and too little time. There was sometimes a lack of students' understanding of the prerequisites for succeeding in group projects concerning problem-solving strategies. These problems are not particular incidents for the Portal collaboration and can happen in any group work in any learning environment.

### 4.3  Arena for Student Active Learning and Social Activities

The Portal delivers learning arenas that are physical, hybrid, online, and formal/informal, which inspire and promote a sense of co-presence and enable the students to create and organize their own additional learning/social arenas or "digital corridors" where they meet up before/after class activity.

Furthermore, they can access local and shared physical/virtual resources made available through the Portal's physical locations or networked connections. The Portal is, in many ways, a universal hub for access to and sharing resources and arenas/workspaces. The Portal provides an excellent experience for students to learn "how to learn" and collaborate in a hybrid environment.

However, net-etiquette to cover all the various interactions/arenas is lacking. In other words, how do we acquaint students with the culture of networked interaction (pitfalls, perks, problems, privacy, and positive outcomes)?

Setting up the Portal for various learning scenarios is a part of the courses at MCT, but sometimes, there is a need to discuss and clarify with the students how they perceive the technology in the Portal. The technology can be a learning object "in itself" or a medium to support teaching and learning activities in the Portal. The perceived control of intangible elements, such as planning and design of the Portal setup, may have more positive effects on learning than control and tweaking technology [52]. At the same time, these activities develop a sense of ownership of the process and use of their Portal. The challenge is knowing when the setup is good enough to support the planned activities and not continue to tweak the buttons. Seeing the technology from both sides is fruitful, but at the end of the day, technology for teaching and learning should primarily be supportive and adapt to students' needs.

According to Torio et al. 2023 [52], there are two main trends in the student's perception of the success of hybrid courses: The importance of live interaction for fostering a fruitful learning experience. Furthermore, projects and other interactive activities are powerful tools for increasing the motivation, level of participation, and learning experience, allowing students to engage more fruitfully with the course content. Despite the additional workload they may represent, students value the outcome since they add value to their learning experience.

As mentioned earlier, findings from Balle et al., 2018 [29] confirm that educator presence in online settings, interactions between students, teachers and content, and designed connections between online and offline activities as well as between campus-related and practice-related activities have a positive influence on students learning outcome, satisfaction, and engagement.

## 5 Conclusion and Final Remarks

On a global scale, the number of students enrolled in tertiary education is estimated to be 660 million worldwide in 2040. In order to deliver lifelong education with sustainable university eco-systems, offering equity, equality, and access for all students, it is not an option just to set up another university building but to be able to deliver hybrid and online learning spaces accessible for all students. "We need a Universities without walls" [15].

On a national level, the updated long-term governmental plan [53] for Norwegian research and HE, 2023–2032, states, "Students will meet both current competence needs and new needs brought about by societal and technological changes. Today's students must prepare for a future work life through solid professional competence and generic skills, including critical and analytical thinking, information processing, innovation, and entrepreneurship". A part of the plan is to deliver decentralized but attractive, relevant, accessible study programs. Norwegian and Sami higher education should also be accessible off campus, close to where people live. It should be possible for people in all stages of life to take higher education and top up their knowledge and skills by taking courses and further and continuing education. More should therefore be done to facilitate high-quality, decentralised, and online education. Establishing new education institutions or more campuses are not necessarily the answer to bringing education closer to the people.

However, the organizational side of creating and running new learning environments or even "just a" hybrid space exposes many barriers. We see inertia from introducing digital strategy at the government level and time/resources/finances dedicated to implementation within the university and faculty level. The top-down transition and anchoring of strategies and symmetrical attempts between cross-campus/universities is often filtered through the organization and does not deliver as the leadership expects. In many ways, one could claim that universities are not rigged or have a shared culture to handle advanced cross-university cooperation, especially concerning hybrid spaces and the development of a shared pedagogical approach.

Based on our experiences and research, the extended PST framework is helpful throughout the whole lifespan of a learning environment. Pedagogy is the most essential element and starting point in the iterative processes running internally and between the framework elements. [39] (p. 11–12). Furthermore, the importance of the human element/interaction through team-based work focusing on peer learning is the foundation for high-quality learning environments. Pedagogical challenges and strategies must have priority. A shift from the traditional focus on physical/space and technology/ infrastructure to these aspects is necessary.

## 5.1 Pedagogy

To develop a sustainable learning environment where students and educators can share and create new knowledge together, we have developed a short, inspiring guide [42] with pedagogical elements that can expand within our Education Spaces Framework (Table 1).

- The teacher takes the role as:

  - A facilitator for learning and communication.
  - A co-designer of learning spaces and sometimes a co-learner of new technologies.

- Focus on developing student ownership of learning
- Transparency in assessment
- Design learning experiences that engage students through collaboration, critical thinking, communication, and creativity.
- Implementing social presence strengthens the physical/hybrid and online learning environments/experiences continuum.
- Facilitate hands-on learning and collaboration-based activities where the students are encouraged to explore, acquire, and create new knowledge that mirrors their needs and interests. Focus on student tasks that should be flexible and open for student choice and where peer learning is one of the leading learning strategies for engaging students.
- Support and encourage student learning autonomy and peer instruction [54].
- Emphasize communication and social bonding in the planning and organization of the pedagogical activity.

These bullet points represent heutagogical design principles (exploration, creation, collaboration, connection, reflection, and knowledge sharing). As suggested by Kavashev (2024) [54], personalized, peer-to-peer, and smart learning activities, aligned with heutagogical principles can foster a conducive online learning environment and promote independent learners. Considering students' interests and motivation can further ensure learner-driven activities in online learning.

We advocate for diverse learning and education spaces that reflect the variety of human interactions. These spaces should support all on-campus, hybrid, and online study modes. They should also empower students to communicate, collaborate, and create "their own" shared learning spaces.

## 5.2 Space

Finding a suitable space for educational purposes within HE was previously solved by setting up a new building. Today, we must find more sustainable solutions to attract, cater, and give flexible access to a variety of new lifelong learners who are used to learning from anywhere, at any time and in any format.

Many Universities offer hybrid or flexible learning, allowing students to "attend" a lecture in the auditorium or watch the streaming or recorded version. For MCT the term hybrid means "participating" not just to "attend". Hence, there is a big difference between an auditorium and our Portal activity. If the auditorium supported the full-blown "participation" with the interaction between students located in-situ and online, communicating, working in teams, talking to the teacher etc., it would require a vast and complex AV system and most likely cause a cognitive overload for the educator handling/controlling several dimensions of activities and inputs and at the same time performing a lecture or a pedagogical plan.

Even though new types of expensive, complex systems with beamforming microphones, camera-tracking, and automated control systems with so-called AI features help, many uncontrollable factors still influence the variation in the learning experience and related activities for students sitting in the auditorium or being online.

Even if the auditorium has a high AV system sending out good quality sound, sound, video and sometimes shared workspaces or using response tools, we do not know what is happening on the receiving end. In which environment is the student, is it good wifi-coverage or bad sound, and what is the size of the receiving screen? All these uncontrollable factors influence the quality of the learning experience and outcomes for the remote student. It will also impact the quality of the technical return signal to the auditorium. In addition, not many remote students would like to see themselves on the big screen in front of the auditorium.

In our Portal, we control and can optimize the whole learning environment, providing a symmetrical experience for all students participating in various learning scenarios containing collaboration, communication, and interaction.

So, we suggest building smaller, similar group rooms with controllable features adapted to the pedagogical strategy and related activities. In addition, we might have a social zone and a larger room for giving small lectures/messages to the whole class. This way, we have small eco-systems that can be interconnected and placed around campus or at a remote campus node.

"Well-designed and properly equipped learning spaces help make some valuable kinds of learning and teaching activities easier to organise, more productive and more likely to happen" Goodyear [44].

## 5.3 Technology

The Portal is a high-tech, advanced learning space where students and teachers work together. Curiously, none of the students mentioned technology as a promoting factor for their learning experience.

Far too often, we trust technology to be the savior of future education instead of building trust between people and mediating this through technology. Just like the emperor in "The Emperor's New Clothes," who is fooled into wearing invisible clothes, educational institutions may adopt new technologies without fully understanding them, fearing they appear outdated. Getting advice from weavers, "experts on learning technologies," promising a digital future that will revolutionize education. It is essential to have individuals who, like the child in the story, question the effectiveness and implications of these technologies from a pedagogical viewpoint. Both scenarios highlight the importance of critical thinking, honesty, and building trust.

Technology is rapidly changing and often causes more disruptions than stability in our educational system. Furthermore, it takes time and resources to implement technological tools within a pedagogical strategy and gain acceptance [55, 56] of its usefulness for students and educators.

For instance, in Norway, there are discussions about the consequences of using mobile technology in primary education and banning AI on exams in HE. However, AI creates new possibilities [57, 58] for learning and teaching, but at the same time, it exposes various layers of trust-related issues. "Trust lies within the complex web of interactions between these AI systems, their intentions and their developers, the actors, the entities, and the regulatory system [59] that comprises the eco-system of the educational sector." [60].

Envision the future of higher education as a continually woven, adaptable fabric to meet the needs of future learners. The threads are the disciplines of study woven together by pedagogy. The loom is the physical/hybrid/virtual space where learning happens. Technology is a tool, subtly integrated, facilitating the weaving process. It is a fabric that covers not just the need for knowledge but also the need for skills, experiences, and personal growth. It is a fabric that reflects our fast-changing world in its design and purpose.

# References

1. Benneworth, P., de Boer, H., File, J., Jongbloed, B., Westerheijden, D.: Engaging in the Modernisation Agenda for European Higher Education (2012)
2. European Commission, High Level Group on the Modernisation of Higher Education :report to the European Commission on improving the quality of teaching and learning in Europe's higher education institutions. LU: Publications Office of the European Union (2013). Accessed 22 May 2023
3. Maassen, P.: The modernisation of european higher education. In: Mary Henkel, A., Amaral, I., Bleiklie, M.C. (eds.) From Governance to Identity: A Festschrift. Higher Education Dynamics, pp. 95–112. Springer, Netherlands, Dordrecht (2008). https://doi.org/10.1007/978-1-4020-8994-7_8
4. Olsen, J., Maassen, P.: European debates on the knowledge institution: the modernization of the university at the European level. In: Maassen, P., Olsen, J. (eds.) University Dynamics and European Integration. Higher Education Dynamics, LNCS, vol. 19, pp. 3–22. Springer, Dordrecht (2007). https://doi.org/10.1007/978-1-4020-5971-1_1
5. Martin, "The Sustainable Development Agenda," United Nations Sustainable Development. https://www.un.org/sustainabledevelopment/development-agenda/. Accessed 17 Jan 2024
6. Miao, F., et al.: Guidelines for ICT in education policies and masterplans (2022)
7. "european strategy for universities". https://education.ec.europa.eu/sites/default/files/2022-01/communication-european-strategy-for-universities-graphic-version.pdf. Accessed 20 Jan 2024
8. Chankseliani, M., McCowan, T.: Higher education and the sustainable development goals. High. Educ. 81(1), 1–8 (2021). https://doi.org/10.1007/s10734-020-00652-w
9. Stensaker, B., Hermansen, H.: Global, Nordic, or institutional visions? An investigation into how Nordic universities are adapting to the SDGs. High. Educ. (2023). https://doi.org/10.1007/s10734-023-01047-3

10. Buerkle, A., O'Dell, A., Matharu, H., Buerkle, L., Ferreira, P.: Recommendations to align higher education teaching with the UN sustainability goals – a scoping survey. Int. J. Educ. Res. Open **5**, 100280 (2023). https://doi.org/10.1016/j.ijedro.2023.100280
11. "What are the 21st-century skills every student needs?," World Economic Forum. https://www.weforum.org/agenda/2016/03/21st-century-skills-future-jobs-students/. Accessed 27 Sep 2017
12. Bellanca, J.A.: 21st Century Skills: Rethinking How Students Learn. Solution Tree Press, Bloomington (2010)
13. Loorbach, D.A., Wittmayer, J.: Transforming universities. Sustain. Sci. (2023). https://doi.org/10.1007/s11625-023-01335-y
14. Ninnemann, K., et al.: Hybrid environments for universities. Waxmann Verlag GmbH (2020). https://doi.org/10.31244/9783830991793
15. Støckert, R., Van der Zanden, P., De Caro-Barek, V.: An education spaces framework to define interactive and collaborative practices over the physical-hybrid-virtual continuum. In: Proceedings of the 16th International Scientific Conference "eLearning and Software for Education," Bucharest: Editura Universitara, pp. 486–496 (2020). https://doi.org/10.12753/2066-026X-21-061
16. "Universities without walls – A vision for 2030." European University Association, 022021. https://eua.eu/component/attachments/attachments.html?id=3079
17. "2024 Higher Education Trend Watch," EDUCAUSE. https://www.educause.edu/ecar/research-publications/higher-education-trend-watch/2024. Accessed 19 Jan 2024
18. "SDG4 Indicators 2023 report". https://unstats.un.org/sdgs/report/2023/Goal-04/. Accessed 17 Jan 2024
19. Cohen, A., Nørgård, R.T., Mor, Y.: Hybrid learning spaces—design, data, didactics. Br. J. Edu. Technol. **51**(4), 1039–1044 (2020). https://doi.org/10.1111/bjet.12964
20. Gil, E., Mor, Y., Dimitriadis, Y., Köppe, C. (eds.): Hybrid Learning Spaces. in Understanding Teaching-Learning Practice. Springer, Cham (2022). https://doi.org/10.1007/978-3-030-88520-5
21. Saichaie, K.: Blended, flipped, and hybrid learning: definitions, developments, and directions. New Dir. Teach. Learn. **2020**(164), 95–104 (2020). https://doi.org/10.1002/tl.20428
22. Bower, M., Dalgarno, B., Kennedy, G.E., Lee, M.J.W., Kenney, J.: Design and implementation factors in blended synchronous learning environments: outcomes from a cross-case analysis. Comput. Educ. **86**, 1–17 (2015). https://doi.org/10.1016/j.compedu.2015.03.006
23. Radcliffe, D.: A pedagogy-space-technology (PST) framework for designing and evaluating learning places. In: Learning Spaces in Higher Education: Positive Outcomes by Design: Proceedings of the Next Generation Learning Spaces 2008 Colloquium, University of Queensland Brisbane, pp. 9–16 (2008)
24. Støckert, R., Jensenius, A.R., Saue, S.: Framework for a novel two-campus master's programme in music, communication and technology between the university of oslo and the norwegian university of science and technology in trondheim. In: ICERI2017 Proceedings, pp. 5831–5840 (2017)
25. Støckert, R., Stoica, G.A.: Finding the right pedagogy and related prerequisites for a two-campus learning environment, ADLRO, 2018. https://doi.org/10.12753/2066-026x-18-030
26. Støckert, R., Bergsland, R., Xambo Sedo, A.: The Notion of Presence in a Telematic Cross-Disciplinary Program for Music,Communication and Technology. Cappelen Damm Akademisk (2020). https://doi.org/10.23865/noasp.108
27. Støckert, R., Refsum Jensenius, A., Xambó Sedó, A., Brandsegg, Ø.: A case study in learning spaces for physical-virtual two-campus interaction. In: von der Heyde, M. (ed.), European Journal of Higher Education IT 2019–1, May 2020. https://www.eunis.org/erai/2019-1/. Accessed 08 Mar 2021

28. Støckert, R.: SALTO - Student active learning in a two campus organization - NTNU. https:// www.ntnu.edu/salto. Accessed 18 Jan 2022
29. (Sandy) Pentland, A.: To Signal Is Human: Real-time data mining unmasks the power of imitation, kith and charisma in our face-to-face social networks. Am. Sci. **98**(3), 204–211 (2010)
30. Balle, S., Petersen, A., Nortvig, A.-M.: A literature review of the factors influencing E-learning and blended learning in relation to learning outcome, student satisfaction and engagement. Electron. J. e-Learn. **16** (2018)
31. Støckert, R., van Der Zanden, P., Caro-Barek, V.D.: A designer's guide to the university learnings space. In: INTED2022 Proceedings, pp. 6366–6375 (2022). https://doi.org/10.21125/inted.2022.1620
32. Schwab, K.: The Fourth Industrial Revolution. Crown, 2017
33. Ellis, R.A., Goodyear, P.: Models of learning space: integrating research on space, place and learning in higher education. Rev. Educ. **4**(2), 149–191 (2016). https://doi.org/10.1002/rev3.3056
34. Oblinger, D.: Leading the transition from classrooms to learning spaces. Educ. Q. **1**(7–12) (2005)
35. Radcliffe, D., Wilson, H., Powell, D., Tibbetts, B.: Designing next generation places of learning: collaboration at the pedagogy-space-technology nexus. Univ. Qld. **1**, 6–20 (2008)
36. Manciaracina, A.G.: Relation among pedagogy, space and technology and users. An implementation of Radcliffe's PST framework. In: EDULEARN19 Proceedings, IATED, pp. 3067–3073 (2019). https://library.iated.org/view/MANCIARACINA2019REL. Accessed 10 Feb 2024
37. Bektashi, L.: Community of Inquiry Framework in Online Learning: Use of Technology, in Technology and the Curriculum: Summer 2018, Power Learning Solutions (2018). https://techandcurriculum.pressbooks.com/chapter/coi-and-online-learning/. Accessed 08 Mar 2021
38. Walisundara, W.: A Review of Literature on the Community of Inquiry Framework, 2017
39. Garrison, D.R., Anderson, T., Archer, W.: Critical inquiry in a text-based environment: computer conferencing in higher education. Internet High. Educ. **2**(2), 87–105 (1999). https://doi.org/10.1016/S1096-7516(00)00016-6
40. De Caro-Barek, V., Lysne, D., Støckert, R., Solbjørg, O., Røren, K.: Dynamic learning spaces—dynamic pedagogy. Students' voices from a master's program focusing on student active learning in a cross-institution two-campus organization. Front. Educ. **8** (2023). https://doi.org/10.3389/feduc.2023.1155374
41. Raes, A.: Exploring student and teacher experiences in hybrid learning environments: does presence matter? Postdigit Sci. Educ. **4**(1), 138–159 (2022). https://doi.org/10.1007/s42438-021-00274-0
42. De Caro-Barek, V., Støckert, R.: From panic to planning: extending the notion of presence to create sustainable digital learning environments (2021)
43. Nykvist, S.S., De Caro-Barek, V., Støckert, R., Lysne, D.A.: Key factors needed for developing a higher education cross-campus learning environment in a nordic context. Front. Educ. **6**, 535 (2021). https://doi.org/10.3389/feduc.2021.763761
44. Buchem, I., Tur, G., Hölterhof, T.: The role of learner control and psychological ownership for self-regulated learning in technology-enhanced learning designs. Differences in e-portfolio use in higher education study programs in Germany and Spain, November 2020
45. Goodyear, P.: Design and co-configuration for hybrid learning: theorising the practices of learning space design. Br. J. Edu. Technol. **51**(4), 1045–1060 (2020). https://doi.org/10.1111/bjet.12925
46. Wrigley, C., Straker, K.: Design thinking pedagogy: the educational design ladder. Innov. Educ. Teach. Int. **54**(4), 374–385 (2017). https://doi.org/10.1080/14703297.2015.1108214

47. C. Fossen, "What is EiT". https://www.ntnu.edu/web/eit/what-is-eit. Accessed 17 Oct 2018
48. Breuer, C., Hüffmeier, J., Hibben, F., Hertel, G.: Trust in teams: a taxonomy of perceived trustworthiness factors and risk-taking behaviors in face-to-face and virtual teams. Hum. Relat. **73**(1), 3–34 (2020). https://doi.org/10.1177/0018726718818721
49. Keller, J.M.: First principles of motivation to learn and e3-learning. Distance Educ. **29**(2), 175–185 (2008). https://doi.org/10.1080/01587910802154970
50. Thibodeaux, T., Harapnuik, D., Cummings, C.: Student perceptions of the influence of choice, ownership, and voice in learning and the learning environment. Int. J. Teach. Learn. High. Educ. **31**(1), 50–62 (2019)
51. Saunders, M., Alcantara, V., Cervantes, L., Del Razo, J., Lopez, R., Perez, W.: Getting to teacher ownership: how schools are creating meaningful change. Annenberg Institute for School Reform at Brown University (2017). https://eric.ed.gov/?id=ED574745. Accessed 13 Feb 2024
52. Lysne, D., De Caro-Barek, V., Støckert, R., Røren, K., Solbjørg, O., Nykvist, S.: Students' motivation and ownership in a cross-campus and online setting. Front. Educ. **8**, 1062767 (2023). https://doi.org/10.3389/feduc.2023.1062767
53. Buchem, I., et al.: Learner control in personal learning environments: a cross-cultural study. Learn. Divers. Cities Futur. **15**(2), 14–53 (2014)
54. "Meld. St. 5 (2022–2023)," Regjeringen.no. https://www.regjeringen.no/no/dokumenter/meld.-st.-5-20222023/id2931400/. Accessed 25 Jan 2024
55. Kavashev, Z.: Heutagogical design principles for online learning: a scoping review. Am. J. Distance Educ. 1–18 (2024). https://doi.org/10.1080/08923647.2024.2303355
56. Davis, F.D.: Perceived usefulness, perceived ease of use, and user acceptance of information technology. MIS Q. **13**(3), 319 (1989). https://doi.org/10.2307/249008
57. Granić, A., Marangunić, N.: Technology acceptance model in educational context: a systematic literature review. Br. J. Educ. Technol. **50** (2019). https://doi.org/10.1111/bjet.12864
58. Bozkurt, A., Karadeniz, A., Baneres, D., Guerrero-Roldán, A.E., Rodríguez, M.E.: Artificial intelligence and reflections from educational landscape: a review of AI studies in half a century. Sustainability **13**(2), Art. no. 2 (2021). https://doi.org/10.3390/su13020800
59. Garg, S.: impact of artificial intelligence in special need education to promote inclusive pedagogy. Int. J. Inf. Educ. Technol. **10** (2020). https://doi.org/10.18178/ijiet.2020.10.7.1418
60. "Artificial Intelligence Act: deal on comprehensive rules for trustworthy AI | News | European Parliament". https://www.europarl.europa.eu/news/en/press-room/20231206IPR15699/artificial-intelligence-act-deal-on-comprehensive-rules-for-trustworthy-ai. Accessed 15 Feb 2024
61. "Project: Artificial Intelligence in Education: Layers of Trust (EduTrust AI)". https://slate.uib.no/projects/artificial-intelligence-in-education-layers-of-trust-edutrust-ai. Accessed 15 Feb 2024

# Promotion of Emotional Learning in Technical and Social Domains: A Systematic Review

Patrick Struger[1] , Benedikt Brünner[1]([⊠]) , and Martin Ebner[2]([⊠])

[1] Institute of Interactive Systems and Data Science, Graz University of Technology, Sandgasse 36/III, 8010 Graz, Austria
{pstruger,bruenner}@student.tugraz.at
[2] Educational Technology, Graz University of Technology, Münzgrabenstraße 36/I, 8010 Graz, Austria
martin.ebner@tugraz.at
https://www.isds.tugraz.at/, https://www.tugraz.at/

**Abstract.** Different learning approaches and new Learning Environment Systems (LES) are evolving rapidly these days and are designed by taking more and more individual skills and personal characteristics and preferences into account. Also Emotional Learning is gaining more importance when it comes to different learning environments in the technical domain as well as in the social context. Emotional Learning can help to support the overall engagement in learning and approaching learning achievements significantly. This paper should give some deeper insights into Emotional Learning, which possibilities exist to support it in a meaningful way and how feedback of emotional states can be obtained in Learning Environment Systems in higher education. For this purpose a literature review was chosen as the underlying research method to explore and find the necessary answers in various scientific articles, encyclopedias and relevant conference papers from different sources. The outcome will show different state-of-the-art approaches and tools to promote Emotional Learning and how to incorporate emotional learning support in Learning Environments.

**Keywords:** Emotional Learning · Social and Emotional Learning (SEL) · Support Emotional Learning · Learning Management Systems · Game based Learning · Education · Literature Review

## 1 Introduction

The more widely used term *Social and Emotional Learning (SEL)* has been used for more than 20 years and has gained importance in learning and teaching environments. Large research efforts and many data-driven studies have shown that SEL highly contributes to the development of empathy, personal skills, and a positive mindset. This results in increased success in educational and working environments, relationships and citizenship [12].

P. Zaphiris and A. Ioannou (Eds.): HCII 2024, LNCS 14723, pp. 241–255, 2024.
https://doi.org/10.1007/978-3-031-61685-3_18

Emotional Intelligence (EI) is the underlying aspect that guarantees Emotional Learning in a meaningful setting. Emotional intelligence involves the ability to perceive, manage, and regulate emotions; promote adaptive thinking; and understand the meaning and consequences of emotions. This process of management, regulation, and adaptation allows an individual to develop intellectually, socially and emotionally [21]. Emotional intelligence is, therefore, strongly correlated with academic performance, since emotional aspects and skills play an important role in human cognition. Students with high emotional skills tend to maintain more social relationships with peers and are being supported by larger networks, indicating positive effects on academic and working performance [15].

To ensure the development and implementation of emotional skills, organizations such as *Collaborative for Academic, Social, and Emotional Learning* (CASEL)[1] and Panorama Education[2] are working on providing assessments and standards in policies as well as guidelines for SEL, which have been accepted by the broader educational community. The five core competencies that ensure purposeful Social and Emotional Learning Environments as defined by CASEL are shown in Fig. 1.

**Fig. 1.** Social and Emotional Learning Core Competencies by CASEL [11].

An increasing number of studies confirm that those (soft) skills play an important role in supporting educational goals but there is still a big lack in research

---

[1] https://casel.org/.
[2] https://www.panoramaed.com/.

of important skills such as *self-control, persistence, professional orientation, academic self-efficacy,* and *social competence* [17].

According to [17] the following research goals are priorities for SEL:

- Developing assessment techniques
- Providing intervention approaches

This literature review provides a closer look at different approaches and possibilities for supporting Emotional Learning in the technical domain. Especially in higher education, learning and teaching environments without technical support or usage of software or data-driven tools can no longer be considered these days. This raises the question of whether current technologies such as *Big Data, Artificial Intelligence, Data Science,* or different approaches for interactive experiences with *Simulation and Animation, Gamification, Augmented Reality (AR), Virtual Reality (VR),* and *Immersive Virtual Reality (IVR)* can construct learning-centered teaching designs [25] and help to promote and support achieving such research goals and positively affect Emotional Learning leading to more efficient collaborations among peers, higher motivation in solving tasks or activities, positive effects on the climate in lecture halls or arousing interest in different educational topics.

Since the connection between emotional development and academic performance based on many studies worldwide is quite strong - especially in countries with well-developed education systems - it is important to promote Emotional Learning in current teaching and learning environments. Therefore, this study addresses the following research questions:

- **RQ1:** Which possibilities exist to support Emotional Learning in a Learning Environment?
- **RQ2:** How to obtain and observe emotional states of students in higher education?

The research methodology and screening process are described in Sect. 2. Section 3 summarizes all relevant findings based on their key attributes for better classification and visualization of correlation purposes. The research questions are addressed in Sect. 4, followed by a deeper analysis and discussion of the outcomes based on different aspects of the included records. Finally, Sect. 6 concludes the review with compact approaches and recommendations concerning the inclusion of Emotional Learning in Learning Environments in higher education.

## 2  Methods

To answer our research questions, we adopted the PICOC methodology [3] and followed the procedures described to perform a systematic literature review.

– *Population:* Students, teachers, or individuals engaged in technical and social domains.
– *Intervention:* Strategies, programs, or interventions aimed at promoting emotional learning.
– *Comparison:* Different types of emotional learning interventions, or variations in delivery methods.
– *Outcome:* Improved emotional intelligence, increased well-being, or better performance in both technical and social domains.
– *Context:* Educational settings where the promotion of emotional learning is relevant.

The research process is systematic and structured, with the aim of collecting, identifying, and critically analyzing the available research studies to provide an accurate understanding of the existing evidence on the topic of interest. [20] We used four digital libraries: Google Scholar[3], Science Direct[4], Research Gate[5], IEEE Xplore[6]. A combination of relevant key phrases "Emotional Learning", "SEL", "Support Emotional Learning", "Learning Management Systems", and "Game based Learning" were used and the following inclusion and exclusion criteria were applied:

– *Period:* Include records from 2011 to 2021. Exclude otherwise
– *Language:* Exclude if not English
– *Type of Literature:* Include articles and papers. Exclude otherwise
– *Type of source:* Include journals and conferences. Exclude otherwise
– *Accessibility:* Exclude not accessible records
– *Relevance to RQs:* Exclude if not relevant

In the databases, 26 records were identified as relevant and were screened by the researchers. For the screening process of the records, the abstract, introduction, and conclusion were considered and evaluated, as well as whether the findings were related to the overall topic of the literature review. The reasons for excluding a record were poor addressing of the topic "Emotional Learning" or strong cultural or ethical differences. After quality assessment, four records were excluded. Two records were not retrieved, the remaining 20 reports were included in this literature review. All records are presented in Table 1. The entire screening and record selection process was adapted from the PRISMA protocol [19], visualised in Fig. 2.

For the data extraction, all findings were inserted into an Excel spreadsheet and listed by their key attributes, such as publication year or citations, in combination with Python scripting for visualization purposes and easier selection by their importance and narrowing the scope later on.

---

[3] https://scholar.google.com (last accessed Sep 2023).
[4] https://www.sciencedirect.com (last accessed Sep 2023).
[5] https://www.researchgate.net (last accessed Sep 2023).
[6] https://ieeexplore.ieee.org (last accessed Sep 2023).

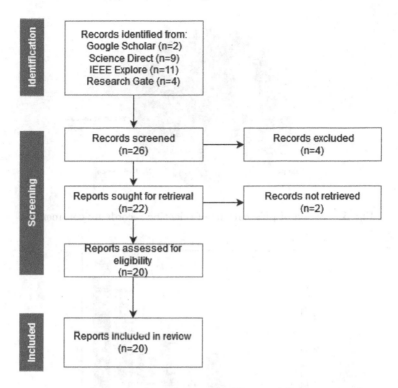

**Fig. 2.** Flow diagram of record selection process, adapted from PRISMA statement [19]

## 3   Findings

This section summarizes the key attributes identified during the data extraction process, the evolving importance of Emotional Learning throughout the past years, the correlation across different domains, and the connection between different cultures and countries.

Figure 3 shows the continents from which the included scientific records were published. We can observe the importance of Emotional Learning as a contribution to educational success in countries with well-developed education systems such as in different parts of Europe, China, and the United States. In case of a collaboration between different continents, every continent gained a count for the published source.

Scientific and psychological publications already mentioned the effects of Emotional Learning during the 1990s. Figure 4 illustrates the years of publication of the identified records. To include technical aspects, new methodologies, and state-of-the-art tools to support and promote Emotional Learning, this review mostly focuses on more recent publications from the last few years.

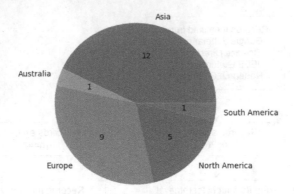

**Fig. 3.** Portion of publications of scientific records by continents

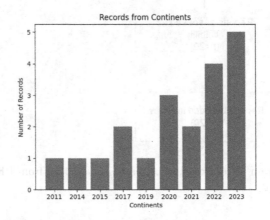

**Fig. 4.** Amount of included publications by years

The main purpose of this literature review is to provide clear answers to the research questions defined in Sect. 1 while considering different domains in educational, technical, and social contexts. Therefore, the included publications emerged from various scientific fields that have an impact on Emotional Learning.

Table 1 lists the specific fields of all identified records as well as their quoted statements. The majority of the records dealt with concepts of the game-based learning approach, followed by data science and online learning environments.

**Table 1.** Specific fields by the identified records

| Field | Records | Quotation |
|---|---|---|
| Online Learning | [9,13,23,24] | "From our results, we discover that sentiment/stress played little part concerning MOOCs in academic performance and was relatively unchanged in online courses between 2019 and 2020" [23] |
| Blended Learning | [27] | "Based on the findings of this study, teacher support has positive effects on behavioral and cognitive engagement, but not on emotional engagement [...] Emotional engagement can be affected by the interface friendliness and interactivity of the online learning platform" [27] |
| Data Science/AI | [2,6,17] | "Affective computer technologies have advanced throughout the years and these advances are direct linked to the same of most significant emotion theories that try to explain what is emotion and what cause emotion." [6] |
| Teaching/Leadership | [9] | "Lecturer charismatic leadership and technology use are each significantly related to student engagement, which predicts students' learning performance and satisfaction" [9] |
| Psychology and Sociology | [21] | "Emotional intelligence is strongly correlated with academic performance, as emotions play a key role in human cognition" [21] |
| Game-based Learning Env. | [7,10,14,16, 26] | "Researchers have further reported that educational computer games can improve students' academic performance as well as motivation and satisfaction." [10] |
| Mobile Learning Management | [1] | "M-learning is advantageous in many ways, it facilitates learning to take place anytime and anywhere, and it enables personalization for both students and instructors" [1] |
| Virtual Learning Environments | [4,8,18,22] | "Immersive virtual reality (IVR) provides great potential to experimentally investigate effects of peers on student learning in class and to strategically deploy virtual peer learners to improve learning" [8] |

# 4    Results

In this section, the literature review is intended to provide clear answers to the previously defined research questions based on the relevant findings of the research task.

## 4.1    Research Question 1: Which Possibilities Exist to Support Emotional Learning in a Learning Environment?

Emotional Learning can be supported by a variety of approaches in the technical domain, as well as in the context of social science.

**Choosing the Right Learning Management Software (LMS):** During the review, it became clear that educational research has strongly shifted into the world of digitization. Rapid developments in computer science, as well as the pandemic, have influenced teaching methods in several ways. Choosing the right LMS for students can be quite challenging in terms of positively influencing learning achievements. In times of *Online and Mobile Learning Management Systems*, or even *Massively Open Online Courses (MOOCs)*[7], the way of presenting educational content and including multimedia tools is a crucial task to promote Social and Emotional Learning. *Adaptive Learning Systems (ALS)* can also lead to better educational performance by adapting interfaces, course flow, organization, or difficulty by considering students' emotional states.

**Game-Based Learning (GBL):** Most included records and studies mentioned GBL as a promising methodology concerning its impact on emotional learning, students' satisfaction, and engagement. Regardless of whether educational content is delivered through a virtual or online learning environment, many studies since the early 2000s have confirmed that the right combination of education and interaction with game objects can have a huge impact on students' behavior, feelings, motivation, and interest regarding the selected topic. Therefore, GBL can improve students' academic performance, overall satisfaction, and motivation by making assessments and evaluations more interactive and engaging [26].

Gamification serves as a very prominent approach to implementing game mechanics in non-gaming environments to enable more interactive experiences and therefore strengthen the bonding between users and platforms by different elements.

Essential elements influencing students' learning behaviour and engagement in game-based environments can be *Levels, Leaderboards, Quests, Points, Badges, Maps, Certificates, Virtual Currencies, Daily-Check-Ins, Avatars, Virtual Environments*, or *Collectibles*.

---

[7] Massively Open Online Courses.

**Project-Based Learning (PBL):** To implement student-centered pedagogic methodologies such as PBL, it is necessary to ensure meaningful learning that induces motivation as well as personal and emotional meaning to students. Alternative scenarios, instead of one correct solution, can offer a place for experimentation and lead students out of their comfort zones for new personal and engaging experiences. In combination with collaboration with peers, this methodology provides even more benefits when it comes to learning experiences and achievements by positively identifying as a valuable member of the group. In this scenario, the lecturer acts as a supporting element instead of the sole source of wisdom to promote innovative and confident future professionals.

The following steps provide insights into the workflow mentioned by [14] to increase student engagement through the project-based learning methodology illustrated in Fig. 5:

- **Problem Exploration**
  Given a problem to be addressed, a given problem is discussed in small groups within brainstorming sessions, for example the construction of an Artificial Intelligence (AI) player for a game.
- **Technology Analysis**
  Identification of approaches, techniques, and knowledge needed to find appropriate solutions, for example exploring AI techniques, learning materials, or collecting further requirements regarding the software to be built.
- **Design of Solution**
  Modelling diagrams, workflows, or software architectures such as UML, class diagrams, or other types of software maps are part of a successful solution design phase.
- **Implementation of Solution**
  In combination with self-organized scheduling and self-defined milestones, accompanied by the lecturer. The focus on implementing the design using self-selected programming languages learned throughout the informatics degree.
- **Testing and Documentation**
  Discussions at this level can be very enriching for the whole class, as students analyze performance and gain practice organizing and showing experimental results. Experiments with several factors, such as iteration cycles for the training samples and parameter tuning.

**Policy Driven:** Among the various factors influencing *Emotional Learning*, many research questions have attempted to promote social and emotional skills that support students' learning experiences and achievements. Choosing the right SEL core competencies to focus on is the first task for SEL instructors and policymakers. Frameworks like the *Collaborative for Academic, Social, and Emotional Learning (CASEL)* framework illustrated in Fig. 1 can help to assess those competence domains on individual levels. The crucial task is to build policies on

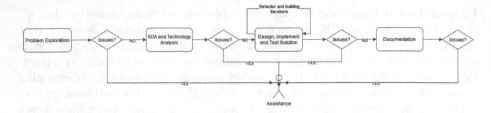

**Fig. 5.** Project-based workflow for increasing students' engagement according to [14]

such frameworks concerning various environmental factors, such as teacher professional development and wellbeing, assessment and learning standards, and school discipline policies and practices.

Policies promoting SEL in higher education could be:

- **Course Design**
  Designing curriculum courses with strategies focusing on SEL competencies such as self-awareness, social awareness, and relationship skills [5]. Completely independent and new courses (for example Positive Psychology: The Science of Well-Being) can also be introduced for this purpose.
- **Pedagogical Approaches**
  In case of more complex learning objectives, division into several more basic approaches instead of introducing overwhelming learning goals can help to prevent frustration, disinterest, or failing. Hands-on activities can provide room for experiments and illuminate learning content from different perspectives, helping students to consider a broader spectrum of engagement points.
- **Campus-wide initiatives**
  Many universities have already established student support services, including counseling, mentoring, health services, and wellness programs that provide resources and support to develop social and emotional skills.

### 4.2 Research Question 2: How to Obtain and Observe Emotional States of Students in Higher Education?

Many LMS offer access to various collections of student data (for example via log files or working with APIs of external multimedia tools), followed by a transformation process to structure them in a meaningful way and visualize them accordingly. These tracing tasks can help reflect on in-depth details and reveal hints for teachers. For example, document access, interaction patterns, completion rates, and time spent on specific learning materials. Some data structures for chat tracing can be described as follows:

```
Chatting <UserName>, <ChannelName>
```

Working with the indicators illustrated in Fig. 6 in game-based learning environments using these structures can support the activity tracing of students and reveal hints for the lecturer (for example, less activity over voice indicated by a "Snowflake" next to the profile picture reveals poor social interaction or less engagement in the group or topic). Despite the available data from the LMS itself, qualitative measures and evaluation of assessments can also be provided in a statistical manner [26]:

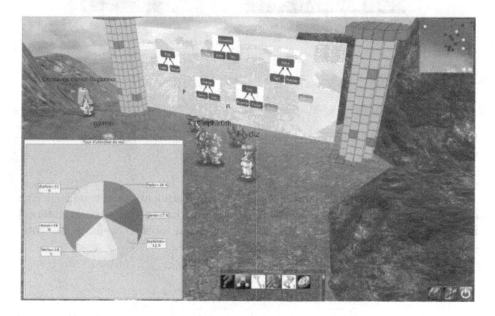

**Fig. 6.** Virtual "post-it" wall and indicator for students' involvement [16]

- **Participation Rate** revealing interaction between game or gamification objects
- **Completion Rate** can reveal emotional disengagement or frustration
- **Time spent** can reveal insights into attraction, difficulty and appealing of educational content
- **Success Rate** revealing effectiveness of assessment/learning objective
- **Conversation Rate** revealing an overview of percentage of module completion

Additionally, auxiliary information systems with the help of specific hardware in combination with machine- or deep-learning techniques (for example image processing in classrooms) as well as Affective Computing[8] remain prominent research topics for obtaining emotional states and student engagement. Further research on feedback methodologies shown in Fig. 7 can help teachers address students specifically and increase overall satisfaction and motivation.

---

[8] Technology that uses AI to recognize human affects and emotions through computers.

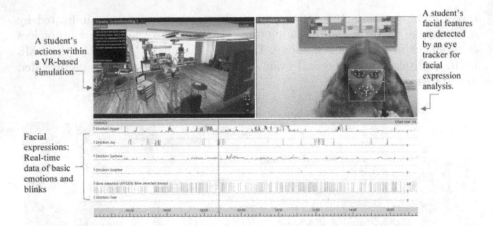

**Fig. 7.** Multi-model data collection while a student is experiencing the VR based simulation [4]

Another way to obtain direct feedback from students is through specific questionnaires after certain learning periods, immediate online surveys, internal feedback channels provided by the LMS or external tools to evaluate students' emotional states, motivation, or satisfaction.

## 5   Discussion

This study aimed to identify different methodologies for supporting Emotional Learning in higher education. This section summarizes the main statements to provide recommendations and reveal approaches in the technical and social domains.

To answer the research questions, this literature review identified several possibilities to support Emotional Learning in higher education. Choosing the right *Learning Management System* is a crucial task to support student behavior, feelings, satisfaction, engagement, and learning outcomes. Simple approaches such as clear interfaces, navigation, or notification systems allow students to share knowledge, collaborate, and communicate with teachers and peers, and can prevent frustration or overload of information. Evaluation through multimedia tools or indicators in LMS can help teachers design interactive and effective learning courses. With *Blended Learning*, there are also flexible approaches that combine digital learning environments with the advantages of approaching emotional feedback via face-to-face learning.

The majority of the included records dealt intensively with the game-based learning approach realized using different technologies, such as *Virtual Reality* or *Educational Video Games*. However, creating educational games for specific topics and needs can be challenging. Meanwhile, there are many reliable tools and apps such as SGAME[9], TinyTap[10], Scratch[11], Bloxels[12], Kahoot[13], Codea[14], and Make It[15] that allow teachers to create customized educational video games regarding topics, learning objectives, difficulty, or language, without programming skills or huge time effort. Gamification is another approach to implement game mechanics in non-gaming environments, such as *Online Learning Platforms* with the aim of enhancing students' interest, satisfaction, or learning outcomes (for example by introducing competitive elements such as a ranking scheme or emotional bonding with virtual avatars).

The identified publications also provide evidence of how *Project-based Learning* can improve students' social and emotional engagement with educational topics. Positive learning achievements through collaboration, emotion-related topics (self-concern and real problems), and sufficient space and time for individual learning can help promote *Emotional Learning*. PBL methodologies assess competent support and guidance provided by instructors or teachers to promote self-sufficient learning. Assessments can be conducted using individually defined milestones of the projects, while feedback can be gathered at all times.

The purpose of this research was to investigate the possibility of obtaining students' emotional states throughout the learning process. Working with feedback solutions provided by the *Learning Management System* is one possibility to provide insights into students' cognitive and emotional engagement as well as learning performance. In addition, ranking systems in gamification approaches can reveal valuable outcomes concerning social and emotional engagement. Supplemented with quick surveys (for example Google Forms), questionnaires such as PANAS[16] or feedback tools like Feedbackr[17], teachers are able to obtain intrinsic data and adapt communication with students, workflow, or difficulty of the course topic.

# 6 Conclusion

Advances and rapid evolution in sociology and technology have paved the way to transfer educational content in many different ways, considering students' personal needs, interests, and cognitive and emotional skills. The literature review proposes a compact and solid summary of how *Emotional Learning* can be promoted in social and technical domains. The results provide teachers, policymakers, developers, and online education service providers with insights, examples, and recommendations for promoting social and emotional learning in higher

---

[9] https://sgame.etsisi.upm.es/.
[10] https://www.tinytap.com/content/.
[11] https://scratch.mit.edu/.
[12] https://play.bloxels.com.
[13] https://kahoot.it/.
[14] https://codea.io/.
[15] https://www.makeit.app/.
[16] https://ogg.osu.edu/media/documents/MB%20Stream/PANAS.pdf.
[17] https://www.feedbackr.io.

education. State-of-the-art technologies reveal big potential in supporting students in their learning experience and help teachers to present educational content in a more convenient and attractive way. However, the majority of included records also mentioned that further research has to be done in the field of *Emotional Learning* and the support of information technology since identification of emotional states and proper reaction to them still remains a major topic in computer science and educational research.

**Disclosure of Interests.** The authors declare that they have no competing interests.

# References

1. Alfalah, A.A.: Factors influencing students' adoption and use of mobile learning management systems (m-LMSs): a quantitative study of saudi arabia. Int. J. Inf. Manag. Data Insights **3**(1), 100143 (2023). https://doi.org/10.1016/j.jjimei.2022.100143
2. Ayvaz, U., Guruler, H.: Real-time detection of students' emotional states in the classroom, pp. 1–4, May 2017. https://doi.org/10.1109/SIU.2017.7960574
3. Carrera-Rivera, A., Ochoa, W., Larrinaga, F., Lasa, G.: How-to conduct a systematic literature review: a quick guide for computer science research. MethodsX **9**, 101895 (2022). https://doi.org/10.1016/j.mex.2022.101895
4. Dubovi, I.: Cognitive and emotional engagement while learning with VR: the perspective of multimodal methodology. Comput. Educ. **183**, 104495 (2022). https://doi.org/10.1016/j.compedu.2022.104495
5. Elmi, C.: Integrating social emotional learning strategies in higher education. Eur. J. Investig. Health Psychol. Educ. **10**(3), 848–858 (2020). https://doi.org/10.3390/ejihpe10030061
6. Faria, A., Almeida, A., Martins, C., Gonçalves, R.: Learning platform: emotional learning. In: 2015 10th Iberian Conference on Information Systems and Technologies, CISTI 2015, July 2015. https://doi.org/10.1109/CISTI.2015.7170392
7. Gordillo, A., Barra, E., Quemada, J.: SGAME: an authoring tool to easily create educational video games by integrating SCORM-compliant learning objects. IEEE Access **9**, 126414–126430 (2021). https://doi.org/10.1109/ACCESS.2021.3111513
8. Hasenbein, L., et al.: Learning with simulated virtual classmates: effects of social-related configurations on students' visual attention and learning experiences in an immersive virtual reality classroom. Comput. Hum. Behav. **133**, 107282 (2022). https://doi.org/10.1016/j.chb.2022.107282
9. Hazzam, J., Wilkins, S.: The influences of lecturer charismatic leadership and technology use on student online engagement, learning performance, and satisfaction. Comput. Educ. **200**, 104809 (2023). https://doi.org/10.1016/j.compedu.2023.104809
10. Hung, C.Y., Kuo, F.O., Chih-Yuan Sun, J., Yu, P.T.: An interactive game approach for improving students' learning performance in multi-touch game-based learning. IEEE Trans. Learn. Technol. **7**(1), 31–37 (2014). https://doi.org/10.1109/TLT.2013.2294806
11. Im, G., Kee jiar, Y., Talib, R.: Development of preschool social emotional inventory for preschoolers: a preliminary study. Int. J. Eval. Res. Educ. (IJERE) **8**, 158 (2019). https://doi.org/10.11591/ijere.v8i1.17798

12. Jones, S.M., Doolittle, E.J.: Social and emotional learning: introducing the issue. Future Child. **27**, 11–3 (2017). https://doi.org/10.1353/FOC.2017.0000
13. Li, W., Wang, H.: Online teaching system combining information feedback and teaching evaluation. In: 2021 11th International Conference on Information Technology in Medicine and Education (ITME), pp. 465–469 (2021). https://doi.org/10.1109/ITME53901.2021.00099
14. Lopez-Gazpio, I.: Gaining student engagement through project-based learning: a competitive 2d game construction case study. IEEE Access **10**, 1881–1892 (2022). https://doi.org/10.1109/ACCESS.2021.3139764
15. Maccann, C., Jiang, Y., Brown, L., Double, K., Bucich, M., Minbashian, A.: Emotional intelligence predicts academic performance: a meta-analysis. Psychol. Bull. **146** (2019). https://doi.org/10.1037/bul0000219
16. Marty, J.C., Carron, T.: Observation of collaborative activities in a game-based learning platform. IEEE Trans. Learn. Technol. **4**(1), 98–110 (2011). https://doi.org/10.1109/TLT.2011.1
17. Liu, M.-C., Huang, M.H.: The use of data science for education: the case of social-emotional learning. Smart Learn. Environ. **4** (2017). https://doi.org/10.1186/s40561-016-0040-4
18. Mosquera, L.: Impact of implementing a virtual learning environment (VLE) in the EFL classroom. Íkala Revista de Lenguaje y Cultura **22**, 479–498 (2017). https://doi.org/10.17533/udea.ikala.v22n03a07
19. Page, M.J., et al.: The PRISMA 2020 statement: an updated guideline for reporting systematic reviews (2021). https://doi.org/10.1136/bmj.n71
20. Pati, D., Lorusso, L.N.: How to write a systematic review of the literature. HERD Health Environ. Res. Des. J. **11**(1), 15–30 (2018). https://doi.org/10.1177/1937586717747384
21. Quílez-Robres, A., Usán, P., Lozano-Blasco, R., Salavera, C.: Emotional intelligence and academic performance: a systematic review and meta-analysis. Think. Skills Creat. **49**, 101355 (2023). https://doi.org/10.1016/j.tsc.2023.101355
22. Silva, M., Teixeira, J., Cavalcante, P., Teichrieb, V.: Perspectives on how to evaluate augmented reality technology tools for education: a systematic review. J. Braz. Comput. Soc. **25** (2019). https://doi.org/10.1186/s13173-019-0084-8
23. Tao, X., et al.: Towards an understanding of the engagement and emotional behaviour of MOOC students using sentiment and semantic features. Comput. Educ. Artif. Intell. **4**, 100116 (2023). https://doi.org/10.1016/j.caeai.2022.100116
24. Toring, H., et al.: Evaluation of students' satisfaction toward an adopted learning management system at Indiana aerospace university: a structural equation modelling approach. Asia Pac. Manag. Rev. **28**(3), 336–346 (2023). https://doi.org/10.1016/j.apmrv.2022.12.002
25. Wei, H.: Research on constructing learning-centered interactive teaching design with the support of information technology. In: 2020 2nd International Conference on Applied Machine Learning (ICAML), pp. 386–390 (2020). https://doi.org/10.1109/ICAML51583.2020.00084
26. Yildirim, O.: Digital Games and Gamification in Education: Chapter 11 - Assessment Based Games and Gamification, pp. 143–153, September 2023
27. Zhao, X., Wang, X., Wei, Y., Wang, J., Jun, T., Zuo, C.: Research on the influence of college students' engagement in blended learning: teacher support, situational interest, and self-regulation, pp. 170–174, September 2020. https://doi.org/10.1109/ISET49818.2020.00045

# Improving Student Team Formation in Design Classrooms Using a Novel Approach

Andrew Twigg(✉) 🆔 and Nikita Valluri

Carnegie Mellon University, Pittsburgh, PA 15213, USA
{atwigg,nvalluri}@andrew.cmu.edu

**Abstract.** This paper proposes a novel method for student team formation, using a combination of student-provided information, instructor guidance, data visualization, and real-time classroom facilitation. There is debate as to the performance of student teams formed by instructor, by student preference, or by random assignment [1]; this new model hybridizes student input with instructor guidance and in-class dialogue. In this new approach, students complete a survey declaring preferences for collaboration style, as well as strengths and skill development goals. This survey data allows the creation of visualizations used to build potential teams, which are then shared with students in conjunction with discussion on the advantages and disadvantages of each team formation strategy. Then through in-class dialogue, teams may be revised in real time, based on student input. It is during this instructor-facilitated discussion when final team composition is determined; this instructor-guided, student-driven process aims to cultivate strong student buy-in and ultimately result in high-performing teams due to direct involvement of students in team formation. The focus of this paper is the methodology, opportunities to improve it, its significance and limitations, and potential future directions.

**Keywords:** Team Formation · Collaboration · Design Education

## 1 Introduction

This study was conducted as a means to improve small team formation in a graduate-level Interaction Design course at the School of Design at Carnegie Mellon University having 25 students; two instructors—Twigg, Dina El-Zanfaly; one teaching assistant; and one external research assistant—Valluri. It was determined by instructors Twigg and El-Zanfaly that teams of four would be ideal, considering project workload, schedule coordination logistics, and classroom management; teams of three would create a high workload on students and too many teams for Twigg and El-Zanfaly to manage, and teams of five might create too many coordination hurdles across all teams. But with 25 students, not all teams could have four individuals. El-Zanfaly and Twigg determined that having most teams comprised of four individuals would be best, so the instructors would plan for six teams to be made: five teams of four students—the preferred team size—and one team of five.

In many instances, classroom teams are formed by instructor, by student preference, or by random assignment, and the merits of these approaches is debated [1]. There are

P. Zaphiris and A. Ioannou (Eds.): HCII 2024, LNCS 14723, pp. 256–271, 2024.
https://doi.org/10.1007/978-3-031-61685-3_19

also tools such as Comprehensive Assessment of Team-Member Effectiveness (CATME) and Team-Maker that use software to assess team members to form teams [2]. But the authors of this paper were not able to identify published team formation methods that use a combination of instructor facilitation and student involvement through the team formation process.

Additionally, while there is literature on the use of visualization for collaborative decision making, it is largely focused on the tools [3] or contexts such as urban planning [4], organizations [5], or big data contexts like "healthcare and command-and-control centers" [6].

Part of the motivation behind this study is to create a method that is easy for instructors to adapt to their own classroom with readily accessible tools such as surveys/forms, spreadsheets, and visualization and collaboration tools such as Figma, Miro, or Mural. Twigg has been piloting a similar team formation approach for several years using these kinds of tools as a means to understand student strengths and preferences, with student-instructor dialogue playing a critical role in final team formation. The method contained herein is an expansion of that approach.

Therefore, using this updated method, students are provided with a survey which includes questions on strengths and growth areas related to the project, preferences for the extent to which they prefer to work in a collaborative manner, and other questions related to collaboration that are used for a separate activity and are not part of this study. During class activities, students are able to see each others' survey responses and initials in the form of data visualizations, and engage in dialogue with the instructor to finalize team formation. Note that in this paper, individualized study data has been anonymized as this paper is not about student data, but instead about the method and tools.

## 2  Methodology

The team formation process has three stages:

1. Student survey response
2. Data analysis, visualization, and synthesis, draft team formation
3. Sharing of results with students, and team finalization through classroom dialogue between instructor and students

### 2.1  Survey

Twigg designed a survey using Google Forms, shown in Fig. 1, based on a similar survey he had designed for prior courses in which students self-reported strengths and collaboration preferences for team formation. The underlying principle of this model is that when students work with others having similar collaboration preferences—working in greater or lesser degrees of direct collaboration—and having complementary skills sets—e.g. being oriented toward conceptual problem solving versus toward applied problem solving—collaboration is easier.

Accordingly, the survey intended to do multiple things: 1) familiarize the instructors with students' learning goals and 2) provide different kinds of information that could potentially be used to compose teams. Student email addresses would be gathered automatically using their school account to help ensure that responses were provided by each individual.

**Survey Questions**

The survey included these prompts; authors' comments are *italicized:*

- Your name
- As a designer, how would you place yourself on a continuum from being solely craft-oriented to being solely concept-oriented? 5 is an even balance between craft and concept

    *There were 11 options, ranging from zero to 11.*

- When working on a team project, where would you place yourself on the scale below, with respect to a preference to work in a highly individual or highly collaborative manner? 5 is an even split between preferences to work individually or collaboratively
- A favorite musician or band of mine is:

    *This is an attention check question.*

**Strengths and Skill Development.** *The purpose of the information gathered in this section was to provide multiple options when composing teams, as well as provide course instructors with information that would allow them to more easily support student learning goals.*

- Please rank each of these project aspects from strongest (1) to weakest (3):

    – Research
    – UX Design
    – UI Design

- Please rank projects aspects you would like to develop during the project in order of most (1) to least (3)

    – Research
    – UX Design
    – UI Design

- A favorite food of mine is:

    *This is an attention check question.*

*The following questions on collaboration values would be used for another activity designed to improve team performance, which students would undertake following team formation. That activity is not discussed in this paper as it is not part of this study, but the questions have been included here because they were included in the same survey activity:*

**Collaboration Values**

1. What do you **value from others** in a collaborative context?
   (E.g. "getting prompt feedback" or "direct communication.")
2. What values do you **hope to bring to the table** in a collaborative context? What do you value of/from yourself in a collaborative context?
   (E.g. "consideration of others" or "deadline adherence.")
3. How do you hope you and your partner(s) will **interact with one another** in collaboration?
   (E.g. "having direct and honest communication" or "making sure that feedback is given in a manner that is constructive and kind.")
4. What are your **fears or concerns** around collaborating with others on a project?
   (E.g. "we cannot find ways to work in an equitable manner" or "team doesn't set mutually agreed upon expectations")
5. Are there any **other collaboration preferences** you haven't mentioned above which you'd like to articulate?
   (Anything else you're thinking about can go here.)

   **And two final questions that could be considered for team formation:**

- What discipline are you coming from?
- Are there any brands that you're particular (sic) interested in working on? (Not required; this does not guarantee team or brand assignment)

*We included these last questions to aid in team formation in the event that other methods didn't provide enough options for team formation, or in the event that the responses provided simple solutions to team formation. The final question was optional as we imagined that some students might not have a preference—which was the case— and we also didn't want students to make assumptions that they would be placed together on a team if they named the same brand.*

## 2.2 Data Analysis, Visualization, and Synthesis

Once responses were stored in a Google Sheet, Twigg removed identifying information to protect privacy and potential occurrence for bias during the process. As seen in Fig. 2, Twigg and Valluri then color coded the responses to the ranking questions (strengths and skill development) in order to more easily see distribution of students in each category.

Using Figma, Twigg and Valluri placed labeled dots representing each student on a series of charts. Student teams would ideally be formed with similar preferences for collaboration style and complementary other dimensions, as explained in the following section.

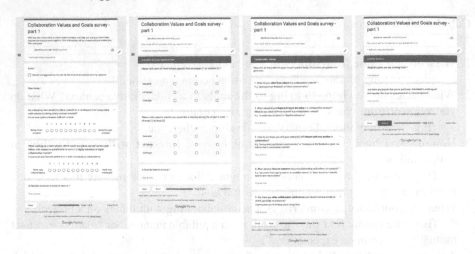

**Fig. 1.** Survey delivered using Google Forms. Survey questions can be read in the preceding text.

| | As a designer, how would you place yourself on a continuum from being solely craft-oriented to being solely concept-oriented? | When working on a team project, where would you place yourself on the scale below, with respect to a preference to work in a highly individual or highly collaborative manner? | Please rank each of these project aspects from strongest (1) to weakest (3) | | | Please rank projects aspects you would like to develop during the project in order of most (1) to least (3) [Research] | | |
|---|---|---|---|---|---|---|---|---|
| | | | Research | UX Design | UI Design | Research | UX Design | UI Design |
| S1 | 6 | 3 | 1 | 3 | 2 | 3 | 1 | 2 |
| S2 | 8 | 7 | 2 | 3 | 1 | 3 | 1 | 2 |
| S3 | 5 | 5 | 3 | 1 | 2 | 2 | 3 | 1 |
| S4 | 4 | 7 | 2 | 3 | 1 | 1 | 3 | 2 |
| S5 | 7 | 2 | 2 | 1 | 3 | 2 | 1 | 3 |
| S6 | 6 | 0 | 1 | 2 | 3 | 2 | 1 | 3 |
| S7 | 5 | 4 | 3 | 2 | 1 | 1 | 2 | 3 |
| S8 | 5 | 5 | 1 | 2 | 3 | 3 | 1 | 2 |
| S9 | 7 | 3 | 3 | 2 | 1 | 1 | 2 | 3 |
| S10 | 7 | 3 | 2 | 1 | 3 | 3 | 1 | 2 |
| S11 | 6 | 3 | 3 | 2 | 1 | 3 | 2 | 1 |
| S12 | 6 | 3 | 3 | 2 | 1 | 2 | 3 | 1 |
| S13 | 6 | 1 | 1 | 2 | 3 | 3 | 1 | 2 |
| S14 | 9 | 7 | 1 | 2 | 3 | 2 | 1 | 3 |
| S15 | 7 | 2 | 3 | 2 | 1 | 1 | 3 | 2 |
| S16 | 2 | 8 | 3 | 2 | 1 | 3 | 1 | 2 |
| S17 | 4 | 8 | 3 | 2 | 1 | 2 | 1 | 3 |
| S18 | 5 | 5 | 2 | 1 | 3 | 3 | 2 | 1 |
| S19 | 7 | 3 | 3 | 2 | 1 | 2 | 1 | 3 |
| S20 | 6 | 5 | 2 | 1 | 3 | 2 | 1 | 3 |
| S21 | 5 | 3 | 3 | 2 | 1 | 2 | 1 | 3 |
| S22 | 6 | 7 | 1 | 2 | 3 | 2 | 1 | 3 |
| S23 | 8 | 6 | 3 | 2 | 1 | 2 | 3 | 1 |
| S24 | 6 | 7 | 2 | 3 | 1 | 1 | 3 | 2 |
| S25 | 6 | 5 | 2 | 1 | 3 | 1 | 2 | 3 |

**Fig. 2.** Image of table of survey responses from Google Sheets. Responses to the final two questions (disciplinary background, brand preference) are not shown; they were not used for team formation and are omitted from this figure as they contain information which may make the students identifiable.

The first chart had two dimensions: collaboration preference on the vertical axis, and craft/concept on the horizontal. This could make visible ideal groupings of students having complementary craft/concept positions while also having similar collaboration preferences. (Fig. 3).

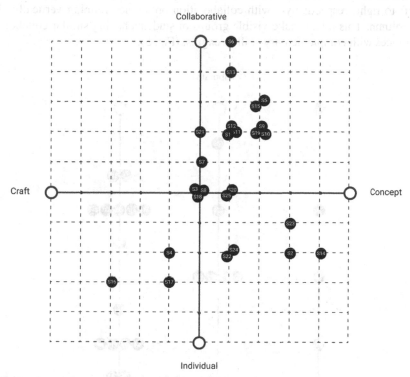

**Fig. 3.** Numbered dots representing students, placed according to collaboration preference on the vertical axis, and craft/concept on the horizontal

However, over the preceding summer, Twigg had been wondering how one might approach forming teams when project aspects might include dimensions beyond those used in Fig. 3. One of the visualization methods he had developed placed the collaboration continuum on the horizontal axis, with a series of parallel axes against which students could be placed based on other areas of consideration (Fig. 4).

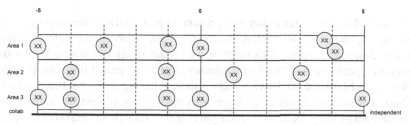

**Fig. 4.** Rendering of how students might be distributed along a series of parallel axes representing focus areas while maintaining a collaboration preference continuum.

Accordingly, a second chart was developed based on the idea shown in Fig. 4. Keeping with the vertical orientation of the collaboration axis seen on the chart in Fig. 4, this visualization used three columns representing skill strengths—Research, UX, and UI left to right, respectively—with collaboration preference running vertically along each column. This might make visible groups of students having similar collaboration preferences with complementary skill strengths. (Fig. 5).

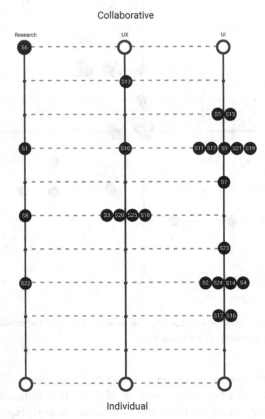

**Fig. 5.** Numbered dots representing students in 3 columns, each representing strength in either Research, UX, or UI design, with vertical placement representing collaboration preference from individual (bottom) to collaborative (top).

The third chart used three columns representing preferred skill development focus—Research, UX, and UI left to right, respectively—with collaboration preference running vertically along each column. This might make visible groups of students having similar collaboration preferences with complementary skill development interests. (Fig. 6).

Instructors El-Zanfaly and Twigg had planned on having six teams, therefore an ideal distribution of students across each focus area might show at least six students having interest in each primary focus area. After plotting data onto these charts (Figs. 3, 5, 6), it was recognized that no particular chart made obvious six teams of four-to-five students having a balance of skill areas and similar collaboration styles.

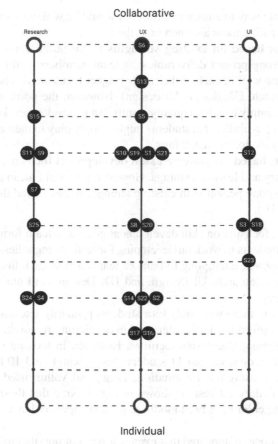

**Fig. 6.** Numbered dots representing students in 3 columns, each representing skill development interest in either Research, UX, or UI design, with vertical placement representing collaboration preference.

## 2.3 Advantages and Disadvantages of Considered Team Formation Criteria

Based on prior experiences with a similar method developed by Twigg, an assumption was made that preferences for collaboration style would remain a factor in any team formation process. Accordingly, each potential team formation strategy offered its own challenges and opportunities:

- **Creating teams based on a concept/craft continuum** didn't adequately address the nature of the project students were being asked to undertake, which would include aspects of conducting research, developing user experiences (UX), and developing user interfaces (UI). While research, UX design, and UI design have elements of concept and craft, the simplicity of a "concept/craft" continuum doesn't discretely consider each of these three necessary project aspects. Conversely, forming teams having a blend of concept development abilities and executional ("craft") abilities might be a simple way to ensure that no team would be without members who could at least conceptualize ideas and then craft them.

- **Creating teams based on existing strengths** might build teams that could more easily create strong project deliverables, as team members could already have the ability to execute well in each of the major project focus areas where they reported strengths (Research, UX design, UI design). However, the point of the course and project was not simply to deliver quality results, but to develop new knowledge. In this model, there's a possibility that students might simply play to their existing strengths and not learn by exploring new things.
- **Creating teams based on preferred skill development focus** presents students an opportunity to try and learn new things. However, this could mean that a team might not have at least one person with existing strength in one of the three project areas (research, UX, UI).

In other words, focusing on skill development goals as a team formation dimension might encourage students to work on developing those skills regardless of their strength in those areas. However, attempting to balance teams across each first preference skill development area—Research, UI Design, and UX Design—did not yield teams with coverage in all areas.

As seen in Fig. 6, there were only four students primarily interested in developing UI design abilities, seven primarily interested in developing research, and 14 primarily interested in developing UX design faculties. However, in looking back at the table, Twigg and Valluri recognized that 11 students had research and 10 had UI design as a secondary interest; using this information, Twigg and Valluri used color to indicate each student's secondary interest, as shown in Fig. 7. Note that these and subsequent visualizations using color have been modified for this paper so they will also reproduce in black and white.

Once this was done, it appeared that even if it was not possible to make teams with at least one student having a primary interest in UI design, it would likely be possible to create teams having a number of individuals with a secondary interest in UI design. Additionally, even though Twigg and El-Zanfaly had agreed to make teams of four and five students; this was done with teams of 3–4 students as well as the preferred 4–5 student teams, just to explore a range of options.

As Twigg and Valluri pivoted to add secondary skill development areas as a consideration in team formation, they attempted to ensure that each team had at least two people in a secondary skill area when no individual represented that area as a primary focus. (Figs. 7, 8) The project would ultimately include UI design as part of the project deliverables; the authors believed having at least two people with a secondary interest in UI design might be a way to allow teams to distribute work on those deliverables among teammates.

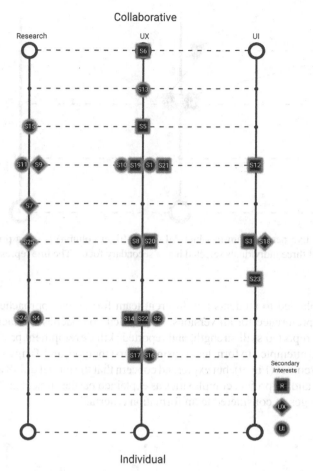

**Fig. 7.** Colors were added to identify secondary skill development interests; visualization has been modified for this paper to change each shape to represent a secondary skill development focus area: a square for "research", a diamond for "UX", and a circle for "UI".

## 2.4   Sharing Visualizations and Team Finalization Through Discussion

Visualizations were shared in class following survey completion. Students were shown visualizations using their initials—initials are not shown here for privacy reasons—in order to help students understand the composition of possible teams that had been formed.

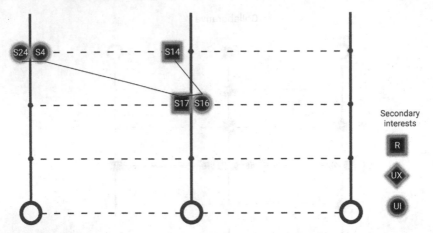

**Fig. 8.** Sample five-person team in which UI design (right column) is not a primary focus for any member, but three individuals selected it as a secondary focus. The line represents connecting team members.

Twigg explained to students the different team formation approaches: one axis of collaboration preference for all versions, with varied approaches for each of the three: concept-craft; reported skill strength, and reported skill development preference. Twigg and Valluri had attempted to form teams using the first method, and Twigg showed a series of the team outcomes (Fig. 9), but expressed concern that the model didn't account for the research, UX, and UI project complexities as explained earlier in Sect. 2.3, "Advantages and disadvantages of considered team formation criteria."

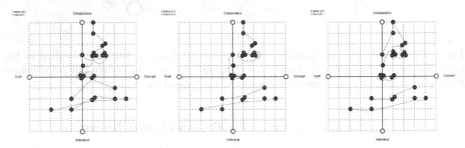

**Fig. 9.** A series of team formation iterations based on various team sizes (7 teams of 3 and 1 of 4; 4 teams of 4 and 3 of 3; 5 teams of 4 and 1 of 5), generating teams based on complementary craft/concept values and similar collaboration preference values. The lines connect dots to create teams.

Twigg then walked through a second visualization based on skill strength—Fig. 5—and explained its limitations as stated earlier in this paper, and that he didn't recommend this option.

Twigg then showed the third set of visualizations —using skill development preference as a dimension—and explained his preference for this version (Fig. 10), based on the reasoning provided earlier in this paper.

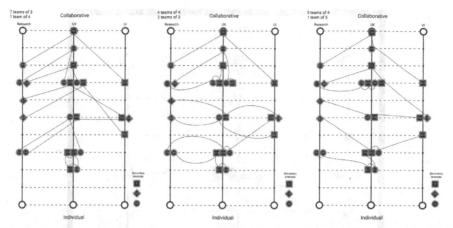

**Fig. 10.** A series of various team formation suggestions based on team size. The left-most variation was the recommended approach, and contained five teams of four people, and one team of five people.

Twigg explained to students that creating five teams of four people, and one team of five people was the best option, referring to factors discussed earlier in this paper. Students were generally on board with this direction, but during conversation it was identified that via this approach, several students who knew each other from a program during the preceding academic year had been placed on teams together. As a result of this point, Twigg facilitated real-time changes to the proposed teams so that none of these students were on the same team, while maintaining the criteria of collaboration preference, paired with primary and secondary skill development areas, which led to the final teams as shown in Fig. 11. These were determined to be the final teams, following additional discussion without further objection or concern.

## 3 Significance and Discussion

### 3.1 Significance

This approach to team formation is intended to provide an alternative to current methods in which teams are determined either by instructor, students, or random assignment. Students are given agency in the formation of teams through several factors: First, students provide information about their collaboration style, then their existing strengths as well as the skills they would like to develop with respect to project aspects. Doing so is intended to alleviate concerns about teams being formed in an opaque manner and without consideration for students' own goals or situation. Instructors can explain the intended purpose of a team formation approach, which is intended to help compel students to buy into the formation of teams having a composition that will both balance student goals and help them develop new skills.

This method provides alternatives to many other team formation approaches, and while there is significant work involved, having the buy-in of students is critical so students do not skeptically enter into work with other students.

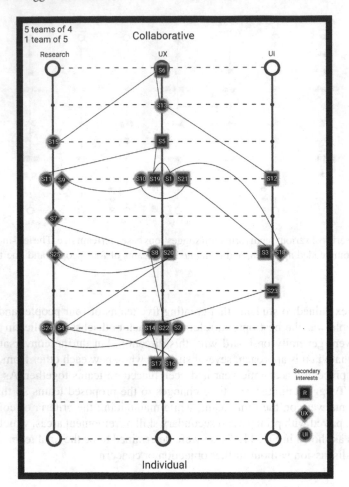

**Fig. 11.** Revised and final teams, based on dialogue between course instructors and students.

## 3.2 Discussion

While the methodology led to the creation of teams which had an alignment in collaboration preference and balance of growth areas, there are limitations with respect to the tool used (here, Google Forms) that compromised ideal data collection.

First, when collecting data with respect to student craft-concept skill balance and collaboration preference, Google Forms has a "linear scale" element (Fig. 12), but it creates discrete positions, each of which have a numeric value. This prevents students from more freely choosing a position, which limits nuanced responses and has an effect of creating clustering on the visualization.

Additionally, placing numeric values on the scale may imply that some responses are preferred over others, e.g. that a value of seven is superior to a value of three. If a student is compelled to choose a higher or lower value because they believe it is better, this would affect positioning on the visualization and thereby affect team formation (Fig. 13).

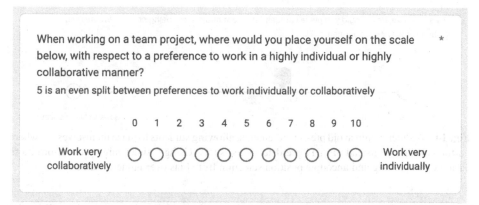

**Fig. 12.** The Google Forms "linear scale" element as presented to students. Students are provided a set of discrete values. Additionally, each response is given a numeric value, which may be interpreted by students as having a better or worse value.

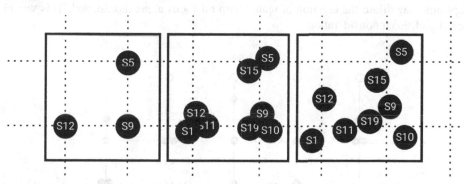

**Fig. 13.** When students choose the same values, each cluster shown would overlap entirely (left). These dots needed to be shifted in order to make all of them visible (center). A slider may afford giving more freedom for value selection on the part of students, which could lead to different distribution (right) which may then lead to different team formation than would arise from the left and center distributions.

It might be preferred that students could use a slide indicator for the craft/concept and collaboration dimensions, instead choosing from 11 positions (Fig. 14). Doing so for this form question might lead to more nuanced responses, which would lead to more nuanced placement on each of those axes, which would help prevent possible overlap (Fig. 13).

This is important because in the current model, a primary aspect of team formation is how similarly individuals have placed themselves on the collaboration axis. Greater nuance may lead to different distribution and to the formation of different teams.

As a designer, how would you place yourself on a continuum from being solely craft-oriented    *
to being solely concept-oriented?

**Fig. 14.** A slider would avoid pre-set increments, allowing students to place themselves anywhere on the continuum instead of in 11 pre-determined spots. Using a slider might then afford more varied chart plotting and uncouple position selection from bias over numeric value.

Additionally, considering the expansion of this visualization method to allow for a greater number of skill areas might afford additional flexibility with respect to team making, as demonstrated in Fig. 15. However, a careful consideration for the number of focus areas might be made in order to allow for the creation of viable teams; too many options may dilute the creation of teams with all focus areas represented. This would need additional consideration.

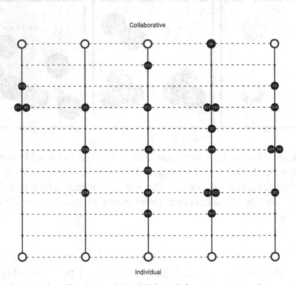

**Fig. 15.** Possible future visualization with additional focus areas and example distribution of students.

Also, due to time, visualization work was completed outside of the classroom; it may be worthwhile for students to participate in creating the data visualizations to more fully understand formation complexity and have more involvement in criteria-based formation. It may also be worth considering whether or not student cohorts would prefer to work with their own data anonymously or in an identifiable manner.

Additionally, developing a tool which automatically visualizes the data, thereby removing the possibility of human error in the visualization stage might be another potential way the current limitation might be addressed. Team suggestions may also be created in a more automated manner.

Finally, part of the motivation behind this work is to create dialogue between the instructor and students in order to increase student acceptance of team formation criteria and resulting teams. Research is needed into team performance, student perception and acceptance of methodology, attitudes toward teams post-formation. Yet this model does provide an alternative to other existing models that may offer both faculty and students more involvement and buy-in where team formation is concerned.

# References

1. Pociask, S.E., Gross, D., Shih, M.-Y.: Does team formation impact student performance, effort and attitudes in a college course employing collaborative learning? JoSoTL **17**(3), 19–33 (2017). https://doi.org/10.14434/v17i3.21364
2. Layton, R.A., Loughry, M.L., Ohland, M.W., Ricco, G.D.: Design and Validation of a Web-Based System for Assigning Members to Teams Using Instructor-Specified Criteria (2010)
3. Oral, E., Chawla, R., Wijkstra, M., Mahyar, N., Dimara, E.: From information to choice: a critical inquiry into visualization tools for decision making. IEEE Trans. Vis. Comput. Graph. 1–11 (2023). https://doi.org/10.1109/TVCG.2023.3326593
4. Bajracharya, S., et al.: Interactive visualization for group decision analysis. Int. J. Inf. Technol. Decis. Mak. **17**(06), 1839–1864 (2018). https://doi.org/10.1142/S0219622018500384
5. Shen-Hsieh, A., Schindl, M.: Data visualization for strategic decision making. In: Case Studies of the CHI2002|AIGA Experience Design FORUM. ACM, Minneapolis Minnesota, pp. 1–17, April 2002. https://doi.org/10.1145/507752.507756
6. Nevo, D., Nevo, S., Kumar, N., Braasch, J., Mathews, K.: Enhancing the visualization of big data to support collaborative decision-making. In: 2015 48th Hawaii International Conference on System Sciences, pp. 121–130. IEEE, HI, USA, January 2015. https://doi.org/10.1109/HICSS.2015.25

# A Proposal for an Interactive Assistant to Support Exploratory Data Analysis in Educational Settings

Andrea Vázquez-Ingelmo[(⊠)] [iD], Alicia García-Holgado[iD], and Jorge Pozo-Zapatero

GRIAL Research Group, Research Institute for Educational Sciences, University of Salamanca, Salamanca, Spain
{andreavazquez,aliciagh,jorpoza07}@usal.es

**Abstract.** In the realm of data science, the critical phases of data pre-processing and exploratory data analysis (EDA) play a fundamental role in ensuring the quality of data for downstream processes. However, these phases often present formidable challenges, characterized by complexity and a plethora of available techniques and tools, which can be overwhelming, especially for users with varying levels of expertise. In response to this challenge, we propose the development of EDAQuest, an interactive assistant designed to guide students and novice professionals through the intricate landscape of data pre-processing and exploratory analysis. EDAQuest's primary objective is to offer a didactic approach that not only enhances users' comprehension but also enables practical application across diverse datasets. Users can anticipate real-time recommendations, invaluable tips, and informative visual aids to enrich their data understanding. Recognizing the diverse nature of data, EDAQuest aims at proficiently handle heterogeneous data sources by customizing pre-processing techniques for each data type, ensuring optimal outcomes and results. This paper provides an overview of the workflow designed to support EDAQuest's developmental prototype.

**Keywords:** data analysis · interactive assistant · human-computer interaction

## 1 Introduction

In data science, the critical stages of data pre-processing and exploratory data analysis (EDA) [1] form the cornerstone of subsequent data processing activities. Their quality significantly impacts the outcomes of later stages. Yet, mastering these phases can be challenging and intricate due to the plethora of techniques and tools available.

The complexity of these initial steps in data science can lead to several issues [2]. Poorly pre-processed or analyzed data can result in misleading insights, which can have far-reaching consequences in decision-making processes and predictive modeling [3–5]. For instance, improperly handled missing data or unaddressed biases can skew results, leading to flawed conclusions. Additionally, the overwhelming variety of tools and methods [6–8] can lead to inefficiency, as users spend excessive time determining the most appropriate approach for their specific needs.

© The Author(s), under exclusive license to Springer Nature Switzerland AG 2024
P. Zaphiris and A. Ioannou (Eds.): HCII 2024, LNCS 14723, pp. 272–281, 2024.
https://doi.org/10.1007/978-3-031-61685-3_20

This situation is particularly daunting for users of all experience levels, as they must sift through a vast range of options to find the most effective and accurate methods for their data analysis tasks.

Therefore, in response to the ever-growing demand for accessible and effective data analysis, we propose "EDAQuest," an interactive assistant currently in its prototype phase. This tool is designed to assist novices and professionals in navigating data analysis tasks. EDAQuest aims to simplify the process of data exploration and pre-processing, making it more approachable for individuals regardless of their prior knowledge or experience in data science. This proposal represents a step towards developing a user-friendly tool that can accommodate the varying needs and expertise levels of its users.

The primary goal of the EDAQuest prototype is to simplify the complexities of data analysis by offering a learning-oriented approach that not only deepens users' understanding but also equips them to practically apply these methods to various datasets. EDAQuest is being designed to provide a dynamic learning experience, featuring real-time suggestions, insightful guidance, and clear visual aids. These elements are intended to enhance users' grasp of the data they are working with, making the analysis process both informative and engaging.

EDAQuest functional features are set to be enhanced by an accompanying educational suite with the goal of explaining the theory behind each data pre-processing and exploratory data analysis (EDA) technique and giving users a solid theoretical base to support the practical skills they develop using the assistant. This integration of theory and practice in EDAQuest is intended to ensure users are equipped to both perform data analysis tasks and understand the concepts behind them.

This paper outlines the conceptual framework of EDAQuest's non-functional prototype, focusing on its intended workflow and design to meet the diverse needs of potential users. We discuss the envisioned features and functionalities of the EDAQuest prototype, illustrating how it aims to make data analysis more accessible and tailored to individual preferences and requirements. It's important to note that this exploration is based on a non-functional prototype, serving as a foundation for understanding the requirements and user stories essential for its future development and validation.

The remainder of this paper is organized in the following manner: Sect. 2 explores the background that laid the foundation for the development of this platform. Section 3 describes the methodology employed during the initial phase of prototyping, including the user stories. Section 4 introduces the initial prototype. Finally, Sect. 5 delves into initial observations and conclusions drawn from this early stage of development.

## 2  Background

EDAQuest was conceived as a response to a key challenge encountered in KoopaML, a platform previously developed by the authors.

The KoopaML platform [9] was developed as a tool to assist users, particularly those without expert-level skills, in constructing and executing machine learning (ML) pipelines. It is tailored specifically for applications in the medical field, offering interfaces that are both user-friendly and educational, facilitating the learning process of applying ML models.

However, the platform's intricate content, including specialized terminology and workflow processes, presented a significant barrier to users fully leveraging its advanced features. To better understand these challenges, medical professionals evaluated KoopaML using the think-aloud protocol [10] which helped gather a preliminary list of enhancements to be implemented.

Building on the insights from the evaluation of KoopaML, we decided to develop a new platform specifically tailored for data analysis. This decision arises from recognizing the need for a specialized solution to address the complexities that users encountered with KoopaML, particularly in terms of understanding the data analysis and navigating its interfaces (Fig. 1).

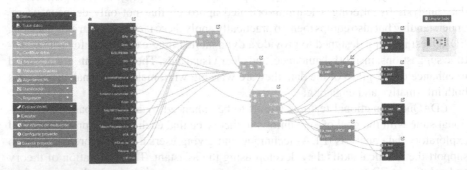

**Fig. 1.** KoopaML interface. Blue nodes represent data uploading and data pre-processing nodes, while pink and purple nodes represent ML models and their evaluation metrics. (Color figure onlie)

This platform is envisioned to harness the strengths of KoopaML while simultaneously tackling its usability challenges. This is achieved by isolating the exploratory data analysis (EDA) aspect of ML pipelines into a distinct interface.

Such separation enables users to concentrate more effectively on data analysis and transformation before delving into machine learning pipeline construction. This clear distinction between data analysis and the ML pipeline itself in EDAQuest is intended to streamline the workflow, making it more user-friendly, efficient, and educative.

## 3   Methodology

### 3.1   User Stories

The development of the EDAQuest platform is anchored in a user-centered approach, prioritizing the needs and perspectives of the end-users in its functionality. This section outlines the user stories, which are instrumental in understanding the objectives and requirements of different user groups interacting with the platform. The user stories follow a consistent format: *As a [type of user], I want [to perform a task] in order to [achieve a result].*

Primary **user profiles.** Final users mainly include: users with limited programming knowledge, professionals used to work with data, users needing tools for algorithm training, users with limited knowledge in artificial intelligence and machine learning algorithms, experienced users in programming or data science.

**Users with limited programming knowledge** may come from various fields and backgrounds, such as healthcare, business, or social sciences, where data analysis plays a crucial role. However, they might not have extensive programming skills. For them, the platform provides an accessible and user-friendly interface to perform data analysis without the need for coding expertise. It empowers them to harness the power of data without barriers.

**Professionals used to work with data**, such as analysts, researchers, or data managers, form another important user group. While they are well-versed in data-related tasks, the platform offers them efficiency and automation in data preprocessing and exploratory analysis. It streamlines their workflow, allowing them to focus on deriving valuable insights from the data.

For **users needing tools for algorithm training** and seeking to delve into the world of machine learning and artificial intelligence, the platform serves as an ideal starting point. It not only guides them through the essential steps of data preparation but also introduces them to the concept of algorithm training. This user group can initiate their machine learning journey with confidence.

Understanding and applying machine learning algorithms can be intimidating for **users with limited knowledge in AI and ML algorithms**. The platform recognizes this challenge and offers a gentle learning curve. Users with limited knowledge in AI and ML can explore curated pathways that gradually introduce them to these advanced topics. They can start with basic concepts and progress at their own pace.

Finally, the platform caters to **experienced users in programming or data science**. While they may possess advanced skills, the platform enhances their capabilities by providing a structured environment for data analysis. It allows them to create custom workflows, trace data transformations, automate repetitive tasks, and collaborate within the user community, fostering a culture of shared learning and expertise.

**Main User Stories.** These main user stories exemplify the platform's commitment to addressing the diverse needs of its users, from those seeking education and guidance to professionals in specialized. In this sense, the platform should focus on versatility, educational modules, and user-friendly features to ensure that all users can achieve their primary objectives efficiently and effectively.

*As a user with limited knowledge in AI and machine learning algorithms, I want a program that teaches me the data transformations and requirements necessary for algorithm training.* This user story addresses the crucial need for education and guidance for individuals who are new to the world of AI and machine learning. It acknowledges that understanding data transformations is fundamental to successful algorithm training.

The platform should respond to this need by offering structured educational modules that walk users through the essential data transformations and prerequisites for algorithm training. It combines theoretical knowledge with practical exercises, ensuring that users not only learn but also apply what they learn effectively.

*As a user with limited programming knowledge, I need a platform that simplifies working with training algorithms.* Professionals from different backgrounds often have their expertise in their respective fields but may lack programming skills. It's vital for them to have a platform that simplifies the technical aspects of working with training algorithms, allowing them to focus on their domain knowledge.

The platform should address this challenge by providing an intuitive and user-friendly interface. It automates complex data preprocessing tasks and simplifies the interaction with training algorithms. This way, cardiologists and similar professionals can leverage their domain expertise without being hindered by technical complexities.

*As a user with limited programming knowledge, I want a platform that helps me correctly prepare a database for algorithm training.* Correctly preparing a database is critical for the success of algorithm training in different fields. Mistakes in data preparation can lead to inaccurate results. This user story emphasizes the need for a platform that ensures data correctness.

The platform should guide users through the precise steps required to prepare a database for algorithm training. This includes data validation checks, recommendations, and data profiling functionalities to help users identify and rectify any issues in their datasets. This ensures the reliability and accuracy of the training process.

*As a professional used to work with data, I seek an easy and automatic way to prepare data for algorithm training.* Even experienced professionals can benefit from a streamlined and automated data preparation process. It saves time and ensures consistency in data handling.

The platform should cater to this need by offering automated data preprocessing workflows. Users can upload their data, and the platform must intelligently apply the necessary transformations and data cleaning operations, including options for customization to allow users to fine-tune the process according to their specific requirements.

**Secondary User Stories.** In addition to the primary objectives outlined in the previous section, the platform should also place a strong emphasis on providing users with the flexibility and control to tailor their data analysis journey to their unique needs and preferences.

The following user stories shed light on how the platform should empower users at every level of expertise, from those new to AI and machine learning to those with prior data handling experience.

Whether it's assisting users in making critical data changes, providing insights into potential data issues, or offering the option to refine data with suggestions, the platform should provide users with the tools and guidance needed to navigate the intricacies of data analysis.

1. As a user needing to work with a dataset, I need the ability to upload my own data files.
2. As a user with limited AI and machine learning knowledge, I seek to choose an objective so the program can guide me through the data treatment process for algorithm training.
3. As a user with limited AI and machine learning knowledge, I want to find objectives with a brief description when I'm unsure of the specific terminology.
4. As a user with some data handling experience, I want to define objectives to have a predefined scheme when using the program.

5. As a user with limited AI and machine learning knowledge, I need to know if the objective I've defined aligns with my actual goal.
6. As a user with some data handling experience, I want to see a summary of my data before uploading to ensure they are the exact data I intend to work with.
7. As a user with limited AI and machine learning knowledge, I would like to know potential issues that may arise with the data I intend to use for a defined objective.
8. As a user with limited AI and machine learning knowledge, I want the program to initially perform the main changes necessary to correctly work with the data I've introduced.
9. As a user with limited AI and machine learning knowledge, I would like to reject the program's process at any step in case of mistakes in data uploading or objective selection.
10. As a user with some data handling experience, I want to view the general characteristics of my data's variables.
11. As a user with some data handling experience, I want to easily see the distribution of my data's variables.
12. As a user with some data handling experience, I want to graphically view the distribution of my data's variables for quick analysis.
13. As a user with limited AI and machine learning knowledge, I would like to make the necessary critical changes for data use.
14. As a user with limited AI and machine learning knowledge, I would like the program to help me refine the data (using suggestions).
15. As a user with limited AI and machine learning knowledge, I would like to view the process of changes made to the data to understand the followed procedure.
16. As an experienced user in programming or data science, I would like a quick way to handle data for subsequent use in algorithm training.

## 3.2 Data Preprocessing Strategies

The methodology for exploratory data analysis (EDA) involves a comprehensive evaluation of each algorithm, focusing on its specific objectives and the data structures it best suits. This section details our strategy for adaptive data preprocessing tailored to these elements.

Our process initiates with a detailed algorithm-specific analysis. Within EDAQuest, every machine learning algorithm is scrutinized to understand its fundamental objectives and the ideal data types it processes. This scrutiny enables us to customize preprocessing steps for each algorithm, thereby optimizing its performance and ensuring more accurate outcomes.

A key aspect of our platform is its focus on the ultimate goals of each analytical task. By aligning our data structuring processes with these end goals, EDAQuest could ensure that the data's format and structure are precisely tuned to meet the desired objectives of the analysis.

Central to EDAQuest is the development of a tailored preprocessing workflow for every dataset. The platform should intelligently offer automated recommendations for data cleaning, normalization, and transformation. These suggestions are specifically based on the unique characteristics of the dataset in question and the requirements of the selected algorithm and objectives.

This innovative approach not only simplifies the EDA process for both novices and experts but also guarantees that data is properly prepared, paving the way for more meaningful and insightful analysis.

## 4   Prototype

The workflow for the proposed platform is described through its initial prototype. First, the user creates a new project and uploads an structured dataset for its exploratory data analysis. During this phase, the user would be able to visually explore the uploaded data through different data visualizations adapted to the data types and distributions.

The subsequent phase entails determining the objective for EDA. Here, the user must specify their goals related to the utilization of the dataset (Fig. 2). This decision shapes the EDA process, as the approach varies significantly between classification and regression methodologies. Users receive guidance through descriptive text and also have the opportunity to create tailored objectives, using predefined options as a foundation.

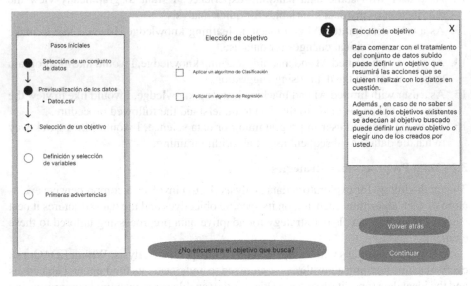

**Fig. 2.** EDAQuest screen for selecting the EDA goal. Contents in Spanish.

Following this stage, users are directed to identify and select the variables to be included in the analysis and machine learning pipeline. Based on their defined objective, they will need to choose both the target variables for prediction and the variables to be used in training, as they will influence the EDA workflow.

Once the preceding information is inputted, the user will be presented with an initial set of alerts concerning their dataset. These warnings will address critical issues such as the presence of potentially problematic empty values, inconsistencies in data types, the need for normalization, among other considerations.

After addressing and confirming the resolution of the identified issues, the user is then guided to the dataset workspace. Here, the dataset is displayed with more detailed warnings about various variables, such as outliers and correlations (as illustrated in Fig. 3).

In this phase, users have the opportunity to implement various system-recommended operations on their dataset. The outcome is a revised version of the dataset, displayed at the bottom of the screen (as shown in Fig. 4). This not only offers a clear view of the changes made but also ensures traceability of the data operations.

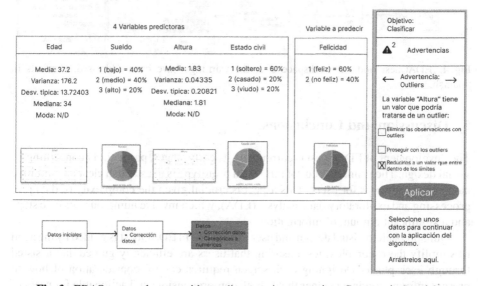

**Fig. 3.** EDAQuest workspace with pending warnings to review. Contents in Spanish.

Ultimately, this application is designed to seamlessly integrate with KoopaML [9]. Once all modifications and cleaning processes are completed on the dataset, users can import it as a data source into KoopaML. This enables users to start constructing a machine learning pipeline using data that has been thoroughly cleaned and preprocessed.

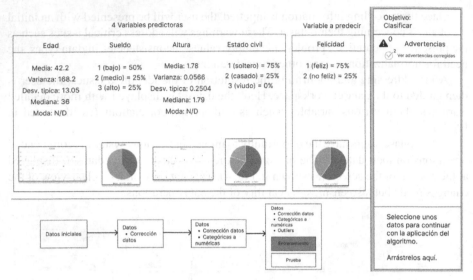

**Fig. 4.** EDAQuest updated workspace after the warnings have been addressed. Contents in Spanish.

## 5   Discussion and Conclusions

The development of EDAQuest is currently in its early stages, particularly concerning its visual design. The primary focus of this initial prototype is to establish clear and intuitive navigation pathways for users. This aspect is crucial given the complexity of data preprocessing and exploratory data analysis (EDA), which involve numerous intricate steps and a significant amount of information.

Our approach to visual design and user experience in EDAQuest is guided by the need to simplify these complexities, ensuring that users are efficiently guided and assisted through each phase. Designing each screen requires careful consideration of how to present information in a manner that is both comprehensible and actionable for users of varying expertise levels and necessities, as identified through the user stories.

One of the pivotal objectives of EDAQuest is to alleviate the burden of data preprocessing from users of KoopaML. This decision stems from user feedback indicating that data preprocessing was a significant challenge when using KoopaML. By separating these processes, EDAQuest aims to provide a more streamlined and focused experience for users engaged in machine learning pipeline construction.

With EDAQuest handling the data preprocessing and providing educational content about these processes, users gain a better theoretical and practical understanding of the steps involved. This educational aspect is particularly beneficial for novices, as it lays a solid foundation for more advanced tasks in KoopaML.

The smooth integration between EDAQuest and KoopaML try to ensure that users can transition effortlessly from data preprocessing in EDAQuest to pipeline construction in KoopaML. This seamless flow aims at improving the users' ability to handle complex data analysis tasks with greater confidence and understanding.

Future steps will involve enhancing the prototype by incorporating valuable insights gained from the feedback provided by our target user group. This iterative process is essential for tailoring our product to meet their specific needs and expectations. Simultaneously, we will start the preliminary phase of EDAQuest's development, laying the groundwork for the project.

**Acknowledgments.** This research was partially funded by the Ministry of Science and Innovation through the AvisSA project grant number (PID2020-118345RB-I00). This work was also supported by national (PI14/00695, PIE14/00066, PI17/00145, DTS19/00098, PI19/00658, PI19/00656 Institute of Health Carlos III, Spanish Ministry of Economy and Competitiveness and co-funded by ERDF/ESF, "Investing in your future") and community (GRS 2033/A/19, GRS 2030/A/19, GRS 2031/A/19, GRS 2032/A/19, SACYL, Junta Castilla y León) competitive grants.

# References

1. Tukey, J.W.: Exploratory data analysis. Reading, MA (1977)
2. Wongsuphasawat, K., Liu, Y., Heer, J.: Goals, process, and challenges of exploratory data analysis: an interview study. arXiv preprint arXiv:1911.00568 (2019)
3. Ferrer, X., van Nuenen, T., Such, J.M., Coté, M., Criado, N.: Bias and discrimination in AI: a cross-disciplinary perspective. IEEE Technol. Soc. Mag. **40**, 72–80 (2021)
4. Zhao, S., Ren, H., Yuan, A., Song, J., Goodman, N., Ermon, S.: Bias and generalization in deep generative models: an empirical study. Adv. Neural Inf. Process. Syst. **31** (2018)
5. Garcia, M.: Racist in the machine: the disturbing implications of algorithmic bias. World Policy J. **33**, 111–117 (2016)
6. Milo, T., Somech, A.: Automating exploratory data analysis via machine learning: an overview. In: Proceedings of the 2020 ACM SIGMOD International Conference on Management of Data, pp. 2617–2622 (Year)
7. Batch, A., Elmqvist, N.: The interactive visualization gap in initial exploratory data analysis. IEEE Trans. Vis. Comput. Graph. **24**, 278–287 (2017)
8. Myatt, G.J.: Making Sense of Data: A Practical Guide to Exploratory Data Analysis and Data Mining. John Wiley & Sons, Hoboken (2007)
9. García-Peñalvo, F., et al.: KoopaML: a graphical platform for building machine learning pipelines adapted to health professionals. Int. J. Interact. Multimed. Artif. Intell. (2023)
10. Jääskeläinen, R.: Think-aloud protocol. Handb. Transl. Stud. **1**, 371–374 (2010)

# Author Index

P. Zaphiris and A. Ioannou (Eds.): HCII 2024, LNCS 14723, pp. 283–285, 2024.
https://doi.org/10.1007/978-3-031-61685-3

Printed in the United States
by Baker & Taylor Publisher Services